This is an authorized facsimile
printed by microfilm/xerography on acid-free paper
in 1982 by
UNIVERSITY MICROFILMS INTERNATIONAL
Ann Arbor, Michigan, U.S.A.
London, England

THE ART
OF
TEACHING AND STUDYING
LANGUAGES.

BY

FRANÇOIS GOUIN,
PROFESSEUR D'ALLEMAND À L'ÉCOLE SUPÉRIEURE ARAGO, PARIS.

TRANSLATED FROM THE FRENCH
BY
HOWARD SWAN
AND
VICTOR BÉTIS,
MEMBRE DE L'ENSEIGNEMENT PUBLIC EN FRANCE.

LONDON:
GEORGE PHILIP & SON, 32 FLEET STREET;
LIVERPOOL: 45 TO 51 SOUTH CASTLE STREET.
1892.

800.7
G69a
t597
cop.2

THE ART

OF

TEACHING AND STUDYING LANGUAGES.

1138177.026

PREFACE.

MANKIND has long passed from the stage in which speech is used for the mere expression of physical facts and desires, to that in which language is employed as the highest tool within the grasp to paint the pictures of poetic imagination, and sway a world-wide audience to noble thoughts and deeds. Not only to satisfy the necessities of travellers in far countries has the study of language been ever desirable, but to penetrate the spirit and genius of Homer, Virgil, Shakespeare, Goethe, Hugo, Dante, it has become, to the cultured of every country, a necessity for the full gift of a liberal education. Since language became literature, the necessity for the mastery over other tongues than his own has forced the attention of student and of professor to the problem of the study of languages; and the great intellectual value of a complete and logical system for the mastery of tongues, if such could be found, is so apparent, that the greatest honour has always been awarded to discoverers in this region, which is still felt, however, to be to a large extent unexplored, or at least unconquered.

The world has this year seen a magnificent celebration of the grand services to the cause of education rendered by Comenius. In spite of this we are still far from having definitely adopted in our schools and college practice the now acknowledged principles perceived by Comenius—that education must be organic and not mechanical, that language teaching, modern and classic, should proceed by dealing with things and not with words and grammatical abstractions, and that before all else education should have direct bearing upon actual life.

The late Mr. W. H. Widgery, M.A., has a very pregnant sentence in almost the first paragraph of his admirable booklet on "The Teaching of Languages in Schools" (D. Nutt), where he says—

"Our great modern reformers, Rousseau, Pestalozzi, Froebel, have been the sources of mighty inspirations; they have pointed out in the rough the paths along which we must travel. They failed in system. We now need rather some powerful organiser, well trained in philosophy, in logic, in psychology, one who will do actual school-work for some years, and then clear for us the jungle of educational literature."

Mr. Widgery evidently looked for his language-organiser to come after many years and after weary labour. This labour is, happily, as will be seen, already in great part accomplished and the work organised; and perhaps no sentence could better express what it is that the work of M. François Gouin, here presented, attempts to perform.

This work might not inaptly be entitled "The Gift of Languages, and How to Acquire it; being an Investigation into Linguistic Psychology." It will be found to appeal, not only to the teacher and the specialist in pedagogic science, but to the student and the general reader, for in its train it draws interesting and far-reaching developments.

It is primarily an investigation into the psychological laws underlying the universal act of learning the mother-tongue by the little child, and, springing therefrom, the exposition of an artificial system of teaching foreign languages—a system which produces peculiarly successful results and endows the learner with the gift for languages: and these results are curiously easy of explanation, being based on the laws of gradual development of the human mind itself.

It may be well to point out at once that the work of M. Gouin is essentially a new departure; it is based upon a close observation of nature—that of the little child at its games weaving its own individuality and learning its native tongue; its mental operations are analysed with extreme care and described with a clearness and simplicity to which one is not always accustomed in subjects so apparently abstruse as that of psychology.

The system set forth is not a variation of the ordinary collection of exercises. That which is therein presented consists of the expression of the real facts of life itself; not accidental facts merely, but those which every one has lived, is now living—external and internal phenomena, deeply imprinted upon the mental background of every human being. And these facts are not seen at hazard; they are grouped, analysed, organised, studied in the exact order of succession which is marked out by Nature. These facts are lived over again, as it were, a second time by remembrance; they are reconstituted as a part of the individuality of the student, who again learns to express them, but this time in a foreign language. Our common life is once more begun at the mother's knee, and lived through with the rapidity of thought; and the conscious knowledge of self thus acquired is obtained as well as the mastery of a foreign language.

The act of speaking and understanding any sentence in one's native tongue may be thus briefly analysed. We may take as example the phrase "The shepherd-dog collects the flock of sheep." The speaker forms in his mind a picture (in this case of a pastoral subject), being a generalisation of many mental photographs; the words, that is, the "sounds," expressing this picture he knows by long association. He utters these sounds in the right order; they strike against the ear of the listener, and the same association between the sound and the mental picture, having to him also long become habitual, arises at once in the mind of the listener. There is here nothing in the nature of translation, but the act is one of pure intuition—seeing in the mind. There is nothing here of printed signs: the signs or letters are but the phantom or symbol of the sounds, carefully analysed phonetically; they also by long habit are associated both with the sounds and with the mental picture, but mental picture, sound, and written symbol of the sound are all distinct elements of what collectively is termed Language; and in learning the language the first two are evidently the most important.

It is in the recognition of the vast part the imagination—or, to be more accurate, the faculty of visualisation—plays in the learning of languages, as in all mental operations, that the originality and success of M. Gouin's "Series" system depends. Not only so, but it opens up an almost unlimited field for the organisation and training of the faculty until now almost unheeded, possibly the principal one the mind exercises (besides that of control of the muscles), namely, the recollection of sense impressions—those of sight, sound, taste, smell, and feeling—but especially the first two—memory of sights and sounds—which may be termed mental visualisation and mental vocalisation. This power of visualisation in the mind, actually denied to a portion of mankind by some physiologists (amongst others Galton himself), is probably the one great and simple faculty of the mind—that which makes man more than the beasts of the field and gives him his mastery over Nature; and the power of converting one mental image into another, and of comparing two mental images, will be found when analysed to be that which we term Reason. So that we might venture the statement that "man is not a reasoning animal," using the word "Reason" as the name for some abstract and abstruse mental operation, but simply "a mental picture-making animal." This theory has far-reaching aspects.

Desirable as the discovery of the rationale of the gift of languages may be and certainly is—for language underlies the acquisition of all knowledge and the study of all arts and sciences—the investigation of this "gift" must be, whether it be recognised or not, in reality the investigation of the rationale of all "gifts" and all powers of the mind. The "gift for languages" once proved to be a method and not an abstruse faculty of the mind, inherited or acquired, is there not an *à priori* reason that the gift for calculation, for drawing, for music, may be, methods? What is it that constitutes talent, and what genius itself? And if we reply, "The strength of the power of mental representation," we are perhaps near to the answer. The extremely important questions such an idea raises are hinted at in this work, and the basis is laid for the initiation of an intuitive method of teaching.

The work of M. Gouin has within it therefore the promise of awakening other discoveries. One of these is hinted at on p. 6, where the act of mental calculation, so wonderfully employed by so-called "calculating prodigies," is suggested for investigation; and, again, on p. 292, where the gift for drawing is alluded to, and the principles of its development are sketched out.

In the definite organisation of language, first into two great divisions of objective and subjective, and then into the groups corresponding, on the objective side, to the varied occurrences in the external world; and on the subjective side, to the varied play of the faculties—in the organisation of the totality of the expressions of any language into concentric groups, viz., of those expressions known by a child of seven, those by a boy of ten, those by a youth of sixteen, and those by a graduate of twenty-one—in all this M. Gouin gives a grouping eminently helpful not only to language teachers, but also to philologists. In the methods of teaching arranged in accordance with the psychological law of the development of individuality in the child, we have not only a possibility of greater efficiency and adaptability in the methods of teaching all subjects, but in the abrogation of the wearisome correction of exercises and construing, and in the presentation of a less abstract grammar, we have a deliverance of both pupils and teachers from their weariest drudgery.

The latter, the exposition of a universal psychological conjugation (Part III. Grammar), calls for some more particular remark. All grammars up to the present have been cast in the same mould, without questioning if this were the only possible one or the best. The form of the word or words and their endings is the material organised by them, and not the thought which underlies these words and endings. The difficulty of accurately fixing the exact thought-subtleties underlying the tense-forms is almost absurd, as the writer well knows, compared with the simplicity of the result when once determined as embodied in a table such as the one given on pages 231 and 238-9. In suggesting a new mould for the setting forth of grammatical forms in lieu of the time-honoured divisions of Passé Indéfini and so forth, clearness of visualisation of the exact act expressed by the verb has been the only guide, and is also the main result aimed at.

PREFACE.

By the present methods we are all well aware that even after four or five years' courses at ordinary school-classes, pupils are certainly usually not able to understand native speakers or lecturers, or capable of speaking correctly and idiomatically themselves, until after some considerable period of residence abroad. Indeed, it is no unusual occurrence to find that students, on the usual methods, may have passed examinations with success, and yet be utterly unable to sustain a simple conversation, or even understand a native speaker. The ordinary class method, so well known by all of us, is here alluded to; other teachers have partly advanced on the lines so thoroughly carried out by M. Gouin. To them all honour!

The reason of the success of M. Gouin's system, and the ill-success of the ordinary class methods, may be briefly summed up as follows:—

The ordinary classical method sets the students (1) to read from a book what they do not yet know how to pronounce; (2) to connect the printed word in one language with another printed word in another language; (3) therefore, to perceive the sense of the foreign language, always through the intermediary of their own language, *i.e.*, by translation, and not as a native, by direct association; (4) more often than not the class exercises given are void of real sense or signification— a set of more or less absurd, illogical (and untrue) statements, having no application whatever to the learner's own individuality, are used for exercises, introduced solely to employ the vocabulary and to illustrate the rules of grammar; lastly, the whole process throughout is abstract and arbitrary, resting on no other foundation than the fancy of the compiler.

To this process the system set forth by M. Gouin is opposed in almost every particular. (1.) The learner has for exercises sentences which bear a distinct and sensible meaning, and are true in substance and in fact; these are linked together in logical sequence of the development of their action, forming separate and simple dramatic scenes of primitive life, giving rise, naturally, to good literary expressions; (2.) the learner has the significance of the word or phrase always given to him or called up in his mind *before* he is introduced to the foreign word or phrase which express it; (3.) the association of the foreign word or phrase is thus not with an English word, but with the actual fact or mental conception which the English word only stands for and expresses; (4.) he is given the pronunciation orally first, and *before* he sees the printed form, and this several times successively and methodically, until it is engraven on his memory; (5.) only after he thoroughly knows the meaning and pronunciation is he allowed to see the written or printed word; and lastly, no rule, no word, no expression, is given in an abstract condition, but always as depending on some concrete fact previously known and directly applying to the student's own individuality.

In this way the foreign language becomes in reality a "language" to the learner, not a slow translation or a set of printed signs; it is associated with actual facts, and expresses his ideas and mental conceptions in the foreign language itself—in other words, the student "thinks in the foreign language."

All that is developed in this work is evidently in strict accordance with the principles which have guided the work of Pestalozzi and of Froebel, as of Herbert Spencer. The Series System indicates, indeed, a direction in which the long acknowledged principles of the Kindergarten system can be carried on into more advanced work—languages, modern and classical, science and technical education; and in this it may serve a doubly useful purpose, for it may give into the hands of teachers the method so long desired of enabling the training of the mind to go hand in hand with the teaching of useful knowledge, while it may also reduce the time necessary for elementary instruction by furnishing more efficient means, and so leave more time for higher and technical education.

To many minds the chapters on the teaching of classical languages will doubtless have most interest, especially at a juncture when the compulsory teaching of Greek at the Universities is hotly challenged as against the spirit of the age. The system of teaching the classics here proposed will unfailingly call forth many and very varied opinions. The author's ideas upon these points are very fully set forth in the chapters on Greek and Latin (Part V., p. 362 *et seq.*).

The original work was written in Geneva, and, it is interesting to learn, was set up and composed in type by the author himself, and printed at his own expense. It was published in 1880 in Paris by G. Fischbacher, 33 Rue de Seine, and has therefore been before the educational world for the last twelve years. It is now out of print. Curiously enough, for such an original and daring work, it has remained entirely unknown to the British public, so far as the present writer can find, until his introduction of it to those interested in educational literature. At the time of the great Paris Exposition of 1889, being interested in language teaching, he had a copy of the work put into his hands by a friend with the remark, "I do not know whether the system has been carried into practice, but the book is an attempt to reconstruct the child's mental life, and is almost as interesting as a novel"—as indeed he found it. Meeting, by a happy coincidence, M. Victor Bétis, the ardent disciple of M. Gouin, who came to England on purpose to introduce the system, the writer has given the time since to preparing a faithful and careful translation of the book, which embodies the life-work of one who may, perhaps, deserve to be enrolled amongst the reorganisers of Pedagogy. This translation, undertaken with the close collaboration throughout of M. Victor Bétis, presents a few modifications in one or two particulars to adapt it to English requirements.

These modifications consist solely in the omission of two or three paragraphs having more direct reference to French schools; the rather important modification of the chapter on grammar (pp. 236–240), due to an extended comparison of the English and French forms of the verbs, leading to a somewhat deeper analysis of the author's investigations into the psychological differences underlying the tense forms of the conjugation; the addition by the author of a scene from "Romeo and Juliet," illustrative of English literature in the form proposed; and the publication in the Appendix of the certificate from M. Lockroy, the French Minister of Public Instruction.

The following facts with reference to the author, M. François Gouin, it may be desirable here to mention. Born in 1831, a native of Normandy, he was educated at the College of Séez. Advised by the professors of the College of Caen to complete his philosophical studies in the German universities—as he relates in the book—he made a dismal failure in his attempt to learn the German language by following out in its simplicity the ordinary or classical method of learning a language, which no one probably has ever before carried to its extreme limits. Studying, on his return, a child, his little nephew of three years old, who had meanwhile learnt to talk its native tongue, he made the discovery which is the keystone of the book, and therefrom worked out his system of "The Art of Teaching and Studying Languages." M. Gouin returned to Germany, and lived for many years in Berlin, eventually holding the position practically equivalent to that of Professor of French to the Berlin Court, and enjoying the personal friendship of Alexander von Humboldt. Nominated by one of the Ministers of Roumania in 1864 to organise the system of public instruction in that country, he left Berlin, but at the revolution resulting in the overthrow of Prince Couza he came to England, and afterwards settled at Geneva, where he established a school, and during this period his book, "L'Art d'Enseigner et d'Etudier les Langues," was written and published. Later he became Director of the Ecole Supérieure of Elbœuf, but left, much to the regret of the inhabitants, who looked to his system to endow the rising generation with the knowledge of languages, and thus to furnish them with the means of becoming the most successful of commercial correspondents.

M. Gouin was then appointed Professor of German at the Ecole Supérieure Arago, Paris, which position he now occupies. Here he taught German, and in his private time Latin and Greek, upon his "Series System," and published further works dealing with the practical part of the method. His book falling into the hands of a certain French gentleman of wealth, M. Tempié, he was accorded the means to carry on experimental classes for the teaching of German in the Ecole Normale d'Instituteurs of Paris, the result of which, as given in the certificate which is found in the Appendix (p. 395), was to demonstrate that a thorough knowledge of the ordinary spoken and written language, ability to understand a native speaker or lecturer, with command of the grammar (and also some knowledge of the literature of the country), with ability to give lessons in the language, was obtained by students in less than one year's course.

One word should be said in reference to the present methods so heavily attacked in this volume. Methods, not men, alone are criticised. There is no possibility of any personal feeling having been imported, for the original work was directed against French methods. Many there are who will welcome this volume as a deliverance from purgatory—those who feel the insufficiency of present methods, as well as those who are already arrayed against the classical process of abstract teaching by grammar and vocabulary. Yet, nevertheless, it would almost have been well to have had a head-line to every page, in the words of the author's preface:—

METHODS AND NOT MEN ARE CRITICISED.

From the interest already shown by many persons of influence to whom the work has been mentioned, it is certain that a large measure of appreciation will be accorded in many directions in England to the life-long task of M. Gouin; and if it is felt that in any way a better study of the beauties of our own or of foreign or classical literature, or the possibility of a more useful and inspiring education can be given by its means, then the small amount of work done in presenting the book in its English dress would have more than ample repayment.

HOWARD SWAN.

RICHMOND, SURREY,
May 1892.

CONTENTS.

PREFACE . . . . PAGE v

PART FIRST.
HISTORY AND CONCEPTION OF THE SYSTEM.

I. Need of a "mental railway" between nations—Character, conditions, and final aim of a good linguistic method—Possibility of its construction—Its prototype in nature . 1

II. Means of demonstrating a truth and of setting forth a system—Analysis and synthesis 7

III. The author attempts to learn the German language—Classical antecedents—The commencement—Hamburg University 8

IV. The first effort—The grammar and irregular verbs—Unsuccessful result 10

V. The study of the roots—Second deception . . . 12

VI. An attempt at conversation—Disgust and fatigue—Reading and translation, their worthlessness demonstrated . . 14

VII. The Ollendorf method—Enchantment—Thirty lessons in ten days—Sad acknowledgment of the master—Delusion 18

VIII. Jacotot and Robertson—Disorder and arbitrariness established as principles—Disconnected steps—The systematic vocabulary by Ploetz 22

IX. Berlin University—Mixing with the Students—Fruitless attendance at the classes 25

CONTENTS.

X. A heroic resolve—Study of the Dictionary—Struggle and victory—Third deception—Futile toil		26
XI. A child of three years old—Development of language in Nature's school—New point of departure—Observation of the child—A clue—Looking at the mill—The intellectual digestion—Saying and doing—The game—Light in the darkness		34
XII. First insight—Transformation of a perception into a conception—The scholastic process compared with that of the child—Secret logic and marvellous order of Nature		39
XIII. Second insight—Principles of classification employed by the child—Order of succession in time—Relation of end to means—The incubation—Secret of the child's memory—Explanation of my failures		42
XIV. Third insight—The child assimilates the mother-tongue sentence by sentence, and not word by word—Revelation of the high value of the verb—The true pivot of the natural system		44
XV. The web of language—Law of its formation—What is the receptive organ of language?—Incomprehensible error of the College		46
XVI. Formation of the individuality by language—Precise definition of the work to be accomplished for the acquisition of the basis of any given language—The idea of Series—A generalisation—The mystic ladder of human individuality		48
XVII. Fourth insight—Two languages in one language—Objective language and subjective language—The relative phrase—Figurative language—Intuition of the system in its totality		52
XVIII. Return to Berlin—The test—A philosophical bout at the University—The triumph—Excuse to the reader		56
XIX. Epilogue and prologue		59

PART SECOND.

CONSTRUCTION AND APPLICATION OF THE SYSTEM.

	PAGE
I. Division of the subject—Order to be followed	60

OBJECTIVE LANGUAGE.

ORGANISATION IN SERIES.

II. Definition and material of the Series .	61
III. Construction of the Series—Outline of the general process to be followed in organising them .	62
IV. Construction of one "theme" of a Series .	67
V. Character and properties of the exercises on the new method	70
1. Logical cohesion and original arrangement of the sentences in the exercises .	70
2. The number of words contained in a lesson .	73
3. Intrinsic value of the terms contained in an ordinary exercise .	74
4. Two kinds of substantives—Common and general nouns—Specific nouns—Their relation .	76
5. Two kinds of verbs—Verbs of ends and verbs of means—Their relation .	77
6. Epitome and general view .	79
7. Mnemonic properties of the method .	80
VI. Critical observations upon the art of composing Series	82
1. The perpetual speech — Written Series — Hidden difficulties .	82
2. A method is a system necessarily artificial .	85
3. Requisite capacities—Pedagogic measure of the Series—Their division into exercises—Construction of these exercises—Rules to be observed .	86
4. Logical linking together of the sentences in an exercise — Order and disorder—The human breath—Measure of the phrase—Placing line by line—The intellectual effort, its extent—Pedagogic measure of a linguistic exercise .	90

CONTENTS.

		PAGE
VII.	Specimens of the Elementary Series	96
	The Pump	99
	The Well	108
	The Spring	111
	The Fire	112
	The Stove	120
VIII.	Co-ordination of the Series—Importance of the Domestic Series	122

OBJECTIVE LANGUAGE.

MODE OF TEACHING THE SERIES.

IX. A Language Lesson 127
    1. Urgent need of a reform in the art of teaching languages 127
    2. The master-organ of language 127
    3. The lesson of the teacher and the work of the pupil—Assimilation—The part of the ear, the eye, and the hand in the study of a language 129
    4. The pronunciation 136
    5. One teacher for three classes 142

SUBJECTIVE LANGUAGE.

ITS ORGANISATION.

X. Classification of the Relative Phrases 144
    1. Definition of the Relative Phrases—Their object and their number in each tongue 144
    2. Two kinds of Relative Phrases—Those perfect or absolute, and the Enclitics 145
    3. Classification of Enclitics—General insight . . 147
    4. Classification of the absolute Relative Phrases—General insight 149

SUBJECTIVE LANGUAGE.

ART OF TEACHING IT.

	PAGE
XI. An ordered conversation carried on by means of the Relative Phrases	159
First Lesson in eight Languages: Latin, Greek, Italian, French, Spanish, German, English, Norwegian	168
XII. Critical observations upon the practice of the Relative Phrases	176
1. Remark upon our Appendices—Double function of the Relative Phrase—Its practical value	176
2. Correspondence of the system with the maternal process—The triumph of art—Correction of exercises—The teacher's power doubled—The question of accent—Free students	177
3. A declaration by a Minister of Education—The keystone of the edifice	180

FIGURATIVE LANGUAGE.

ITS ORGANISATION.

XIII. Object of this study—Two problems to be solved	182
XIV. Metaphorical themes	183
1. Origin of the metaphor—Its constituent elements—Its definition	183
2. Ordinary symbolism—Construction of the metaphorical themes	186

THE ART OF TEACHING METAPHORS.

XV. Two kinds of processes	189
1. Intrinsic rank of the figurative language—How assimilated in ordinary life—The part remaining to be done by Art	189
2. Search for a connecting link between the metaphorical theme and that of the Series—Idea of Dominants—Crossing and harmonious progress of the two languages	192
XVI. Still another question	195

CONTENTS.

PART THIRD.
GRAMMAR.

	PAGE
I. Two opinions upon the practical value of grammar	196
II. Definition and division	197

STUDY OF THE VERB.

EXERCISES IN THE CONJUGATIONS (FIRST WEEK).

III. Indicative (present acts) 198
   1. First exercise 198
   2. Second exercise 199
   3. Third exercise 200
IV. Critical examination of the process 201
   1. Properties of our exercise in verbs . . . 201
   2. Upon the unity of the conjugation . . . 203
   3. Our process and that of nature—Awakening of the grammatical sense—The indicative mood, the form of the present tense, and the third person—The Series of the Verb 207
   4. Summary and conclusion—Grammatical teaching must be reformed, not abolished 209

EXERCISES IN CONJUGATION (SECOND WEEK).

V. Indicative mood—Acts past, present, and future . . 211
   1. Six times or six periods—Definite times and indefinite times—Moments of precision 211
   2. Natural association of the forms of the verbs with the times—The tense intuition 215
   3. The ordinary period of time (yesterday, to-day, to-morrow, &c.)—The false period of time of the grammars (the past, the present, the future) . . 220
   4. Erroneous notions of the tenses in the grammars—Various causes of these errors: disdain of observation, traditional logomachy, confusion of the tense and the act, vain symmetry 222

CONTENTS.   xxi

	PAGE
VI. Our practice in the forms of the Indicative	227
1. First exercise—Simple and momentary acts	227
2. Second exercise—Continuous and habitual acts	232
3. Third exercise—Two acts occurring within the same period of time — Simultaneous acts — Imperfect, anterior, and posterior acts—The pluperfect acts	235

EXERCISES IN CONJUGATION (THIRD WEEK.)

VII. The Conditional and the Subjunctives	244
1. First exercise—The Conditional	244
2. Second exercise—The Subjunctives	246

STUDY OF THE SENTENCE.

ELEMENTS OF THE SENTENCE, THEIR FUNCTIONS.

VIII. Spoken Analysis of the Sentence	250
1. Various functions of the terms of a sentence—The pupil's initiation into this knowledge	250
2. A starting-point and a direction	252
IX. The complements—Cases or inflections—Declensions	253
1. The art of declining out of school	253
2. The art of declining at school	259
3. Practice of the declensions in our system	261
4. Parallel of the two processes	266
X. The Preposition	268
XI. The Prefix	271

CONSTRUCTION.

XII. Two sorts of construction—Natural order and logical order	276
XIII. Practical study of the construction in an ancient or modern foreign language	279
1. Construction by the ordinary process	279
2. Construction by our method	281

THE MODAL PHRASES.

	PAGE
XIV. Classification and practice	284
1. Definition of the modal phrase—Its constituent elements—Their relations	284
2. Establishment of the moods—Vicious circle of the Classical school—Our process	285
3. Ordinary practice of the modal phrases and the moods—Our process	286

ANNEXES AND COROLLARIES OF THE SYSTEM.

I. The Orthography—Spelling	288
II. Reading	289
III. Drawing—Its relation to language—The illustrated Series	292
IV. The time necessary to learn a language	294
V. The teaching of languages brought within the reach of all—Linguistic aptitudes of women	299
VI. Can a language be learnt without a teacher?	301

PART FOURTH.

STUDY OF THE CLASSICS.

LITERARY SERIES.

Outline of a new process for translating, reading, and assimilating the classical authors.

I. Putting a literary work into Series	305
1. Principle and point of departure	305
2. Transcription of a classical work into literature lessons	306
3. Specimens of transcriptions	308
"The Lion and the Gnat"	309
"Canis et Lupus"	311
"Die Drei Spinnerinnen"	313
"Romeo and Juliet"	320
II. Elaboration of a Literary Series—Our method of teaching	325
1. One of La Fontaine's Fables	325
2. A page of Virgil	333

THE LANGUAGES BY THE SCIENCES AND THE SCIENCES BY THE LANGUAGES.

	PAGE
I. The solidarity of the sciences and the languages	341
II. The languages by history and history by the languages	343
1. Necessity for a reform in the teaching of history	343
2. History put into Series	345
"The battle of Rossbach"	348
3. The teaching of the history lessons	350
4. Geographical Series	355
III. The languages by the natural sciences and *vice versa*	356
IV. The languages and the exact sciences	359

PART FIFTH.
GREEK AND LATIN.

I. The value of Greek and Latin	362
1. The interest of the race	362
2. The interest of the individual	364
II. Condemnation of the processes applied to the study of ancient languages	367
1. Ten years and ten masters	367
2. The dictionary, or the discipline of the vicious circle	369
III. The fear of improvement—Sceptical disdain of the official schools and their secret aversion to reform	376
1. A last contest	376
2. Solution of the conflict	380
IV. The dying dialects—An ark of safety	383

APPENDIX.

I. Three French Series lessons	386
II. Co-ordinated acts—Author's text	389
III. "Le Lion et le Moucheron"	392
IV. Certificate of the French Minister of Public Instruction	395

INDEX	397

THE ART OF TEACHING AND STUDYING LANGUAGES.

PART FIRST.

HISTORY AND CONCEPTION OF THE SYSTEM.

I.

NEED OF A "MENTAL RAILWAY" BETWEEN NATIONS—CHARACTER, CONDITIONS, AND FINAL AIM OF A GOOD LINGUISTIC METHOD—POSSIBILITY OF ITS CONSTRUCTION—ITS PROTOTYPE IN NATURE.

THE feeling which leads nations to become acquainted with each other and to penetrate farther and farther into each other's territories is one which it is useless to resist. It is in vain that despotism constructs frontiers bristling with fortresses and cannon; in vain that the spirit of absolutism strives to multiply the germs of discord between nation and nation, and to imprison the races each within the barren confines of its own unhealthy egotism.

Steam and electricity have drawn nations nearer together than were neighbouring villages in the olden times. By their means every movement, every aspiration is made known and reported from one to the other, is revealed and published hour by hour. A proximity, an interpenetration of the nations such as this, renders more imperative day by day the need for mankind to be able to speak to and understand each other, to exchange their ideas and the fruits of their activities.

Unfortunately, however moral and legitimate the demand may be for the complete satisfaction of this need, a barrier is opposed which until now has been almost insurmountable, namely, the difference of language. To what, then, should fall the task of throwing down, or at least of levelling up, this obstacle of Nature? Evidently to science, to teaching, to the school.

Alongside the material railway needed to enable our bodies to communicate, it is absolutely necessary to construct a "mental railway" for the intercourse of minds. This mental railway must take the form of a linguistic method that shall enable a person, by means of the language, to enter into and assimilate the intelligence, and the spirit of a foreign nation, not as now, in a period of ten or of twenty years, and in so doing to expend the third part of a lifetime, but in the space between two equinoxes, or, for those of trained will, in the space of a single season. On the day when this new species of locomotive is definitely organised and put at the service of men of thought and will, the brotherhood of nations will cease to be a vain and empty word—a word which Governments laugh to scorn, and peace as well as liberty will perhaps have found their most solid foundation.

Nations would never strive to cut each other's throats if they understood each other thoroughly, and if a healthy and moral hospitality drew them together. However great the perverse ambition of those who excite the races to make war upon each other, their efforts must inevitably fall to the ground if opposed to a universal league waging a continual crusade in the cause of the most sacred interests of humanity.

Nothing, therefore, could be better than this "mental railway" to prepare and hasten the development of that Areopagus which sooner or later—vowed inwardly by all men of heart—will effectually close the temple of war by curtailing and disarming for ever the sanguinary fury of political ambition. From this point of view a good linguistic method is not merely a scientific and a literary work, but a humanitarian and a moral one. As such, it is worthy of the greatest efforts of the profession of teaching, and perhaps takes the lead of all other scholastic undertakings.

"But the world is old," say the numerous friends of routine —those who have lived in it, those who live for it, and those who live by it—"the world is old, and that which the masterminds who have preceded us must have sought and could not discover—the solution of this grand problem—can we flatter ourselves that we can discover?"

If the world is old to-day, it was already old sixty years ago; and if, sixty years ago, every one had taken this reason, so dear to all quietists, to comfort themselves in idleness, we should never have had to this very hour the knowledge of either steam, or electricity, or the thousand other forces which science and industry have already begun to subdue or to transform as into new organs of our race.

Nations do not grow old; they change, and in so doing they remain eternally young. If the men of the last century were to awake to-day, they would have some difficulty in recognising the present generation as their children. They would at first, perhaps, believe in the accession of a new race. Pascal himself, at the sight of natural forces so magnificently conquered, so cunningly adapted to the needs of modern life, might well feel inclined to take us for magicians. Would he not be wonderstruck at the marvels executed by engineering and the omnipotence of calculation? Would he recognise in our sciences, in our industries, in our arts, the corollaries of his own discoveries and his own profound intuitions? Before the marvels of chemistry even Lavoisier, the father of this science, might well stand speechless.

"Nil mortalibus arduum est!" This statement, which in the ode of Horace sounds like a hyperbole, has become a living reality. Lightning itself and all the indomitable energies which the giants, sons of the earth, drew from the contact with mother earth, are now practically at the beck and call of man—"Sub ditione hominis."

In spite of this, or rather because of this, the earth is still young, extremely young; for the power of mankind is, above all, a growth. It is, as yet, hardly at the beginning. His success has, it is true, given to man a consciousness of his power; this is much, no doubt, but it is a commencement and not an end.

Considered from the moral point of view, can it be said that the world has attained to years of discretion? Which of us is in possession of the true knowledge of good and evil? Look around towards the four points of the compass and say whether the nations most resemble men actually and incontestably free, or children under tutelage. No, the world is not old, and the era of discovery, so far from being closed, has but just opened. Great inventions are the daughters of Necessity, and when Necessity has spoken, man seeks and always finds.

Before the advent of the railway, it may be said that nations lived so far apart that the need of speaking to and of understanding each other did not really exist. It made itself felt slightly at the frontiers, and for this Nature herself has provided.[1] But to-day, thanks to the locomotive, nations are next door to each other. Necessity wills that they shall be able to talk together with intimacy, that they shall have no more secrets one from the other, that they shall not betray one another, that at last they shall know and understand one another mutually and to the utmost depths of their natures.

The material railway has long been built, and it calls inevitably for the mental railway of which we have spoken. In reality this, if we but knew it, is the end of which the other is simply the means. Each cause must have its effect, and tends thereto until this has been realised. In the historical development of the human race that which was an "end" during one generation becomes a "means" to the next; that which to-day seems to us an "effect," to-morrow will be a "cause," and will have the virtues of a cause together with its character.

Material railway, mental railway: have we here a vain antithesis? Can the latter be constructed, and will it ever be constructed? Why not, we may ask, if for it there is, as we have seen, a historical necessity—a necessity of civilisation? Why not, if Nature possesses already the marvellous machinery which, in the child, weaves in so short a time the wondrous fabric of the human individuality out of the raw material of language? Why not, if the method sought for is working every day under our very eyes; if the child practises it continually with so much success as to assimilate the idiom of his native soil; and if all that is needful to transform it definitely into a general instrument of the mind is to submit the maternal process to the work of exegesis commanded by the profound saying of Bacon, "Interpretanda est natura"?

Our individual efforts to conquer the language of the countries which surround us, the love of children, the constant and assiduous search for the laws which must preside over the

---

[1] Frontier races speaking both languages (Trans.).

curious and rapid development of language in early years, the long philological studies, these have perhaps enabled us to discover some of the principles of this method, which, when perfected both by time and by practice, might well be called by the name of the "NATURAL METHOD."

To those who *à priori* tell us, "Your system, whatever it may be, and however ingenious it may be, can only represent a chimerical idea, or else it is simply a trick and a delusion, you are seeking to square the circle"—to those we answer as did the Greek sage to the sophist who denied that movement existed—the philosopher simply walked. We on our part point to the child—the little child who knows how to speak a language at three years of age, who has learnt it whilst playing round his mother, who speaks it in a way in which most of us would be proud of being able to speak the language of any of our neighbours. Yes, Nature has already solved the problem that we are investigating, and she holds a permanent school for early infancy, in which we can, if we wish, at any time take part, and where we may be able to study her never-failing processes.

Unhappily the child has remained up to the present a hackneyed riddle which we have never taken sufficient trouble to decipher or even to examine. In the feverish and changeful rush of its life we have not kept sight of the regular and mathematical development which has been effected in its mind by (or through) language. In the turmoil of its acts, sensations and feelings so diverse and multifold, we have hitherto been able to perceive only a pure game of chance. We have never been able to conceive that possibly there might be, or that we might find in this something resembling a method; that we might find somewhat of order, that is to say, a "principle of order." Yet the little child, which at the age of two years utters nothing but meaningless exclamations, at the age of three finds itself in possession of a complete language. How does it accomplish this? Does this miracle admit of explanation or not? Is it a problem of which there is a possibility of finding the unknown quantity?

It is instinct, says one. It is a gift of Nature, reply others. Very convenient answers, no doubt, having the remarkable property of equally well solving all questions of an intellectual and moral nature.

When Henri Mondeux,[1] in his appearances before the colleges, and even before the Académie des Sciences at Paris, stood up on the platform, and, without pens or paper, solved intuitively and in a few seconds problems which it had taken Arago eight days to calculate, the professors wagged their heads, and they also said, "It is a gift!" And thanks to this superb word, thanks to this impious disdain, the university has left buried with Henri Mondeux a method of calculation which, applied to steam, to electricity, to modern industry, might to-day have increased tenfold the power of mankind.[2]

No, the marvellous aptitude of children for assimilating a language is not a "gift;" it is the result of a process admirably carried out, resting upon principles as yet imperfectly apprehended, and often in entire contradiction to those which the usual systems now proclaim. Given a child of four or five years with a Greek or a Chinese nurse: is it true, or is it not true, that this child will speak Greek or will speak Chinese at the end of six months in a manner that will confound the greatest philologists in the world? And is it true, on the other hand, that if this same child had as masters these same philologists, at the end of six months it would know practically nothing of either of these languages? Therefore the child by the side of his nurse would have a gift or faculty which it would lose by the side of the savants!

Gift and instinct—these are two words, two sayings void of sense, to which man still turns to excuse his idleness or conceal his ignorance.

To conclude our preamble: the child learns in six months, in a year at the outside, to talk and also to think. The youth or the adult having to do but a portion of this work, since he already knows how to think, should therefore be able without trouble to learn in six months, or in a year at the outside, to speak any given language, be it Chinese, Japanese, Arabic, Sanscrit; German, English, or French. And he certainly can do this on condition that he follow the special process known

---

[1] A famous French calculating boy (Trans.).

[2] It may not be uninteresting to state here that one of the disciples of the author has worked out the theory and the method of this wonderful mental calculation, as the result of the hint given above, with extremely interesting and successful results, which will be embodied in a work on intuitive calculation (Trans.).

and so well applied by our own mothers. Nature has set herself the problem in equations: it is for us to clear the fractions and determine the unknown.

II.

MEANS OF DEMONSTRATING A TRUTH AND OF SETTING FORTH A SYSTEM—ANALYSIS AND SYNTHESIS.

When a teacher puts a question before the little public of his class, we may suppose that he knows the solution of it. In the same way when a writer upon pedagogy or the science of teaching undertakes to bring forward a new method to the larger public, he should be, or believe himself to be, in possession of a certain number of practical truths until that time more or less unknown. It is not, therefore, a discovery so much as a demonstration which he proposes to make.

Now there are, as is well known, two means of demonstrating a scientific theorem, or, in fact, a thesis of any kind whatsoever. We may either combine or turn about the data in order to discover the necessary constant relations which these facts bear one towards the other; or else, knowing these relations beforehand, we may bring them about or establish them in the first place, and then by a series of logical deductions arrive at the particular truth which results from these relations.

In reality these two processes are two portions of the same whole. The first, usually termed "analysis," is the rational part of the demonstration, since it establishes the necessary relations of things. The second, usually termed "synthesis," is the practical part, since it develops and brings to light the truths which lie in the germ within these relations. We may add that the one is the necessary complement of the other. Without the first the second leaves something arbitrary and unexplained. On the other hand, without synthesis and deduction, analysis remains but a barren effort, like a word half articulated or a circle abruptly and awkwardly broken through.

Therefore, to explain our present method as clearly as possible, that is, to demonstrate the practical truths embodied in the system, we must have recourse to the double process of analysis and synthesis. But in what can the analysis consist in a case such as this? It should be the same, for example, as the explanation of the process which has given us porcelain, or the web from the Jacquard loom, which would be an account of the successive experiments by which the two inventors have attained the realisation of their conception. It is, therefore, by the history of what we may term our "discovery" that we are invited by logic to begin the explanation of the system.

The reader is asked to pardon the intrusion of the author's personality in a work of this kind; but for an author the interest of the idea and his success take precedence over every other consideration, and in the name of logic, and for the sake of clearness of exposition, we may perhaps be permitted to begin the treatise by an account of the author's personal experiences.

We should like to point out before commencing that this linguistic method is, so far as we know, the first yet brought forward which begins by the advancement of a theory; it is indeed the first which even admits of a theory, or which it has been possible to form into a distinct system. Jacotot, Robertson, Ollendorf, &c., have in reality nothing to do with theory; their works, as we shall show, do not rest upon any real principle of psychology; they either consider themselves superior to all principles, or more probably the possibility of a theory never occurred to them.

III.

THE AUTHOR ATTEMPTS TO LEARN THE GERMAN LANGUAGE— CLASSICAL ANTECEDENTS—THE COMMENCEMENT—HAMBURG UNIVERSITY.

On leaving what are termed by our masters "solid studies," I embraced, both by taste and by vocation, the career of teaching. I was at first in charge of a fifth (lower middle) class, and in the intervals of the lessons I had to prepare students for the Baccalaureat.[1] Besides this, I followed assiduously the Academy courses in literature and science, most of these being given at hours when I was at liberty. This first stage, and these university studies, in our lovely town of Caen, were

---

[1] The French matriculation, considered equal to a degree (Trans.).

to last four years. I threw myself into the methods and the classical proceedings with all the ardour of which one is capable in the early days of youth.

For the purpose of argument I will grant that this zeal occasionally did develop sundry small prodigies. For instance, at my first attempt, a student who had never before learnt any Latin was taken in hand by me one October, and in the October following he passed his examination at the head of the section. All which is to indicate that I must have known, to have practised it, both the strength and the weakness of the classical method of teaching, which I shall attack and combat later on.

My professors at the university (of whom I may be allowed to mention the revered names of MM. A. Charma and Ch. Hippeau), believing they had distinguished certain philosophical aptitudes in their pupil, engaged me to cross the Rhine and go to listen, if not to the great masters of the German school, Hegel and Schelling, at least to the last echoes of their voices and the doctrines of their successors. I departed with joy, furnished with precious letters of introduction to many of the celebrities of the day.

To cross the North Sea, to leave Havre and alight at Hamburg, did not require a great effort. The first and greatest obstacle to conquer was not the distance, but the language, for I hardly knew the German characters; but at the age at which I was then, nothing is deemed impossible, and I thoroughly expected at the end of a few weeks to be able to speak German, at any rate, as well as the children of the place. It seemed to me that a living language might be somehow assimilated in the very air of the country.

Hamburg was thus my first stage. My idea was there to conquer the foundation of the language, then to proceed to Berlin to enter the university. Hamburg had, moreover, an academy with many able professors and largely frequented by students. Every class was crowded with earnest students of both sexes, a striking and humiliating contrast to the unfortunate French universities, usually neglected by the people, and practically unknown to the district ever since the time when the State constituted them its exclusive property. I had thus ready to my hand an excellent means both of controlling my progress and of habituating my ears to the accent and to the language of German science. I promised myself to profit well by such a good opportunity, and to make considerable use of this pleasure.

The carrier pigeon, before taking its flight, mounts straight upwards into the air, and, seeking its way, measures the space it has to traverse. To estimate approximately and to fix in my own mind the distance between the point of departure and the point of arrival, I resolved to listen at the very first at least once to each of the professors, and see how much of his thought I should be able to grasp by the attentive observation of his gesture and accent. Alas! I can only state my absolute incapability of penetrating a solitary one of the ideas so eagerly and so religiously gathered up by a crowd of students whose happiness I envied. I was therefore compelled to set to work, commencing "at the very beginning."

IV.

THE FIRST EFFORT—THE GRAMMAR AND IRREGULAR VERBS—UNSUCCESSFUL RESULT.

For the study of languages I knew but one process—a process without any particular name—the classical process. My faith in the grammar, the dictionary, the translation from and into the foreign language, was entire and above suspicion. To my mind the value and the efficacy of this "universal" process were indisputable. Was it not the final outcome of the experience and the science of mankind? To learn first words, then the rules for grouping these words, and of these to make up sentences, this seemed to me to include the whole art, the whole secret, the whole philosophy of the teaching of languages. Was it not thus that I had learnt Latin myself, and had afterwards taught it to others? Was it not to this process that I owed what knowledge I possessed of Greek?

When I thought about it seriously, my knowledge of Greek and Latin appeared to me, it is true, insufficient for a living language, and the thought of the length of time I had devoted to their study would sometimes come to trouble the serenity of my confidence and to disquiet the hope that I had of mastering German in a few weeks; but a word, a saying, an inward voice, had the virtue of chasing away all these troublesome thoughts. "Those are dead languages," I said to myself, "and German is a spoken language." And this simple antithesis sufficed to put to flight every objection, every importunate suggestion.

I had armed myself after leaving Havre with a grammar and a dictionary. I applied myself resolutely to the study of the grammar. I divided it into seven or eight portions, and I devoured it, I assimilated it in a week. Declensions, strong, weak, and mixed; conjugations, regular and irregular; adverbs, prefixes, and propositions, syntax and method, all passed under my eye, upon my tongue, and into my memory— all with the exception of the table of irregular verbs. This was divided into two parts and imposed as a task for the two following days.

In my previous studies I had given more than a year to learn the Latin grammar; in ten days I had mastered the grammar of the German language. This victory swelled my courage, and I hastened forthwith to the Academy in order to measure the extent of this first step and to realise the power acquired.

But alas! in vain did I strain my ears; in vain my eye strove to interpret the slightest movements of the lips of the professor; in vain I passed from the first class room to a second; not a word, not a single word would penetrate to my understanding. Nay, more than this, I did not even distinguish a single one of the grammatical forms so newly studied; I did not recognise even a single one of the irregular verbs just freshly learnt, though they must certainly have fallen in crowds from the lips of the speaker.

For a moment I was prostrated. Then musing over the extent of my first effort, I consoled myself for this deception or for this failure by reflecting that I had familiarised myself as yet with rules and terminations only, and that with respect to the foundation of the language itself, I knew only its 248 irregular verbs. All that was needful again to give me courage was the explanation or reason of my failure; and I thought I had found it in nothing more serious than the foregoing consideration. What now had to be done, therefore, was to attack the foundations of the German language. But where was I to find these foundations and how detach them from their surroundings?

V.

THE STUDY OF THE ROOTS—SECOND DECEPTION.

When, in my school-days, I had been learning Greek, I had studied Lancelot's book of roots. Full of faith in the promise of the professors, who, without being certain of it themselves, yet assured us that it sufficed to thoroughly know the two thousand root words to know Greek thoroughly, I had perhaps ten times learnt, ten times forgotten, and ten times more reconquered the "Garden of Greek Roots," which finally became for me a kind of breviary which I repeated over every morning.

The promise of my masters, it is true, was not fulfilled, and although I was perhaps a better Hellenist than any other of my co-disciples at the university, I could not altogether deceive myself. I was very far from being able to read and enjoy Thucydides and Plato as I could read and enjoy the authors of my native land. But Greek was a "dead language," and no doubt there was, for a knowledge of dead languages, a point which one could never expect to pass. This reflection tranquillised me by deluding me as to the real value of my classical knowledge.

So that if by the "Garden of Greek Roots" I had not altogether arrived at the promised land, I did not feel that I had the right to draw from this an argument against the efficacy of the German roots. German being a living language, the process which was defective for Greek might yet be excellent for German. One should be careful not to prejudge. A remedy which might be impotent upon a dead body may very easily produce an effect upon a living being.

Far from confirming this objection, reason reminded me that there should be, and in fact there was, for each language a foundation, a substance, as for every other thing; and that this foundation, this substance, is nothing else than the collection of the roots, namely, that part, that unalterable element of the language which supports and nourishes the varied and variable assemblage of cases and of conjugations as a plant supports and maintains the phenomena of efflorescence.

I made up my mind, therefore, to treat German exactly by the same process as Greek, and I visited all the booksellers of

Hamburg to procure a book of this description, which, vastly to my astonishment, was not to be found. Nevertheless, German was, I reflected, a language constructed after the manner of Greek. Ought not the study of the roots to be made the subject of the first lesson of all the courses in philology? Could it be possible for this science to have any other point of departure?

I deemed it impossible that a collection of German roots should not exist; and, in spite of the denials of the booksellers, I set myself to work to find this book, and to look through all their shops (they spoke French), and I ended at last by discovering in the corner of a shelf the treasure I sought.

It was quite a small book, bearing the name of a Jesuit father; a very complete collection, and with the roots arranged in alphabetical order. If my memory serves me, this booklet contained eight or nine hundred roots. The smallness of this number, I must confess, somewhat disenchanted me; it disconcerted and almost discouraged me. If, indeed, with the two thousand Greek roots I had arrived at no very practical result, how could I hope to achieve anything practical by a study which only required half so great an effort?

A thousand roots, I said to myself at last, after having counted and recounted the columns of the book; it is, at any rate, so much gained. Let us begin, afterwards we will see if anything more complete can be discovered.

Four days afterwards the Jesuit father's work had passed into my memory. I gave myself four days more to look through and digest my grammar, my 248 irregular verbs, and my 800 roots. This time I thought I really possessed the foundation of the language, as well as the laws and the secret of its forms, regular and irregular.

If the method was good—and how could I doubt it?—was it not the grammatical and classical method? If the masters of my *alma mater* were not deceived—and how should they be?—themselves the representatives and the ministers of the wisdom of the university? If, in a word, I had not completely mistaken the reality of my efforts and the amount of work accomplished, I ought now to possess the German language, doubtless not in all the amplitude of its riches, but sufficiently at any rate to listen, to read, to penetrate whatever was within the reach of a person of ordinary intelligence.

I hastened to the academy, content within myself, and filled with confidence, tasting in advance the double pleasure of hearing science through a foreign dialect, and of feeling my small personality suddenly increased by half in mastering the speech of a vast country.

Imagine then, if it be possible, the astonishment at first, then the stupefaction, then the degradation by which I was overtaken after the first quarter of an hour at the lecture I attended, when I had to submit to the evidence, and to confess to myself that I was, so far as regards the spoken language, exactly in the same state as upon the first day; that I did not understand a word, not a syllable, and that all my efforts had been made in pure waste, or at least had produced no appreciable result.

This was no longer a mere deception—it was a failure; nay, more than this, it was a defeat. My *amour propre* was deeply touched; my courage and the confidence I felt in my energy were greatly diminished thereby. I sorrowfully wandered back to my lodgings, seeking the causes of my incapability, and unfortunately this time unable to give myself any explanation.

VI.

AN ATTEMPT AT CONVERSATION—DISGUST AND FATIGUE—READING AND TRANSLATION, THEIR WORTHLESSNESS DEMONSTRATED.

I now attempted to converse with my hosts. Up to this time I had neglected, or rather disdained, this means, as being too slow, too uncertain, too casual, too troublesome, especially for those to whom I spoke. However, I had taken rooms at a hairdresser's; I could hardly have been in a better school. So I drew myself together for another effort, and each day found me established for long hours in the hairdresser's saloon, where I attempted to follow the conversation, hazarding from time to time a sentence carefully prepared beforehand, awkwardly constructed with the aid of my roots and grammar, and apparently always possessing the property of astonishing and hugely amusing the customers.

Meanwhile the days passed and the weeks also, and truly I could not see what I had gained from one morning to the other. I considered that the sundry conventional phrases I could now exchange with the frequenters of the house were really not worth the pains I had given either to gather or to retain them. I felt, besides, that to converse with me was an undertaking hardly less painful than with a deaf-mute. Moreover, I had an intense desire, an ardent thirst for order and logic, to which the scraps of ordinary conversation, more or less vapid and continually interrupted, corresponded but ill. This want of order enervated and fatigued me beyond measure. Studied in this manner, a language appeared to me under the guise of a Penelope's web, where the work of the night destroyed that of the day.

Seeing no limit to a work thus carried on at haphazard, I suddenly broke off with a process that could lead me to nothing, and I returned to reading—translation by the aid of the dictionary. The prodigal son, who had one moment wandered from the straight path, entered once more upon classic ways. The depth of the ideas translated would prove no obstacle, nay, rather for a student of philosophy should possess an attraction; so I went direct to Goethe and Schiller.

If I had been able to doubt for one instant the wisdom and the infallibility of the university, "Et si mens non læva fuisset," I should have been able,—indeed, I ought to have been forced, from this moment to appreciate at its true value the study of roots and the vocabulary in general, that exercise so much extolled by all scholastic bodies.

Practically, in spite of the perfect knowledge I believed I had acquired of the roots of the German language, although I was able to repeat them by heart from one end to the other, and although I had saturated myself with them every morning before breakfast, yet when I opened the first page of my author, I found I could recognise hardly any of the words I had acquired, though the page must have contained many of them.

If perchance one of them seemed to me to be a little better known or less strange than the others, its inner sense always escaped me; this I could never find, and above all could never precisely fix. It was exactly as one recalls having seen a person somewhere without being able to call to mind either his name or what he was.

When my glance fell upon a word of my native tongue, the idea represented by this word shone or sparkled forth, so to speak, under my eyes. The word became transfigured with a certain mysterious element of life. I beheld no longer mere letters; I saw the idea itself.

Strange that this phenomenon would not occur for the German word, even when I had been able to determine its meaning by the aid of the dictionary. The word was always as a dead body stretched upon the paper. Its meaning shone not forth under my gaze; I could draw forth neither the idea nor the life.

"Tragen," for instance, was for me but an arbitrary assemblage of six letters, perfectly incapable of revealing to me the effort or the special movement it had the mission to represent. The hour was yet far distant when I should ask myself the reason of this difference, or should seek the explanation of this curious phenomenon. Other trials were needed to open my eyes.

So my work on the roots and the irregular verbs seemed to have been made in vain. Nevertheless I could not bring myself to believe this seriously. "The fire smoulders under the ashes," I assured myself, "and will brighten up little by little. We must read, read, read, day in and day out; translate, translate continually; hunt, hunt a hundred times after the same word in the dictionary; catch it a hundred times, a hundred times release it; we shall finish by taming it."

The first day I had much difficulty in deciphering even one page, and I was not sure I had not made a dozen blunders in this. The second page seemed to be equally difficult with the first. For a week I worried and tossed about my dictionary. In this week I had hardly interpreted the meaning of eight pages, and the ninth did not promise to be less obscure or less laborious than the preceding.

I felt I was not advancing, that I should never by this means arrive at the knowledge of the language in its totality, that the words did not grave themselves upon my memory, and that my work this time was indeed a Penelope's web. Translation might be a useful and necessary exercise for the study of Greek and Latin; it appeared to me to be far less fruitful for living languages.

For the first time in my life I dared to question the efficacy of the classical methods of the university. I still maintained them, it is true, for the ancient tongues; but I boldly condemned them for modern languages, and these are the considerations upon which I grounded my judgment.

"To translate a volume of 300 pages would take some 300 days; this is a whole scholastic year: and, moreover, would this work be profitable except to a person who should set himself to learn the pages of the book by heart as he translated them? Now no one can ignore the fact that by the time he had mastered the last page he would probably have forgotten at least 290 pages. Moreover, this book is far from containing the whole of the language, with all its terms and all its forms.

"At school, when we had finished construing a book of Herodotus, we were made to pass to Thucydides. Now, I never found that the interpretation of the first book facilitated very much the interpretation of the second. The same verb, it is true, reappeared often, but nearly always with a different signification. Each sentence was an enigma which must be deciphered with the aid of a dictionary.

"Translation is not merely a slow and painful process, but it leads to nothing and can lead to nothing. Suppose that I have translated the entire volume, there is every evidence that I should not be in a state either to speak or understand speech, or even to read readily a second volume."

The means was therefore judged, and condemned for ever. I closed my Goethe and my Schiller, decided not to reopen these books until the day that I could speak the language of their authors.

However, I had not arrived at my goal; I judged it, indeed, farther away than ever, for my faith was beginning to be shaken. What new proceeding should I next essay? To what artifice could I have recourse? For it was indeed necessary that I should learn German; I *would* learn German. The thing could not be impossible; the little children learnt it easily enough; the hairdresser's babies prattled around me, saying all they wished to say, understanding all that was said to them, answering to all that was asked of them, and this without having learnt either grammar or roots or irregular verbs, and without ever having worried a dictionary.

VII.

THE OLLENDORF METHOD — ENCHANTMENT — THIRTY LESSONS IN TEN DAYS — A DOUBT — SAD ACKNOWLEDGMENT OF THE MASTER — DELUSION.

I paid another visit to the booksellers of Hamburg, and telling them of my unfortunate experiences, I begged them to let me into the secret of the persons who learn German, or rather of those who had really arrived at learning it.

They immediately offered me Ollendorf's book, and bade me pay especial attention to these words, "fifty-fourth edition." The whole world then studied this book! There was no doubt of it; it was certainly here that all the foreigners who spoke German had learnt that language. I bought the celebrated method; I read the preface attentively, then I meditated and I pondered for some time over this promise, "German in ninety lessons."

Three months added to the long weeks sacrificed to my unfruitful trials represented a period which exceeded considerably the time I had judged necessary for a first initiation into the ordinary language, and from this would result an annoying delay which would derange all my plans for study at the Berlin University. I therefore put the question to myself, if I could not, by stubborn efforts, accomplish in six weeks the work which an ordinary student would achieve in three months? It was a thing that might be tried. I divided my day into three parts, and in each I placed a lesson of Ollendorf.

It is unnecessary to say more than that success recompensed my zeal, and each day saw me at the end of my triple task. I should like to retrace here for the benefit both of teachers and of students the impressions which I felt in passing abruptly from the classic methods to these new methods, which might be aptly termed "extra-scholastic."

1. Instead of isolated words, as abstract as logarithms, such as the roots and irregular verbs, connected together by the purely fortuitous circumstance of the similarity of their initial letters, Ollendorf produced words ready set in their phrases, the meaning of which was consequently definitely fixed, and which had for connection, if not logical relationship, at any

rate those of the immediate wants of life and of every-day usage.

"Have you a knife?"—"Yes, I have a knife."
"Have you any shoes?"—"Yes, I have some shoes."

2. The grammar, instead of being presented as an undigested mass of abstractions, of theories more or less obscure, of rules and exceptions regulating *à priori*, and from the heights of a special book, matters unknown to the pupil, was hidden beneath the kindly form of counsel given as the necessity for it arose, passing immediately into practice, embodying itself in actual facts and in habitual locutions to which one had recourse a hundred times a day.

3. It was no longer by the figurative literary language of classical authors that the pupil was forced to begin. It was the expression of the life of every day, the expression of the most ordinary phenomena that Ollendorf presented to us, or pretended to present to us, and this in doses having the appearance of being regulated according to the measure of a partial effort of the mind.

This linguist gave the actual, objective world for the foundation of his edifice; the world of facts, not of pure idealities and abstractions. With him we commenced no longer at the topmost summit, as we had done at college when learning Greek and Latin, where metaphorical language was the kind almost exclusively cultivated, and was in reality the only language held in honour.

4. The same word reappeared indefinitely; sprung upon one abruptly, incoherently, *apropos* of nothing, and subduing by its very frequency both the eye and the ear. This want of order, this desultoriness appeared to me to conform perfectly with the ordinary method of life.

Ollendorf's method was decidedly based upon Nature: it was certainly a natural method. As such it could not fail to lead to the point at which the child, whose infallible method Ollendorf seemed to have copied, so quickly and easily arrives.

These numerous advantages amply accounted to me for the favour which the new method enjoyed, and the vogue which had raised it to twenty editions a year. After the arid proceedings of the classical methods, and the intellectual fatigue which results from these, Ollendorf's book spread before those who still had the courage to study languages like a delicious oasis, where real and living beings were once more encountered, instead of the sempiternal and odiously abstract phantasms of the classical solitudes.

I found one thing only to object to in the book, and this was its smallness. My repeated checks had rendered me distrustful. Its weight seemed to me, at first glance, too light to equal that of a complete idiomatic system; its volume appeared to me too restricted to contain the whole material of a human language. But the promise of the author was formal, and formally inscribed in the preface to the reader. This promise had been repeated, republished fifty-four times in fifty-four editions. Had I the right to doubt a statement whose truthfulness no one until that time had publicly contested?

So I boldly entered my new skiff, making regularly my three knots a day. After an uninterrupted effort, a struggle without quarter for a whole fortnight, I had conquered, and completely conquered, the half of the book, thoroughly learning off each exercise, repeating it, copying it out, taking each lesson as a subject, elaborating it, treating it in all imaginable ways.

During this time I severely denied myself all attempts at conversation with the family at whose house I was staying. To be able to construct as well as to understand a sentence, I considered it was necessary first to be in possession of all its elements. A single unknown term sufficed to render it either impossible or incomprehensible. I did not desire to expose myself to a failure which might affect or diminish my courage. I did not feel myself yet sufficiently assured to dare to challenge the doubt.

After the forty-fifth lesson I was seized with a great temptation to attend one of the Academy classes. But the fear of a fresh defeat, which might paralyse all my forces, restrained me. "When I have finished," I said to myself, "I will no longer deny myself this pleasure. Yet another week, and then another. Patience till then, and courage."

The third week passed and the fourth. I had mastered the whole of Ollendorf. Did I know German? Perhaps,—but indeed I was hardly sure of it.

From the third week doubts had begun to assail me, which

I repulsed as suggestions of the Evil One. The nearer I approached to the end of the book, the faster they arose,— numerous, importunate, pointing out thousands of forms, thousands of words, forgotten or wilfully omitted by the author. They became truly terrible when at the foot of one of the last pages I came upon a note where the master, taking each of his disciples, as it were, to one side, acknowledged in confidence that the work was but roughed out, and invited him to invent and construct by himself similar exercises to those given, assuring him that he would shortly be able to compose them.

Up to this point I had implicitly believed in the words of the master. To believe in him any further was clearly impossible. I candidly avowed myself incompetent for what he termed the completion of the undertaking, which was in reality that of teaching myself a language I did not know. Without going to the Academy for the proof or the demonstration of the fact, I understood that I had been once more deceived.

Talking was, as a matter of fact, equally difficult, or perhaps I should say equally impossible, as a month ago, and the conversations in the hairdresser's shop did not seem to be less impenetrable than at the date of my arrival. I was at a loss especially at every point for the verbs, and these the most common and essential. Having represented throughout the book nothing but written words, having never in reality translated any of the perceptions or conceptions proper to myself,—when I wished to express these, all the words learnt by heart immediately took flight, and I found myself exactly in the condition of Tantalus, and this without being able to discover the sins that were costing me this chastisement.

That which had led astray my inexperience in the Ollendorf method was above all its contrast with the classical method and the deserved criticism it indirectly administered. I was not to discover till much later the prodigious errors of the pedagogic art that had presided over this miserable compilation of words.

For the present, all my wrath was poured upon the bookseller who had praised and sold me the drug. At first he entrenched himself behind the time-honoured formula, "Well, anyhow that's the book every one buys;" then changing his tune, he drew forth from his shelves two other books and cast them towards me—Robertson and Jacotot. I piously carried away these two fresh masters.

VIII.

JACOTOT AND ROBERTSON—DISORDER AND ARBITRARINESS ESTA-
BLISHED AS PRINCIPLES—DISCONNECTED STEPS—THE SYSTE-
MATIC VOCABULARY BY PLŒTZ.

"All is in all," said Jacotot.
This time, instead of yielding myself blindly to the good faith of my guide, I determined to examine, to scrutinise attentively, his ways and means; to judge beforehand, if possible, the point of arrival by the point of departure; to read the last lesson of the book by the light of the first.

Ollendorf proceeded by irregular bounds, by leaps and somersaults. His principle was disorder—intentional and systematic disorder. His logic consisted in mocking at logic. In this he thought himself in accord with Nature. I had thought so too in the first instance, as others besides myself had thought, for the book was in its fifty-fourth edition.

Jacotot, on the other hand, played as his imagination led him with the diverse sources of the association of ideas, linked word to word, perception to perception, thought to thought, sentence to sentence, everything to everything. From the acorn he went to the oak, from the oak to the carpenter's axe, from the axe to the ship, from the ship to the sea, from the sea to the clouds; from the clouds he descended again upon the plain to go to the tillers of the soil, to the harvests, to the flourmills, to the rivers, &c. All was in all, and all roads led to Rome. He laid the plan of the teaching which was to return to us later from Germany under the name of "object-lessons."

Nothing then seemed more contradictory than these two systems. Which was the better? for the choice had to be made. After meditating long over them, I thought I perceived that the two systems, apparently so opposed, touched at a point, and that this point was a vice, and a fundamental vice, which took from both the right to arrogate the name of a "Method." Both rested upon "the arbitrary," and a frightful arbitrary it was. If indeed Ollendorf could not state exactly why from the bread-knife he jumped to the Englishman's or the Spaniard's jackboot, rather than to the back of an elephant or the planet Saturn; why he admitted the verb "to dance," and refused access to the verb "to abstain,"—so, on his side, Jacotot would have been greatly embarrassed to explain why, instead of going from the acorn to the ship, he did not go to the roof of the Louvre or the belfry of Notre-Dame.

Although this latter system seemed to me to be certainly superior to the former, still I felt that to yield myself to Jacotot was to embark in a vessel unprovided with compass or rudder. It was a thousand chances to one that I should ever touch port, but rather should drift about continually on a limitless ocean, only to hear in the end the new pilot cry out to me, as the other had done, "Now try and find your way by yourself."

The perception of this first vice enabled me to espy a crowd of others. I felt the weight of the book also, and I found it quite as light as that of Ollendorf. I turned over its 120 or 160 lessons, and I came to the conclusion that the frame was decidedly much too small to contain the human language, whose imposing mass and infinitude of detail I was now beginning to realise. I closed the book and I opened Robertson.

I found him occupied in dissecting, I think, a page of "Gil Blas," pirouetting about in a hundred different ways on each word, turning and twisting each sentence about endlessly, putting questions and giving answers often more than extravagant, then finally inviting the reader to set himself to work in the same way, and create from his own inner consciousness and from the same material a chapter as long as that of the teacher. A single paragraph of Gil Blas thus ended by developing into a large volume.

Evidently for Robertson as for Jacotot "all was in all." Their proceedings differed but in this, that Jacotot applied himself more particularly to make substantive spring from substantive, intentionally neglecting the verb as too rebellious for his purpose. Robertson, on the other hand, exerted himself to make sentence spring from sentence, and consequently verb from verb. This he did by proceeding by questions and answers, by having recourse to what he termed the "Socratic method."

I put to Robertson these two questions:—

1. How many pages of "Gil Blas" approximately would be required, developed in this manner, for one to be sure of having gathered and assorted the whole of the forms, the whole of the

terms of the German language; meaning of course the language of ordinary life?

2. The collection having been made, how much time should I require to read it over and repeat it in order to fully assimilate the contents; by which I mean, to be in a condition that, given an idea, not of Lesage or Fénélon, of Addison or Swift, but of my own, in which I should be able instantaneously and intuitively to find the exact and adequate expression for it?

I turned the leaves over and over and backwards and forwards, and I found no answer to either of these questions. I therefore condemned Robertson's method on the same indictment as that of Jacotot, supporting my judgment on the same considerations.

A certain book was, at this epoch, greatly in vogue at the German schools—a book specially prepared for the study of French. This was the "Systematic Vocabulary" by Plœtz. The two languages ran side by side in this book. If it was good for the one, it should be equally good for the other. Plœtz at this time was teaching French with great success in the "Gymnase Français" at Berlin. I know not how it was that it occurred to none of the booksellers to offer me this book. It was not until much later, when I no longer had any need for it, that it fell under my notice. I afterwards became acquainted with Plœtz himself, and often discussed with him the merits and defects of his book.

In my judgment the "Systematic Vocabulary" lacked, in order to be a real method, merely that which was lacking to Pygmalion's statue to make it Galatea, namely, life. Quite sufficient, one may say. It is nevertheless true that Plœtz was upon the right track. If he had allowed himself to study the little child, and then to recast his book upon the model of the as yet unpublished proceedings of Nature, instead of leaving it in the state of dry and abstract category, of incomplete nomenclature, always more or less arbitrary, then the NATURAL METHOD would have been constructed twenty-five years sooner. He did not try this; one can only suppose that the idea did not occur to him.

The book made the fortune of its author without producing the results sought for by him. The best criticism upon this first book is the later work of Plœtz himself. The "Vocabulary" being always found incapable of giving the student the knowledge and usage of the language studied, the author, in order to supply the deficiencies of his work, was obliged to have recourse to the composition of an indefinite series of dialogues, themes, and exercises in the same style as the attempts of Ollendorf and Robertson.

Even supposing good luck had at the time placed in my hands this new instrument, incontestably more perfect than the preceding ones, should I have been able to make better use of it than the author himself? Evidently not. I have, therefore, little to regret in not having earlier become acquainted with the "Systematic Vocabulary."

IX.

BERLIN UNIVERSITY—MIXING WITH THE STUDENTS—FRUITLESS ATTENDANCE AT THE CLASSES.

As the sick person, feeling himself at the end of his strength, seeks for change of air and surroundings, so now I felt an irresistible desire for change of place. I left Hamburg—sojourn of misfortune, witness of my many defeats—and I departed for Berlin. My first care was to become acquainted with the persons to whom I had letters of introduction, to make inquiries of them as to the scientific resources afforded by the technical schools of the capital. Almost every one talked, and liked to talk, French; and I never ceased wondering how all these people had learnt this language. Every one encouraged me to frequent as much as possible the company of the students, assuring me that this was the shortest means of becoming able to understand and speak German—the first thing, of course, to which I must attain.

To be well received by the various students' societies was easy enough. The French were much liked at this epoch; they were feasted and petted by every one. But what was most difficult was to get any of these young people to converse in German with a Frenchman. I soon recognised that the greater part of them sought my society with the interested motive of exercising their French. At first I let them do as they wished—I had talked alone long enough in Hamburg. But I was not long in taking steps to counteract this abuse, and, recalling myself to duty, I forbade myself all further conversation in French. Visits and friends at once began to decrease. I already knew how apt my German conversations were to produce this effect.

I needed something to take the place of the chattings and socialities of the students, which, moreover, appeared to me not particularly profitable. So I resolved, for a next trial, to attend the university courses, and to do this perseveringly from morning until night. I wished to see whether my ear would not in time become accustomed to the sounds of the German words and the accent of the phrases; and whether, like the child, by sheer force of bending the attention and sense of hearing to them, I could not become able intuitively to penetrate the meaning of the expressions used by the professor.

I persevered thus for a whole week, listening without understanding a word to discourses which seemed to me to form one continuous sound, and which, if they had been written down, would have formed a single word on a single line three-quarters of an hour long. In other words, on the last day of the week, as on the first, I could distinguish neither the words, nor the sentences, nor the periods of the professor. I had sat and watched for seven or eight hours a day, various mouths alternately opening and shutting, and this was all.

Such an entirely negative result demonstrated to me that the new means was no means at all, and that I might attend the German university for a thousand years under these conditions without learning German.

What was I to do next? Had I not tried everything? Was a Frenchman really a being incapable of learning any other language than his own? No, for I had seen some simple workmen who had come from France some time after myself, who apparently could understand everything and talk about everything with the first-comer. What was it that held in such utter incapability a young professor gifted with a strong memory and a will perhaps even stronger still?

X.

A HEROIC RESOLVE—STUDY OF THE DICTIONARY—STRUGGLE AND VICTORY—THIRD DECEPTION—FUTILE TOIL.

There still remained one last method . . . but one so strange, so extraordinary, so unusual—I might say, so heroic—that I hardly dared propose it to myself. This supreme means was nothing else than to learn off the whole dictionary. "My ear," I told myself, "is not sufficiently familiarised, first with the terminations, then with the body of the words—that part from which the idea ought to shine and spring forth instantaneously.

"Now a resolute and persevering study of the dictionary would evidently produce this double result. In fact, the same termination as well as the same root-word striking thousands and thousands of times upon the eye, the ear, and the mind—the inner sense of this termination and this root, the idea hidden in these two elements of the language—would end by shining forth with the sound itself, and by being substituted, so to speak, for it.

"Therefore, if I could assimilate the whole dictionary, with the 30,000 words it contains, there was every evidence that, every term being no longer a sound but an idea, I should be able to follow and understand every conversation, read every book, and, by reason of this double exercise, arrive in a very short space of time at being able to speak fluently myself."

"But to learn off the dictionary," added my thoughts, "what an extravagance! Was ever such an idea entertained before? It was absurd on the face of it, and quite unrealisable. There must be some other means of arriving at the same result. The child learns no dictionaries by heart; and even supposing such a desperate means should enable me to succeed, it was certainly not a method I could recommend to any one else. If none other existed, no one would, of a surety, ever undertake to learn German." Such were the reflections and objections by which I myself combated this strange idea.

After a time the human mind becomes familiarised with situations and resolutions which at first appeared impossible and utterly repugnant. Seeking a fresh way and finding none, I fell back naturally on my dictionary, and returned in spite of myself to my latest notion.

"It is quite true," I reflected, "that the child learns to speak without opening the dictionary; but it is also true that it finds itself in conditions far other than those in which I am placed—conditions extremely favourable, in which I cannot hope again to place myself, and which I am powerless artificially to re-establish. Besides, the child has before it an indefinite time, such as I have not now at my disposal. The hours glide away slowly for the child, but for me day devours day, month courses after month. Cost what it may, I must go forward. I am forced to turn, like Alexander, to any remedy, however violent, only let the effect be prompt."

My will began to waver. From day to day the thought of the dictionary gained ground. My reason even allowed itself to be subdued, and gradually passed over to the enemy. The finishing stroke was given by a sudden consideration and an argument which seemed to me final. I thought: "Is not learning the dictionary in reality the work which is imposed when we study the classical tongues? Would it not be simply carrying out at a stroke by a continued—a Herculean—effort what we are supposed to accomplish at college, little by little, in the space of nine years, that is to say, by nine times 360 partial efforts? Is not the pupil obliged to cull the words of a language one by one, during nine or ten years, from the dictionary?

"If he has been made to seek diligently for them, instead of having them offered directly to him, so that he could serve himself with them from hand to hand, this is apparently because the research itself is held to be advantageous and profitable for him. Indeed, thus to hold an expression in his memory during the time required by its research, its determination, its organisation, and its application to a given thought, is not all this to submit it to a kind of incubation thoroughly suitable for the purpose of opening out and fixing this expression in the mind?"

I took again the path toward the classical teaching, and after having made the *amende honorable*, I entered again into grace. I exalted, I glorified its principles and its fundamental process. Despair had brought about, between routine and my mind, a full and complete reconciliation, and without asking myself the question whether the nine times 360 efforts were always crowned with success, I exclaimed—

"There is but one wisdom in the world, that in which I have been brought up; the wisdom of the university! I will study the dictionary as they do at college, as the university requires. But I will study it with a vigour which will certainly gain me the plaudits of the masters who have sung me the praises of the Greek roots. The frequency of repetition, a repetition occasioned by daily needs, will supply, and more than supply, the 'incubation' occasioned by the constant use of the vocabulary."

Thereupon I took up my dictionary. I weighed it again and again in my hands; I counted its pages, and the number of words in a page, then I did a sum in multiplication. "Three hundred pages," I said to myself, "and thirty thousand words!"

"If this can be learnt off, if the task be feasible, it must be accomplished within a month. For no one need flatter himself that he could retain for very long without practice a mass like this learnt under these conditions. The new matter will soon have covered up and obliterated what had gone before. Besides, there is the question of fatigue. Thirty days of superhuman work is a task which a man of my age and constitution can undertake at a pinch, but there is no use in abusing one's strength for nothing, and an effort such as this could not be indefinitely prolonged.

"So, three hundred pages in thirty days; this is ten pages a day. Can I do it? And if I manage it to-day, could I do it to-morrow, and the next day, ten days following, twenty days following? Let us try."

The next day, at six o'clock in the morning, I opened my dictionary, and at noon I had accomplished my first task. It was a good augury, but I did not yet dare to judge of the final result. To prevent every cause of discouragement, to avoid every annoying interruption from without, I thought it prudent to resort to measures under whose protection I had been able to study first my roots and then the lessons of Ollendorf. I put myself, and declared myself, in quarantine, and prohibited every walk and every dialogue which was not an absolute necessity. I placed my recompense at the end of the month, the most lovely of all recompenses; a lesson in philosophy at last understood at the university!

The second day a fresh fight, and at noon, victory! And in the afternoon I had time to look over yesterday's field of battle. The eighth day I achieved my eighth triumph. Three more such efforts and the German language will be tamed.

The second week's struggle placed the second quarter of the dictionary in my power. Fifteen thousand words were in my memory. To turn back was impossible. My courage was exalted, my confidence in the coming success was absolute; my happiness was complete.

Should I for a moment break my quarantine and go to hear a lesson, just one lesson at the university? I bravely resisted the temptation, and persevered in my first resolve, desiring absolutely to keep whole and entire the surprise which was to come at the end of the month.

The third week gave me the third quarter of the dictionary; the thirtieth day I turned page 314, the last; and, more triumphant than Cæsar, I exclaimed, "Vici!" That same evening I went to seek my crown at the university—a crown surely well merited.

To comprehend what now happened to me it is necessary to have studied profoundly, as I have since been able to do, the question of language; to have determined accurately the conditions in which mankind, infant or adult, must be placed that they may be able to learn any language, no matter which.

I understood not a word—not a single word!

I shall be refused credence by him who, keeping his faith in the classical methods, has studied only Greek and Latin (I will not say learnt), and in whom faith in the dictionary is anchored by a practice of ten, twenty, or thirty years.

He will never believe that, knowing thoroughly the elements of a language from the first to the last, I should not know thoroughly the language itself, at any rate sufficiently to understand it spoken or written. He will rather prefer to deny that I was really in possession of the grammar and the vocabulary.

He also will not less refuse me belief who, having studied a living language, did not, through force of circumstances or by his own determination, confine himself exclusively to the classical process, and who making nought of the inflexible logic which caused me to push the precepts of the college to their last extremities, had the good sense to yield himself idly to the free and easy course of things, and learnt like the little child learns, "laughing and playing."

He will not believe that a book written expressly to be an aid to the study of languages might prove an obstacle to the study of these languages. I certainly would not have believed it myself if I had not gone through the whole experience.

And nevertheless I repeat, "I did not understand a word—not a single word." And I permit no one to doubt the sincerity of this statement. "Not a word—not one single word."

Feeling unable to bring my mind to acknowledge such a result as this, I returned the next day, the day after that, every day, to listen to the professors whom I judged to be the most clear and interesting, those who seemed to be most popular with the scholars. But their lectures remained for me just as impenetrable, as strange, as they had been when first I had listened at Hamburg.

If I could not hear, perhaps at least I could read. I looked up my Goethe and Schiller again; but the trial was not very much more successful than it had been at Hamburg after the study of the roots. It took me half a day to decipher two or three pages, and then I was not absolutely sure of having found the real meaning of all the sentences.

No one need be surprised at this double failure. I shall demonstrate further on that it is exactly what should have happened, and I hope to lay bare the true causes of this obstinate incapability. I may be allowed to say at once, however, that this incapability was due, not to any native or national incapacity of the writer, but solely to the process which was applied by him, and which he now intends to arraign.

Since that time I have sometimes been "reproached" with having what is termed the "gift for languages." If I had it not then, perhaps I have "acquired" it. Six months after this struggle, the outlines of which with its first wanderings I have attempted to sketch, I required no more than four months to learn any language; and I actually did learn several, one after the other, of those I thought would be most useful to me; but by following out an entirely different process, and, as one may well imagine, "without learning off any more dictionaries by heart."

One of my university professors wrote one day this judgment on the margin of a dissertation which I had submitted to him: "Faculty of following long and far the same idea." The preceding history proves that this faculty—which excludes more or less a certain mobility of mind sometimes extremely necessary—is not always a good quality—above all, a practical quality. What came next goes to demonstrate that I was still the same in the year in which I undertook to learn German.

The process I followed was defective. The proof of this was visible and palpable. Any other person than myself would have been convinced of his error, and, uttering maledictions upon his dictionary, would have flung it away together with the roots of the Reverend Father. But I was too obstinate to believe that I was not on the right path, or that there could be another, shorter and better. Hence the next reasoning and the next resolution was this:—

"I have learnt the dictionary, but I do not know it thoroughly. I have been able to know it thoroughly, for a time and partially, ten pages by ten pages, but not in any constant manner in its entirety. This alone explains my failure, and indicates at the same time the means to remedy the matter.

"I must go through my dictionary again, and in such a way that what is learnt yesterday and to-day will be repeated to-morrow, and so on until the thirtieth day's task, which will carry me through the whole vocabulary. In this manner the vocabulary will become a part of myself, and this time I shall be able to affirm unhesitatingly that I really do know the German language."

So I recommenced my work upon this plan, and I indeed perceived that I had forgotten much. This discovery almost gave me pleasure; it confirmed my judgment and justified my latest measures.

I will spare the reader my further struggles. I will say simply that my will triumphed over all obstacles, and that at the end of a fortnight I had again traversed the greater part of the dictionary. I knew it so thoroughly that I could go through the whole of it in two hours, and so saturate myself with it every morning. Almost at a glance I could take in the eighty words of a column, translating them mentally as rapidly as the eye could see them. I should add that I went every day to pass several hours at the university, but that my hope of arriving at a comprehension of the words of the professors was deceived, always deceived, deceived to the very end.

Alas! I can say it now; it all depended upon a very small error. I had simply mistaken the organ. The organ of language—ask the little child—is not the eye; it is the ear. The eye is made for colours, and not for sounds and words. Now all I had hitherto learnt, I had learnt by the eye. The word was in my eye and not in my ear. The fact expressed by it had not penetrated to, was not graven upon, my intellectual substance, had never been received by my faculty of representation. This was why I was deaf though yet I heard, and both deaf and dumb though I was able to speak. Fool that I had been! I had studied by the eye, and I wished to understand by my ears. I had set myself to represent printed characters instead of representing real facts and living ideas. I had wearied my arms to strengthen my legs.

In a future chapter I shall show the consequences of this unfortunate misunderstanding, or rather this fundamental vice of the classical teaching.

This tension, continuous and contrary to Nature, of the organ of sight, this forced precipitancy of the visual act, produced what it was bound to produce, a disease of the eyesight. My left eye was first attacked and refused service, then my right eye also became affected, and the doctor condemned me to remain blind for a month. This was quite time enough for me to forget my vocabulary, which resided, as I have said, essentially in my eye; and for words, this organ is without true memory, not having the wherewithal to "retain" them.

As soon as I had recovered sight, I opened my dictionary, and for the third time I passed the contents under my eye. After which my ardour moderated. What other means was there indeed of "following longer and farther"—I will not say my idea, but the process I had adopted?

As I ought not, however, to allow the seed thus sown at the expense of so many efforts to perish, I made the resolution to recite the seventh part only of the dictionary every day, so as to look it through at least once a week. And because matters would not take place differently, I simply waited patiently for time to fructify my labours.

I had been introduced by my professors to some of the most eminent as well as the most distinguished minds of the time. I now gave to visiting them all the moments I could tear from my roots, my grammar, my vocabulary, my authors, and my always "incomprehensible" lessons at the university.

Spring came, and after spring the holidays. The fine

weather and the summer sun once more called up pictures of the country within me. I resolved to go back to my native soil, and I departed with the fixed intention of returning to Berlin, and of again joining the classes, to pursue the work I had commenced.

XI.

A CHILD OF THREE YEARS OLD—DEVELOPMENT OF LANGUAGE IN NATURE'S SCHOOL—NEW POINT OF DEPARTURE—OBSERVATION OF THE CHILD—A CLUE—LOOKING AT THE MILL—THE INTELLECTUAL DIGESTION—SAYING AND DOING—THE GAME—A LIGHT IN THE DARKNESS.

In taking leave of home ten months before, I had kissed good-bye to one of my little nephews, a child of two and a half years, who was beginning to run about, but could not yet talk.

When I entered the house on my return, he began chatting with me about all sort of things quite like a little man. Although I had but just returned to France, the question of language, as one can well imagine, was my constant preoccupation, and would remain so until I had triumphed over this obstacle. To this point everything I saw, everything I heard, now had reference.

This language, so living and so thoroughly real, within the power of such a tiny mortal, handled with so much ease, applied to everything with so much surety, so much precision, so much relevancy—this phenomenon could not but strike me forcibly. It was impossible not to make a comparison at once between the child and myself, his process and my own. "What!" I thought, "this child and I have been working for the same time, each at a language. He playing round his mother, running after flowers, butterflies, and birds, without weariness, without apparent effort, without even being conscious of his work, is able to say all he thinks, express all he sees, understand all he hears; and when he began his work his intelligence was yet a 'futurity,' a glimmer, a hope. And I, versed in the sciences, versed in literature, versed in philosophy, armed with a powerful will, gifted with a trained memory, guided by an enlightened reason, furnished besides with books and all the aids of science, have arrived at nothing, or at practically nothing!"

"How happy should I be if I could talk German as this little child could talk French; if I could express in German the simple facts which came to his tongue so instantaneously and so spontaneously, and this without seeking either words or rules to construct his sentences."

A doubt accompanied with a heavy anger rose in my mind. "The linguistic science of the college," I exclaimed, "has deceived me, has misguided me, has led me completely astray. The classical method, with its grammar, its dictionary, and its translations, is a delusion—nothing but a delusion.

"Nature knows and applies another method. Her method is infallible; this is an undeniable, indisputable fact. And with this method all children are equally apt in learning languages. Do they not all learn their mother-tongue, and this within a time sensibly the same? Was Jacotot really so wrong when he proclaimed the equality of intellects? For languages at least his assertion had a foundation. In the school of Nature this equality was real enough. Where is the child born under normal conditions of whom Nature despairs, whom she declares incapable of learning its mother-tongue, and of speaking it, at the latest, at four years of age?"

But to criticise is always easier than to do. I now knew my process to be essentially defective. But how? In what? I had judged the tree by its fruit only, not as yet from its inner nature—from itself.

To perceive anything, we must first have light upon it. Falsehood cannot be well distinguished but in the light of truth. To judge the value of my previous process, as one might say, with a full knowledge of the brief, some definite point of support was necessary; in other words, I required a term of comparison. This term of comparison was a better method—in the present case, the method of Nature.

Leaving the classic system, therefore, entirely on one side, I said to myself, "To surprise Nature's secret I must watch this child."

To tell the truth, I had been deceived so many times during the last year, and the work of Nature seemed to me so confused, so complex, so tangled, so disordered, so desultory, and so arbitrary, that I despaired of discovering anything at all. Was there really anything to discover? Why had it not been discovered already?

I did not, therefore, delude myself. Nevertheless I held in my hand at any rate a slight clue, and however frail, loose, lightly attached, and insecure it might be, yet I took the utmost pains never to release my hold of it. This was the guiding thread which was to lead me through this dark labyrinth of ends and means, of causes and effects, that I had entered with such temerity, and finally was to aid me in emerging therefrom with honour, after having found and slain the monster.

This guiding clue was the following simple reflection :— "The child has not yet seen everything, has not yet perceived everything. I should like to surprise him in the presence of some phenomenon entirely fresh to him, and see what he would do—on the one hand to express this phenomenon to himself in the aggregate and in all its details, and then to assimilate the expressions gathered, attempted, or invented by him on the occasion of this phenomenon."

One day the mother said to the child, "Would you like to come along with me ? I am going to the mill; you have never seen a mill; it will amuse you." I was present; I heard the proposition; and the words, "you have never seen a mill," recalled my watchword to me.

The little lad went along with his mother. He went over the mill from top to bottom. He wanted to see everything, to hear the name of everything, to understand about everything. Everything had to be explained to him. He went up everywhere, went into every corner, stopped before the tick-tack, listening long in mute astonishment. He curiously examined the bolters, the millstones, the hoppers. He made the men open the flour-store; he pulled back the curtain of the bran-room, admired the turning of the pans and belts, gazed with a sort of dread at the rotation of the shafting and the gearing of the cog-wheels, watched the action of the levers, the pulleys, the cranes lifting through space the sacks stuffed full of wheat. All the time his eyes eagerly followed the millers, whitened with flour, moving about here and there, loading and unloading sacks, emptying some, filling others, stopping the motion of the wheels, silencing one clattering wheel and then starting another.

Finally the child was led to the great water-wheels outside. He lingered long in ecstasy before these indefatigable workers, and before the mighty, splashing column of water, which, issuing from the mill-pond, already full to overflowing, rushed white with foam along the mill-race, fell in roaring torrents into the floats of the water-wheel, setting and keeping in motion with thunderous roar the giant wheels, with all this immense and marvellous mechanism turning at full speed beneath their impulsion, driving, devouring the work with a bewildering rapidity.

He came away deafened, stunned, astounded, and went back home absorbed in thought. He pondered continually over what he had seen, striving to digest this vast and prolonged perception. I kept my eyes upon him, wondering what could be passing within him, what use he was going to make of this newly acquired knowledge, and, above all, how he was going to express it.

In the child the intellectual digestion, like the physical digestion, operates rapidly. This is doubtless owing to the fact that it never overloads its imagination any more than its digestive organs.

At the end of an hour he had shaken off his burden. Speech returned. He manifested an immense desire to recount to everybody what he had seen. So he told his story, and told it again and again ten times over, always with variants, forgetting some of the details, returning on his track to repair his forgetfulness, and passing from fact to fact, from phrase to phrase, by the same familiar transition, "and then . . . and then . . ." He was still digesting, but now it was on his own account; I mean, he did not stay to think any further over his perception; he was conceiving it, putting it in order, moulding it into a conception of his own.

After the discourse came the action; after Saying came Doing. He tormented his mother till she had made him half a dozen little sacks; he tormented his uncle till he had built him a mill. He led the way to a tiny streamlet of water near by; and here, whether I would or no, I had to dig a mill-race, make a waterfall, drive in two supports, smooth two flat pieces of wood, find a branch of willow, cut two clefts in it, stick the two pallets in these clefts; in short, manufacture a simulacrum of a large wheel, and then, lastly, place this wheel beneath the waterfall and arrange it so that it would turn and the mill would work.

The uncle lent himself with great willingness to all these

fantasies, and acquitted himself in the enterprise as well as he could. During all this time I watched each movement of the importunate little fellow attentively. I noted each of his words, each of his reflections, striving to read the interior thought through the work or the external pre-occupation.

When the mill was definitely mounted and set agoing, the little miller filled his sacks with sand, loaded them on his shoulder with a simulated effort accompanied with a grimace; then, bent and grunting beneath the weight, carried his grain to the mill, shot it out and ground it, so reproducing the scene of the real mill—not as he had seen it, but as he had afterwards "conceived" it to himself, as he had "generalised" it.

Whilst doing all this, he expressed all his acts aloud, dwelling most particularly upon one word—and this word was the "verb," always the verb. The other terms came and tumbled about as they might. Ten times the same sack was emptied, refilled, carried to the mill, and its contents ground in imagination.

It was during the course of this operation, carried out again and again without ceasing, "repeated aloud," that a flash of light suddenly shot across my mind, and I exclaimed softly to myself, "I have found it! Now I understand!" And following with a fresh interest this precious operation by means of which I had caught a glimpse of the secret so long sought after. I caught sight of a fresh art, that of learning a language. Testing at leisure the truth of my first intuition, and finding it conform more and more to the reality, I wandered about repeating to myself the words of the poet, "Je vois, j'entends, je sais "—"I see, I hear, I know!"

What had I seen in this short and fugitive instant? What was it that had been made clear to me? This I will now attempt to explain.

* * * *

The foregoing recital will serve as preface or introduction to the general system I am wishing to set forth; it will serve as a beacon-light to the reader who has decided to follow me across the labyrinth of theses and of facts, of principles and of consequences, of precepts and criticisms contained in this treatise. For what had appeared to me in this short moment of time—for me ever memorable—was a whole system, a system of Nature weaving and building up the individuality of man upon and by language. It was the system of which, in this book, I propose to retrace the principal lines and the general construction.

XII.

FIRST INSIGHT — TRANSFORMATION OF A PERCEPTION INTO A CONCEPTION — THE SCHOLASTIC PROCESS COMPARED WITH THAT OF THE CHILD — SECRET LOGIC AND MARVELLOUS ORDER OF NATURE.

While before the mill, the child's mind had taken a passive and entirely receptive attitude; but after the hour of "intellectual digestion" he had changed the part he played, and reacting upon the impressions thus received and experienced, he had worked upon them as upon raw material, and had transformed them into realities, or, if the term be preferred, into "subjective images," that is to say, into ideas. To this phase—the passive attitude of perception—had succeeded the active phase—the reactionary attitude, first of the reflection, then of the conception. In other terms, he no longer saw in reality; he "saw in the mind's eye;" he represented.

"To see in the mind's eye"—let us not forget this fact, this psychological moment. It is the point of departure of Nature's method; it will be the first basis of our linguistic method. We shall not commence either by declining or conjugating verbs, nor by the recitation of abstract rules, nor by mumbling over scores of roots or columns of a vocabulary. We shall commence by representing to ourselves—"seeing in the mind's eye"—real and tangible facts—facts already perceived by us and already transformed by the reflection and conception into constituent parts of our own individuality.

It was because I had represented to myself nothing but "abstract words," and not real facts, grafted in reality upon my individuality, so becoming an integral part of my being, that I had foundered so often in my laborious voyage across the grammar, the roots, the lessons of Ollendorf, and the dictionary.

This was the first truth or first principle I now caught sight of, one which thoroughly explained to me the incapability, the sterility, the utter uselessness of all my previous efforts. Was this the whole of what I saw? No, indeed! In this humble scene of the mill, reproduced or rather acted before me, I had read and heard many other truths, many other principles, many other lessons.

The child had represented to himself the complex phenomenon of the mill; but under what form had he represented this phenomenon? What form had he given to the original perception? Had the double work of reflection and conception altered, modified in any way the immediate perception? Was this representation at first ordered or disordered? Was it a picture, a confused incoherent mass of facts and ideas, a chance throwing together of remembrances, recalling one of Ollendorf's lessons, arranged in a similar way, and justifying the point of departure and the intentionally "illogical" process gloried in and brought into fashion by this linguist? No, no! most certainly no.

It is not disorder which presides over the secret and curious work of reflection and conception. It is a principle, or rather it is a need diametrically opposed to this; it is that indeed which makes the mind what it is. To reflect, to conceive, is "to set in order"—to set the details of a perception in order.

The linguistic work of a child does not take place by chance, day by day, the sport of the fleeting impressions of the moment, as the greater number of linguists proclaim, and as I myself had at one time imagined. The child follows, on the contrary, a marvellously straight line—an order, a logic absolutely irreproachable, which we will presently reveal; one which is the secret of this prodigious memory that allows a little child of four years old to assimilate in a year the several thousand terms of the language of ordinary life, with all the phrases and turns of expression derived therefrom, without including the forms termed grammatical.

Thus the child had reflected, had conceived, had cast in the mould of a certain "concept" the complex perception of the phenomena of the mill. Consequently he must have set his perception in order—I repeat "set in order,"—this perception being the sum total of the phenomena perceived by him in the presence of the mill.

Was it upon this plan that I had myself worked when I had forced my eye, never my inner sense, to course at full speed over the thirty thousand terms, the thirty thousand abstractions of the vulgar tongue, classed, moreover, in alphabetical order, that is, by the accident of their initial letter? Could I expect anything else than to sustain check after check, mortification after mortification?

The child sets in order each of his perceptions intellectually, gliding upon those that have gone before, upon the knowledge already "acquired," stopping abruptly before new ones, rearing, so to speak, at them, loitering curiously around them, working upon them, until he has set these also in order in their turn and transformed them, like his previous perceptions, into knowledge henceforth "acquired."

It is the irregular course of a botanist through wood and field; neglecting the common plants, he stays only before those species to him unknown and new. It is the flight of the bee in the meadows, which hovers over one blossom, passes by another already visited and harvested, dips into a third, sucks a fourth, and on another freshly opened stays and plunders long.

By this play, this action, this toil, apparently so arbitrary, so fantastic, so desultory, but yet in reality so logical and so easily understood, the child deceives the most attentive observer. The observer indeed watches for the child always in the wrong place, seeks always where his mind cannot be, requiring order where the child cannot possibly place it, and neglecting or disdaining precisely those facts where he always does place it.

What the child is incapable of establishing is the order of the succession of its perceptions. It cannot make, for instance, the presentation of the mill come immediately after that of the harvest or of the threshing. But what it can and does mould, what it can and does set in order, is the detail of each separate perception. At whatever hour of its life a fresh phenomenon occurs, the child looks at this phenomenon, studies it, puts the details into their order, and transforms it at last into "knowledge."

The ordinary philosopher, not being able to perceive in the succession of the child's perceptions an order which does not exist, concludes therefrom that in the mind of man all linguistic work is done in disorder, is brought about by chance. The secret work accomplished by the mind upon each particular perception escapes his notice.

Thus, not hour by hour and day by day, but from perception

to perception, progresses and develops the illimitable fabric of a human individuality, which fabric constitutes the psychological or mental ground-work of the individual himself.

XIII.

SECOND INSIGHT—PRINCIPLES OF CLASSIFICATION EMPLOYED BY THE CHILD—ORDER OF SUCCESSION IN TIME—RELATION OF END TO MEANS—THE INCUBATION—SECRET OF THE CHILD'S MEMORY—EXPLANATION OF MY FAILURES.

The child conceives, that is, sets each of its perceptions in order. Who can dispute this? But to set in order is to classify; and to classify, a rule, a constant principle of classification is necessary. Without this, order becomes disorder. Therefore a further question is presented. What is the rule followed by a child when it organises and mentally sets one of its complex perceptions in order?

Psychology acknowledges six or seven various relationships by which the mind of man associates ideas one with another. Among these relationships is that of "succession or contiguity in time." It was this that the child observed by me had adopted. He classed in his imagination all the facts relative to the mill, according to their order in succession of time, attaining by this means the most profound, the most logical of all relationships—we may say the sole scientific one of the seven; that of cause and effect.

First of all, he filled his little sacks with grain,
    then—he hoisted them on his shoulder,
    then—he carried them to the mill,
    then—he emptied the contents before the mill,
    then—he gave them to be ground in an imaginary mill.
Meanwhile, the water ran out of the mill-pond,
    then—it flowed along the mill-race,
    then—fell upon the wheel,
    then—this wheel turned round,
    then—the mill worked,
    then—the mill ground the corn,
    then—the flour was sifted,
    then—the flour was put into the sacks, &c., &c.

The child represented, and repeated always in the same order, the totality of the facts which constituted his general perception of the mill; and when he recounted what he had seen, he joined, as we have said, all the sentences together invariably by the conjunction "and then."

The order of succession in time was not, however, the only relationship which presided over his conception and regulated it. To work as he worked, to group the facts as he grouped them, the child must evidently have grasped the second relationship, that of "means to an end."

To grind the corn was the final or supreme aim, and this aim or end was attained by the diverse means we have just enumerated, which formed the material of the child's game.[1]

The first relationship, that of succession in time, serves to aggregate the various elements of the conception. The second, that of means to an end, binds them together, enframes them, gives them that unity without which there is and can be no "conception."

Perception of the relation of succession in time, perception of the relation of means to an end, these are the instruments of logic with which Nature has provided childhood; these are the loom and shuttle which elaborate the marvellous web of language, and by it the individuality of each one of us.

To this primitive logic join an incubation of five or six days, the repetition of the same game by the indefatigable and insatiable player, until the moment when a new perception arrives to distract him from the previous one, and you have the secret of the prodigious memory of the child, which, without having learned by heart either grammar, or authors, or roots, or vocabulary, but after having played some sixty games similar to that of the mill, finds itself shortly in possession of its mother-tongue.

Let us keep well before us these three articles of the natural method—relationship of succession in time, relationship of means to an end, and the incubation. Let us place these carefully on one side; they should form also the basis of our artificial system.

I had therefore at last discovered the logic of Nature, the

---

[1] This desire for the perception of the relationship of means to an end is so universal, that a child's first question when placed in front of an object is always, "What is that for? What does it do?" (Trans.).

logic of the little child. What a light it threw upon all my learned proceedings! Comparing from this new point of view my own work with that of the child, I could explain more and more to myself both the triumphs of the ignorant baby and the defeats of the professor.

The child had proceeded from one "complex" perception to another "complex" perception, and I, from one abstract word to another abstract word, from one abstract phrase to another abstract phrase.

The child had transformed its perceptions into conceptions, and I had travestied the living word in characters purely typographic.

The child had submitted each of his conceptions to the innate logic of the mind; and I, although I had studied the roots, the grammar, the dictionary—although I had learnt the lessons of Ollendorf and of Robertson—I had begun to work at hazard, to learn everything in the greatest disorder possible, under the pretext of better exercising myself and of hardening my memory.

The child sets its conceptions in order in its mind, and I disposed the letters of words in my eye.

I had therefore taken exactly the opposite course to that of Nature. I had worked on a system exactly contrary to Nature's; and thus I had arrived at a point which Nature never approaches.

XIV.

THIRD INSIGHT—THE CHILD ASSIMILATES THE MOTHER-TONGUE SENTENCE BY SENTENCE, AND NOT WORD BY WORD—REVELATION OF THE HIGH VALUE OF THE VERB—THE TRUE PIVOT OF THE NATURAL SYSTEM.

My intuition could not rest simply here. I could not but remark that the child, in going from one fact to another fact, proceeded not from one word to another word, but from one sentence to another sentence. This was a revelation of the highest importance, which condemned the ancient system, together with the course of declensions and dictionary, and opened out to pedagogic science a new path with a new horizon.

In the school of Nature the child does not spell; never

does it spell isolated words. It knows, understands, enounces nothing but complete sentences. Each isolated word is an abstraction; the child does not comprehend abstractions. It is by synthesis that the human mind commences its growth. The faculty of analysis is the fruit of age, of experience, of reflection.

The child's first word, even if monosyllabic, is not a simple word, but a phrase, a complete sentence: the enunciation imperfect, but formed from a judgment fully complete. The child of three conquers, assimilates the mother-tongue not word by word, but phrase by phrase, sentence by sentence. We will also put on one side this precious article of the natural system, with it to endow, later on, our artificial system.

Finally, the child, going from act to act, articulated either aloud or softly to himself the expression of this act; and this expression was necessarily the verb. This was the last revelation (or the last but one), and perhaps the most important.

How shall I trace what this revelation was to me? The verb! Why, it was the soul of the sentence. The verb was the foundation upon which the child, little by little, built up his sentence. The verb was the germ from which, piece by piece, sprang and blossomed forth the sentence itself. The verb! Why, when we have this element of the sentence, we have all; when this is lacking, we have nothing. The verb! This, then, was the link by which the child attached sentence to sentence, perception to perception, conception to conception.

In the classical process, as in the methods of Ollendorf and his co-workers, it was the substantive that played the principal part; and in the process of Nature it was the "verb."

The verb! The method which rested upon the substantive, in reality rested upon space which contained the substances. Now space having neither height nor depth, beginning nor end, the method which took it for a basis was condemned to be and to remain eternally illogical, arbitrary, disordered.

When is it, in reality, that you name the sky? When and in relation to what do you name the earth? When this knife? When the floor? And in the name of what principle, by what association of ideas, do you pass from one to the other: from the spoon to the horse, from the fish to the spoke of a wheel. The arbitrary, and nothing but the arbitrary, will govern your system.

" Have you a hat ? "

" No, but I am eating a beet-root," writes, or might write, Ollendorf.

Considered by itself and divorced from time, space is the region of chaos and disorder. Therefore every method based upon the substantive cannot represent, and does not represent in reality, anything but a vain jugglery.

" Have you a hat ? "—" Yes, I have a hat."
" Have you a broom ? "—" Yes, I have a broom."

The verb! The method which is based upon the verb is based in reality upon time. The German term " *Zeit-wort* " (time-word) is a whole chapter of psychology. In time and by time everything is in order, because everything in it is successive, everything springs from something else. The method which rests upon the verb is therefore based upon a principle of order.

We will take up this theme again in another place. We will establish, when the proper moment arrives, the immense value of the verb, and assign to it the part and place belonging to it in a linguistic method which desires to rival the method of Nature. For the moment, it suffices to say that the verb appeared to us as the pivot or axis of the linguistic method practised by Nature. This sole insight contained in germ a whole revelation in the art of teaching languages.

XV.

THE WEB OF LANGUAGE—LAW OF ITS FORMATION—WHAT IS THE RECEPTIVE ORGAN OF LANGUAGE ?—INCOMPREHENSIBLE ERROR OF THE COLLEGE.

Nature and the child had now both in great part given up their secrets; there remained only to draw the conclusion. The conclusion was as instantaneous as vision—" Ab uno didiceram omnia "—from one I learnt all.

Whence had the child drawn the terms which he had used to express such a complex scene as that of the mill? Assuredly it was not from a dictionary, nor from a grammar, nor from any book whatever; for he did not know how to read. He obtained them from his mother or from the persons who had answered his questions at the time of his visit to the mill.

Among these expressions some were "special," and therefore new to him. These he had gathered immediately, directly, upon the fact itself together with the perception. The others—and these formed the greater number—were the terms already acquired by him, having served to translate his anterior perceptions.

The purely linguistic effort of the child had been therefore in reality very slight, hardly perceptible to himself. The work by which he assimilated a new element, a new knowledge with new locutions, had been a game which had given him a very similar pleasure to that of trying on a new jacket; and, in fact, the new perception of the mill with its expression constituted for his mind a veritable "new" adornment.

On the one hand, this alliance, this forced mixture of the old with the new; on the other hand, this grafting of the new upon the old, enabled me to catch sight for the first time in its true light of the web of language. I saw that to express each new perception, it was necessary, so to speak, to employ the whole of the vocabulary already acquired. Here the formula of Jacotot, "All is in all," found a just application. Language appeared to me under the form of an embroidery, where the same thread ran from end to end, always identical in itself, yet nevertheless creating constantly varying designs by combining with its neighbours.

I drew from this fact, hitherto unobserved or neglected, the important practical consequences which are contained within it, and I formulated at last for myself the law which presides over the formation of a language. This I shall attempt to formulate anew and more explicitly with regard to the construction of the system over which this same law must equally preside.

Which, now, was the receptive organ of language? In the scene of the mill, certain "special" locutions had arisen. Was it to the sight, or to the touch, or rather to the hearing, that they had been confided? Happily for him, the child not yet knowing either how to read or to write, it was his ear that had received and transmitted them to his inner sense.

The process of Nature was therefore again in utter contradiction to that of the school. At school languages are taught by books; consequently it is the eye, and not the ear, which is required to transmit the locutions to the mind. At school the eye is the receptive organ of language. It was thus to my eye that I had given my roots and my vocabulary. This is why the spoken words would never enter my understanding. And which was right—the School or Nature?

To ask the question is to answer it; and a little child had given me the answer. The eye is made to perceive colours and forms; the ear is made to perceive sounds and words. How is it that philology has never seen and prescribed this? How is it that linguists have never applied this? How is it that they have hitherto obstinately confided to the eye a part which appertains only to the ear?

XVI.

FORMATION OF THE INDIVIDUALITY BY LANGUAGE — PRECISE DEFINITION OF THE WORK TO BE ACCOMPLISHED FOR THE ACQUISITION OF THE BASIS OF ANY GIVEN LANGUAGE—THE IDEA OF SERIES—A GENERALISATION—THE MYSTIC LADDER OF HUMAN INDIVIDUALITY.

I had now in my hands all the elements and all the principles of a system; but I had not yet the system itself. What was needed? A simple generalisation, and this generalisation was made at once. I said:—

"The same process which the child had used to express and translate his perception and then his conception of the mill must have already been employed by him to express, for instance, all that he knew of the mower and of haymaking—all that he knew of the reaper and of the harvest—all that he knew of the woodcutter, the weaver, the blacksmith—all that he knew of the dog, the sheep, the horse, the cow—all that he knew of the birds—all that he knew of the insect—all that he knew of the plant—all that he knew of the power and the play of the elements—all that he knew of man himself from the baby in the cradle to the old man tottering to the grave."

It was at this moment that I began to perceive in its vast extent, and also in its marvellous genesis, that which is called an "individuality," and for the first time I understood what is meant by the words "to learn a language."

To learn a language was to translate into this language not Ollendorf, not Goethe, not Virgil, not Homer, but the vast book of our own individuality. Now this book is composed of a multitude of chapters analogous to the episode of the mill. To learn German, then, what I had to do was to reconstitute the whole of my individuality, to form it anew piece by piece, to take again one by one all my perceptions, and treat them exactly as does the little child.

This work appeared to me at first stupendous. Then it became simplified all at once in view of this consideration: each perception, such as that of the mill, represented not a solitary fact, but a totality, a group of facts more or less extensive. I counted approximately these groups, and I saw that there might be some fifty of them.

It was therefore a book of fifty chapters that I had to compose as the child had composed that of the mill. His work had been as rapid as it was easy; mine should be the same. Moreover, the child's individuality is formed within the revolution of a year and under the influences of the various scenes which unrolled before him in the four seasons. The linguistic work had therefore very precise limits, and the book which had to translate a perfectly definite development could not itself be without end.

The work was still further simplified when, my reflection dwelling upon a special chapter of my own individuality, I perceived that the material of this chapter represented in reality a "series" of ends, realised one after the other by a series of means, such as I had already gained a glimpse of in the scene of the mill. Each chapter—that is, each general perception—was a complete book, or might be made to furnish one. To treat this conveniently and easily, it was important to divide it into parts, and now I had found a division as simple as it was natural—the division into "ends" sought.

I will ask the reader to permit me here to reproduce the two examples which I myself employed to fix my thought, and which became the point of departure of a vast and definitive generalisation.

"If I follow the growth of an oak," I said to myself, "from the time the acorn falls to the ground to the moment when, now an oak itself, it produces an acorn in its turn, I shall have named all the phenomena of which this tree is the occasion or the cause. In the history of a single tree I shall have the history of all trees, and in the expression of the development of a single plant I shall have the expression of the development of all plants. I shall have nothing more to ask of the dictionary than certain substantives, the names of certain species. In this way I shall have translated an important chapter of my individuality, and this while thinking immediately and directly in German.

"But every end is expressed by a verb, and every means is equally expressed by a verb. Now, to write the history of a plant is to determine and then to express, on the one hand, the diverse ends which Nature seems to propose in view of the development of this plant; on the other, the means by which she realises each of these ends.

"The whole of this work must therefore be carried out upon and by the verb, and not by means of the substantives, which will never be able to yield me anything but the names of the parts of the tree.

"Moreover, each verb expressing an end, a means, or a state of being, will it not forcibly drag along with it as subject or complement the name of the organ in which occurs the action translated by the verb?

"Whilst conquering the verbs, therefore, I shall obtain as well all the substantives and other terms specially appertaining to vegetable life. 'Ends and means,' two facts, or rather two ideas, I had already caught sight of in the child's work around his mill. 'Series of verbs,' expressing a series of means, was not this the litany which the child ceaselessly recited when he loaded, unloaded, and carried his corn to the mill?

>The acorn sprouts.
>The oak plant takes root.
>The shoot sprouts out of the earth.
>The sap rises.
>The sapling throws out leaves.
>The stalk buds.
>The stalk blossoms.
>The flower blooms.
>The fruit forms.
>The fruit ripens.
>The fruit falls, &c., &c.

"These are some of the general aims of Nature. They will

form the divisions of the chapter entitled 'The Plant.' The total of the means by which each of these ends is realised will form the subject-matter of each division. I shall thus have a series of themes corresponding to a series of ends or aims. I shall call the whole of this chapter 'The Series of the Plant.'

"Here again is a farmyard," I continued to myself, "and here is a hen. This bird has before itself, the whole day long, a series of ends which it realises one after the other by a series of means. If I follow this fowl attentively from the moment it awakes till the evening when it goes back to roost; if I express in German all these ends and all these means, I shall have translated a new chapter of my individuality, a chapter which will be the expression not only of the existence of this bird, but of all its species; not only so, but of every kind of bird. I shall find arising from this material, as from that of the oak, a series of themes corresponding to the series of ends, and I should call, or I might call, this new chapter 'The Series of the Fowl or the Bird.'"

"Series!" For some time now I had had the thing. The name was still missing which was needed definitely to fix my conception. This name I had now found, or rather "captured;" and a final effort was to consecrate it as one to be definitely adopted. I had calculated that the human individuality—my own, at all events—could be written in fifty chapters. I soon substituted for this expression that of "fifty series."

I had sketched out rapidly the series of a growing plant and the series of a living being. My conception could therefore be applied to the whole of Nature. I actually so applied it, and in the light of this idea I first perceived the law of the progressive work which had presided over the development of my own personality. Then leaving myself, I sought to realise the development by language of every thinking and speaking being. Then arose before my eyes that which might be called "the mystic ladder" of the human individuality, a ladder whose innumerable steps stretched from earth to heaven. Marvelling inwardly, I sketched out its form. From it resulted the system I shall now attempt to construct.

XVII.

FOURTH INSIGHT—TWO LANGUAGES IN ONE LANGUAGE—OBJECTIVE LANGUAGE AND SUBJECTIVE LANGUAGE—THE RELATIVE PHRASE—FIGURATIVE LANGUAGE—INTUITION OF THE SYSTEM IN ITS TOTALITY.

But had I really yet seen everything? Was the whole language really comprised within the fifty or sixty chapters, however large they might be, that I had now enumerated to myself?

It was as the ocean in the great waters of the earth. But in the ocean there are two oceans: an ocean of water and an ocean of living beings. The first contains, nourishes, maintains the second, yet without being identical with it.

In a language were there not also two languages, one language for external facts and another language for internal facts? And what connection was there between the two? Was not that which I had already perceived merely the first of these? Where, then, was the second? Without doubt it should be found in the first, as the effect is found in the cause. But the effect never is the cause. What was necessary, therefore, was to separate these two languages in order to consider and study them apart, and so to learn to know them better, at first by themselves, and afterwards in their reciprocal play upon each other.

In the spoken scene of the mill I had, as a matter of fact, noticed two languages, parallel, and profoundly, essentially different, which, like two currents, spread out and developed themselves side by side without ever being confounded together.

At every moment the child interposed in his story or his action expressions or reflections such as the following: "That's all right!—now, then!—there you are!—that's it!—that's fine! —I think that . . .—I should like to . . .—I think I'd better . . .—I'm going to try to . . . &c., &c.

These locutions appeared to me to have nothing, absolutely nothing, in common with those that translated the facts relative to the mill: filling a sack—carrying a sack—emptying a sack—grinding the corn—the water falling from the mill-race —the wheel turning—the mill going, &c., &c. I saw here two categories, two species of expression which it was impossible to resolve one into the other. From the differences of consequence I naturally concluded difference of principle. From the effect I ascended to the cause, and I discovered a second source of language in the depths and in the secret energies of the human mind itself.

"Man," I said to myself, "does not merely perceive the phenomena of the external world. He judges them, he appreciates them, that is, he reacts upon them. By the contact with exterior facts the mind is awakened and the struggle is begun. The mind is a force gifted with diverse faculties, each of which operates in its own way. It enjoys this and is pained by that; it approves this and blames that; it wishes for this and repels that; it believes this and doubts that, and so forth.

"These movements, these internal facts, are as capable of receiving names as are the external facts. Hence, a new language, that which translates the facts and activities of the soul. These facts and activities are so varied, their slight differences, are so fine, so delicate, and, moreover, so numerous, that this second language might well be as rich as the first."

We shall see hereafter how well founded was this suspicion when the attempt is made to arrange the categories of the innumerable abstract forms of any given language.

As before, I had the idea together with the thing, but as yet I had no name with which to fix it. The language which translated the complex play of the faculties of the soul never having been separated or distinguished from the other by any philologist, was a language as yet "nameless." In order better to understand these myself, I gave them distinct names. That which translated the facts of the external world I termed "objective language." That which translated the facts and operations of the soul I termed "subjective language." Thus:—

>   The wheel turns,
>   The mill goes,
>   The grindstones crush the wheat, &c.,

belong to the objective language.

>   That's right,
>   It is true,
>   It is false,
>   I wish to . . .
>   You think that . . .

form part of the subjective language.

"Subjective," however, was a generic designation. I required and I sought a "specific" designation. I soon perceived that a subjective locution only expressed a fraction of a thought, was only the part of a whole. It resembled the form abstracted or separated from its basis—of a line abstracted from the surface, of the surface abstracted from the solid.

"That's right;
He wishes to . . ."

But what is right? What is it that he wishes to do? Every subjective locution was applied to, was connected with, an objective fact, and had some relation to this fact. I thought, therefore, to define it by terming it "Relative Phrase." And since then, however imperfect this denomination may be, no other has presented itself to me which has seemed to be more appropriate to the idea.

Contemplating from the heights of their resources this objective language and this subjective language, I saw how, in Nature, they perpetually crossed each other, how they ran concurrently to form the marvellous warp and woof of which I have so often spoken. A double problem now remained to be solved, an arduous problem withal: first, to systematise the subjective language, to gather and classify it in such a way that it might be easily assimilated; then to find the secret of attaching the exercise of it to that of the objective language or of the Series properly so called.

In Nature the two languages progressed side by side, developing themselves harmoniously, one gearing or working into the other. No sooner does a fact of the external world present itself than immediately the mind takes possession of it and judges it. A linguistic system cut according to the pattern of Nature must be required to reproduce this beautiful harmony. What had to be done, therefore, was to invent some connection, some gearing at least equally practical with that of Nature.

A more and more profound study of the "relative phrase," joined to an inspiration as happy as it was unexpected, suddenly revealed to me the secret sought after. I will not dwell here upon this important discovery: it should form the subject of a special chapter. I will confine myself to saying that Art triumphed over Nature, by permitting the young learner as well as the adult to learn in a few months that part of the subjective language which the child assimilates but imperfectly in the space of a year.

The child observed by me had not arrived at the age when abstract ideas are produced or sought to be embodied in symbolic language and metaphor. But the subjective language was already in his mouth; and this language, which rested upon abstraction, led me forcibly and by foresight to study the problem of the figurative language. It was not difficult for me to establish the true relationship between this third language and the former two, and to postulate that the figurative language was grafted upon the objective language and implied the previous development of this.

I again ask the reader's permission to leave the study of this question to an ulterior chapter, in which, developing at leisure my insight, I shall attempt to organise the figurative language itself and to harmonise it with the two others in imitation of Nature, and, if possible, better than Nature.

I had started from the system of the objective language. I had returned thereto by way of the symbolical language. The voyage round the linguistic world was achieved; the circle was perfect; the vision seemed complete. One thing remained to be done, and this imposed itself upon me with the authority of a duty—to prolong indefinitely this intuition, and finally to convert it into reality, that is to say, into a well-thought-out system.

If sometimes, and for certain minds, I have been obscure or apocalyptic in the setting forth of this linguistic revelation; if, above all, I have not been complete, I beg the reader to have patience. The same facts, the same principles, the same problems will be taken up again, discussed separately one after the other, sounded at leisure, and, I hope, the whole brought into the full light of day.

XVIII.

RETURN TO BERLIN—THE TEST—A PHILOSOPHICAL BOUT AT THE UNIVERSITY—THE TRIUMPH—EXCUSE TO THE READER.

The best-constructed mechanism requires to be tested at least once. In the same way the most ingenious and the most logical of systems requires to be put to the trial, must be seen, at least once, at work.

I started again for Berlin, for it had been sufficiently demonstrated to me that it was by the living voice that a language was transmitted, and never by books or by solitary studies. A little child, more clever in this than all the doctors of the university, had proved to me that the veritable receptive organ of language was the ear, and not the eye. The fifty series which translated or expressed the sum total of my individuality—the whole book of my existence—these I must live over again in German, must conceive over again in German, and for this I must first hear them in German. This time it was the ear that should, as in Nature, play the principal part.

I boarded and lodged with an excellent family of Saxon origin, and at my particular request the children were given over to my charge. Their greatest desire had always been to learn French; there was therefore an exchange of services between us. We established ourselves around a table, and we began the study of the series such as I had conceived after the episode of the mill.

This is not the place to recount how I directed the lessons, or rather the conversations, and how, in the manner of Socrates, and of the little child itself, I managed to draw out from my little interlocutors successively all the German expressions corresponding to the details of my French series. This belongs to a future chapter ("Practice of the Method, or the Art of Teaching"). I have only to declare that the grammar, the roots, the dictionary, together with Ollendorf and Robertson, were pitilessly banished from our table.

From the second day I felt I was on the right road. Not only was the work deliciously easy—easy, in fact, as a game—but that which we assimilated in an hour was prodigious; and once entered by way of the ear, it was imprinted upon the memory, and never after became effaced. My sense of hearing was not long in recovering its pristine vigour, and this vigour often surprised even myself. After an hour of conversation I was able to repeat, without making a mistake in a single word, a series of ten or fifteen pages—300 or 400 sentences—and my young hosts could do as much in French.

At the end of a week I began to comprehend ordinary conversations. My tongue spontaneously became loosened, and like the child, spontaneously I began to speak. Like the child, I found words, and the correct words, to say all that I wished. Like the child, too, and intuitively, I applied the grammar, and my speeches all at once lost the sad property of making everybody laugh. In short, at the end of two months "I dreamt in German."

A fortnight after, in a philosophical bout at the university—"in disputatione philosophicâ"—I made a speech in German. The subject proposed (I can never forget it) was the comparison of the formula of Descartes, "Je pense, donc je suis," with the formula of Hegel, "Das reine Nichts und das reine Sein sind identisch." After a long and lively debate (in German, be it understood), the French student was proclaimed victor. I knew German!

I have had it said to me, and others doubtless will say it again, "But your long work previously must have been of considerable assistance to you, possibly even without your being aware of it yourself." Reader, be not deceived in this respect.

This anterior work had, on the contrary, hindered me—hindered me to the utmost extent, and this for two reasons: the first, because it had completely falsified my pronunciation; the second, because there was not a single verb in the whole language to which I did not attribute a meaning quite other than its true one. So that I had a double task to execute: first to forget, afterwards to re-learn; and the latter was by no means the most difficult and troublesome of the two. But beyond this, my little friends, who had not suffered the penance either of grammar or of dictionary, at the end of three months dreamt in French as easily as did their tutor in German.

I should, however, be unjust towards the dictionary if I did not acknowledge that the study of it has rendered me a great, a really great, service. It has cured me of, or preserved me from, all fear of dictionaries. Henceforth I could read or study a dictionary, be it as thick as that of Littré, as I could any other book. Were it not for this benefit, I should hardly have dared to undertake a task of which I shall speak hereafter, which constitutes an essential part of my system.

Reader, my story has been long, possibly wearisome. I pray you excuse it. This hour of struggle, fierce as it may have been, counts amongst the most delightful of my life. It is for this I love to return to it; it is for this I love to recount it, as the veteran does the battles in which he has fought; and when I begin, I know not when to finish.

This introduction to " The Art of Teaching and Studying Languages" was the subject of a lecture given at the Palace of the Paris Exhibition in October 1878, under the auspices of the Congrès Libre de l'Enseignement.

XIX.

EPILOGUE AND PROLOGUE.

In this first part analysis has bodied forth the general features of the linguistic system of Nature. Gathering together with care the definitions, the axioms, the principles developed by this analysis, and combining them as logically as possible, we will endeavour to reconstruct synthetically this same system, and, by simplifying it, to raise it to the dignity of an art. The synthesis being the analysis reversed, many repetitions will be inevitable—indeed, indispensable. We trust the reader, in view of the importance of this object, will not find them too tedious.

Before commencing, let us put a question to ourselves which without doubt every reader will ask of us. We have just spelt out the first page of a hitherto unpublished book of Nature. When we shall have finished it, shall we have revealed the whole child? Shall we have revealed the whole art of Nature herself? Shall we have penetrated all her secrets? Will she have hidden from our eyes none of her artifices? To this we must reply in the words of Pascal, "We shall never know the whole of anything."

Nevertheless the book will have been opened, and if we know not how to read all therein, others after us will be more fortunate, and the practical science of language will be at last constituted, like all other sciences, upon the immediate observation of Nature, the only true rational basis of human knowledge, and the only fruitful one.

PART SECOND.

CONSTRUCTION AND APPLICATION OF THE SYSTEM.

I.

DIVISION OF THE SUBJECT—ORDER TO BE FOLLOWED.

THE method, properly so called, will divide itself essentially and naturally into three chapters, corresponding to the three constituent parts of the whole human language. It should treat of the objective language, of the subjective language, and of the figurative language. Let us repeat the definitions already given.

The objective language is the expression of the phenomena perceived by us in the exterior world.

The subjective language is the expression of the play of the faculties of the soul.

The figurative language is the expression of the purely ideal, that is, of the abstract idea by means of symbols borrowed from the exterior world.

Where shall we begin? Where shall we finish? The objective language is the occasion of the subjective language. It precedes it as the cause precedes the effect, as action precedes reaction. It is, moreover, the substratum upon which it rests. Without the external phenomena, the exercise of a mental faculty has no reason for existence. Lastly, it is by the objective language that the child begins. The child seems, even for some considerable time, to know and exercise this language to the exclusion of the two others.

The figurative language itself rests upon the objective language, which feeds it and furnishes it with images. Further, abstraction being a product of the play of the intellectual faculties, the language which translates this abstraction presupposes the awakening of these faculties. Therefore the subjective language takes its birth before the figurative language, and consequently must always precede it.

Both Nature and reason show us clearly the order to follow. We shall commence by the objective language, we shall continue by the subjective language, and we shall finish by the figurative language.

These chapters admit in their turn, and require, a subdivision: firstly, the theoretical organisation of each of these languages; secondly, the practical art of teaching them.

OBJECTIVE LANGUAGE.

ORGANISATION IN SERIES.

II.

DEFINITION AND MATERIAL OF THE SERIES.

By a linguistic Series I understand a linked sequence of statements, of scenes, of descriptions, of "themes" in point of fact, all bearing upon the same order of facts, by expressing successively all the moments and all the phenomena known by us, and reproducing these in the order of their natural development. Our series have as their object the facts which present—

    The man.
    The quadruped.
    The bird.
    The reptile.
    The insect.
    The plant.
    The elements.

The species which enter into each of these great divisions form the material of the series. Thus the Elements give the Series of the River, the Series of the Sea, the Series of the Storm, the Series of the Sun, &c., &c. It is a treatise on cosmography and of elementary natural science.

The plant gives the Series of the Vine, the Series of the

Apple-Tree, the Series of the Corn, that of the Grasses, that of the Walnut, &c., &c. It is a treatise on botany and agriculture.

The insect gives the Series of the Bee, of the Ant, of the Butterfly, of the Spider, of the Beetle, &c., &c. It is a vast chapter of natural history.

The bird gives the numerous set of Series of the Domestic Fowls, the Singing-Birds, the Birds of Prey, &c., &c. Another large chapter of natural history.

The quadruped gives the Series of the Domestic Animals (sheep, cow, horse, &c.), the Series of the Rodents, the Series of the Carnivora, &c. A further and vast chapter of natural history.

Man gives for Series :—the Child, the Student, the Young Man, Mature Age, the Trades, the Arts, &c., &c.

III.

CONSTRUCTION OF THE SERIES—OUTLINE OF THE GENERAL PROCESS TO BE FOLLOWED IN ORGANISING THEM.

A Series follows the being it is dealing with, first in the life of one day, then in its life during the four seasons of the year. It thus embraces the totality of its existence, and consequently reproduces the totality of the terms which the language possesses for the expression of all that we know about this being.

Each " end " proposed by the being in question forms the " motive," the title of one theme, and the successive " means " by which the being attains this end form the material or the development of the theme. Suppose we have to construct the Series of the Bird. The following are some of the ends which will be proposed by this being, and to which it will tend :—

1. A couple will pair.
2. The pair will make a nest.
3. The hen-bird will lay.
4. The hen-bird will sit.
5. The young will be hatched.
6. The father and mother will feed them.
7. The nestlings will grow, will be fledged.
8. The brood will leave the nest.

CONSTRUCTION OF THE SERIES.

This is a sequence or series of ends, but this is not a series of themes or elaborated descriptions.

What is it that has to be done to draw from this series a series of themes? We must consider, and say:—

1. How the birds pair.
2. How they build their nest.
3. How and under what conditions the eggs are laid.
4. How the incubation takes place.
5. How the hatching is accomplished.
6. How and with what the father and mother feed the brood.
7. How the nestlings quit the nest.
8. How the little birds learn to fly, &c.,

and the numerous accidents which arise from the bird's relation with the elements and with the other species of animals which make war upon it, or upon which it makes war itself.

Here is a second example. Suppose we have to construct the Series of any species of "Plant." Determine first of all the series of ends that the plant itself, or that Nature, seems to desire:—

1. The seed is planted in the ground.
2. The seed sprouts.
3. The plant takes root.
4. The plant grows.
5. The stalk develops.
6. The plant puts forth leaves.
7. The plant buds.
8. The plant blossoms.
9. The flower is fertilised.
10. The fruit hardens.
11. The fruit increases in size.
12. The fruit ripens.
13. The seed falls and propagates the plant, &c.,

and the numerous diverse facts which arise from the relation of the plant either with the elements or with animated beings.

Develop each of these ends, and you will obtain as many themes. More than this, each of these ends will be in itself a mine of secondary ends; each species of plant will give you a small treatise full of interest, in which, one by one, all the problems of botanical science will be thoroughly traversed. This is what I term a Series.

I will cite a third example. Suppose the Series of the Bee is to be constructed. This is the series of facts or general aims:—

> First, the swarm builds the honey-combs,
>   then—the workers provide a store of wax,
>   then—they gather the honey from the flowers,
>   then—they store this honey,
>   then—they defend their treasure against enemies who wish to steal it,
>   then—the queen-bee takes her marriage-flight,
>   then—the queen breeds,
>   then—the workers wall up the royal cells,
>   then—the eggs are hatched,
>   then—the grubs change form,
>   then—the nurses take care of the new-born,
>   then—a new swarm is formed,
>   then—the new queens fight the old queen,
>   then—the hive swarms,
>   then—the exiled swarm flies off to establish a new colony, &c., &c.

Add to this the various possible accidents (inclement weather, enemies, disease), both for the life of one day and for the various seasons, and you will have a monograph of the insect as interesting as any romance, and from which, if required, the material for a couple of hundred chapters or more might be drawn.

Develop properly each of these chapters and you will obtain a series of themes wherein can be placed practically the whole of the terms that the language possesses to express all that we know about the insect world in general.

The Series of the Ant may follow that of the Bee. It will give many valuable terms, whose meanings it is difficult to fix, both for architecture and for the art of warfare; for the ant is by nature both warrior and architect. Any other insect observed by Réaumur, and described in his immortal memoirs, would furnish material for still other series equally interesting with the foregoing, and not less rich in terms of all kinds.

In the same way the Series of the quadrupeds may be constructed; in the same way that of the reptiles, that of the fishes, that of the elements; and thus also, and before all the others, those which represent the development of the life of man through one day, through the seasons, through the historic eras, through the arts and the manifold labours of industry.

Suppose now that a student has conquered the Series of the Elements, the Plant, the Insect, the Fish, the Amphibious Animals, the Bird, the Quadruped, and the Man, will he know the whole language? the whole language translating exterior facts, the expression of the "non-ego"—in a word, the whole objective language? Yes!

Indeed, what remains to be expressed beyond these facts? Language can only express that which we know of the world wherein we exist. Now our Series claim to exhaust the general phenomena of the objective world. The severe order which presides over their construction does not allow a single detail of these phenomena to remain unexpressed. The whole of our Series includes, or ought to include, the objective language in its totality. The whole vocabulary should be found therein, and is, in point of fact, found therein. When arranging our system, as soon as we constructed a series, we went through the whole of the thirty thousand words of the ordinary language. We inserted in this series the terms which we might have overlooked, but which belong naturally thereto. Then we crossed out in the dictionary all the words contained in the series. At the end of about the fifteenth complete series, the whole of the dictionary was found to be crossed through.

This number "fifteen" is an answer, admitting of no reply, to a grave objection which has often been addressed to us, and certainly will be so again. "Granted," we are told, "that the whole language is to be found in your Series; that may very well be; it is even evident it must be so. But would not the study of such Series as these be 'infinite'?"

We reply: The number of Series is, or might become, immense, because it might be made equal to the number of the different species. But the human language happily has not the same dimensions. Language only expresses or represents general facts, and, moreover, has very precise—I should even say, very restricted—limits.

Write the history of any single quadruped—of the quadruped which presents the most varied existence or which is best known to us—that is, develop its Series (of the sheep, horse, or cow, for example), and you will find therein all the terms the language possesses for the genus "quadruped" as a whole.

Write or develop the Series of a single bird—the one best known to you (that of the hen, for example)—and you will have all that part of the language which expresses the whole of the general phenomena special to the genus "bird."

The single Series of the bee will give that part of the language appertaining to the phenomena of the "insect" in general.

The "wheat" or any other plant chosen will give the whole of the terms appertaining to the phenomena of vegetation in general, &c., &c.

From whence it results that to know any language it suffices to know thoroughly fifteen or twenty general series, subdivided, as we have previously set forth, in fifty or sixty special series.[1] The remainder would be no more than exercises in reading, and scientific treatises, in which will be reproduced, with the infinite variety of Nature, facts analogous to these, and expressed in the same general terms.

When I state that a Series will give all the terms the language possesses for any similar order of facts, I should explain further. These terms are not substantives or isolated words, as the reader might imagine if I were not to apprise him of it. This method knows "sentences" only. It is therefore, and with good reason, the enemy of the vocabulary.

It is not the substantives naming, in any order whatsoever, all the parts of the tree, all the parts of the insect, all the parts of the bird, all the parts of the quadruped, which constitute this method, but the expression of phenomena and the detail of the existence of each kind of being. It is not the cold and hackneyed enumeration of the constituent parts of this being that our method proposes; it is rather the representation of the life itself in its movement and in its natural

---

[1] For instance, the Series of the Bread would be a General Series, of which those of the Ploughman, the Reaper, the Miller, the Baker, &c., would be Special Series. Each separate scene in any of these will form a "theme" or exercise (Trans.).

development. It is not the name of the organs which it aspires to give, but it is the play of these organs which it first reveals in order to express.

In a word, in the classical process and in the pretended methods of Robertson, Ollendorf, Jacotot, and others, it is the substantive, wittingly or unwittingly, that plays the principal part. In ours it is the verb that plays the principal part; the verb—we have already said it, and cannot repeat it too often—the verb, soul of the sentence; the verb, that which translates the movement and the action, and which manifests the life; the verb, principal organism of speech, the living centre around which, in the phrase, gravitate all the nouns, whether subject or complement, with all their train of prepositions and adjectives. This sole difference, we think, opens an abyss between the ordinary processes and our method.

Before we proceed to draw the numerous theoretical and practical consequences which unfold themselves from the substitution of the verb for the substantive as the first principle of language, let us say, or rather repeat, that our method is a method solely by this adoption of the verb as base. In reality, he who says "Method" says "Order." But from the substantive we can neither pass logically to the verb, nor to the adjective, nor to the adverb, nor to the sentence; much less still from one sentence to another sentence.

From the verb, on the other hand, we go straight to the substantive and adjective which are called up around it, as we have just said, either as subject or as complement. And from one verb, that is, from one action, we pass quite naturally to another verb—that is, to another action—consequent upon or complementary to the first. A linguistic system, therefore, which takes the verb as base is founded upon a principle of order. This system consequently may become a "Method" in the true sense of the word.

IV.

CONSTRUCTION OF ONE THEME OF A SERIES.

We have just seen what it is that constitutes a linguistic series, considered in its general development and its principal divisions. It now remains to explain how a simple element, a simple exercise,[1] any particular theme of a given series, is elaborated. For this purpose we will choose one of the series which translates that which we term the common life, that is, the ordinary everyday life of mankind; say the "Series of the Fire." And in this series we will take an exercise or theme capable of giving rise to the enunciation of the greater part of our principles—that, for example, which has as its title "The Maid Chops a Log of Wood."

To chop a log of wood,—this is the end. What are the means employed?

To chop wood, we require a hatchet.
Therefore, first of all:— she goes to seek this hatchet;
then what does she do?—she takes a log of wood;
then what does she do?—she goes up to the chopping-block;
then what does she do?—she kneels down near this block;
then what does she do?—she places the wood on the block;
then what does she do?—she raises the hatchet;
then what does she do?—she brings down the hatchet;
what follows? . . . —the hatchet cleaves the air;
then what happens? . —the hatchet strikes the wood;
then what happens? . —the blade buries itself in the wood;
and then? . . . . —the blade cleaves the wood;
and then? . . . . —the two pieces fall to the ground;
and then? . . . . —the woman picks up the two pieces;
and then? . . . . —she chops them again and again to the size desired;
and then? . . . . —she stands up again;
and then? . . . . —she carries the hatchet back to its place.

The end is attained. The exercise is therefore finished: the theme is complete.

Before examining the contents of this exercise and taking stock of the process which creates it, let us transcribe it under the form which experience has definitely shown us to be the most practical.

---

[1] The word "exercise" is used here, and throughout the book, in a definite sense, as a lesson which includes a certain portion of the language, and not a merely fugitive lesson of words or tenses (Trans.).

The maid chops a log of wood.

———

— The maid goes and seeks her hatchet,   seeks
the maid takes a log of wood,   takes
the maid draws near to the chopping-block,   draws near
the maid kneels down near this block,   kneels down
the maid places the log of wood upright upon this block.   places

— The maid raises her hatchet,   raises
the maid brings down her hatchet,   brings down
the hatchet cleaves the air,   cleaves
the blade strikes the wood,   strikes
the blade buries itself in the wood,   buries itself
the blade cleaves the wood,   cleaves
the two pieces fall to the ground.   fall

— The maid picks up these pieces,   picks up
the maid chops them again and again to the size desired,   chops again
the maid stands up again,   stands up
the maid carries back the hatchet to its place.   carries back

*   *   *   *

.. Maid (housewife, cook, servant, domestic, girl, woman, person, hewer of wood, she, &c.)
2. Chopping-block (block, log, billet, article, thing, object, it, &c.)
3. Place (right place, proper place, spot, corner, post, position, location, &c.)
4. Blade (edge, cutting edge, sharp edge, keen edge, iron, steel, metal, it, &c.)
5. Hatchet (axe, wood-axe, chopper, chopping-knife, cleaver, cutter, bill, billhook, instrument, tool, edge tool, implement, it, this, that, &c.)

We have many times met with persons who, after having heard a single exercise such as the above set forth, have not only understood our method in its general idea, but who have instantaneously grasped the whole mechanism of it almost to the point of themselves being able to develop the system therefrom out of hand as clearly and directly as we should have been able to do it ourselves. Amongst others, of those linguists who have a name, we may be permitted to mention M. Eichhoff, who, at the end of a class inspection at the College of Caen, conjured us, so to speak, to complete a method which could and must, according to his opinion, render the grandest service to the teaching of languages.

This facility of comprehension results from the fact that each exercise contains the whole method—is the method in miniature. And it was by an intuition of the same nature, relative to the linguistic development provoked by the spectacle of a mill and observed upon a very young child, that we ourselves discovered, or believe we have discovered, the true process of Nature in the formation of language, and that, in one and the same glance, we gained both an insight into the details and a survey of the whole general development of the present system.

We may now proceed to consider the reflections called up both by the basis, and by the form of the preceding theme.

V.

CHARACTER AND PROPERTIES OF THE EXERCISES ON THE NEW METHOD.

1. *Logical cohesion and original arrangement of the sentences in the exercises.*

In the table of the exercise given, we see first of all the enunciation of a general action—that of chopping wood—then the development of this action in and by a species of definition. It is therefore a general act defined by a series of particular acts. Considered from another point of view, that of logic, this exercise presents:—

    1. A general end, unique and simple—to chop wood.
    2. A group, a series of means conducive to this end.

The relation of end to means is therefore the "logical connection" which binds together the title of this exercise with its development. But the diverse pieces that serve for this development, are they also bound together amongst themselves, and upon what relationship is their association founded ?

The logic which in our method links sentence to sentence is not the more or less artificial, and more or less arbitrary logic of the printed book in general ; it is that which may be called "the logic of nature," a logic accessible, or rather familiar, to everybody—one which the little child understands and practises equally with the man of genius.

The relationship of succession in time—this is the natural cement which in our exercises unites phrase to phrase and sentence to sentence. This relationship, let it be borne in mind, constitutes in itself alone the elementary logic of the human mind. It is by it that thought begins. The mind perceives it while perceiving movement, and it is by it that we are led to the perception of more profound relationships, those of cause to effect, of principle to consequence, of end to means.

A simple, a very simple expression presides over and suffices for the genesis of our themes ; the words " and then." This is an expression or a relationship understood all the world over ; it is an expression or relationship pre-eminently that of the child when it attempts to tell others its little tales :— "and then . . ."

Hence the peculiar form under which our exercises are presented to the listener ; hence the disposition of our phrases upon the paper itself. Each has its own line, each occupies a special line. In this manner the book itself aids us in distinguishing, in analysing the thoughts, brings out the unity of the sentences, isolates them in order better to manifest them, instead of holding them confounded together, as do the ordinary printed books.

A true linguistic method is certainly subject to conditions other than those of an ordinary book. It cannot aim at too great clearness, at too much precision. It should, to the highest point attainable, put in evidence each element of the language, which for us means every sentence. This is why, in our exercises, the sentences progress in single file ; being elaborated separately, being born, so to speak, beneath our very eyes, one after the other in a regulated succession, each presenting a complete whole, on which are concentrated all the rays of the eye as well as all the energies of the intelligence, upon which the mind, which aspires to assimilate the idea together with its expression, lingers and rests at leisure.

So therefore, in our exercises, all is bound together, strictly and logically; the title is strictly connected with its development; the pieces of this development are strictly connected among themselves. And yet in all this everything is distinct; the title is perfectly distinct from its development; the end is distinct from the means; the means are distinct from each other. If perfection consist in the union of these two extremes, our system should attain this point to the nearest possible limit.

In the exercise already cited it will be noticed that certain guiding-points are marked by the sign (—). These signs are intended, on the one hand, to determine rigorously the diverse moments of the action, on the other, to indicate to the teacher, when he is giving the lesson, the precise points at which he should stop, both to repeat it himself and to ask the pupil to recite it. These signs mark, so to speak, the number and extent of the steps that the pupil must take to conquer a given theme.

It is better, in fact, to banish the arbitrary as far as it can be found possible, not only from the method itself, but also from its application. In itself the general disposition of our exercises, considered as linguistic reading lessons, already, we think, incontestably offer considerable advantages. In the chapter on the employment of the method or the art of teaching, we shall see this same disposition acquire a prime importance.

If we sum up what we have just said, we shall find therein the five following facts to be noted:—

1. Each exercise is composed of two parts, to wit, of a title, and of a certain number of phrases which develop and define this title by analysing it.

2. The title expresses an end, a simple end; and the body of the exercise expresses the means, the equally simple means, by which the end is attained.

3. One sole relationship, always the same from one end of the exercise to the other, that of succession in time, enjoys,

to the exclusion of all others, the privilege of connecting the end with the means.

4. The means are enounced in the same order in which they succeed each other, or should succeed each other, in view of an end to be attained; and the sentences which translate these means are written line by line.

5. The various moments of the action are distinguished with care, and separated one from another by a sign or guiding mark, in order to assure a logical exposition and an easy assimilation.

Such is the art, or, more modestly, such are the principles which preside at the genesis of all our exercises. We shall see farther on how much these dispositions have in common with the processes of Nature.

2. *The number of words contained in a lesson.*

Let us now take stock of the gross value of our exercise. We will count first of all the number of words which it contains, and then estimate their intrinsic value. The main body of the exercise gives sixteen different verbs (twenty-two words), (go, seek, take, draw near, kneel down, place, raise, bring down, strike, bury, cleave, fall, pick up, chop, stand up, carry back); twelve nouns (maid, log, wood, axe, hatchet, block, air, blade, piece, ground, size, place); three adjectives (upright, (..), desired); five prepositions (of, to, upon, in, near); six pronouns (her, she, this, these, itself, its); in all, forty-eight separate words. So much for the body of the exercise itself.

Now look at the appendix placed at the foot of our small table. It contains about forty words entirely different from the others. These new terms are intended to be substituted for their equivalents in the exercise, according to a process which we shall set forth in the chapter "On the Art of Teaching a Language." We give them for this reason the name of "equivalents or substitutes," that of "synonyms" not being sufficiently general, or only applying accidentally.

Therefore, in sum total, the preceding exercise would contain over eighty different words. We do not count therein the adjectives and adverbs that each phrase of the exercise might include and calls for naturally, such as: maid (industrious, quick, active, strong, &c.); blade (hard, shining, cutting, sharp, &c.); verbs (rapidly, quickly, firmly, then, afterwards, &c.).

If we reflect that the ordinary language, that which suffices for the wants of everyday life, hardly amounts at most to more than ten thousand words, it will be easy to calculate what is the number of exercises analogous to this which will be necessary to yield what may be called the first basis of the language. This interesting calculation we shall make in detail a little farther on.

3. *Intrinsic value of the terms contained in an ordinary exercise.*

Let us now estimate the intrinsic value of the terms contained in our exercise. And first of all, some may possibly be astonished at the comparative commonness of the fact chosen by us. We shall reply provisionally that the method does not contain only these series translating common life, but that it can be raised, and as a matter of fact is raised, to the extreme heights of science as well as of poetry—the poetry of nature and the poetry of truth. Here indeed is wherein it triumphs. Consequently, if we do not disdain these every-day facts, if we deem it well to express them, and to accord them a place in our work, it is because they are imposed upon us by a certain character of utility and of practical necessity.

We will reply further once again, that to learn a given language is to translate into this language the whole of our individuality. Now " fire," and all that appertains thereto, certainly occupies a page in the book of our perceptions and our remembrances. Therefore the Series of the Fire has the right to figure in our method.

Let us add that fire is the symbol of love, and therefore the source of those elevated metaphors by means of which the life of the heart is expressed and manifested. The heart is set on fire, glows, burns, is consumed, &c., like the wood which the housewife arranges upon the hearth. Thus, again, the passions take fire, grow cold, smoulder, die away, are stirred, spring from their ashes, revive, &c.

Our humble scene of the fireside is therefore found to conceal the precious terms of the language of the heart. Consequently the Series of the Fire has a double value; it serves for the practical and material life; it serves also for the moral life.

Thus it is with the greater part of the series which translate common life. The life of every day, the life of every one of us, the terms by which each series expresses a certain order of tangible facts, serve at the same time to render a certain order of psychological facts; in other words, to interpret a phase of the soul. For this reason our set of everyday series takes a very high position. Humble as they are, who can dare to despise them?

So much having been said, let us return to our exercise of chopping wood, and from the standpoint of utility let us weigh attentively in the balance all the terms which it offers to us.

Take the exercise piece by piece, and examine each piece by itself, and pick out, if you can, one single expression; quote one word, any single word, to which you are not obliged to have recourse a hundred times a day! We know that in order to act we must think, and that thinking is talking to one's self by means of this interior speech, which always stands ready within us, which is the first minister of the reason and the will, and which analyses, secretes ceaselessly our thoughts and our volitions; distributes them, classifies them as regards an action, in the double category of ends and of means.

Dialogue or monologue, our speech is continual. Language is a constant need of the mind. This granted, let us see first of all if the verbs of our exercise are often to be found upon the pathway of thought, if they serve this thought, and how they serve it.

Seek.—What is there that we do not seek, from the garments with which we clothe our bodies to the glory which adorns our life?

Draw near.—We draw near both to the table which bears our meals, and to the truth or perfection for which our nature longs.

Take.—We take both the bread which nourishes our body and the courage which sustains us morally.

Place.—We place our foot on the ground, and we also place faith in our cherished beliefs.

Raise.—We raise a glass of water to our lips, or a difficulty to mental progress.

Fall.—The fruit in the orchard falls, and so also does the man whose will is abandoned to evil or whose intelligence strays in the paths of error.

OBJECTIVE LANGUAGE.

Pick up.—We pick up not only the tool that has dropped from our hands, but the moral force which begins to fail under misfortune.

Carry.—Do we not see carried, not only the basket on the arm or the burden on the shoulder, but dismay to the ranks of an enemy, complaints to the officers of law, or a new hope of life to a condemned prisoner?

Open any good dictionary at these verbs, and from the length of the columns devoted to them, judge whether these are the idle words in a language. We can then appreciate at their true value the expressions which form so large a part of the web of the ordinary language; and appreciating this common language itself, we shall appreciate the series which translate it.

Let us next consider the substantives and the terms of relationship contained in this same exercise. These words are not idle in themselves:—Axe, log, wood, maid, air, blade, piece, earth, size, place. Nor these:—Servant, domestic, girl, woman, article, thing, place, spot, position, post, sharp, steel, metal, chopper, billhook, instrument, tool, &c. Nor these:—Of, near, on, in, to, &c.

Have these terms, all of which enter into our exercise, the appearance of being idle and low simply because they are grouped and organised; or is it rather that they serve to express a scene which is too humble, too familiar? To most persons there will be no necessity for maintaining the importance of simplicity in the early lessons, and we shall presently demonstrate the importance of order, that is, a regular grouping—a logical organisation relative to the normal action of the memory—and we shall state besides the extreme value, from the linguistic point of view, of the ordinary every-day facts of life and of their expression.

4. *Two kinds of substantives—Common and general nouns—Specific nouns—Their relation.*

Compared one with another, the substantives in our lesson present two characters profoundly diverse: some are specific, others are general. Axe is a specific noun; it designates the species. Instrument is a noun relatively general; it marks a kind. Of these two species of nouns, one is more necessary than the other. The specific substantives are more important than the general substantives. The general terms are, so to speak, terms of luxury, which the language can upon necessity do without. A kind of pronoun, or substitute, as we have named them, they are there for the convenience, sometimes for the elegance, more often for the rapidity of language.

The specific substantives, on the other hand, are indispensable. Therefore the word "axe" will always have its correspondent, its translation relatively exact in a foreign language, while the general term, such as instrument or tool, will seldom find an equivalent which affords exactly the same extension, or which presents an adequate signification.

Our exercise, therefore, which yields us in its first part, a series of purely specific nouns, and which, in its second part, bears a list of general terms corresponding to the specific nouns, cannot possibly be made to proceed with more strictness of method, nor to be more practical or more complete.

Further than this, the specific nouns are found repeated almost at every line; so that it may be said that the frequency of repetition of each term is proportional to the relative value of this term. This is also noticeable in the practice of ordinary language. For ten times that a child will say axe or chopper when speaking of the instrument that bears this name, he will hardly once make use of its general name of "tool."

5. *Two kinds of verbs—Verbs of ends and verbs of means— Their relation.*

Like the nouns, the verbs also, when compared amongst themselves, present two distinct species which all serious philology should recognise. Verbs of one species designate the ends; verbs of the other species express the means employed to attain these ends. Thus, to draw water, this is an end. To take the pitcher—to carry it to the spring—to dip it in the water—to fill it with water—to draw it out of the water—to carry it to the house: these are the means. This distinction established, let us ask ourselves a question similar to that which we asked ourselves relative to the substantives. Which are the most important, the verbs expressing "ends" or the verbs expressing "means"? Or are they rather of equal value?

Between these two species of verbs there exists the same relation as between the larger and the smaller pieces of coinage. The large pieces have a greater value in themselves, the small pieces are most indispensable for every-day transactions, and at need can serve instead of the former. The smaller pieces circulate largely in commerce. What should we do without them? The larger pieces, on the other hand, could be reduced to the least possible number, or even totally disappear, as indeed has happened at a period not greatly distant from the present, as, in fact, is still the case in certain countries. Such exactly is the relation which exists between the verbs which express ends and those which express means.

The verbs of means form a current coinage absolutely necessary for commerce. The verbs of ends are useful without being indispensable. Their utility is analogous to that of the larger pieces of money. They abbreviate and simplify the language, and consequently accelerate and facilitate the exchange of ideas between man and man. But they can be perfectly well replaced by verbs of means, and this substitution does, in fact, take place at every instant in practice. Instead of saying, "Close the door," we often say, "Pull the door to;" instead of saying, "Ring the bell," we often say, "Pull the bell." Pull, in these cases, is not the end; it is the means. It is this fundamental distinction which has rendered possible both the organisation of our series and the construction of our exercises.

Considered separately and outside the action, outside the mind which conceives this action or the will which desires it, all verbs have the same character—a character to which no name is given, because every name is the result of a distinction, and every name presupposes a distinction. Verbs, therefore, only express ends and means relatively and not absolutely.

It can now be understood how and why philology, exclusively preoccupied with the meanings and the absolute value of words, without any regard for the intrinsic mental value of the acts which these words may translate, has never notified, has never caught sight of, the double character with which the verb can be clothed in the practice of language.

We repeat, these two characters, which seem to have escaped the sagacity of the philologists, have nothing in them of the absolute. They are essentially relative; the same verb which here expresses an end, elsewhere will express a means. An example will throw a little light upon our thought.

To open the door of the woodshed is an end in relation to the act of turning the key in the lock, which is the means of attaining this end. But opening the door of the woodshed is only a means by relation to the end of going to fetch some wood. Going to fetch wood in its turn is a means by relation to the superior end of lighting the fire. Lighting the fire itself is a means by relation to the more general end of heating the room or of cooking the meal. The value of the verbs is, therefore, like that of the actions, one which we might call a "shifting" value.

In this series of ends and means, in this ascending hierarchy, as in the machinery of human industry, the most important and the most essential wheels are just those which are the most elementary, the very smallest, and apparently the least precious. Take, lift up, lay down, carry, leave, turn, push, open, shut, stretch, &c., these are the elementary essential wheels of the language; these are the true "roots" of tongues. You will find them at the base of all actions; you will come across them at every line from the pen of the author, at every phrase in the mouth of the orator. Nay, more, the grand, the metaphoric style hardly admits, as verbs, others than these "vulgar" verbs, and this because, in their quality as expressions of the current tongue, they surpass all other verbs in clearness and precision; and because, all the world making constant use of them, they are "understanded of the people."

6. *Epitome and general view.*

The natural development of the man, of the animal, of the plant, of the elements, can be conceived as a series of diverse ends, realised or attained by a certain number of means. There are, therefore, two species of verbs in the language, and this language is not and cannot be other than the expression of this development. Some verbs there are which express "ends," other verbs express "means."

The verbs of ends are not absolutely necessary; the verbs of means are indispensable. The greater part of the ends require for their attainment the action of a certain number of means. Therefore for one single verb which expresses an end there are several verbs which express means.

Our existence is one "continued conversation," either with

ourselves or with our fellows—one continual entertainment or talk, in which we express aloud or to ourselves our ideas, our sensations, our beliefs, our perceptions, our sentiments, our volitions, our actions. An end perceived or pursued by us involves always the perception, and therefore the expression—articulated or mental—of the means necessary to the realisation of this end; and the same end involves always the employment, and consequently the expression of the same means.

Therefore, already the verbs of means, in reality and in the ordinary practice of language, repeat themselves with as great frequency as the verbs of ends. But we should further point out that even this equality is not the true relation between these two sorts of verbs from the point of view of frequency. In reality there is not a single means which does not serve as such to a whole crowd of diverse ends. Therefore, in practice, the verbs of means are repeated with far greater frequency than are the verbs of ends.

Each of our exercises faithfully reflects all of these distinctions, reproduces and manifests all of these relationships.

1. The ends are found therein perfectly distinct the one from the other.
2. Each end is distinct from its means.
3. The verbs of means are repeated ceaselessly from one end to another end, from one series to another series.

To all these observations upon the inner constitution of our exercises we need to add one other relative to these observations themselves. The method ought not to be judged solely from the manner in which we here present it. Language being the most direct and immediate product of the human mind, the theory of its development is, and cannot but be, at bottom a chapter of psychology; and whatever efforts are made to render its principles intelligible to the whole world, these principles will always present themselves with that character inherent to all principle—I mean, of abstraction.

7. *Mnemonic properties of the method.*

Let us examine our theme from a new, that is, the purely practical point of view. This theme that we have given, is it within the reach of every intelligence, within the grasp of every memory; in other words, is it possible of easy assimilation?

The exercise itself is a sufficient answer. Read it over once more, and say if you know of one child so deprived of intelligence as, first, not to be able to understand this theme, then not to be able to imagine in all its details the fact which this theme expresses, and further, to repeat it to you, however weak his memory may be, as soon as you have properly and methodically given it to him, that is, placed it before him in the true order in which the facts take place, carefully detaching the sentences one from the other.

Make the experiment upon the least gifted of your scholars, and if you are in the least expert, you will inevitably arrive at this joyful conclusion, that before the study of language, with a method conformable to that of Nature, all intelligences are sensibly equal—a conclusion, I am well aware, contrary to the prejudices of scholastic teaching, and unfortunately antipathetic alike to the instinct and to the interest of the professors, who too often avoid placing the burden upon their own shoulders, preferring to shield themselves behind allegations of stupidity upon the part of the pupil rather than admit the possibility of error in the more convenient methods of routine.

Therefore we may claim, at least, that our lessons are accessible to all intelligences, are within the reach of all memories. Their conception is as instantaneous as perception, their assimilation as rapid as speech. Two things specially contribute to this result:—

1. The perfect simplicity of the sentences, which are reduced almost throughout to three terms,—a subject, a verb, and a complement, without making use of incidentals.

2. The logical connection which links together all the sentences of each exercise.

And if our themes are easy of assimilation, easy in the mother-tongue, they are also relatively easy of assimilation in a foreign tongue, provided always that the process of giving the lesson is a rational one, like that which we shall shortly attempt to describe.

Our exercises afford one other fact that deserves notice, and on the practical values of which it is well to insist. Not only do the verbs of the sentences call forth around them a crowd of words; not only do the substantives, as we have said, gather of themselves towards these verbs, either as subjects or as complements, but these nouns are repeated, or may be repeated, quite naturally almost at every phrase.

Count how many times in our exercise recur the words maid, axe, block, wood, &c., and from this how many times what we have termed their "substitutes" might themselves be repeated.

This special form of our exercises offers very considerable advantages in practice.

1. Each phrase expressing a detail, a new fact, the repetition of the same subjects and the same complements has not the character of an ordinary repetition, of a repetition pure and simple. Owing to this new detail, this step made in advance in each phrase, neither tediousness nor fatigue is to be feared.

2. This natural repetition of the same nouns, this constant and periodic return of the thought towards the same object, this reiterated effort of the representative or visualising faculty upon the same idea, is not all this the graver's tool which engraves the ideas and their expressions upon the memory?

3. This same repetition, this perpetual recurrence of the same sounds, is not this the essential condition, is not this the most sure and solid guarantee of a good pronunciation?

4. The listener, feeling himself safe in this repetition of subjects and complements, turns the principal effort of his attention quite naturally upon the verb. But the verb, which is the soul of the phrase, the most important and precious element of the sentence, is at the same time the most difficult to conquer and to keep. It is important, therefore, that the attention should be fixed entirely upon this term. Now, by means of the before-mentioned evolution, all the visual rays of the intelligence are verily concentrated upon a solitary fact, the action—upon a solitary word, the verb.

Is it possible to place the memory under more advantageous conditions? Would it be possible for any one to propose better conditions?

VI.

CRITICAL OBSERVATIONS UPON THE ART OF COMPOSING SERIES.

1. *The perpetual speech—Written series—Hidden difficulties.*

Each one of us in reality, from the first dawn of intelligence, forms series, constructs exercises, works out themes. Was it not in seeing a child of three so doing that we ourselves gained an insight into this system—the formidable work of the human mind creating for itself, spinning for itself a language conditioned to its life?

The humble nursemaid forms a series, or at least a theme analogous to our own, when, leading the baby towards the door, she says to it—

Walk, baby;	that's the way!
now, go towards the door;	that's it!
now, you've got there;	bravo!
lift up your little arm;	capital!
take hold of the handle;	that's quite right!
turn the handle;	how strong you are!
open the door;	what a clever little baby!
now, pull the door open;	you little darling! &c., &c.

It has already been stated that in any language there are two languages. It is therefore by design that we have here disposed in two columns the text which the ordinary books present confounded together in spite of their diversity. We shall return at the proper time to this distinction; for the moment let us pass on.

The mother or the nurse makes a series also when she dresses the little child, a series which she repeats every morning, always the same in substance; and she makes a lesson of this series when she says—

Come along!
let me put on your frock;
put your little head through;
give me your little arm;
pass your little arm into the little sleeve;
now let us button the sleeve, &c., &c.

I omit the reflections and terms of endearment with which she knows so well how to season each of her phrases, and which form part of what we have called "the subjective language or relative phrases."

Our life is a perpetual talk. You cannot open a door without mentally expressing each movement necessary to arrive at this end, without commanding yourself to do it, as the nurse commanded it aloud to her baby. It is this constant and permanent exercise which alone can explain this prodigious facility, this miraculous mobility of language which flashes forth with an idea like the thunder with the lightning, which walks with the thought and runs with it like the shadow with its substance, lingering when it lingers, hurrying when it hurries, going up hill and down dale without ever asking for respite.

Has it never happened to you in the railway train to find yourself listening to two foreigners conversing together in an unknown tongue? Which is it that has most astonished you, the intellectual power which, in the interval between two stations, can thus reel off, by linking them together, the myriads of ideas; or this language which strikes them off as quickly as they are produced, without fatigue and without cessation?

I repeat, life from one end to the other, even in sleep, is a perpetual talk. In the light of this fact one can already judge of those methods and those masters, and those astonishing Government regulations, innocently proposing to teach or to have taught any language in giving or voting for it one hour, two hours, three hours a week, that is, five to ten full days a year.

If, therefore, each of us constructs these series ceaselessly and almost unawares even to himself, and if it is true that by dint of striking one may become a smith, one might be led to believe that nothing is more easy than to build up the system of which we have thus laid the foundations. And this indeed is the conviction which at first is forced upon whoever is desirous of listening to the explanation of the system; and possibly this very fact is a presumption in favour of the system, if the words of Pascal are true, "Seeing a good book, you expected to find an author; you are quite astonished to find nothing but a man."

But any one on setting to work will soon find himself stumbling against unforeseen obstacles; and this method, so natural when listened to, so natural when an experienced teacher applies it before you, immediately appears bristling with difficulties to the most skilful person who undertakes to construct—I will not say the system entire, I will not say even one series—but the most lowly of the exercises. This results from the first conditions that the system must fulfil in order to be what it ought to be—a system conformable to the nature of the human mind, a system truly "psychologic." We will endeavour to establish the most important of these conditions.

2. *A method is a system necessarily artificial.*

A method can never, and must never, repeat Nature, or it is no longer a method. This would be simply a plagiarism—less than a plagiarism—a bald caricature. To reproduce Nature without tracing, without copying her, is the sphere of art. A linguistic method is essentially an art. Now an art cannot in itself be "natural." It is indeed inspired by, and ought to be inspired by, Nature; but it exists in order to vanquish Nature, to do better than Nature. Art is the rival of Nature, it is not Nature herself. To become art, Nature must be recast in the mould of a human concept. Let us therefore confess it from the first, and declare it aloud: our method does not admit, it refuses, this qualification of "natural;" and if it is not yet an art, it is the roughed-out model of an art—it is an "attempt at an art," as we have named it, as we ought to name it.

Let no one therefore bring against us the absurd reproach of having found only an "artificial" method. A method cannot be other than artificial, and it is so much the better the more it is artificial, that is, the more it resembles an art, the more it is endowed with the means proper to vanquish Nature itself. In the sense in which we understand the word artificial, let us remark that it certainly does not exclude simplicity. On the contrary, it requires it; for is not simplicity a first condition, an essential virtue of all that bears the name of art? If the expression "natural method" has any signification, it is that which is contained in the profound saying of Bacon, "Interpretanda est natura"—nature must be interpreted.

Steam is a natural force, an agent every day producing numerous phenomena which may be called "natural;" but put to the service of man, it becomes an "artificial" force. The railway train set in motion by steam is not a natural fact. The natural force condensed, so to speak, by the will and by the industry of man, provided by him with a special organism, produces that which we all know: a thing which is not in Nature, a thing consequently artificial, and, let us add, a thing far superior to that which would be realised by Nature if left to herself. The telegraph, again, is not a product of Nature, but the true offspring of man, who has endowed electricity with an organism appropriate to his social wants. In these creations art has magnificently and gloriously vanquished Nature.

So it should also be with a good linguistic method. Psychology will interrogate Nature, and will ask of her a primitive, an original force, a principle; then it will adapt a special organism to this principle, and the system will be of good repute if it can produce, for instance, within the duration of a single season, that which Nature can only achieve in the space of one or of several years. The system will be defective if it cannot compete with Nature either in the quantity or in the quality of the products. By its fruit the tree shall be judged.

A linguistic method is an art, or should tend to become one; such is the idea which has been kept in view in the construction of our own method, and which has guided us in our work.

3. *Requisite capacities—Pedagogic measure of the series—Their division into exercises—Construction of these exercises— Rules to be observed.*

The first condition requisite for composing a series is to have lived it. To write the Series of the Fisherman, one must have fished or seen some one fishing. To write the Series of the Hunter, one must have hunted or have followed the hunters. To write that of the Shepherd, one must have tended sheep or lived with shepherds. To write the Series of the Harvest, one must have reaped corn. To be able to speak of the sea, one must have voyaged. To write the Series of the Oak or the Fir, it is necessary to have studied the tree, not in a book, or according to a cold and dry nomenclature, but in itself, in its living reality, and to have followed it, if possible, from its first germ and its first cell unto the most complete of its fruits. And so for the rest. The construction of the fabric desired demands, therefore, an observing mind which has long been in immediate contact with Nature, and which, after having widely lived the life of the fields and the life of the people, has embraced with passion and devotion the study of the sciences and of literature.

This is what might be called the subjective condition of the enterprise. Let us pass to the objective conditions.

A series being given to develop, it is necessary before aught else to trace its limits and to settle upon its contents. This first operation already offers considerable difficulties. Too long, the series will fatigue the child; too short, it will not occupy its imagination for a sufficiently long duration of time. The intellectual incubation not having the desired length, the hatching will not take place. Neither the phenomena itself nor its expression will be able to take root in the moral substance. They will leave in the memory, like the shooting-star in the heavens, nothing but an ephemeral trace.

Upon what, therefore, must we base our measure? Can Nature here also serve us as guide? Has she some wise indication, some model to offer us?

We have seen, in the first place, that the child begins by playing at games of the facts and occupations of serious life; we have seen also that he lingers a determinate time upon each of his games. This time is the measure sought. It is by the ordinary duration of a child's game that the duration of a series, and so the extent of its development, should be regulated. Cut according to this pattern the series will interest the scholar without risk of fatiguing him.

If necessary, we can divide and subdivide the material; and by making several series, to some extent concentric, spring from the same subject, we can treat them each at its proper time, at determined intervals; so leading the pupil's imagination back periodically, as is done in Nature, towards facts in appearance identical, in reality always diverse, we might even say, always new.

The distribution of the general matter in chapters, that is, in different and special themes or exercises, and the construction of these exercises themselves, have also their difficulties. Each exercise, indeed, should form a complete whole in itself, an independent whole, without ceasing to be a natural and necessary link of the series. Moreover, each exercise should be conceived under a form which strikes the imagination, should be developed with a certain movement which interests and captivates the mind, while remaining accurately faithful to the reality. A word, a simple detail sometimes, suffices to produce this effect; one must know how to find it. All this necessitates very careful work, which cannot be accomplished without long experience and a clear idea of the end to be attained.

Upon the testimony of several sufficiently able persons who have attempted to write some of the series on the model of our own, this work, in appearance so simple, would seem to be of considerable difficulty. It is usually not easy to say where to begin or where to end any particular theme. It is still more difficult to say precisely to what depth the analysis of the phenomenon described should be pushed. The temptation arises, indeed, at every instance of forcing matters, and of doing violence to Nature in order to attain such or such an expression. The ploughshare too readily buries itself in the soil, or, to speak more directly, one becomes lost amongst details. An exercise composed under these conditions is defective in itself and indigestible by the student. The pupil's mind cannot assimilate it. He feels a miserable hesitation, a repugnance that paralyses part of his forces.

It can soon be recognised if an exercise has attained the wished-for perfection, when, in the first place, its contents attract the attention of the class and impress it, and, in the next, when several of the more moderately gifted pupils dispute, at the first reading, the honour of repeating it. The tailor who is jealous of his good repute will not deliver a suit until after he has carefully fitted it to his customer. The pedagogue who has a love and respect for his art, before publishing his work will submit it to the natural test he has always to his hand, and will prove it long and conscientiously upon his class. The pleasure and the ardour of his scholars are the true touchstones of the school-book.

It is in the highest degree necessary that the lesson given by the master should do nothing but awaken in the mind of the pupil a conception, a representation, which already exists in his imagination. The method must not propose, at any rate at first and in the elementary series, to endow the pupil's mind with fresh ideas, but to translate those which are already there; to express his individuality, such as it is, without changing anything thereof, in a new tongue; to re-make, to reconstruct this individuality in French, in German, in Greek, in Latin, &c.

Nay, more than this: the method proposes, and proposes essentially, to place the pupil in those conditions under which he will be enabled to re-think his own being, to take up again and re-read the book of his existence, to re-live his Ego in German, in Greek, in French, &c. For example, if the pupil has never seen a mill, you will not give him the series of the miller to study, but you will first take him to a mill, or wait till he has the opportunity of visiting one. Your series will then reawaken his perceptions, will set them in order and organise them perhaps, but will not create them. The expression will not precede the idea or the perception, but will follow it: it will not shape it, it will clothe it. So much for the general direction.

The same precepts apply not less rigorously to the details. Your Series of the Miller—we are supposed to be still speaking of the mill—will not contain more facts than those which are to be found in the imagination and in the recollection of every ordinary person who has seen a mill.

Experience has proved to us that too direct or too immediate an observation of Nature is unfavourable to the pedagogic description of a phenomenon. Like the artist, designer, or painter, the pedagogic artist should be placed at such a distance that the secondary or too individual details are effaced or disappear, and that the general features only remain.

The most propitious position in which to write the pedagogic or linguistic description of a mill is not that in which the eye, fully regarding this mill and actually contemplating it, embraces the mechanism and the action in the smallest details, but rather that where this mill appears to us through the prism of a recollection still strong, after having passed into an intellectual concept, and having there been lopped, pruned, ridded of all that is too individual, that is, of all that is not essential and truly general.

We here touch upon one of the greatest difficulties of the system, not only as to its teaching, but as to its construction. It is this hidden difficulty which prevents the teachers, otherwise able, of whom we have spoken, from creating an acceptable exercise. Either they lost themselves among the details, individualising too much, copying Nature too closely; or else did not follow Nature closely enough, wandering astray in the vagueness of a generality without character, and without attraction for the child, and therefore without profit.

4. *Logical linking together of the sentences in an exercise—Order and disorder—The human breath—Measure of the phrase—Placing line by line—The intellectual effort, its extent—Pedagogic measure of a linguistic exercise.*

We have already established the high value of the relationship of succession in time. We have said that it forms in itself alone the elementary logic of the human mind, and that it is before all the logic of the child, the only one it understands well, and the only one it knows how to apply. The pedagogue, therefore, in constructing an exercise, will practically employ only this relationship. He may, however, from time to time use the relationship of cause and effect, the most familiar to the child after the former. He will use very rarely, and only by exception, the relationship of "the whole to the part," which is a relationship neither logical nor constant, but altogether accidental, fortuitous, and generally arbitrary.

The most ordinary judgment knows how to discern that which goes before from that which comes after, knows how to distinguish the cause from the effect, the end from the means, the whole from the part. There is here, therefore, no really serious difficulty. If any arises with reference to the arrangement or order of the sentences, it does not belong to this arrangement itself. It comes from something more abstruse; it belongs to the nature of the conception, to the separation of the exercises, or to the progression of the series, and consequently the problem enters into that of the previous one.

With reference to this arrangement or order, let us say that the logic, severe, inflexible, constant, which links exercise to exercise, sentence to sentence, makes of our labour an essentially original work, without precedent as without model, and places an abyss between our method and all others bearing this name.

It is necessary to repeat it: the attempts of Ollendorf, of Robertson, of Jacotot, and of others, are not methods at all. Who says "method" says "order." Now, all these books offer, in reality, nothing but a hideous confusion, a frightful muddle, worse even than the fortuitous sequence of the dictionary.

"Have you a hat?"—"Yes, I have a hat."

"Have you a table?"—"Yes, I have a table."

"What knife have you, that of the Englishmen or that of the Spaniards?"—"No, I have the basket of the Jew."

There you have the logic of Ollendorf!

What, think you, is the natural relationship which connects these four words: hat, table, knife, basket? And how could it be hoped that I should dispose within my memory, by means of this astounding jugglery, the thirty thousand words of the vocabulary and the sixty thousand turns of expression of the ordinary language? Can we, then, be astonished that routine still continues to rule supreme in the school, and that the universities still always prefer the ancient way of Charlemagne or King Edward to the impossible paths traced by the modern linguists?

Instead of studying words upon the facts and by the facts they express, and in the eternal order in which these facts are developed—as does the little child, and with such good results—the scholar studies the words for themselves as absolute sounds, or rather as "abstract numbers." The unforeseen, the unconnected—disorder, in a word—these are the ordinary and universally received springs that are set in action in the handbooks written for the study of languages. There "disorder" is raised to the height of a principle; the unforeseen and the strange are converted into a mnemotechnic means. A singular proceeding this, which proscribes order and annihilates logic and reason, to strengthen the memory, as if the true memory was not the faculty which classes facts and sets them logically in order within the mind.

This error—I should say this aberration—evidently proceeds from a defect of observation already notified by us. The authors of these methods have not reflected that Nature had solved the problem of language long before them; "that she holds," as we have said, "for early childhood a permanent and open school, at which we could assist, and where we could study her always infallible processes. In the turmoil of the child's life, so feverish and fitful, they have not caught sight of the regular development which takes place in the child's mind by language and for language. In the hurried and confused succession of its acts, sensations, and fantasies, so diverse and manifold, they could see nothing but a 'pure game of chance;' and have never imagined that there could be therein anything which resembled order—a principle of order."

This is why, imitating Nature, as they call it, they have erected disorder into a principle, and have inscribed in letters of gold upon their books: "NATURAL METHOD!"

"Have you a hat?"—"Yes, I have a hat, but my brother has the Frenchman's fork."

"Have you been to sea?"—"No, but I have been skating," . . . &c.

Robertson, Jacotot, and their followers mark time, as it were, upon the same substantive to the point of vertigo; or again, without regard to common-sense, without pity for the reason, they will turn over and over and over again [like Prendergast], one and the same sentence, and work it about—unhappy collection of words!—until it is thoroughly worn to rags.

Everything that is developed in Nature, animal or vegetable, is subject to fixed immutable laws. The life of the child does not escape therefrom any more than the rest of Nature. We have defined it thus: "A series of general ends which it proposes either aloud or to itself, and which it attains one after the other by successive and perfectly determinate means." Here there is sequence; here there is order. Who can deny it? By its inward speech the child talks, explaining all that it feels, all that it wishes, all that it desires. Language, the faithful and constant acolyte of all its internal developments, participates thus itself, and from the beginning, in this order. Therefore chance does not preside over the development of language any more than it does over anything else.

This, philological linguists, is what you will learn first of all in the school for little children kept by Nature, if you are neither blind nor deaf, if you are not distraught, and if you can become teachable. Only be observant and you will learn many other things. But above all be logical; then have the courage to burn, if it is necessary, what until now you have held in respect or even reverence.

Our method, therefore, is right, a thousand times right, when it links series to series, exercise to exercise, sentence to sentence. It is right again, when, among the various relationships by which the human mind can associate two ideas, it has chosen the most simple of all, that which is familiar to the child, "the relationship of succession in time." It is by reason of this solely, by this double character of logic and of simplicity, that it is a "method;" and if a method could arrogate to itself the title of "natural," it should be that one which, appropriating the secret processes of Nature, simplifies them, sets them in order, or combines them until it has made of them a veritable "organ."

We have stated the principal conditions which each exercise should satisfy as to its contents and as to its form; a second problem remains to be solved, not less important than the preceding ones, and beset with equal difficulties—"Where shall an exercise begin, and where finish?" In other terms, can we assign a limit to its length? What shall be this limit? And upon what data or upon what principle shall we take our stand in order to establish it?

As animal life is developed by a series of pulsations which are resolved into a series of "breaths," so intelligence is developed by a series of "conceptions" which are resolved into a series of "ends;" and the will of man is developed by a series of "efforts" which are resolved into a series of "acts." If the human breathing is regulated, if it is subject to a certain measure which it does not exceed, the human conception and the human effort should also have their measure. It is easy to demonstrate that these measures do actually exist.

Must not the sentence, or, if you will, the phrase, be trimmed according to the length of the human breath? Why does rhetoric repel and condemn all phrases that are inordinately long? Why does a sentence whose verb is loaded with four or five complements appear to us heavy, detestable? Is it not precisely because it exceeds the effort of the lungs, because it cannot be held within the duration of a breath, because it overflows and exhausts it?

And why also, in certain German books, do the sentences, dragging in their train incidents of every kind, so often appear obscure? Why must they be read over and over several times before we can penetrate to the sense? It is because each partial effort of the intelligence, as each effort of the lungs, has a precise limit, and when the expression of an idea exceeds the dimensions of a conception, the mind is obliged to retrace its steps, and, in order to take possession of the idea, to decompose the expression of it, that is, to reduce each part to the normal length of an ordinary conception, exactly as we break up a piece of bread in mouthfuls before putting it into the mouth.

The ear is subject to the same conditions. From continuous

sounds, without intervals, a melody will never be made. The reading of the most beautiful book in the world, given in one breath—if the thing were possible—without stop, without repose, would fatigue, confuse, deafen the ear, without transmitting a single idea to the seat of intelligence.

So also is it with the eye and its glance, and so also with all the senses. Each has its proper movement, each has its period, each has a constant arc of oscillation or vibration. We may draw from this two consequences of the greatest importance for a linguistic method :—

1. In the first place, the phrase will always be a simple sentence, and this sentence will be as short as possible, that is, the verb will always appear therein with one complement or with two complements, rarely with three. Consequently we shall usually be able to write the sentence in one line.

Hence the original method of arrangement of our exercises, where each phrase is on one line, and where each phrase has its line to itself. Our phrases never, therefore, exceed the dimensions of an ordinary conception, even of a little child, whose phrases are eminently and necessarily brief. The shortest breath can compass each of them. By this relationship, therefore, the method is put into perfect accordance with the lessons, prescriptions, and dictates of Nature.

2. The second consequence is of still greater importance. The theme, the exercise, each link of a series will have a precise measure which it should never exceed. We have studied, from this point of view, some of the principal literary masterpieces, and this is what we have discovered :

The ideas or general conceptions found therein succeed each other at intervals of an almost mathematical regularity. The complete development of each idea is found to occupy from twenty-two to twenty-seven sentences or complete phrases. To cite an example, the most beautiful scenes of Virgil, his most beautiful pictures, are all presented under these conditions, all without exception (see, for example, the transcription of the Æneid on our system). It is interesting to read them through again and to count them. Homer observes the same rule perhaps more strictly still, even when he nods; and the great prose writers are not less faithful to it in all the languages known to us.

This discovery, if it be one, is worthy of being taken into

serious consideration. It will yield precious and fruitful precepts for the science of teaching. Let us attempt to raise this fact to the height of a rule or a law, by submitting it to the double test of reasoning and of experience. Let us first hear the verdict of experience.

When, before a well-disciplined class, I develop a linguistic exercise, be it in Greek, in Latin, in German, or in English, each pupil remains seriously attentive up to the twentieth, the twenty-second, or the twenty-fourth sentence. Of this attention of the pupil I have as guarantee, first of all, his looks, which will be fixed upon me, and then his good behaviour. After the twenty-fifth sentence involuntary nervous movements begin to show themselves. Legs begin to shift, feet scrape on the floor, papers rustle, and faces lengthen. Evidently the wits are wandering in quest of other things. The human patience is at an end; the intellectual force is overloaded; the limit of voluntary effort is overstepped. The bow bent to excess is relaxed. In fine, the souls have flown elsewhere. The menace and fear of a punishment is now necessary, or rather, the interval necessitated by this diversion(!), to recall them momentarily to the tree of knowledge.

I say momentarily, for you will never succeed, whatever your talents and the charm of your language, whatever the ability, the resources, the artifices of your discipline, you will never succeed for a longer time—with profit, be it understood—in holding your class prisoner. And your severity will be, in reality, a want of tact, if not a cruelty, betraying an entire ignorance of the elementary laws of the intelligence which you have in charge to direct and to form.

At this moment, what is absolutely necessary is a rest, a release, an interval, or rather a diversion; for the mind does not rest, and never remains absolutely idle. But what diversion shall we choose that may be of profit to the intellectual effort that our lesson has just provoked, that may sustain it, complete it, render it fruitful? This we will give farther on, in the chapter upon "The Use of the Method." The extreme limit of a linguistic theme is therefore settled. Where shall we place its lower limit?

In order that an intellectual effort may become fruitful, the mind must take this effort seriously; it must work upon itself, must become heated, must bestow pains to produce a result; in a word, this intellectual effort must be submitted, in order to be hatched, to an incubation of a determined period of time. Experience has proved to us, and continues to prove every day, that an exercise which contains less than eighteen sentences fulfils but ill the conditions which result from the preceding principle. The pupil disdains and despises it as being too far beneath his power. He does not stay thereat the time desired; he is not sufficiently interested; he does not ponder over or "incubate" it, and therefore he does not assimilate it.

The length of an exercise will vary, therefore, from twenty-two to twenty-seven sentences, from twenty to thirty at the outside. This is the verdict of our personal experience. It fully agrees with the result of our study of the great writers. Each one may, if he pleases, experiment in his turn, and pronounce thereupon.

But if we submit the verdict of experience to the verdict of reason, the second will only confirm the first. In fact, have we not established in principle that every effort of the intelligence has a determinate measure? that every conception has a definite amplitude, both when it is developed solitarily in the mind of its author, and when it clothes a form in order to penetrate to the minds of others? in fine, that all intellectual development, to become durable, must be submitted to a kind of incubation? Reason, therefore, lays down the fact in principle; experience settles the question with exactitude.

VII.

SPECIMENS OF THE ELEMENTARY SERIES.

To precepts we judge it useful to add examples. Instead of referring the reader to the book of the Series or to the method itself, we will attempt to build up before him one or two of these series. We will choose them amongst the shortest and the most rudimentary—say the Series of the Pump or of Water, and the Series of the Fire.

1. *The Series of the Pump.*

Let us remark first of all that this series, elementary though it may be, is not that by which the method should, or in practice does, begin. The development and the expression of facts more rudimentary still, such as to walk, to dress one's-self, to open a door, to shut a door, to go downstairs, to go upstairs, &c., should precede it, and, so to speak, prepare the way for it. It will rest upon these facts, as a theorem in geometry rests upon those which precede it. It may recall them in mentioning them, but will not go to the length of describing them in detail afresh. So much said, let us analyse the common act of "drawing water from the pump."

Let us commence by decomposing it into its separate moments. For myself, I involuntarily picture in my mind the first pump I ever saw, that which stood in front of my childhood's home. There I picture to myself the kitchen where my mother busied herself, and I always see the utensil which she used when she went to draw water, to wit, an iron-bound wooden bucket with a handle.

Will the reader be good enough to picture to himself, as I have done, a "real" pump and a "real" kitchen, actually known to him, those which he now knows, or used to know best of all? The earliest impressions are so profound and so living, that in all probability his mind will be transplanted, like my own, spontaneously to the home of his childhood. If this takes place involuntarily, so much the better; if not, it should be done voluntarily. For what is required to be translated is not a sequence of hackneyed phrases written down upon paper, but a page of our own individuality—a page which is to be found written in the depths of the memory of every one of us upon the bed-rock of our intellectual substance.

The personality of the reader is other than my own. Consequently, neither the pump, nor the kitchen, nor the bucket, which each of us pictures to himself, is identical. We shall therefore avoid with care every detail which might be purely individual, every means which would not be decidedly general. Facts which are too special, instead of facilitating the work of representation, would interfere with it. Our pen-and-ink picture must confine itself to awakening the mind, to calling it to the work, without ever hindering either the liberty or the spontaneity of its movements.

This limitation has in view, it must be understood, only the written series. It does not apply at all to the series as taught.

Confronted with the reality, it will always be allowable to the teacher to modify our exercise, and to push matters to more minute particulars.

To go and fetch water from the pump is a complex act, in which three distinct divisions may be counted :—

1. Going to the pump.
2. Pumping the water.
3. Carrying the water back to the kitchen.

The Series of the Pump will furnish us, therefore, with three exercises. If it is considered better to leave to the maid this domestic work, we should develop this short series in the following manner :—

THE PUMP.

I.

The maid goes to the pump.

— The maid takes hold of the pail by the handle,   takes hold
the maid lifts up the pail,   lifts up
the maid goes across the kitchen,   goes across
the maid opens the door,   opens
the maid crosses the threshold,   crosses
the maid goes out of the kitchen,   goes out
the maid turns round,   turns round
the maid shuts the door.   shuts

— The maid leaves the kitchen,   leaves
the maid moves away from the kitchen,   moves away
the maid turns towards the pump,   turns towards
the maid draws near to the pump,   draws near
the maid comes to the pump,   comes
the maid stops at the pump,   stops
the maid lifts the pail,   lifts
the maid puts out her arm,   puts out
the maid sets down the pail under the spout of   sets down
the maid lets go the pail handle.   [the pump, lets go

*   *   *   *   *

1. Maid (woman, girl, servant girl, housemaid, servant, man, lad, boy, domestic, servitor . . .).
2. Pail (bucket, water-can, pitcher, jug, ewer, bowl, tub, pot, vessel, utensil . . .).
3. Kitchen (house, homestead, dwelling, domicile . . .).

THE PUMP.

II.

The maid pumps some water.

— She puts out her hand,   puts out
she grasps the pump handle,   grasps
she raises the pump handle,   raises
she lowers the pump handle,   lowers
she raises the pump handle,   raises
she lowers the pump handle,   lowers
the pump handle creaks,   creaks
the pump shakes.   shakes

— The water rises in the pump,   rises
the water flows along the spout,   flows
the water falls into the pail,   falls
the water strikes the bottom of the pail,   strikes
the water splashes at the bottom of the pail,   splashes
the water swirls round in the pail,   swirls
the water foams in the pail,   foams
the water rises in the pail,   rises
the water rises and rises higher and higher,   rises
it fills the pail,   fills
the maid lets go the pump handle.   lets go

* * * * *

1. Pump handle (the handle, arm, lever, machine, thing . . .).
2. Pump (the body of the pump, the cylinder, the interior, the inside . . .).
3. Spout (the conduit, the channel . . .).

THE PUMP.

III.

The maid carries the water to the kitchen.

— The maid bends down towards the pail,   bends down
takes the pail by the handle,   takes
and draws it out from under the spout,   draws out
she closes her left hand,   closes
she presses her fist against her hip,   presses
she leans to the left-hand side,   leans
and thus balances the weight of the water.   balances

— She turns her back to the pump,   turns
she leaves the pump,   leaves
she moves away from the pump,   moves away
she turns towards the kitchen,   turns towards
she comes to the door,   comes
she opens the door,   opens
she crosses the threshold,   crosses
she goes into the kitchen.   goes in

— She shuts the door,   shuts
she goes across the kitchen,   goes across
she carries the pail of water to its place,   carries
she bends down,   bends down
and sets down the pail of water gently on the   sets down
she lets go the handle,   [ground,   lets go
straightens herself,   straightens
and takes breath;   takes breath
she then uses the water for the ordinary pur-   uses
    poses of her housework.

*   *   *   *   *

Place (spot, position, corner, sink . . .).

The reader shall decide for himself if these three exercises are properly constructed according to the rules previously laid down. We should, however, like to draw his attention to sundry facts which could not be raised in the general explanation of the method:—

1. Not only do the same substantives and the same verbs reappear indefinitely, but whole groups of phrases are repeated from one exercise to the other. Such, for example, is the case with the whole of the phrases which translate the fact of locomotion (to leave, to move farther away, to turn towards, to draw near to, to come to, to stop at). These complex elements are at the same time a cement which bind together and fix the whole, a valuable bridge upon which the imagination passes without effort from the known to the unknown. After these elements have been conquered analytically, they would be included in one single verb. For example, the six phrases which correspond to the six verbs mentioned are contained in the phrase "The maid goes to the pump." In one step, therefore, we have now taken six, and it is thus that the forward march is continually accelerating, and the scholar ends by really pulling on the seven-leagued boots.

2. I am not at all sure that it is possible to define any one substantive exactly, but I defy the greatest philologist in the world ever to define even one of the best known, the simplest, and the most common of the verbs—and, indeed, especially one of this kind. Now, observe: the knowledge which science is incapable of yielding up to us, our exercises give to the child intuitively, as is the case in Nature. What we mean is that in our method each verb is defined by the particular place it occupies, either in the recital or upon the paper. For example, to leave is not to move farther away. To leave represents one moment of the locomotion, and to move farther away represents that which follows and is complementary to it. The second verb limits the first, that is to say, defines it, and *vice versâ*. This delimitation of one act by another act, of one verb by another verb, is the only definition possible with these kinds of expression, a definition purely intuitive. Let us further recall to the reader that each exercise is the definition of its title.

3. Exercise II. shows us the working of the pump. There is here a pitfall to be avoided. We might be tempted to go

into scientific details of the interior working of the machine and to explain, in passing, an interesting chapter of physics. Our series would thereupon cease to be elementary. It would no longer reproduce a perception, a personal conception of the scholar. Moreover, the matter of it could only be assimilated by a person to some extent scientific. Let us, however, at once say that this part is only deferred, and that later on, in a series concentric to the one just given, the complete working of the pump would be scientifically set forth and explained.

4. The Series of the Pump has, as its natural complement, the parallel Series of the Well and the Spring. We think it useful to sketch out the principal exercises of these latter; in the first place, in order to afford a glimpse of what developments and expressions, of what resources and linguistic riches, are contained in the most elementary acts of ordinary existence; and in the next place, in order to establish and obtain acceptance of this truth, that the expression of every-day life, the domestic life, is the fundamental basis and bed-rock of the human language—a truth hardly more than suspected in spite of its evidence—and one which no linguist up to the present day has thought of thoroughly applying and exploiting.

Moreover, without this insight, we should have some difficulty in treating the chapter which should round off and make complete the theory of the construction of the system, to wit, the co-ordination of the Series.

5. At the foot of each of our exercises is seen a collection of terms destined to be substituted orally for their equivalents in the exercise proper. These appendices only occupy this place for the present occasion, and solely for the purpose of facilitating our explanation. The definitive method relegates them to the end of the Series. Their presence at the foot of the pages, indeed, impedes and hinders the regular progress of the exercises, conceals and weakens their logical sequence, unnecessarily overloads the Series, and disturbs the general economy, taking away from it its character of simplicity.

Besides this, these terms themselves are susceptible of a certain organisation. They can and ought to be arranged according to their degree of generality, so that they may be defined, as are the verbs, one by another, and by the intrinsic mental value they occupy in each table. Let us add also that their number being sometimes fairly large, there would often be a risk of their encumbering the pages and of preventing the development of the ordinary exercises. Consequently, it is better to assign them a separate place. We shall therefore suppress them in the exercises which follow, believing that the few examples already given will suffice to show how these species of terms are treated by our method.

This grouping and the establishment of their intrinsic value itself necessitates considerable work. After a series is constructed what we do is to read through the entire dictionary, and carefully gather every term which can relate closely, or more distantly, to the development of this series. This done, we organise the material so found.

The Series of the Well comprises four exercises as follows:—

1. The housewife goes to the well.
2. The housewife lets down the bucket into the well.
3. The housewife draws up the bucket.
4. The housewife carries the bucket of water to the kitchen.

In order not to load our text with too many examples, we leave on one side all such exercises as would arise from the possible and ordinary accidents which are connected with this series and complete it. We will simply point out that, as an aim can be attained, it can also be missed. An aim missed is what we term an accident. The maid who upsets the water in carrying it to the kitchen would miss her aim. This fact constitutes an accident. The development of the indirect and complementary series of the accidents is hardly less rich in terms and sentences than the development of the direct series itself.

The well which I picture to myself is that of our village, the first, I suppose, that I ever observed. As with the pump, the pupil and the reader are invited to do likewise, that is to say, to call to memory a real well and one known to themselves.

There exist several kinds of wells, or at least of mechanical arrangements for drawing water. We have thought it best to start with the most ordinary, if not the most simple—that system having the windlass as its basis. In the vast development which the whole set of the series presents, the occasion will not be lacking for the description of the working of other systems, and from thence to glean the special locutions to which they give rise. This observation applies to all the series, each one having what may be called its "variants."

A SERIES IN A SINGLE SENTENCE.

Exercise I. presents a crowd of verbs, of sentences even, already employed in the Series of the Pump. We have elsewhere touched upon the advantages of this natural repetition, so exactly in accordance with that of the "perpetual talk."

Exercise IV., "The housewife carries the water to the kitchen," being identical with Exercise III. of the Series of the Pump, we have summed this up in the line which forms the title to this latter exercise; and in the new exercise the sign (*), which is placed at this line, notifies the teacher or the pupil to return to the analytical development of the fact expressed, in case it is found not properly fixed in the memory. But the analysis of this fact having been, so to speak, exhausted, it would be equally idle and ridiculous to reproduce it on the paper. It is by the living voice, and not by the written or printed exercise, that the repetition mentioned should be carried out. It will be seen from this that he who has been able to assimilate the three exercises of the pump, here clears, in a single line, the space of twenty-four lines.

The Series of the "Spring" of water would be developed, similarly to that of the pump, in three exercises:—

1. Going to the spring.
2. Drawing the water.
3. Carrying the water to the kitchen.

For the reasons we have just given, these three exercises will be reduced naturally to one only. In this single exercise, so formed, the first and third will be represented simply by the enunciation of their titles, which will be indicated, if it be desired, by the sign (*).

In the same way that an exercise can be thus reduced to a single sentence, so also an entire series might be brought into a single exercise, and again to a single sentence. For example, in the Series of the Baker, when the dough has to be prepared, water will be required. The single sentence, "The baker goes and draws some water," will thus sum up an entire series. It is in this linguistic synthesis that the seven-leagued boots of which we spoke a few pages back are to be found; and we do not fear to affirm that here the hyperbole is, if anything, below the reality.

Our series, as they are thus constructed, furnish, therefore, constant occasion to turn back both to those already studied, as well as to the separate exercises. And it is this, we should add, that provides a permanent test, as convenient as it is easy, for the teacher to examine and report upon the degree of assimilation of the series previously elaborated. This property of our themes and our series does away with a drudgery more barren even than it is wearisome, that of the correction of the pupils' exercise-books, which always costs so many hours, and is usually productive of little, save the disgust of the pupil, and the discouragement, the lukewarmness, and the indifference of the teacher.

Instead of correcting, we do over again. This is simpler, more profitable, and infinitely more expeditious. Is it not by circulating that the sap purifies and corrects its acerbities? We wish our processes of instruction to be "organic" and not "mechanical."

Our abridged Series of the Fire will be represented by two parallel or concentric series,—that of the fire on the ordinary hearth, and that of the fire in the stove. The Series of the Spring was based upon that of the Pump; the Series of the Fire in the Stove will be based upon that of the Fire on the Hearth. To light a fire is an act that can have the most diverse final aims. It is needful, therefore, to state that to heat the room is the sole motive of the action developed by the present series. Furthermore, all the observations which the Series of the Water occasioned equally apply to the development of these two new facts of domestic life.

We will decompose the first into eight exercises:—

1. The housewife goes to the woodshed.
2. The housewife gets some wood.
3. The housewife lays the fire.
4. The housewife lights the fire.
5. The wood burns.
6. The wood consumes.
7. The housewife mends the fire.
8. The housewife puts out the fire.

We shall defer, as with the Series of the Water, the possible and ordinary accidents which might give material for an indirect and complementary series.

The theatre in which my imagination places and sees this new scene is still the house in which I was born. The instruments of fire for us are reduced to their indispensable elements: a woodshed, some wood, a fireplace, a grate, some firedogs, and a chimney. Fires are lighted in many other places: under the baker's oven, in the limekiln, in the fields, in the forest, in the forge, in the workshop, &c., &c. These various fires will be the objects of as many series, similar and at the same time complementary, which will rest upon the first without repeating it, and will give rise to a host of special expressions and new sentences. A detail, and consequently an expression, relative to fire which would not be comprised in the first series will certainly find its place in one of the others.

As there are subsidiary and completing series, so there are subsidiary and completing exercises. The exercise of the fire affords us an example.

The act "to unlock the door" being given for development, we must not descend at first into the extreme limits of analysis. We must guard ourselves, for instance, from speaking in the early lessons of the working of the bolt and of the hasp, and of the movements of the spring in the lock. However, these facts requiring to be placed and named somewhere, they are reserved for other and later series, where there will be further doors to be opened. The primitive theme will reappear, but more or less modified, charged with fresh details yielded to us by a closer and closer analysis. We shall thus penetrate gradually to the very heart of the phenomenon, until we have definitely exhausted it, and possess the totality of its expression. It is necessary also to remember, in considering the early lessons, that the fundamental literary expressions have taken their rise from habitual acts of simple and primitive life.

The Series of the Stove is reduced to two exercises:—

    1. Chopping the wood.
    2. Lighting the stove.

The other acts having been written out in the previous series, need not figure herein. The Exercise I. (chopping wood) has already been given as a model: we will, however, reproduce it in its place, so as to present the complete series, and to ensure its continuity.

THE WELL.

I.

The maid goes to draw water at the well.

— The maid takes her bucket,   takes
the maid goes out of the house,   goes out
the maid bends her steps towards the well,   bends her steps
the maid draws near to the well,   draws near
the maid gets to the well,   gets to
the maid stops at the well,   stops at
and sets down the bucket on the brink of the well.   sets down

— The maid leans over the well,   leans
she stretches out her arm,   stretches out
she catches hold of the chain,   catches hold
she draws this chain towards her,   draws
she opens the hook,   opens
places the handle of the bucket in the hook,   places
and closes this hook.   closes

— She puts one hand to the crank,   puts
and with the other pushes the bucket into the mouth of the well,   pushes
the bucket swings to and fro over the depths,   swings
the chain rattles,   rattles
and makes the depths resound.   makes resound

* * * * *

THE WELL.

II.

The maid lets down the bucket into the well.

― She turns the crank,   turns
the windlass turns round,   turns round
the windlass creaks in its bearings,   creaks
the rope uncoils,   uncoils
the windlass is stripped rapidly,   is stripped
the bucket goes down into the well,   goes down
swings from side to side,   swings
catches against the sides,   catches
and the depths boom hoarsely.   boom

― The bucket goes down, down, down,   goes down
the bucket is lost to sight in the gloom,   is lost
the bucket gets near to the water,   gets near
the bucket reaches the water,   reaches
the bottom of the bucket strikes the surface of the water,   strikes
the bucket turns over on the water,   turns over
the water rushes into the bucket,   rushes
the bucket turns up straight again in the water,   turns up straight
the bucket sinks to the bottom,   sinks
and is filled with water.   is filled

― A dull sound comes up from below,   comes up
the drawer of water hears this sound,   hears
the drawer of water stops turning,   stops
and seats herself for a moment on the crank handle.   seats herself

*   *   *   *   *

THE WELL.

III.

The maid winds up the bucket.

— The maid rises from her seat,   rises
grasps the crank handle with both hands,   grasps
winds up the rope one turn,   winds up
and so draws the bucket out of the water;   draws out
she lets the rope go again,   lets go
plunges the bucket into the water again,   plunges
draws up the bucket once more,   draws up
tests to see if it is full,   tests
and then turns the handle vigorously.   turns

— The windlass turns round,   turns round
the windlass creaks and creaks,   creaks
the rope coils up round the windlass,   coils up
covers up the windlass little by little,   covers up
the bucket rises towards the mouth of the well,   rises
the water drips off the bucket,   drips
the bucket gets near to the well-mouth,   gets near
and comes to the level of the brink.   comes to

— The maid stops turning,   stops
seizes the handle of the bucket with her left hand,   seizes
brings the bucket over to the edge of the well,   brings
lets go the crank handle,   lets go
opens the hook,   opens
unhooks the bucket,   unhooks
flings back the chain into the well,   flings
and carries away the bucket of water to the kitchen.(*)   carries

*   *   *   *   *

THE SPRING.

I.

The girl draws water at the spring.

— She takes the bucket,   takes
and goes away to the spring,(*)   goes away
she stops at the brink of the spring,   stops
she bends over the brink,   bends
and dips the bucket in the water,   dips
the bucket displaces the water,   displaces
the water rushes into the bucket,   rushes
making a gurgling sound;   making
the water fills the bucket.   fills

— The girl draws the bucket out of the spring,   draws out
the overflow runs over the edge of the bucket,   runs over
streams down the sides of the bucket,   streams down
and falls back into the spring;   falls back
the girl sets down the bucket on the brink,   sets down
and takes a breath.   takes

— Finally, she catches hold of the handle of   catches hold
    the bucket with one hand,
takes up the bucket,   takes up
puts the other hand to her hip,   puts
leans her body over to the left,   leans
balances the weight of the water,   balances
leaves the spring,   leaves
and carries the water to the kitchen.(*)   carries

* * * * *

THE FIRE.

I.

The housewife[1] goes to the woodshed.

— The key of the woodshed is hanging on a nail,   is hanging
the cook takes down this key,   takes down
the cook goes out of the kitchen,   goes out
the cook leaves the kitchen,   leaves
the cook goes away from the kitchen,   goes away
the cook goes towards the woodshed,   goes towards
the cook draws near to the woodshed,   draws near
the cook gets to the door,   gets to
the cook stops at the door.   stops

— She puts out her hand,   puts out
inserts the key into the keyhole,   inserts
turns the key in the lock,   turns
the bolt shoots back from the hasp;   shoots back
the cook opens the door,   opens
she lets go of the key,   lets go
she pulls the door,   pulls
the door yields,   yields
the door turns on its hinges,   turns
the door creaks on its hinges.   creaks

— The cook crosses the doorstep,   crosses
enters the woodshed,   enters
and goes across the woodshed.   goes across

*   *   *   *   *

[1] The cook, housemaid, servant . . .

THE FIRE.

II.

The cook fetches wood.

— The cook goes up to the heap of wood,   goes up to
she stops near the heap of wood,   stops near
she puts out her right hand,   puts out
she catches hold of a piece of wood,   catches hold
she lifts up this piece of wood,   lifts up
she places it upon her left arm,   places
she takes a second piece,   takes
and places it beside the first,   places
she takes a third piece,   takes
she takes a fourth piece,   takes
she takes a whole armful of wood.   takes

— She goes up to a bundle of twigs, a faggot,   goes up to
she takes a handful of twigs,   takes
puts the twigs upon the larger pieces,   puts
and clasps the whole in her arms;   clasps
she goes out of the woodshed,   goes out
crosses the doorstep again,   crosses
pushes the door to,   pushes to
turns the key in the lock,   turns
locks the door,   locks
draws the key out of the lock,   draws out
returns to the kitchen,   returns
throws the wood into the woodbox,   throws
and hangs up the key on its nail.   hangs up

THE FIRE.

III.

The housemaid lays the fire.

— The housemaid takes some twigs,   takes
bends her knee,   bends
places the twigs against her knee,   places
and bends the wood,   doubles back
the wood gives way,   gives way
the wood bends more and more,   bends
the wood cracks,   cracks
the wood breaks,   breaks
the splinters fly over the kitchen;   fly
the housemaid doubles up the twigs,   doubles up
stoops down to the hearth,   stoops down
and lays the twigs on the firedogs.   lays

— She stands up again,   stands up again
goes back to the woodbox,   goes back
takes some bigger pieces of wood,   takes
carries them to the fireplace,   carries
bends down to the hearth,   bends down
places the logs on the twigs,   places
fetches a handful of shavings,   fetches
and stuffs them in beneath the twigs.   stuffs in

* * * * *

THE FIRE.

IV.

The servant lights the fire.

— The servant takes a box of matches,   takes
she opens the matchbox,   opens
she takes out a match,   takes out
she shuts up the matchbox,   shuts up
she strikes the match on the cover,   strikes
the match takes fire,   takes fire
the match smokes,   smokes
the match flames,   flames
the match burns,   burns
and spreads a smell of burning over the kitchen.   spreads

— The servant bends down to the hearth,   bends down
puts out her hand,   puts out
puts the match under the shavings,   puts
holds the match under the shavings,   holds
the shavings take fire,   take fire
the servant leaves go of the match,   leaves go
stands up again,   stands up
looks at her fire burning,   looks
and puts back the box of matches in its place.   puts back

* * * * *

THE FIRE.

V.

The wood burns.

— The match sets fire to the shavings,   sets fire
the shavings catch light,   catch light
the shavings smoke,   smoke
the shavings burst into flames,   burst into flames
the shavings blaze,   blaze
the shavings burn,   burn
the shavings set fire to the twigs,   set fire
and the twigs catch fire.   catch fire

— The twigs smoke,   smoke
the twigs burst into flames,   burst into flames
the twigs blaze,   blaze
the twigs burn,   burn
the twigs crackle,   crackle
and throw out sparks all around;   throw out
the twigs set fire to the logs of wood,   set fire
the logs take fire.   take fire

— The logs smoke,   smoke
the logs burst into flames,   burst into flames
the logs blaze,   blaze
the logs burn,   burn
the logs crackle.   crackle

* * * * *

THE FIRE.

VI.

The wood burns away.

— Smoke is given off by the wood,   is given off
the smoke rises up the chimney,   rises
and deposits soot all the way up the chimney-   deposits
the smoke issues from the chimney-pot, [shaft,   issues
rises up in the air like a blue column,   rises
curves over under the wind,   curves
floats away into space,   floats
melts away into space,   melts
becomes gradually lost,   becomes lost
and finally disappears.   disappears

— Meanwhile,
the flames lick and lick the logs,   lick
the flames devour these logs,   devour
the flames consume these logs,   consume
transform the logs into charcoal,   transform
reduce the charcoal to ashes,   reduce
both the ashes and the charcoal fall to the hearth,   fall
gradually heap up on the hearth,   heap up
and form a glowing mass of red-hot embers,   form
a great heat is given out by the hot embers,   is given off
spreads all around,   spreads
and heats the surrounding air.   heats

* * * * *

THE FIRE.

VII.

The housewife mends the fire.

―――

— The fire burns and burns away,   burns
the embers are consumed little by little,   are consumed
the fire gets low for want of fuel;   gets low
the housewife notices this,   notices
she takes up the tongs,   takes up
stirs the firebrands together,   stirs
rakes out the ashes from underneath,   rakes out
puts the tongs back in their place,   puts back
and then puts on some more wood.   puts on

— A pair of bellows are hanging near the chimney-piece;   are hanging
the woman takes down these bellows,   takes down
places the nozzle to the fire,   places
then she blows and blows,   blows
the air rushes hissing out of the nozzle,   rushes
comes against the red-hot embers,   comes against
and brightens up the fire.   brightens up

— The flames spring up from the charcoal,   spring up
the flames lick and lick the wood,   lick
heat the wood,   heat
the wood blazes,   blazes
the woman blows, blows, and keeps on blowing;   blows
presently she stops blowing,   stops
and hangs up the bellows on their nail.   hangs up

* * * * *

THE FIRE.

VIII.

The housewife puts out the fire.

— The fire burns for one hour,   burns
the fire burns for two hours,   burns
the fire burns all day long,   burns
the fire burns until the evening,   burns
the fire burns until bedtime.   burns

— When bedtime comes,   comes
the housewife takes the fire-shovel,   takes
rakes the hot embers together on the hearth,   rakes together
takes a shovelful of the ashes,   takes
empties the ashes upon the burning brands,   empties
covers them up with ashes,   covers up
puts back the shovel in its place,   puts back
and the fire smoulders under the ashes.   smoulders

— The woman takes up the tongs,   takes up
removes the firebrands from the grate,   removes
and stands them on end against the chimney,   stands
a thick smoke is given off by them,   is given off
and escapes up the chimney;   escapes
the burnt part crickles;   crickles
combustion ceases,   ceases
the ends of the burnt logs become covered   become covered
the fire dies away little by little, [with ash,   dies away
and at last goes right out.   goes out

*   *   *   *   *

THE STOVE.

I.

The girl chops some wood.

—The girl goes and seeks a piece of wood,   goes and seeks
she takes a hatchet,   takes
she draws near to the block,   draws near
she places the wood on this block,   places
she raises the hatchet,   raises
she brings down the hatchet,   brings down
the blade strikes against the wood,   strikes against
the blade penetrates the wood,   penetrates
the blade cleaves the wood,   cleaves
the pieces fall right and left.   fall

—The girl picks up one of the pieces,   picks up
places it upon the block,   places
raises her hatchet,   raises
brings down her hatchet,   brings down
and chops the piece of wood,   chops
she chops another piece, and then another,   chops
she chops up all the wood.   chops

—She puts down her hatchet,   puts down
gathers up the pieces into her apron,   gathers up
takes one or two logs and some shavings,   takes
and carries them to the stove.   carries

*   *   *   *   *

THE STOVE.

II.

The girl lights the stove.

— She puts the wood down in front of the stove,   puts down
she crouches down in front of the stove,   crouches down
she opens the door of the stove,   opens
she removes the ashes,   removes
she cleans out the stove,   cleans out
she puts in the shavings first,   puts in
then she puts in the chopped firewood on top of these,   puts in
and she places the logs upon the firewood.   places

— This done,   done
she takes a match,   takes
strikes the match,   strikes
lights the match,   lights
puts the light to the shavings,   puts
and closes the stove-door.   closes

— The fire is communicated to the firewood,   is communicated
the firewood blazes;   blazes
the fire is communicated to the logs,   is communicated
the logs burn,   burn
the flames rush up the stove-pipe,   rush up
the stove roars.   roars

— The smoke escapes up the stove-pipe,   escapes
the stove-pipe gets hot,   gets hot
the stove gets hot,   gets hot
and radiates heat all over the room.   radiates

*   *   *   *   *

VIII.

CO-ORDINATION OF THE SERIES—IMPORTANCE OF THE DOMESTIC SERIES.

For every fabric made there is a beginning and an end. The life of a tree commences at the germ and ends with the fruit. At what point shall our method take its birth? By what series shall it begin? Upon what series shall it come to an end? What order shall be assigned to its development?

We have said that the speech of mankind is perpetual, and that its linguistic development takes place by a continual creation of series which our method has taken, or claims to have taken, as models. We will now go further: we will say that to think is to speak. Speech and thought are identical. In other words, man does not think; he speaks. Thought and word are certainly two distinct names. So are hatchet and implement, yet no one would pretend that they represent two different facts. One is the specific name, the other is the general name of one and the same thing.

So it is with the two names "thought" and "word." "Word" is the specific name, the true name, the proper name or noun; "thought" is a "common" name or noun.

The word is a principle: it is the mind itself in process of development, and the mind only develops, in point of fact, by the word. But what has provoked its development, and what continues to provoke it? It is action, that is to say, movement. The word starts under the impression and the perception of movement, as does the waterwheel under the impact of the water. Here we have the true origin of language.

The development of this theme would take a thick volume; prudence bids us stop. We will content ourselves by saying that if this grave problem has remained unsolved up to the present day, it is because the data were false. It has been stated, in fact, as an axiom, not only that thought was essentially different from speech, but that it actually gave rise to speech, that speech was subordinate to it. Now the reverse is the truth. Man does not speak his thought; he thinks his speech; and this thought itself is still speech.

The child speaks from its birth, that is to say, as soon as its organism is finished and complete. Its first word is the cry it utters on entering the world. And this speech is determined, set free by what? By the shock produced on its organism by the double action of air and light. It is movement which endowed and still endows our species with language; and it is by the word, and not by thought, that the mind of man has its beginning.

It is without doubt the duty of an author of a linguistic method to give his opinion, at least incidentally, upon the origin of facts produced by a "force" which he undertakes to discipline.

The inarticulate language corresponds to the syncretic phase of human life. The world, in fact, appearing before the primitive perception as an undivided whole, calls for a single name only, a monosyllabic noun. This will be the "article" under one of its forms—*a, e, i, o, u, om, um, el, le, das, the,* . . .

We will pass over this preparatory period, its creations not being those that we are seeking to set in order and reproduce. We will pass at once to the analytic phase, that in which the mind begins to unravel, to batter down, by the aid of speech, the primeval chaos. At this moment the linguistic development of man takes place perceptibly, I repeat, by a continuous creation of series. Henceforward we may be allowed to rest upon this fact as axiomatic.

This stipulated, in what sphere and under what influence does the child elaborate its first series? To ask this question is to answer it. Evidently it is under the influence of its mother and inside its father's house. We designate this work by the name of the "Domestic Series."

The varied and manifold actions of the mother of the family around the hearthstone, this is the material of the child's first linguistic exercises. And let there be no mistake here. This material is prodigiously rich; so rich, indeed, that the day the child is strong enough to cross the paternal threshold, and venture out under the vault of heaven, he is already able to analyse and to put into words the great unknown world that lies spread before him.

Consequently our thanks once again are due to our mothers, whose blessed words for us have added the life of the mind to the life of the body. Consequently, also, our respect is due to the most common, the most elementary of the series. They constitute the marvellous organ of nutrition by which speech is fed and strengthened the whole life long. Do you know why it is that the adult arrives so seldom at assimilating another language than his own? It is because he usually never thinks of translating these rudimentary series which form what might be called his first words, that is to say, the first basis of his individuality. Every one knows how worthless and unenduring must be a building of which the foundation has either been forgotten or neglected.

The method will commence, therefore, by the "Domestic Series." But what limits shall we assign to their development?

The child does not wait until he has finished the whole of the series of indoors before he tackles those of outdoors. From the first days of his life, in the arms of grandmamma or of one of his sisters, he will go out into the open air, will drink in the light, and will take into his eye the vast heaven, with the sun, the moon, and the stars. The Series of the Fire that burns on the hearthstone does not commence at the woodbox, but at the woodshed. The Series of the Water does not begin at the basin where the sponge is soaked to wash baby's limbs, but rather at the pump or at the wayside spring.

If, therefore, the Series of the Water and the Fire have one end in the room where the child lives, they have their other end out of doors; and thus with almost all of these earlier series. But so soon as the child knows one end, he wishes to know the other; from effects he goes back continually towards the causes, and will neither rest himself nor leave you to rest until he has completed the series already partly executed in the house. Hence his insatiable curiosity; hence his passion for the open air and the surroundings of the dwelling. It is here, indeed, that he completes his first knowledge and lays the beginnings of further progress.

The final aim of the acts translated by the Domestic Series is the "immediate" satisfaction of the every-day wants of human nature. This, indeed, is the characteristic by which a Domestic Series is known. Its starting-point will be the first act which prepares for this immediate satisfaction. The Domestic Series of the fire, for instance, will not go right back to the action of the woodman who fells the tree. This action, preceding by more than one day the moment at which the fire is lighted, can no longer be said to prepare for the "immediate" satisfaction of an every-day want.

The Domestic Series themselves require to be classified, co-ordinated among themselves. Upon what rule will this co-ordination take place? What order are we to adopt?

They will be regulated upon the order itself in which the general wants of every-day life require and receive their satisfaction. Thus will be obtained a natural co-ordination, perfectly in accordance with the child's hidden series. To get the breakfast ready, we need the fire; the Series of the Fire will, therefore, precede that of the breakfast. So far the Domestic Series; now for the others.

In searching, outside the house, for the first threads of the Domestic Series, the child, finding himself confronted by fresh facts, immediately sketches out, almost without knowing it, series of a new kind; those of the animals, those of the insects, those of the reptiles, those of the plants, those of the elements. . . . These series constitute the "Rural Series," which come directly and immediately after the Domestic Series. It therefore remains to classify these amongst themselves.

What the child knows best is always mankind. Those Rural Series in which mankind takes part are at the same time the most interesting, the easiest, and the richest in developments. They are besides the most useful and the most instructive, inasmuch as they relate directly to the first needs of life. The Rural Series should, therefore, be classified according to the importance of the part played in them by mankind.

The being that the child understands best after man is the animal, and before all others the domestic animals. The Series of the Shepherd presents the life of mankind reduced to its greatest simplicity, alongside the life of the two domestic animals, the dog and the sheep, which always have the sympathies of childhood, and it is the Series of the Shepherd, therefore, which appears to us the best qualified to open the grand chapter of the Rural Series. After the shepherd will come the tiller of the soil, then the harvester, &c. The rule followed by us may be formulated thus: to proceed from the best known to the least known, from the most living to the least living.

The Rural Series will lead us straight to the ordinary country trades, those which prepare or crown the action of mankind out of doors. We shall then open a third chapter, that of the "Technical Series." We shall classify them, as we did the previous ones, according to the degree of utility of the fact which they translate, according to the relation, more or less immediate, of this fact to the needs of mankind.

After the child has contemplated for some time the acts and scenes of serious life, the idea comes to him to play at them. This mimic play is the natural transition from the conception to the action, that is, to contest. It leads very shortly to the game properly so called, the game of emulation, to the struggle of man against man, in which are seen force arrayed against force, skill against skill, trick against trick.

The mimic games, which do nothing but reproduce the series —domestic, rural, or technical—can give rise to no new kind of series. It is far otherwise with the games of emulation. These occupy a considerable place not only in the life of man, but in the domain of language. For them the method will open a fourth chapter, to which it will give the title, "Series of the Games."

The succession of the games is usually regulated by the succession of the seasons. "Festivals," says the poet, "open and close the great labours of life." We shall put the Series of the Games in the same order that Nature or tradition have already done.

The games and festivals, with the trades, will lead us to the door of art and of science. At the end of its fourth chapter the method will, therefore, have both exhausted and placed in order the whole of the ordinary objective language.

We should not think of spreading before the reader here the whole network of our series, and of enumerating all our marches and counter-marches. But we are satisfied in being able to show that their co-ordination is not, and ought not to be, founded upon the arbitrary, and that before establishing this co-ordination we have taken pains to unravel the more or less tangled skein of the linguistic developments of mankind. It is, therefore, Nature once more, attentively observed and interpreted, that has furnished us, for this new labour, with both a rule and a direction.

OBJECTIVE LANGUAGE.

MODE OF TEACHING THE SERIES.

IX.

A LANGUAGE LESSON.

1. Urgent need of a reform in the art of teaching languages.

We will suppose the method constructed, constructed according to the rules which we have just laid down—constructed with the most consummate art: in short, in accordance at all points with our ideal. Would the reform projected by us be accomplished? We do not hesitate to declare that nothing will be done if the art of teaching is not itself reformed. The best constituted plant will be struck barren, or will yield but abortive fruit, if, during the time of fructification, it is taken from the vivifying action of the light and the heat of the sun, to be placed in a cellar and submitted to the influence of a lamp or stove.

The spoken method must, therefore, be reformed equally with the written method. But how are we to reach an art so personal as that of teaching? The quality of the voice, the accentuation, the rise and fall of the speech, the gesture, the look, these are things that defy all regulation. We grant it: like eloquence, the art of teaching comes from the heart. But the art of speaking well has its rules. Then why should not the art of teaching well?

The truth is, that a large part of the present teaching not only cannot be authorised upon any real pedagogic principle, but violates at pleasure the least controvertible prescriptions, not only of science, but of ordinary common-sense. The art of teaching languages, therefore, calls imperatively for a reform. We may, perhaps, be permitted to point out a few of its essential features.

2. The master-organ of language.

First of all, what is the natural organ of language, the receptive organ? Is it the eye? is it the hand? or is it the ear? A puerile question, you will say, and one which bears its own answer. A question of the first importance, we reply, and so little settled, that in all the methods for teaching languages, almost without exception, and in all the schools, the problem is solved exactly the wrong way.

For it is writing—that is to say, the touch; that is to say, the hand—that is there taken as the "master-organ." It is reading—that is to say, the sight; that is to say, the eye—that occupies the second place, often even disputing the first with the before-mentioned organ. The ear comes last of all. No one, we think, will contradict us upon this point.

Has this proceeding anything in common with Nature? Is this programme due to any inspiration, any indication whatever gathered from Nature? Does Nature allow the child to read and write, does she even allow him to speak, before he has already in his ear a large part of the language?

What motive can it have been that has led the school to adopt exactly the reverse order, and to direct the development of a fully gifted child, a child who has the use of all his senses, as if it had to work upon a "deaf mute"? Yes; the school has certainly forgotten to consult Nature upon the part the ear should play in the teaching of languages. Upon this point, as upon so many others, the school has taken as guiding compass chance and thoughtlessness.

The ear is the natural organ, the first organ, the most immediate organ of language. To substitute for it the eye or the hand, as is done in all the schools at the present time, is to commit a capital blunder, which in itself alone condemns the greatest philologist in the world to be unable to accomplish in twenty years what the humblest nursemaid can achieve in six months. It is this proceeding, so absolutely contrary to Nature, which explains both the disgust inspired in childhood by the study of foreign languages and the certificates of incapacity which routine delivers to so many children. The child who, with his mother and in playing, has been able to learn a first language, surely this same child is not utterly incapable of learning a second one.

Let us state it as impressively as we can: the incapacity of the child is the incapacity of the teacher and the defectiveness of the method. *To learn to speak no matter what language is a thing as natural and easy to a child as learning to fly is to a bird.* For ourselves, however serious may seem the engagement, we would undertake to make ourselves responsible and to guarantee the development and real progress in a foreign language of any child, however backward, who "loves a game and knows how to play."

The child who shows himself eager and intelligent in playing cannot but be eager and intelligent in studying. It is the part of teaching to know how to assume the character which it must and can always have; that it should be as easy, interesting, and attractive as a game, and that it should know how to carry out each day, or rather each hour, a real and perceptible development in the mental and moral nature of the child. Playing itself, perhaps, only owes its own irresistible attraction to the development it provokes.

To conclude: If we desire to obtain surely and rapidly a development of the intellectual force, we must choose and put to work the organ capable of producing this development. Obedient, therefore, to the prescriptions of Nature, we will begin, like her, by intrusting the language-lesson to the ear.

3. *The lesson of the teacher and the work of the pupil—Assimilation—The part of the ear, the eye, and the hand in the study of a language.*

We will suppose the occasion to be a lesson in French, beginning with the exercise by which we generally initiate pupils into our method: "I open the door of the class-room." First of all, I briefly enounce this aim, and present it as such. Then I set forth in the native tongue of the children the successive means by which this end can be attained, to wit:—

— I walk towards the door,	I walk
I draw near to the door,	I draw near
I draw nearer and nearer,	I draw nearer
I get to the door,	I get to
I stop at the door.	I stop
— I stretch out my arm,	I stretch out
I take hold of the handle,	I take hold
I turn the handle,	I turn
I open the door,	I open
I pull the door.	I pull

I.

— The door moves,   moves
the door turns on its hinges,   turns
the door turns and turns,   turns
I open the door wide,   I open
I let go the handle.   I let go

The end proposed is attained, my volition is realised; I stop. My exercise is dictated and written not upon the paper, but in the ears; and by way of the ears it has penetrated into the minds.

One of the pupils, the weakest or the most distracted, should now go through this analysis again in English, and the whole class should be invited to imagine clearly to themselves not only the end, but the successive means by which it can be attained.

This done, and when the whole class have "thought" the exercise, the teacher once more takes the first phrase in English, detaches the verb—I walk, and thereupon throws the French [1] verb—*marche*, upon which he emphasises by repeating it several times over slowly—*marche, marche, marche.*

He then calls for the second sentence, "I draw near to the door," separates the verb "draw near," then pronounces the French verb—*approche*, leans upon it, accentuates it forcibly, as he did with the first.

He calls for the third sentence, and treats it in the same manner. He attacks the fourth, then the fifth, and arrives at the end of the paragraph. He has now given what I term the first step.

The sign (—) at the beginning of the paragraph indicates at the same time both a rest and a repetition. The teacher, therefore, begins once more this first "step," that is to say, the verbs which represent the sentences. He repeats them, if necessary, a third time.

Now let us see what has taken place, or ought to have taken place. In the first place, it is certainly the ear which has played the chief part; it is the ear, first, which has received the lesson in English and transmitted it, not to the eye, but to the imagination. The exercise has been, not read, but thought —an entirely different matter. It is the ear again which has received the first-fruits of the French; and the sounds *marche, approche, arrive, arrête* are identified, not with the words walk,

---

[1] Or the German, if it is a German lesson.

draw near, get to, stop, &c., but with the ideas, the perceptions, the representations revealed by these words. There has been no "translation" of English words, but a direct and immediate translation of ideas or perceptions. The English verb has simply served as a bridge for passing from one bank to the other, but a bridge that has been drawn up as soon as the passage was effected.

In other words, we have made the class "think in French." The third repetition could be done, and ought to be done, without the aid of the English. The first effort has succeeded; our first end is attained. What proves this to us is that hand which is raised over there; one of the scholars wishes to repeat what he has heard. All eyes are turned towards him, and each mouth attempts to articulate in a low voice what he articulates aloud.

The effort of the hearer has not been divided between all the portions of the sentence—article, pronoun, adverb, preposition, case, subjects, attributes, complements. It has been concentrated with care upon one and the same point, upon a single element, the essential element, the generating element of the sentence, "the verb." Therefore be not astonished if all the class are found to know thoroughly the "step" given, and if that pupil, reputed to be the least gifted of his companions, knows it equally well with the cleverest. Both have learnt their mother-tongue within sensibly the same time and with the same ease. It appears that our process has re-established, at any rate with regard to languages, the native equality of intellects! Here is a result worthy of the most serious consideration. We leave the reader the pleasure of drawing the inferences of this fact.

The second step is elaborated in the same manner as the first; and the third, if there is one, like the two others.

The conquest of the exercise is accomplished so far as regards the verbs. How about the other terms?

I take up the theme once more, and giving beforehand each French verb, henceforward well known, I build up upon this the sentence which corresponds thereto. I seek the subject first, and place it in front of the verb. I next seek the complement, and, determining grammatically the case desired, I place it after the verb. I thus arrive at the end of the first step. Each subject has reappeared so many times; the same complement has returned so often under the same form, that this once going through really suffices to set down and engrave upon each memory the exercise in its totality.

The work here is reduced, therefore, to the task of thinking the exercise by the verb and in the verb; and when the verb is conquered, the learner finds himself suddenly, and without need of any fresh effort, in possession of all the rest. From this results a considerable simplification, worthy of the best attention of linguists. We earnestly beg that our experience may be repeated and our assertion verified.

The work we have just described is so simple, so elementary, so easy both for teacher and pupil, that we are almost ashamed, every time we are obliged to have recourse to all these words and circumlocutions, to explain a process that any child of six years old thoroughly comprehends at the end of five minutes' practice. We are tempted, at every time, to substitute, as did the Grecian philosopher, action for explanation, of throwing down our pen and of appealing to a demonstration before the class. A single lesson, indeed, shows the whole system, and never fails to convert the attentive listener to our side. The most obstinate prejudice always gives way before this living demonstration.

The exercise is conquered—conquered in its totality. All the class has repeated, or is capable of repeating it. To what task shall we next pass?

Here is the moment to treat a question previously reserved. We have said that after the oral elaboration of each exercise should come a release, a rest, a diversion useful to the work already accomplished. What shall this diversion be?

All intellectual development, to be durable, must be submitted—we repeat it once more—to a species of "incubation." The mind must brood for a certain time over each one of its morsels of knowledge. This is a law of Nature which pedagogic science will have to inscribe at the head of its code. This mental incubation is an essential condition of all real progress. It is not enough, in fact, to acquire knowledge; it must be "taken possession of." Our work, to be entirely in accordance with reason and with Nature, must count two distinct moments :—

First, conquest—and that by active force;
Then, thinking over and taking possession.

METHOD OF TEACHING THE SERIES.

The first act has been accomplished. The mind is, so to speak, exhausted by it. It is right to grant it a rest before demanding a fresh effort.

To take possession of knowledge is to make it pass successively by way of all the senses. Now, our exercise has been confided to the ear by the lesson given by the teacher, and is graven upon the imagination. It should now be confided to the eye by reading, then to the touch by writing. Each pupil should now open his book and read, then open his exercise-book and write:—

J'ouvre la porte.

— Je marche vers la porte,   je marche
je m'approche de la porte,   je m'approche
je m'approche et m'approche encore,   je m'approche
j'arrive à la porte,   j'arrive
je m'arrête à la porte.   je m'arrête

— J'allonge le bras,   j'allonge
je prends la poignée,   je prends
je tourne la poignée,   je tourne
j'ouvre la porte,   j'ouvre
je tire la porte.   je tire

— La porte cède,   cède
la porte tourne sur ses gonds,   tourne
la porte tourne et tourne encore,   tourne
j'ouvre la porte toute grande,   j'ouvre
je lâche la poignée.   je lâche

The exercise will thus have passed by way of the scholar's three principal senses; the lesson will have penetrated into his inner nature, and it will be equally indestructible. This is the rest promised; this is the diversion useful to the work already accomplished. While the class is writing, let us discuss sundry considerations relative to the present proceeding.

Before everything else, it must be understood that the eye and the hand only take possession of the exercise *after* the ear has entirely conquered it for itself and transmitted it to the mind. Indeed, change the order, and begin by the writing, or even by the reading lesson, as is now everywhere done, and the lesson ceases to be fruitful. The pupil no longer thinks—he translates; he no longer assimilates—he dwells upon the written word, the written line. The visualising faculty is no longer brought into play to look at the fact itself taking place before it, but is content to notice the place of the expressions of this fact in the book, to remark if this expression is to be seen on one page or over-leaf, at the top of the page, or at the bottom, or in the middle.

What is the consequence? The consequence is that the lesson now only yields the fruits we know of old. The child leaves the morsel of intellectual food which he has been able for one brief instant to separate by the reading, carelessly to fall back into the book; giving it back faithfully to the book, instead of seeking to wrest it therefrom. Truly there is little profit in such morsels.

On the other hand, transmitted as we have set forth, the lesson passes (one cannot repeat it too often), really passes into the nature of the pupil, and never more becomes rubbed out, whether he have or have not what routine calls a "memory." It must also be well understood that the exercise taught is not any exercise, no matter what, but a page of our method; that is to say, a picture whose details are logically linked together, linked together by the most natural of all relationships, that of causation, or rather that of succession in time, a relationship that the feeblest mind can grasp, and which becomes the all-powerful auxiliary of the memory, which it creates even if this does not already exist.

The class upon which we have operated is supposed to be composed of pupils new to the system or of beginners. These will write out the exercise by simply copying it. But at the end of one month's practice the programme will be modified; they will no longer copy—they will write it out of their heads. Will they be able to do it? you ask. How can they possibly carry out this task?

The pupil who has gone through a single series, a general series, has assimilated (like the little child who has arrived at being able to express his daily life) all that is most essential of the language. After our Series of the Shepherd, for instance, the pupil finds himself in possession of nearly all the elementary verbs of the language he is studying, that is to say, of those by means of which all ordinary matters can be expressed. An exercise which, at the beginning, would have taken a quarter of an hour or more, may henceforth be given in five minutes at the outside.

The teacher's labour is, therefore, simplified and considerably abridged. At the end of five minutes the pupil is sufficiently familiarised with the exercise to open his book. Then, covering with one hand the text of the sentences, he goes down the column of verbs step by step, and upon each verb he attempts to reconstruct, as did the teacher, the corresponding sentence of which the verb recalls to him the idea. As is seen, at this moment the effort of the pupil is partially substituted for the effort of the teacher. After a simple and short period of listening, the pupil elaborates and conquers by himself the proposed exercise. We have arrived at the "personal" work.

In two or three minutes the pupil will have reconstructed the exercise, sentence by sentence. He then writes down in his exercise-book the column of verbs, closes his book, and to the left, opposite each verb, he composes and writes out his sentence. This phrase is his own work; he has drawn the whole phrase out of his own conception. The process followed has permitted (and this is not one of the least of its merits) the thought of the master or the expression of the book to become the personal work of the pupil. This is the second stage established by our method, and it is not the last.

His strength increasing quickly under such a system, the pupil will be very shortly able to reproduce the whole exercise, verbs and sentences. That day he will have put on the garb of manhood. Henceforward, it will no longer be an isolated exercise that he will be given to digest at a time, but an entire series, all that can issue from the teacher's mouth in the space of a quarter of an hour at first, then of half an hour, then of a whole hour. But at this rate the fifty or sixty partial series which translate the entire life, which exhaust the whole generality of our conceptions, will soon themselves be exhausted. What shall we do then? Will the book be closed and the work declared finished?

Before replying to this question, we wish to develop two points which have an immediate connection with the process of teaching, of which we have just sketched out the general features.

4. *The pronunciation.*

Submitted to the discipline which we have explained, will our pupils acquire what is termed a good accent, a good pronunciation? The child speaks with a good accent, pronounces correctly, when his nurse or his mother speaks with a good accent and pronounces correctly. Where, indeed, can he acquire a bad accent if he never hears any other than a good accent? How should he be likely to pronounce badly when he has never heard anything pronounced other than well? How is it, then, that so many people pronounce so badly the foreign languages that they have begun to learn at school?

We believe we have found the true answer to the enigma. The first great cause of a bad accent is reading—reading undertaken at the wrong time, too soon. The second cause is reading degenerating into a bad habit; and the third cause still seems to us to be reading. Let us explain.

Is it more difficult to pronounce "boosh" than "bowch"? Evidently not. In French, the word written *bouche* (mouth) is pronounced *boosh*, and not *bowch*. If, therefore, you pronounce the French word *bouche* to me before I have seen how this sound is represented in writing; if the sound *boosh* strikes my ears before the letters *b o u c h e* strike my eyes, I should have no reason for finding the French pronunciation at all odd, though I might, perhaps, its spelling. As is seen, the thing is turned the other way round; and if one learns French without being able to read it, as the little child does, there will be no longer much greater difficulty in pronouncing it than in pronouncing words in English. This is perfectly evident.

"How about the spelling?" you will ask. The spelling! You would learn it like the young French children learn it, as you yourselves have learnt the English spelling, ten times more difficult than the French; and this without letting the study of the spelling spoil your already acquired pronunciation. Besides, the spelling is a thing that can be reformed—the pronunciation hardly at all. We must choose between the two evils.

The modern Greek child of four or five years old, who has hardly yet left his nurse, does he or does he not know how to pronounce this beautiful language better than the most learned of our philologists? Every one will answer yes, and our philologist before the others. We will allow this child to grow up. We will send him to school, and suppose that he is made to begin the study of, say, English. The first thing they will do at the school, as we all know, is to put into his hands either a grammar or a dictionary, or probably both.

How will our scholar read the first English word that comes before his eyes? He will undoubtedly read it in the way he knows how to read—as if it were Greek; he will pronounce it as if it were Greek; he will accentuate it as if it were Greek. How should he do otherwise? And this false sound, this false accent, issuing from his mouth, ascends to his ears, and is graven, is bitten thereon. And the teacher must be clever who will efface this first impression. It is, then, the reading which does the harm, and the more the child reads and repeats his word, that is, the more diligently he works, the more the evil is aggravated, until the time may arrive when he becomes absolutely incapable of reform. Our young Greek is then condemned for life to pronounce English badly, whatever effort he may make, whatever discipline he may submit to. Even with our own method it would be extremely difficult, if not impossible, to alter. The fruit has been vitiated at the germ.

If our young Greek, on the other hand, had been, on principle, deprived of all books; if his eye had been guarded from the sight of the English spelling, if he had had the companionship of an Englishman who would never write a word for him, he would then have acquired the exact English accent, as he had already acquired the exact Greek accent with his nurse.

The foreigner who comes to our colleges with a first tinge of the language often leaves without having greatly corrected his first accent. On the other hand, those who have never studied, speak and pronounce almost as well as their teacher at the end of six months. Any of us could do the same if we would submit ourselves to a rational process of learning.

The first cause, therefore, of a false accent and pronunciation is the study of languages by means of reading. Neither the temperament, nor the throat, nor the larynx are to blame. With a Greek nurse, the child will talk Greek like a Greek; with a German nurse he will talk German like a German; with a French nurse he will talk French like a Frenchman, and so for other languages.

In other terms, and to close the subject, we have mistaken "the organ." Nature has funished us with ears for the study of languages; we have thought it possible to substitute the eye in their place. Here is the primal fall, here the original sin in the present teaching. Our method returns to the order of Nature; it should arrive, and it does in fact arrive, at the same result as Nature.

What must we say of those books where the author, amusing himself by figuring the pronunciation of each word, superposes an artificial and abstract language upon the real language, abusing the human patience and force to the point of desiring to paint upon the student's eye the thirty thousand words of the dictionary along with the thirty thousand shadows of these words? If such a labour were possible, this would mean the learning of two languages in order to know one. These, nevertheless, are the aberrations which govern schools, and maintain whole legions of printers and compositors.

We never allow any child to read or to write any exercise that he has not heard, that he has not repeated, that he has not assimilated; any lesson which is not in his ears, which is not at the end of his tongue, as a pianist has a tune in his ears and at the end of his fingers. The pronunciation of our pupils, therefore, will not be wrong, unless that of the teacher himself is wrong.

Like the little child, our school mocks and laughs at all these pretended difficulties of pronunciation—English, French, German, Greek, &c.; or rather, it never encounters these kinds of obstacles upon its path. It gives the pronunciation of each word as each word is met with in our series, and it does not preoccupy itself with building up theories or formulating rules to settle—months or years in advance—the pronunciation of them.

When a word occurs in an exercise taught by us, it occurs under the form of a "spoken word," that is to say, together with its pronunciation, and not as a vain assemblage of printed characters. When once the word "mouth" has been translated by the spoken French word "*bouche*," it is impossible to hear, without laughing, any one translate it by any other sound.

"Without laughing!" This expression, or rather this fact, is one of the bitterest criticisms of the ordinary teaching. Can you cite a class where the most monstrous pronunciation excites the least hilarity? Is it the same outside the class-room? Pronounce once before a young Greek the superb "Polusphloisboio!" and in the burst of laughter that your learned pronunciation will provoke, you will be able to judge if your teaching is on the right path.

The pedagogic error which we point out is decried by every one; yet such is the fixity of tenure enjoyed in the schools by the opposite process to that which we are prescribing, so much has it passed into a habit, and, in appearance, so convenient is it for the ease of the teacher, that we almost tremble for fear of being neither understood nor even accorded a hearing. I say "tremble," for if this prescription of the manner of teaching is neglected, our method will remain as sterile as all the others.

Address the ear, then, first of all and principally. Afterwards take as auxiliaries the eye and the hand in reading and writing. The ear is the prime minister of the intelligence. It is the sense which watches with the greatest constancy and fidelity at its gateway; it is the one that the intelligence listens to most willingly, the one that speaks with the greatest authority and the greatest intimacy, the one that guards longest its depositions. Let the eye, then, reign over the dominion of colours and forms, and restore to the ear a function which the schoolmen and pedantry have forced the eye to usurp. The memory will thereupon gain a vigour hitherto unknown, and will recover that power which so astonishes and confounds us in the little child.

"But I cannot remember these verbs; I must see them written down," exclaims the adult who, trained in the ordinary schools, is subjected for the first time to our discipline. What? Do you hear the little child make this remark to his mother? Can *he* not go direct from the fact to the word without passing by the intermediary of the written representation? Our nature, upon this point, has been so deformed by our scholastic habits, that to arrive at the reality we have first to pass by way of the shadow. Is not the written word the shadow of the spoken word, and so the shadow of the idea?

A man who, from some accident, has been obliged to renounce the use of his arms, and who has learnt to use his feet in their place—this is the image of our adult learners. He has been "atrophied" by pedagogic science. When the ear is called, it is the eye that answers, leaving the sense of hearing slumbering peacefully at the door, and communicating—ill or well, as the case may be—with the intelligence in its place. Hence this cry of distress :—"If only I might see the words written down!"

It is precisely these "written words" that have paralysed your linguistic sense. Renounce them, I pray you, courageously, as the cause of all evil. Strike against this pernicious habit. Accustom yourself to learn only by listening, that is, by going directly from the fact to the articulated, the spoken word. Your sense of hearing will promptly awake from its torpor, and, after a few days' practice, will completely recover its native activity and energy.

The little child stammers and lisps long over each word newly pronounced in his presence. This is because the ear is far more docile than the tongue. The word is in the ear long before being on the tongue. But do not fear. The ear has received the correct imprint of the sound: it will act as tuning-fork, correcting and regulating the attempts and efforts of the tongue. The same fact is reproduced in our teaching. The pupil has in his ear the accent of a phrase before the tongue is able to reproduce it exactly. Be careful, therefore, not to get impatient if the pronunciation of your pupil be not perfect at the first lesson. The essential thing is that the spoken word shall be deposited within the ear, that it vibrate and resound therein, before the tongue has attempted to reproduce it. It is the ear that must give the law to the tongue, not the tongue to the ear. The spoken sound must reside in the ear as a type or ideal to which afterwards the tongue will conform to fashion its products.

Do not, therefore, attempt to obtain a perfect pronunciation at the first lesson. Talk yourself, talk continually. At the commencement let the pupil speak as little as possible; it is in his ear and not on his tongue that it is important to fix the word or the phrase. When the spring is abundant it will flow of itself, and the liquid supplied by it will have the advantage of being pure.

Let us not forget that the little child listens for two years before constructing a phrase, and that he has possession of both the sound and its idea, that is, the spoken word, long before attempting to produce it himself. For languages Nature appears to us to be the best of teachers; let us strive to follow out all her prescriptions.

In concluding this chapter, we think it will be useful to formulate a grave corollary which results therefrom, and which we will develop farther on. "The spoken word must precede in everything and everywhere the word as read or as written. Therefore, the only really fruitful exercise is that of the translation of facts into the foreign language by the intermediary of the professor."

It results from this that our system condemns, à priori, the exercise of translation from the foreign language, as understood and practised until now. In this it is again found in perfect accord with the process of Nature. Is it by making translations from other languages, think you, that the little baby learns its mother-tongue? The reading of a foreign author cannot of itself be fruitful, except upon the condition of its being transformed by pedagogic art into a series of statements to be reconstructed in the language of the author by the intermediary of the professor. To prohibit translation into the language studied, and to replace it by translation from this language, is to render the study of languages "absolutely impossible." We shall farther on demonstrate this, and, while pointing out the evil, we shall indicate the remedy, which will be a "New Method" of reading, translating, and assimilating the works of classical authors.

And let no one imagine that these principles apply only to the study of living languages. There are not, and it is impossible that there should be, two right ways of learning a language, be this language ancient or modern. The governing body of a university which should be so ill-advised, under whatsoever pretext, as to prohibit (as is done in certain countries) all translation into the language studied, would only prove that it possesses no correct information upon the art of teaching languages.

Be certain of this, that it is only by thinking directly in the language studied that you will arrive at reading fluently a page of Virgil or a page of Homer. From the height of a long experience, I venture to denounce translation as the true cause of our ignorance in which we are of those two unfortunate ancient languages, which we study all our lives and know never.

It is too true: the ordinary collections of exercises seem to become more and more absurd, and consequently perfectly impotent. But who is responsible for this result? Is it the exercises themselves or those who fabricate them? The child in the family only does and only hears exercises in the language he is studying. Does he succeed or no in learning the language there spoken? If yes, it is because the process is a good one: we must preserve it.

It is not the abolition of this exercise which the head-masters must decree; it is its reform which they must strive to provoke.

5. *One teacher for three classes.*

While the class is taking possession of the lesson by writing it out, the teacher is idle. How could he best occupy his time? Should he give it to rest or to supervision? We believe we employ ours more profitably by passing into an adjoining class-room and giving a second lesson. We have spoken of pupils of three kinds, more or less advanced, treating and elaborating the series in three different manners. These three classes may be very easily taken in charge by a single teacher. If each lesson is properly carried out, the moment at which the teacher reappears in the first class will coincide exactly with the moment at which this class finishes the work proposed. One teacher, therefore, with our method of teaching, is worth three.

And if the teaching of science were susceptible also of reformation—of reformation in the sense which a future chapter will indicate — our system would carry into the pedagogic machinery a simplification of very considerable extent.

We trust we may be permitted, in the interest of the cause pleaded, once more to bring our own personality to the front. By the aid of our linguistic, historic, and scientific methods, we have carried on three classes simultaneously with more ease, and infinitely greater success, than before we had carried on, at college, a single class by means of the ordinary methods.

At the risk of sinning against modesty, we will state another result. If one teacher is worth three, one year of our method is worth two, or even more, of those passed under the ordinary curriculum. There is not one of our boys who cannot subdue in one year, and this without pain and fatigue, the work of two, and often of three years of college. And this should not be otherwise, because by teaching the sciences by the languages, and the languages by the sciences, we necessarily gain a considerable amount of time, without counting the numerous advantages assured to us by a plan of progress logically and severely drawn up.

This is not all. No one thoroughly knows a science or an art until he has taught it himself to others. This is specially true of languages. Now, the simplicity of our linguistic exercises, added to the simplicity of our process of teaching, allows any of our pupils to give the lesson of any of the series learnt by them almost as well as the teacher could do it himself. And not only is this exercise possible, but we recommend it, we impose it upon our students. It represents, in our eyes, the last phase of assimilation.

Our method amply provides, therefore, for the multiplication of teachers. If anything hinders the progress of our school, it will not be the scarcity, but rather the superabundance of embryo teachers. "And the discipline, impositions?" we shall doubtless be asked. Discipline! We speak after a long experience. Discipline, such as you understand by the word, is only necessary in classes where the studies are a torture instead of being a pleasure.

SUBJECTIVE LANGUAGE.
Its Organisation.
X.
CLASSIFICATION OF THE RELATIVE PHRASES.

1. *Definition of the relative phrases—Their object and their number in each tongue.*

In every language there are two languages. The one translates the facts of the external world, the other translates the facts and gestures of the soul or the mind. The first constitutes the "objective" language, the second constitutes the "subjective" language. These two languages are irreducible in terms of each other. The first forms the material of our series; the second is the source of what we term "Relative Phrases." The relative phrases are destined to translate the complex play of the soul's faculties, that is, to express our ideas, our judgments, our sentiments, &c.

"Man," we have said, "does not only perceive the phenomena of the external world; he appreciates them, judges them, that is, he reacts upon them. He enjoys this and dislikes that, he approves this and blames that, he believes this and doubts that." The expression of each of these movements, of each of these operations, is a "relative phrase":—

I am glad . . .	I want you to . . .
I am sorry . . .	Attempt to . . .
I think that . . .	That is good.
I hope that . . .	That is bad.
I wish that . . .	It is true.
I believe that . . .	It is false.
I am certain that . . .	It is easy.
Do what you can to . . .	It is difficult.
Try to . . .	You must . . .
I wish you would . . .	It is important to . . .
Have the kindness to . . .	I regret that . . . &c., &c.

These are "relative phrases."

These expressions do not stand alone. They rest upon the expression of another fact; they have a "relation" to another fact. Hence the name "relative phrase," by which we think we can venture provisionally to designate them. This lin-

guistic distinction, as far as we are aware, has never before
been made by any one, although a prodigious number of these
formulæ enter into the web of each distinct language or
dialect. It has, therefore, been necessary for us to invent,
or at least employ, a special name to represent this species of
locution.

The relative phrases are to the language what mortar is to
stones. It is they which bind the parts together. Without
them the knowledge of the series or the possession of the
"objective language" would be almost barren. The real or
apparent dualism presented by the human personality is reproduced in the language itself. Its two constituent parts
cannot subsist separately.

We have made a most careful collection of these expressions
from the most finished works in the languages studied by us—
dictionaries and classical masterpieces. Our manuscripts contain, for each tongue, about sixty thousand of these phrases.
But let the reader be reassured. This number, like that of
the series, can be very greatly reduced. By organising the
material of the subjective language in a certain manner, our
method will enable every one to conquer in playing, and without
wearisome and exhaustive application, this formidable mass
which represents for each language the spirit and the genius
of the people who speak it. Nature solves this problem every
day; then why should not pedagogic science also solve it?

2. *Two kinds of relative phrases—Those perfect or absolute,
and the enclitics.*

The relative phrases are susceptible of division and subdivision. In the first place, they divide themselves naturally
into two vast species. Phrases of one species express complete
judgments, as :—

    It is true.
    It is false.
    I am satisfied.
    You have spoken well.
    You have done ill, &c.

Phrases of the other species express judgments; incomplete, imperfect, and unfinished phrases, they express volitions,
beliefs, efforts, feelings, &c., of which the object is expressed
by a second phrase :—

It is necessary to → work hard
I want you to → attend well.
I think → you can manage it.
I hope that → you will succeed.
Try to → conquer the difficulty.
I should like you to → succeed, &c., &c.

The first are relative phrases, properly so called, which might be named "perfect." We term the second species "enclitic" ("hung upon"), because they are as it were suspended from or inclined against the expression of a second fact which serves them as complement. "I want you to" leans or is inclined upon "attend well."

Every language has about seven hundred words giving birth to these enclitic phrases. This uniformity has nothing very surprising in it. As a matter of fact, the number of faculties is the same with all men. Therefore the enclitics which express in precise terms the play of these faculties ought to be equal in number in all tongues. To him who seeks properly, each phrase has its equivalent in the language of his neighbours. We can affirm that it is the same with the simple or perfect relative phrases, and that the richness or the poverty of a language in these expressions is, in fact, nothing but the richness or poverty of mind of him who makes this judgment. We have followed, step by step, five or six modern besides the classic languages, and must declare that, in this respect, none of them has proved weaker than the others.

This remark is of great importance. It is sufficient, in point of fact, to draw up in a first language—in French or English, for example—the complete system of relative phrases, and this system will hold valid for all other languages. Is not the mother's process the same in all latitudes? A good method, one truly inspired by Nature, should itself admit of but one manner of proceeding, whatever might be the language to be studied. In this our method offers the closest analogy with the natural process.

For the relative phrases as for the series, our system, when once constructed in one language, will really be done for all languages. We shall no longer hear of a "special method" for learning German, of a "special method" for learning French, of a "special method" for learning Arabic or Sanskrit, &c. There will be "*The* method of studying languages."

We shall see shortly how the grammar itself becomes ONE,

as the human mind is ONE. Let us return to our work of classification; and, in the first place, we will attempt to classify the "enclitics."

3. *Classification of Enclitics—General insight.*

The enclitics, as we have said, express and translate the complete play of the faculties of the soul. If psychology were a thoroughly developed science, we could borrow from it the list of these faculties, and we should then only have to group around each of these the expressions which relate thereto. Thus the expressions: I believe that—I think that—I fancy that—I doubt whether—It seems to me that, &c., relate evidently to faith, or the faculty of believing. The expressions: try to—attempt to, evidently belong to the will, or to the faculty of willing. Unfortunately psychologists are not agreed either as to the number or the essence of the faculties of the mind. The linguist is therefore obliged to work here to some extent at his risk and peril; but at least his way is clearly traced.

First of all, he will consider the relative phrases one by one; he will determine with the closest possible accuracy to which faculty of the mind they are related, and will again divide them into a certain number of natural groups psychologically distinct, so producing from this linguistic labour a work in itself fundamentally philosophical.

The numerous expressions ranged around any one faculty might also, in their turn, be distributed in secondary groups corresponding to the various moments of this faculty. Each faculty, in fact, has distinct moments, passes through various phases and various states. For example: belief, certainty, uncertainty, doubt, hope, &c., are all diverse states of the faculty of believing; as love, hate, desire, resolution, &c., are distinct states or movements of the faculty of willing.

The linguist will determine these moments, and will determine his classification accordingly. The relative phrases which compose these secondary groups can only be, and in fact only are, synonymous locutions, expressing the various shades of meaning of the same idea, the same conception, the same volition, or the same judgment—synonyms which can be themselves classified by basing them upon the relationship of the most general to the least general, or *vice versâ*. If this work were properly carried out, the pupil who should practise the relative phrases would have studied, at the same time, an important chapter of psychology.

Let us take the number of these faculties of the mind or soul as twelve, and let us grant to each of them twenty different moments or states, a supposition which is evidently exaggerated. Twelve times 20 are 240. Each language would thus comprise at most 240 simple enclitic phrases, elementary and irreducible, types of all the others, of which all the others are varieties. This number is found to be entirely in accordance with the verdict of experience or of direct observation. The child of five years old has not two hundred enclitic phrases at his disposition; but those he does employ form part of the 240 types of which we have just spoken. The child does not say—

"Have the kindness to → pass me the bread."
"I invite you to → come and play with me."

He will say, far more simply, for example :—

"Please → pass me the bread."
"I want you to → come and play with me!"

Provided with this light mental outfit, the child cannot, indeed, understand everything, but he can say everything. Ourselves, when we wish to undertake the study of a foreign language, the first thing we do is carefully to collect and assimilate the 150 or 200 enclitic phrases chosen according to the before-mentioned process. At that moment we are not yet able to understand all we hear, but, like the little child, we can say all we wish, if besides this we possess the whole of the ordinary series. Finally, who would believe it? The Æneid itself does not contain 300 different enclitic phrases. If this number sufficed for Virgil, assuredly it can suffice for others.

The three or four thousand enclitic locutions or formulæ can therefore be reduced to 200 primary enclitics. This reduction appears to us to deserve the attention of linguists. To study these 200 formulæ abstractly or separately would be the work of two or three days. To study them afterwards in their various shades of meaning would be a longer task, but relatively easy if these formulæ were properly classified and logically set in order.

As a matter of fact, to learn them in the way we have set forth is not even a task; it is a GAME. Yes, a game! Why should it not be a game? Ask yourselves if the little child, when he was learning his own set of phrases, saw therein anything else than a mere game. Let us once learn to set about it as he set about it, and it might be, nay, it necessarily will be, for us as for him, a game—nothing but a GAME.

4. *Classification of the absolute Relative Phrases—General insight.*

The absolute or perfect Relative Phrases translate, like the Enclitics, but under another form, the diverse states or movements of the inner nature. To classify them, it was necessary to compare them among themselves, and to determine their common characteristics. We have devoted many long evenings to this work; the following are some of the heads under which we have found that the locutions contained in our voluminous collection might be placed : Praise—Blame—Advice—Wish—Reprimand—Admonition—Encouragement—Menace.

It must be understood that these categories are thrown together at hazard, and not by any process of reasoning. They appear here only in the light of examples or of indications. We give them to show simply that the definite classification is to be made, like that of the enclitics, upon an essentially psychological basis. This important work must form the object of a special treatise.

The classification arrived at could not remain at this first generalisation. Indeed, several of the orders of phrases established were found to be represented by columns of ten to twenty thousand expressions. I had distributed the material in orders; it was now necessary to seek to divide these orders into species. For long this problem appeared to me insoluble; and what caused me most to despair was that alongside this problem I perceived a third, equally important and not less difficult of solution.

In Nature the two languages gear together, as we have said, one into the other, developing harmoniously side by side, the one aiding and pushing forward the other. Even supposing it were possible to discover a principle for subdividing the above orders into species how was I to be able to cross the yawning chasm which separated the Ego from the Non-Ego? how was I to ally in the same exercise or in the same oral lesson the subjective language with the objective language? how, in point of fact, was I to wed the relative phrase to the phrase of the series?

After long meditations and trials of every kind, I eventually caught a glimpse, by a sudden intuition, of the true and unique relation by which the two languages could be linked together. And this relation was so simple—so simple—was so natural and so close to me all the time, that I actually felt sorry for myself. So much labour for so small a thing! Such long researches to find what was under my very hand! The disproportion between my efforts and their result was enough to make a child laugh.

The third problem was, therefore, seen to be solved before the second. But while examining more closely the solution found, I perceived that it contained within it that of the second, and presented a means as simple as it was practical of subdividing the orders in question into species.

At the same time, the secret process by which Nature transformed, for the child, the study of the subjective element of language into a game, was explained and laid bare; and this process, by its perfect conformity with the solution already found, justified our conception. But let us hasten to descend from these generalities and approach directly the problem itself.

In order to prepare the reader for the full understanding of the solution announced, we will conduct him for a moment to the school of Nature, and we will interpret before him the object-lesson and the language-lesson which the nursemaid gives, unconsciously, to the little baby in her charge, when she amuses it, for instance, in making it open the door. For this purpose, we may be allowed to give once more a well-known exercise :—

Walk, my pretty;	That's it!
Go towards the door;	That's very good!
Now you've got there;	Bravo!
Lift up your little arm;	Capital!
Take hold of the handle;	That's the way!
Turn the handle;	How strong you are!
Open the door;	What a clever little man!
Pull the door open;	There's a little darling! &c. &c.

This exercise, which every one of us has done, or rather played, under a mother's direction, is in miniature the system which we believe we have wrested from Nature. It contains it, as the acorn contains the oak. Never can the saying, "All is in all," be invoked more truly or to better purpose.

The left-hand column represents the series or the objective

language; the right-hand column represents the relative phrase or the subjective language; and these two languages, so diverse and so opposite as they seem, are here united to form one and the self-same exercise. Let us here add, that each phrase of the right-hand column expressing a judgment "relative" to the corresponding objective fact, the name "relative phrase" is seen to be sufficiently justified.

Philologists, linguists, and grammarians! To weigh these expressions, so widely different one from the other, you have only known up to the present moment of the use of balances in which substantive is weighed against substantive, pronoun against pronoun, adjective against adjective. These scales are good, perhaps, for the weighing of syllables, but they are not made for the weighing of ideas. Your logical and grammatical analyses have found nothing which essentially distinguishes the sentence

"How strong you are,"

from the sentence

"Lift up your little arm,"

while the most ignorant of mothers has the knowledge of their difference, and knows exceedingly well how to translate it and make it understood by the child.

"What is her secret?" you ask me. It is a secret which you know full well yourselves; it is a process with which you are just as familiar as she is, and which you practise continually.

Living speech is not solely composed of syllables—of words and sounds. You may, perhaps, have heard a talking-machine. What difference do you find between the phrase articulated by these ingenious pieces of mechanism and that which is uttered by the mouth of man? The speech of an automatic speaking-machine affects you disagreeably. It is wierd, hollow, unearthly—the speech of a corpse. What is lacking for it to sound like the speech of a living man? A thing that art can never give. This thing is called "THE ACCENT."

Now we have it! It is by the accent—the stress-accent of the voice—that the mother initiates her child into the subjective language; it is by the accent that she teaches it to distinguish the words which express an external fact from the words which translate a movement or a state of the soul.

And the baby—a better analyst here than Noel et Chapsal [or Lindley Murray]—interprets admirably its mother's accent, and according to the note of this accent classes such and such an expression in the objective language, and such another expression in the subjective language. Without this virtue of the natural accent confusion would be inevitable. Where, otherwise, is the reason that should hinder the baby from translating the sound " How strong you are " by " Lift up your arm," and the sound " Lift up your arm " by " How strong you are ?"

A child assists in a conversation between grown-up persons. He assists in his own style, that is, by playing about and by attending, in appearance at least, to anything else than the conversation. An hour after, the next day perhaps, one is astonished to hear issue from his mouth, suddenly and *àpropos* of nothing, a form of expression which he had never articulated before, and of which the sense, more or less abstract, seems altogether beyond his age. Whence has the child taken this expression ? Assuredly he has not evolved it from his inner consciousness ? Go back in your mind to the conversation which took place this morning or yesterday, and there is the place where you will indubitably find it.

Quite a young child remarked to us a little while ago, " The weather is dark; I really should not be surprised if it rained hard. It has been snowing up on the mountain. The deuce ! the winter has begun early !" Now, " I really should not be surprised " and " The deuce ! " are expressions which certainly do not belong to the vocabulary of the little child. He must, therefore, have taken them from some remark or other made in his presence.

This explanation is generally held to be quite sufficient. We declare, however, that it does not entirely satisfy us, and we put this question: Why and how is it that he has retained out of a long conversation this phrase and not another ? Why has he fastened by preference upon an abstract expression that he does not understand, or that he interprets as often as not the wrong way round ?

He retains it, we may perhaps be told, simply because it seems strange to him. This reason would be a good one if it were a question of an isolated term—of a proper name, for instance. But we are speaking here of a complex form of expression, of an expression composed of words ordinarily well known to him, and consequently not having even the attraction of novelty.

We put the problem, therefore, once more: Why this phrase and not another ? And why is this expression, instead of

THE ACCENT.

belonging to the objective language, always found to belong to the subjective language? "It is instinct," replies one. "It is a gift of Nature," adds another. We have already said what we think of this solution, and of the persons who propose it. The following is our own:—

The child has taken from a certain conversation this expression, and not another, simply because the expression in question was accentuated in a different manner from all the others. Yes, accentuated! Everything is in this. The accent! Is not this the speech employed by the lower species? Is not this the language of the animals, a universal language? Is not the accent the signature of the soul in the phrase? Attempt to speak, to read; attempt even to think without accentuating your words either aloud or to yourself. It cannot be done.

In the monologue of its mother or its nurse, how is it that the child can distinguish the absolute phrase from the relative phrase, the objective language from the subjective language, the expression of the tangible fact from the expression of the pure idea, the translation of the act from the translation of the judgment made upon this act? Between the mother and her child I do not see any other interpreter, nor is there any other interpreter, than "the accent."

"Mamma," asked a little French child once in our hearing, "Mamma, what does 'sacristie' mean?"

"My child, it is the little room where the priest puts on his robes," answered the mother.

"Oh, no! It is not that sort of sacristy at all. When any one lets fall something, and picks it up again, and then it falls again, they say 'sacr-r-risti!'"

This definition is an entire revelation. It demonstrates that the accent, and nothing but the accent, had given to this child the consciousness of the inner signification of a doubly figurative locution. In conversation, the author of a relative phrase, without knowing or without wishing it, isolates it by accentuating it; raises it, so to speak, above the level of the rest of the conversation by a special intonation. The child then catches it as it flies; or, if you will, it vibrates more strongly than the rest in his ear, and is imprinted thereon in less ephemeral characters. This is why and this is how his tongue attempts to reproduce this expression an hour after, a day after he has heard it.

Let us now see what use the child makes of a relative

expression recently acquired. Follow him attentively, and you will notice that the new phrase will be found at the tip of his tongue quite as often as the newest of his toys is seen in his hands. He serves this formula, as one might say, with every kind of sauce. He applies it, wrongly or rightly, to all his conceptions. He uses it for talking to his rocking-horse, to his carriages or their coachmen; he uses it to apostrophise his wooden Punch and Judy or his living pets. He thus rapidly appropriates and assimilates this particular expression. Presently he will listen to another conversation; he will pick out a new relative phrase, and will assimilate this like the first.

There you have the whole process of Nature. Was I not right when I stated that even the study of the abstract and subjective part of the language is for the child simply a game? We have here evidently arrived at the end of the phenomenon. We may here halt awhile, in order to meditate upon the process of Nature, to extract therefrom the precepts it may contain, and finally to engraft them upon our own method.

In the school of Nature the subjective language and the objective language are developed simultaneously and parallel with each other. They advance together and side by side, harmoniously, and without ever becoming confused; the accent marking them each with a character of its own. What would happen if we were to advise the study of the various groups of the objective expressions separately in a special vocabulary? We are able to reply to this question, having made at our own expense the experiment of this deplorable proceeding. All your efforts would be, and necessarily, made in pure waste. They will even be prejudicial to you, inasmuch as you will have to pull down before you can rebuild.

If one reflects for a moment, it will be seen that it cannot possibly be otherwise. The relative phrases are formed to lean or rest upon some other thing. In themselves they present only empty, hollow forms, as vague and fugitive as bubbles of air, applying at one and the same time to everything and to nothing.

> Try to . . .
> Would you please . . .
> I want you to . . .
> I exhort you to . . .
> It is important to . . .
> Reflect that . . . &c., &c.

You might read these forms of expression over and over

again till they became thoroughly imprinted upon your eye; you might train your tongue as much as you pleased to articulate this indefinite sequence of sounds; when you have reached, as you supposed, the end of this wearisome exercise, you will find yourself just at the point where the author of these lines found himself after having thought he had passed the entire dictionary into his memory.

A man is not a joiner, and cannot pass himself for one simply because he has just made the purchase of a complete kit of joiner's tools. Nor will he become one any the sooner by twisting and turning about indefinitely in his hands and contentedly contemplating the tools which he now regards as his stock-in-trade. The mere acquisition has not advanced him one single step in his art. So also is it with him who by sheer force of reading over and over again—that is, of regarding the same syllables—has succeeded in heaping together the whole of the forms of the subjective language in what he is pleased to call his memory. He would not be less awkward, less affected, if it were necessary for him to converse for a few moments, than our raw joiner if any one gave him a window to make, or rather, a simple mortice to cut.

We repeat, no one will ever learn a language by studying isolated words, disconnected expressions, and abstract and equally disconnected rules. Nature absolutely condemns this process. Unhappy is he who works in opposition to Nature! But how are we to put the indications and the teachings of Nature into practice? How are we to introduce Nature's process into the schools?

Perhaps we have discovered this secret. The reader shall judge.

The general motive, the sole motive which gave rise to the relative expressions employed by the mother or the nurse in the lesson of the door, is the manner in which the child carries out his task, realises his intention, attains the 'end which he proposed to himself, or which others had proposed for him. Now the whole subjective language flows from a similar source. There is not a single relative expression which cannot be made to have for "motive" the manner in which an end has been attained, is being attained, or will be attained. Was it not this motive which inspired our mother to utter the following expressions?—" Bravo ! " " Very good ! " " That's it ! " " That's

SUBJECTIVE LANGUAGE.

the way!" "Capital!" "Splendid!" "How strong you are!" &c.

Well, the manner in which the scholar himself has carried out, is carrying out, or will carry out his task, that is to say, has recited, is reciting, or will recite any given exercise, has been adopted by us in our method as the "general motive" of all the subjective forms of expression imaginable. And amongst those which figure in our immense collection not a single one escapes this generalisation. How indeed should it escape? To recite a lesson, to repeat an exercise, is an aim or an end like all other ends. Now a relative expression, from the very fact that it is "relative," can only arise *àpropos* of a determinate fact or aim.

Besides this, phrases like the following:—

> I think that . . .
> Try to . . .
> Take care,
> I congratulate you,

are absolutely independent of the nature of the aim; they cannot be conceived as special to such or such an aim, but can be applied to all indifferently, and with the same effect. To open a door, to go and draw water, to study a lesson, these are aims perfectly distinct. Yet the expression, "I think that," can be adapted, when required, just as well to one as to the others.

> I think that → he has opened the door.
> I think that → she has gone to draw some water.
> I think that → you have studied this lesson.

A relative expression is, and can only be, dependent upon the conception of the person employing it.

This granted, it is evident that the aim of reciting well or reproducing correctly a linguistic lesson, is in itself alone capable of supporting the whole of the relative phrases of any given language, and in whatever number they may be presented. This conclusion is important, extremely important! However simple, however puerile and innocent the dialectic that has led us to this point may appear, this conclusion victoriously cuts the gordian knot of the practical teaching of the subjective language.

What, in point of fact, was it that we were in search of? Was it not the "species" which would allow us to subdivide the orders previously determined upon? Well, if we have not yet obtained these species, we have the source from whence they will spring forth in emulation, as it were, of each other.

The recitation or the reproduction, more or less correct, of a given exercise is a "general motive," that is to say, a motive essentially complex, one including within itself a crowd of other secondary and special motives. We will quote a few of these:—

The pupil knows,	or he does not know.
He pronounces well,	or he pronounces ill.
He constructs his phrase well,	or he constructs it ill.
He goes too fast,	or too slowly.
He experiences a difficulty,	or he does not.
He is sure of himself,	or he is not.
He has a good memory,	or a bad memory.
He studies with method,	or without method.
He takes pains,	or he does not take pains.
He imagines the facts well,	or he imagines them ill.
He speaks with thinking,	or without thinking.
He recites by heart,	or by reflection.
He analyses the facts well,	or analyses them ill.
He goes into all the details,	or he forgets them.
He applies the grammar,	or he does not apply it,
&c., &c.	

In a word, the whole arsenal of the pedagogic principles and maxims may be utilised. Each precept furnishes the teacher with a natural motive around which he can group at will an illimitable number of relative phrases, while varying, according to the needs of the pupils or of the class, the moods, tenses, persons—exercising to-day the positive form, to-morrow the negative form, another day the interrogative or the exclamatory form, &c.[1]

Let us point out in passing that the use of these expressions makes or may make of the language-lesson an admirable lesson in psychology and in pedagogic science itself, as well as in

---

[1] Thus employed, with the foregoing motives, the Relative phrases constitute what are here termed "Interlocutory Sentences" (Trans.).

grammar; I will also add, in morality—the religion of work being therein recommended, preached, and glorified by every word of the teacher.

The aggregate of these special motives constitutes the aggregate of the species which we were seeking for the purpose of subdividing our "orders," and so completing our classification. When, in a general treatise, the relative phrases are classified and the whole subjective language thoroughly organised, there will then only remain to make therefrom extracts or partial treatises appropriate to every age. One of these will reproduce, for example, the relative phrases familiar to the child of seven; another will contain the subjective language practised by a child of ten; a third will be destined for the youth; and a fourth will be composed for the use of the adult. (Separate treatises upon the subjective language and graduated collections of relative phrases will form part of the practical part of the system.)

These new categories will present, besides, many incontestable advantages. By their aid the work will be graduated, and the steepness of the mountain to be scaled will be proportionately lessened. The elementary extracts will naturally present those relative phrases which are the simplest, the most usual, and the most indispensable, those which form the types or the roots of all the others. Hence the most necessary phrases will be first learnt. This labour will afford a kind of "practical" classification of the species themselves.

As we have already stated, the dialectic that has enabled us to discover these species has at the same time afforded the means of allying the subjective language to the objective language, of "wedding" the relative phrase to the phrase of the series. The theoretic question is therefore solved. Let us now pass to the purely practical part.

We rely upon this both to enlighten and to confirm our theory itself, as well as dissipate any doubts that the reader may have still preserved upon the didactic virtue of the system.

It was by meditating long and deeply upon the dualism presented by language, as by all Nature; it was by following attentively and opposing one against the other the two currents therein manifested; it was by disentangling and severely separating the subjective element from the objective element;

it was by isolating the first in order to be able to contemplate it face to face; it was by following the idea to the extremest limit, as certain philosophers would say; in plain terms, it was by determining with greater and greater precision the general part played, the supreme and exclusive function of the relative phrase in the language, that we have been enabled to conceive the possibility of forming it into the pedagogic organ which we have just explained, and which we shall see presently in action.

SUBJECTIVE LANGUAGE.

Art of Teaching It.

XI.

AN ORDERED CONVERSATION CARRIED ON BY MEANS OF THE RELATIVE PHRASES.

To thoroughly grasp the linguistic operation brought about in our system of teaching by the relative phrase, it would be necessary for the reader to give at least a few moments' attendance at one of our classes. A lesson held in dialogue, as ours is held, is extremely difficult to represent upon paper. It loses its movement, and with this a great part of its clearness and of its interest. We will, nevertheless, attempt, as it is the only means within our reach of presenting an exercise to the public, to give a lesson by means of writing. The imagination of the reader must do its best to supply what is lacking, amongst other things the accent—so penetrating and so effective—of the living speech, and the wonderfully communicative play of the physiognomy.

As a basis of operations we propose to take the known theme—

To open the door.

In order to be understood by every one, we will go through the process first of all in English. Before we begin, let us make quite clear the exact moment at which the teacher appears before the pupils. The teacher is supposed to have already given the lesson, and the pupil to have elaborated it. Consequently we are at the point where recitation by the pupil commences.

Teacher.—Here is a door: to open it, what is it you do?
Pupil.—First of all, I walk towards the door.
Teacher.—Capital! And then what do you do?
Pupil.—I draw nearer to the door.
Teacher.—Capital! And then what do you do?
Pupil.—I get to the door.
Teacher.—Capital! And then what do you do?
Pupil.—I stop at the door.
Teacher.—Capital! And then what do you do?
Pupil.—I stretch out my arm.
Teacher.—Capital! And then what do you do?
Pupil.—I take hold of the handle.
Teacher.—Capital! And then what do you do next?
Pupil.—I turn the handle.
Teacher.—Capital! And what do you do after that?
Pupil.—I pull the door.
Teacher.—Capital! And then what happens?
Pupil.—The door moves.
Teacher.—Capital! And after that what happens?
Pupil.—The door turns on its hinges.
Teacher.—Capital! And then what do you do?
Pupil.—I leave go the handle.
Teacher.—Capital! The aim is attained and the lesson finished.

We will transcribe this dialogue under another form, where the two languages are distinct without ceasing to be united, without ceasing to be geared one into the other, and to complete each other mutually.

THE PUPIL.	THE TEACHER.
To open the door:	
I walk towards the door	Capital! And then? ...
I draw nearer to the door.	Capital! And then? ...
I get to the door.	Capital! And then? ...
I stop at the door.	Capital! And then? ...
I stretch out my arm.	Capital! And then? ...
I take hold of the handle.	Capital! And then? ...

AN ORDERED CONVERSATION.

THE PUPIL.	THE TEACHER.
I turn the handle.	Capital! And then? ...
I pull the door.	Capital! And then? ...
The door moves.	Capital! And then? ...
The door turns on its hinges.	Capital! And then? ...
I let go the handle.	Capital!

The expression "capital!" may be replaced by the expressions—

Bravo!	You couldn't do better.
That's right!	That is very well learnt.
Very good!	You have worked hard.
That's it!	I am pleased with you.
You have it!	I congratulate you.
Exactly!	&c., &c.,

and the thousand relative phrases by which satisfaction can be expressed.

The above is a specimen of what we call, and have the right to call, "an ordered conversation carried on by means of the relative phrases." And this conversation is carried on, or can be carried on, according to the language studied by the pupils, in Latin, in Greek, in Arabic, or in Chinese, just as well as in German, in Russian, in French, or in English.

Now, I would ask, Has this locution, "Capital!" by the effect of this exercise, entered into the pupil's memory? Is it assimilated by his understanding? If you doubt it, try the experiment. This expression is not only in his memory—it is part of his very nature, and is there for ever. And what has been done for one expression can be done and will be done for twenty thousand expressions.

Another fact is to be noted, from whence springs a new and important consequence. If a class of a hundred had heard and understood this lesson, who is there, even without having taken part personally in the conversation, who would not have in his ear or upon his tongue this expression—"capital!" —or its equivalent in the foreign language? Our method, therefore, answers admirably to the need so universally felt of a collective method of teaching. A lesson like the preceding, given before a thousand hearers, would be as profitable to the last as to the first, provided only that the teacher's voice would carry so far.

Finally, we have hitherto placed the relative phrase or interlocutory sentence in the mouth of the teacher: there is nothing to prevent it coming from the mouth of one or of several of the pupils themselves, who, turn and turn about, acting as leader of their class, would guide the conversation, while the teacher would pass to the adjacent classes or divisions. While one harvest is ripening, two others might be sown.

For three classes ONE teacher.

This is a refrain which we shall yet repeat more than once as finale to our chapters. In Nature, one child can and does teach another child to talk. Is it so terribly difficult, think you, for a pupil to direct a conversation like the preceding, in no matter what language? Under these conditions the pedagogic apprenticeship may commence early and has some chance of being successful.

We shall, of course, have the question of disorderliness again thrown in our teeth. We answer: Disorderliness is the daughter of inaction and of weariness. Now our lesson or ordered conversation permits neither the one nor the other. Varied in the subjects of the lessons, varied in the details of these lessons, alive and holding the attention like speech itself, it stimulates the curiosity continually, occupies the visualising faculty continually, and until the very end keeps the attentive force upon the strain. There are schools in which the ill-omened words, "strict and lax discipline," are practically unknown. Apparently these schools are organised upon different methods to others that we know of, as much for the scholars as for the teachers. We may take it, at any rate, for certain that our opinions with reference to schools will change on that day that the methods themselves change. In any case, a man to keep discipline will be less difficult to find and less costly than a professor equipped by science in the way that we desire.

"Capital!" is an absolute relative expression. Let us now take an enclitic phrase; for example, the phrase, as commonplace as it is frequent—

Will you kindly . . .

USE OF ENCLITIC PHRASES.

and let us rest this upon the simple motive of "to continue." The lesson will be presented as follows :—

PUPIL.	TEACHER.
I walk towards the door.	Will you kindly continue?
I draw near to the door.	Will you kindly continue?
I get to the door.	Will you kindly continue?
I stop at the door.	Will you kindly continue?
I stretch out my arm.	Will you kindly continue?
I take hold of the handle.	Will you kindly continue?
I turn the handle.	Will you kindly continue?
I pull the door.	Will you kindly continue?
The door moves.	Will you kindly continue?
The door turns on its hinges.	Will you kindly continue?
I let go the handle.	The exercise is finished.

Instead of the enclitic phrase, "Will you kindly," we can substitute—

Have the kindness to → continue.
Have the goodness to → continue.
Be so good as to → continue.
Please → continue.
Try to; endeavour to → continue.
Do all you can to → continue.
Do your best to → continue.
Will you please → continue?
I beg you to → continue.
I should like you to → continue.
You are requested to → continue.
I think → you can continue.
I hope → you will continue.

and the thousand expressions by which we can formulate an invitation, a counsel, an order, a recommendation, &c.

We have in the above a second example of an "ordered conversation carried on by means of relative phrases," a conversation which progresses not blindly and at haphazard, but where each step is counted and regularly marked off in the total journey to be accomplished—a conversation where each expression exercised passes definitely from the "debtor" to the "creditor" side. In other terms, having given a good classification of the relative phrases, the master and the pupil know to-day, will know to-morrow, will also know in two months, exactly what they have done and what remains for them to do. But this is a statement of account that can never be rendered by the teacher, however conscientious he may be, who follows the ordinary course of lessons.

In olden days, at the end of the first week I should have been greatly embarrassed if required to recount the number and the kind of expressions that I had been able to give to my pupils. I imagine that more than one of the teachers now practising would feel the same difficulty. It is, in fact, a zigzag course to which we are condemned by the process termed classical—a course in which we traverse the same road over and over again a hundred times—a course in which each advance is annulled by a retreat, and one consequently which never allows us to arrive at our destination. We are pleased to hope that a thorough classification and a judicious use of relative phrases will furnish the remedy for this vice in language teaching, and that the professor of languages will find therein the guiding thread of which he stands in so great a need.

Now that the reader understands—at least we hope he does—our manner of proceeding and the mode of teaching the subjective language, we will remove the relative phrase from the place we have given to it for the occasion at the right hand of the exercise, and we will write it once only, and as appendix, at the foot of this exercise. We shall thus economise space and labour in the composition, and permit the two languages to develop freely. We ought indeed to point out that neither the sentences which compose the exercises of our series nor the relative expressions which our collection contains are always as simple or as short as are the phrases which figure in the preceding example. Instead of one relative phrase we shall be able to write three or four at the foot of each exercise; and the teacher will deal with them, one after the other, exactly in the manner shown in the example above. Instead of asking a single pupil to repeat the phrase, he will ask three or four different pupils to do so, having at hand the material for many such dialogues.

Moreover, this arrangement of the text permits one last detail to be added which our first exercise lacked, to be faithfully represented upon paper. We have stated in a previous

A COMPLETE EXERCISE.

chapter that the pupil, like the teacher, should find and then enounce "first of all" the verb of each sentence. Now, in the text which we have presented as definitive for the exercises of the series, the verb is found repeated at the right-hand side of the sentence. Perhaps the reader would better follow our course, and would better understand the economy of our lesson if the column of verbs were placed at the left hand of the exercise instead of being placed to the right. Let us, in his favour, make this slight change. It is better here to subordinate practical convenience to clearness of exposition.

Here, then, at least is the form under which it seems to us that our lesson may be fully comprehended by every person of intelligence who cares to do so. The exercise presents its three parts, set out in three columns, and in the following order:—

1. The verb.
2. The complete sentence.
3. The relative phrase or interlocutory sentence.

The place of the last is indicated by the letters R.ph., and its text relegated to the foot of the exercise.

PUPIL.

I wish to open the door.
To do this :   MASTER.

walk	I walk towards the door.	R. ph.
draw near	I draw near to the door.	R. ph.
get to	I get to the door.	R. ph.
stop	I stop at the door.	R. ph.
stretch out	I stretch out my arm.	R. ph.
take hold	I take hold of the handle.	R. ph.
turn	I turn the handle.	R. ph.
pull	I pull the door.	R. ph.
moves	The door moves.	R. ph.
turns	The door turns on its hinges.	R. ph.
let go	I let go the handle.	R. ph.

*   *   *   *

MASTER.—Continue, go on—and :

1. Try to → pronounce well.
2. Do your best to → pronounce well.
3. Do your utmost to → pronounce well.
4. Keep trying to → pronounce well.

Our too short appendix presents only a few relative phrases, and we have chosen by preference perfectly simple enclitics. The motive upon which they rest is that of the pronunciation, and the hook (⌒) is a sign which we have adopted to represent the relation of these expressions with the fact to which they apply, which they are, so to speak, "hooked upon." However few, for want of space, these expressions may be, and therefore however little variation there may be in them, they certainly suffice, in the first place, to give a correct idea of our process, and, in the next place, to afford a glimpse of the use that linguistic science may make of this element of the language.

A language-lesson thus constructed in English is perhaps insufficient for a decisive, peremptory demonstration of the excellence of the new process. Presented in a foreign tongue, this same lesson will be more striking, and certainly more convincing. It is the night that makes us appreciate the day. At the risk, therefore, of overloading our text, we will repeat the above lesson in the eight following languages :—English, French, German, Italian, Spanish, Norwegian, Latin, and Greek. We would give it also in Russian and Arabic if this would serve any useful purpose.

The last two words of our programme (Latin and Greek) will let loose upon us a perfect tempest from the Classicists. "Your system," the pure Humanists will exclaim, "may be an excellent one for living languages, but do not touch the sacred ark of the dead languages: you can do nothing but profane these grand monuments." In a future chapter, entitled "Greek and Latin," we shall suitably reply to this strange dogma. Provisionally, and to justify to some extent our audacity, let us remark that the linguistic process of the mother of a family at Rome or at Athens—so at least it seems to us—must have been exactly the same as that practised by the mother of a family at this present day in London, in Paris, or in St. Petersburg. And let us also emphasise, to dissipate the pious alarm of our opponents, the statement that no phrase or expression employed by us will ever be risked—that is, fabricated by the sole aid of the dictionary.

Our veneration and love for the ancient languages is so profound and sincere, that we have imposed upon ourselves, in their honour, a task which perhaps would frighten more than one of the purists scandalised by our temerity—to wit, we have dissected, sentence by sentence, the works of the principal Greek and Latin authors. This done, in the first place, the expressions belonging to the objective language have been distributed in the vast pigeon-holes of our series and of our exercises; and in the next place, the relative phrases have been arranged in the categories to which they are called by the classification of which we have already established the grand outlines.

By the aid of this double work, a dead language may be treated exactly in the same way as a living language. But there is something further; we are enabled to present to whoever desires it the language of whichever writer he prefers. In our manuscripts, each sentence bears the name of its author, with the number of the chapter and the number of the line. It was, in fact, of first importance to obviate this grave objection:—"Your Latin and your Greek are made-up Latin and made-up Greek."

We think we may make the following declaration: That the day upon which the student has assimilated our series and our relative phrases, Greek and Latin, he will have assimilated Virgil, Cicero, Sallust, Quintillian, &c., Homer, Herodotus, Xenophon, Plato, &c., and he will be able to read and understand these authors exactly as he understands the masterpieces of his native tongue.

So much said, we will commence by the Latin lesson.

Latin. **OSTIUM APERIO.**

pergo	Ad ostium pergo.
appropinquo	ad ostium appropinquo.
advenio	ad ostium advenio.
subsisto	ad ostium subsisto.
extendo	brachium extendo.
apprehendo	ansam apprehendo.
torqueo	ansam torqueo.
recludo	ostium recludo.
adduco	ostium adduco.
sequitur	sequitur ostium.
vertitur	cardinibus vertitur ostium.
pando	ostium pando.
dimitto	ostii ansam dimitto.

1. Optime dictum!
  Amabo ut → persequaris.
  Pergratum mihi feceris si → persequi volueris.
  Placet-ne tibi → progredi?

2. Perge, te precor, et . . .
  Conare ut → bene dicas.
  Da operam ut → bene dicas.
  Cave ne → perperam pronunties.
  Te hortor ad → bene dicendum.

3. Ne parcas operæ:
  Tua refert ut → in dies proficias.
  Non te pœnitebit → laborem insumpsisse.

4. Macte animo!
  Gaudeo quod → in dies proficis.
  Tibi sane continget → tuum assequi propositum.
  Non dubito quin → brevi latine locuturus sis.

Greek. ἈΝΟΙΓΩ ΤΗΝ ΘΥΡΑΝ.

Ἔρχομαι   ἔρχομαι πρὸς τὴν θύραν.
πλησιάζω   πλησιάζω τῇ θύρᾳ.
παρα-γίνομαι   παραγίνομαι τῇ θύρᾳ.
ἐφ-ίσταμαι   ἐφίσταμαι ἐγγὺς τῆς θύρας.
ἐκ-τείνω   ἐκτείνω τὴν χεῖρα.
ἐφ-άπτομαι   ἐφάπτομαι τῆς κορώνης.
στρέφω   στρέφω τὴν κορώνην.
ἀν-οίγω   ἀνοίγω τὴν θύραν.
ἐπ-ερύω   ἐπερύω τὴν θύραν.
εἴκει   ἡ θύρα εἴκει.
στρέφεται   ἡ θύρα στρέφεται ἐπὶ τοῖς στροφεῦσι.
ἀφ-ίημι   ἀφίημι τὴν κορώνην.

1. Κάλλιστα εἶπες!
  παρακαλῶ σε → καλῶς λέγειν.
  παρακαλῶ σε → διατελεῖν λέγοντα.
  διάτεινε → ὀρθῶς λέγειν.
  ἆρά γε φίλον σοι → διατελεῖν τὸν λόγον;

2. Διατείνου λέγων, και . . .
  ἀπότεινε τὸν λόγον . . . (Plato)
  ἀπότεινε τὴν ὁδόν . . . (Lucien)
  πειρῶ → ὀρθῶς λέγειν.
  σπούδασον ὅπως → ἀκριβῶς λέγῃς.
  ἐπιμελοῦ ὅπως → κάλον λέγῃς.

3. Κάμνε ὡς ὅτι μάλιστα . . .
  σοὶ γὰρ συμφέρει → προκόπτειν.
  οὐ σοὶ μεταμελήσει → πεπονῆσθαι.

4. Θάρρει! μὴ ἀποκάμνε . . .
  διαπράξῃ ὥστε → Ἑλληνιστὶ λαλεῖν.
  ἐλπίζω → σε ταχὺ σκοποῦ τεύξεσθαι.
  φήμ' ἐγώ → σε ταχὺ Ἑλλάδα γλῶσσαν ἥσειν.
  σαφῶς οἶδα ὅτι → σὺ ταχὺ ἑλληνίζειν ἐπιστήσῃ.

Italian.   **10) APRO LA PORTA.**

vado	Vado alla porta.
mi avvicino	mi avvicino alla porta.
arrivo	arrivo alla porta.
mi fermo	mi fermo alla porta.
stendo	stendo il braccio
prendo	prendo la maniglia della porta.
giro	giro la maniglia della porta.
tiro	tiro la porta.
cede	la porta cede.
gira	la porta gira sui suoi cardini.
lascio	lascio la maniglia della porta.

1. Bene! Benissimo!
   Abbiate la bontà di → continuare.
   Abbiate la compiacenza di → continuare.
   Volete voi avere la bontà di → continuare?
   Dimostrate che → sapete il seguito.
   Fate vedere che → sapete la continuazione.

2. Continuate, io vi prego, e . . .
   Cercate di → pronunziare bene.
   Fate tutto il possibile per → pronunciare bene.

3. Studiate con zelo:
   Bisogna che → voi facciate dei progressi.
   Non vi pentirete di → aver lavorato.

4. Fatevi coraggio!
   Arriverete ben presto a → sapere la lingua.
   Spero che → voi arriverete al vostro intento.
   Vi prometto che → in sei mesi voi saprete la lingua.
   Siate sicuro che → in sei . . .

FIRST LESSON IN EIGHT LANGUAGES.

French. **J'OUVRE LA PORTE.**

marche	Je marche vers la porte.
m'approche	je m'approche de la porte.
arrive	j'arrive à la porte.
m'arrête	je m'arrête à la porte.
allonge	j'allonge le bras.
prends	je prends la poignée.
tourne	je tourne la poignée.
tire	je tire la porte.
cède	la porte cède.
tourne	la porte tourne sur ses gonds.
lâche	je lâche la poignée.

1. Très bien !
   Ayez la bonté de → continuer.
   Faites-moi le plaisir de → continuer.
   Ayez la complaisance de → continuer.
   Je vous prie de → continuer.
   Montrez que → vous savez le reste.

2. Continuez, s'il vous plaît, et . . .
   Tâchez de → bien prononcer.
   Faites tous vos efforts pour → bien prononcer.
   Faites votre possible pour → bien prononcer.

3. Appliquez vous :
   Il importe que → vous fassiez des progrès.
   Vous ne regretterez pas → d'avoir bien travaillé.

4. Courage !
   Vous parviendrez → à apprendre la langue en six mois.
   J'espère que → vous atteindrez bientôt le but.
   Soyez certain que → dans six mois vous saurez parler Français.

SUBJECTIVE LANGUAGE.

Spanish. **YO) ABRO LA PUERTA.**

    voy   Voy hácia la puerta.
    me aproximo   me aproximo de la puerta.
    llego   llego á la puerta.
    me paro   me paro cerca de la puerta.
    alargo   alargo el brazo.
    tomo   tomo la empuñadura.
    volteo   volteo la empuñadura.
    halo   halo la puerta.
    cede   la puerta cede.
    gira   la puerta gira sobre suz goznes.
    suelto   suelto la empuñadura.

1. ¡ Muy bien !
   Tenga la bondad de → continuar.
   Hágame el favor de → continuar.
   ¿ Quiere Vd. tener la bondad de → continuar ?

2. Continúe, si me hace el favor, y . . .
   Trate de → pronunciar bien.
   Haga todo lo posible para → pronunciar bien.

3. Apliquese :
   Es conveniente que → Vd. haga progresos.
   Vd. no se arrepentirá de → haber trabajado.

4. ¡ Animo !
   Vd. llegará á → saber pronto el idioma.
   Espero que → Vd. sabrá la lengua en seis meses.
   Os prometo que → Vd. sabrá la lengua en seis meses.
   Esté seguro que → Vd. sabrá la lengua en seis meses.

German.   **ICH ÖFFNE DIE THÜR.**

schreite zu	Ich schreite auf die Thür zu.
nähere mich	Ich nähere mich der Thür.
komme an	Ich komme bei der Thür an.
bleibe stehen	Ich bleibe bei der Thür stehen.
strecke aus	Ich strecke den Arm aus.
fasse an	Ich fasse den Griff an.
drehe um	Ich drehe den Griff um.
mache auf	Ich mache die Thür auf.
ziehe an	Ich ziehe die Thür heran.
gibt nach	Die Thür gibt nach.
dreht sich	Die Thür dreht sich auf den Angeln.
lasse los	Ich lasse den Griff los.

1. Ganz richtig!
 Seien Sie so gut — und fahren Sie fort.
 Thun Sie mir den Gefallen — fortzufahren.
 Wollen Sie so gut sein und — fortfahren?

2. Ich bitte, fahren Sie fort, und . . .
 suchen Sie — richtig auszusprechen.
 machen Sie, daß — Sie richtig aussprechen.
 bemühen Sie sich — richtig auszusprechen.
 thun Sie Ihr Möglichstes, um — keinen Fehler zu machen.

3. Schaffe fleißig:
 es liegt dir viel daran — Fortschritte zu machen.
 Du wirst es nicht bereuen — fleißig studiert zu haben.

4. Fassen Sie Muth:
 gewiß gelingt es Ihnen — die Sprache in sechs Monaten zu erlernen.
 ich hoffe, daß — Sie zu Ihrem Zwecke gelangen werden.

SUBJECTIVE LANGUAGE.

English.   **I OPEN THE DOOR.**

walk	I walk towards the door.
draw near	I draw near to the door.
get to	I get to the door.
stop	I stop at the door.
stretch out	I stretch out my arm.
take hold	I take hold of the handle.
turn	I turn the handle.
pull	I pull the door.
moves	The door moves.
turns	The door turns on its hinges
let go	I let go the door handle.

1. Quite right! Very good!
   Have the kindness to → continue.
   Will you have the kindness to → continue?
   Be so good as to → continue.
   I beg you to → continue.
   Let us see that → you know the rest.

2. Go on, please, and . . .
   Try to → pronounce well.
   Endeavour to → pronounce well.
   Do your utmost → to pronounce well.

3. Take pains; work hard:
   It is important that → you should make progress.
   You will not regret → having worked hard.

4. Be of good cheer! Take courage!
   You will very soon be able to → speak English.
   I hope → we shall soon see a good result.
   You will soon succeed → in learning English.
   Rest assured that → in six months you will speak English well.

FIRST LESSON IN EIGHT LANGUAGES.

Norwegian. **JEG AABNER DŒREN.**[1]

gaar	Jeg gaar henimod Dœren.
nærmer mig	Jeg nærmer mig Dœren.
kommer	Jeg kommer til Dœren.
standser	Jeg standser ved Dœren.
udstrækker	Jeg udstrækker Armen.
tager	Jeg tager Dœrgrebet.
dreier	Jeg dreier Dœrgrebet om.
trækker	Jeg trækker Dœren til mig.
giver efter	Dœren giver efter.
dreier sig	Dœren dreier sig paa sine Hængsler.
slipper	Jeg slipper Dœrgrebet.

1. Meget godt!
   Vær saa god → at fortsætte.
   Hav den Godhed → at fortsætte.
   Vil De have den Godhed → at fortsætte.
   Vis at → De kjender Resten.

2. Vær saa god at blive ved, og . . .
   Bestræb Dem → for at udtale godt.
   Gjør Deres Bedste → for at udtale godt.

3. Vær flittig;
   Det er nødvendigt at → De gjør Fremskridt.
   Det vil ikke angre at → De har arbeidet godt.

4. Tag Mod!
   Det vil lykkes Dem → at lære Sproget i sex Maaneder.
   Jeg haaber at → De vil naa Maalet.
   Jeg lover Dem at → De vil lære Sproget paa sex Maaneder.
   Vær forvisset om at → De vil lære Sproget paa sex Maaneder.

---

[1] The Norwegian barred o is replaced by œ.

XII.

CRITICAL OBSERVATIONS UPON THE PRACTICE OF THE RELATIVE PHRASES.

1. *Remark upon our appendices—Double function of the Relative Phrase—Its practical value.*

We do not wish our system of the subjective language to be judged alone upon the semblance of organisation presented by the above appendices. In the first place, our limited space does not allow any really methodical and didactic arrangement of the matter. The relative phrase appears therein, furthermore, in an unfavourable light, and under a strange and almost bizzare form. We shall appeal, therefore, from these mutilated groups to our special treatises.

In the next place, and more especially, these expressions have been taken, so to speak, at hazard, and solely with the view of awakening certain reminiscences of college life. Lhomond, to whom we several times refer, and for a reason, seems to have had some slight idea of this subjective language. The third part of his Grammar, in fact,—that to which he gives the title "Latin method,"—is nothing else than a small treatise upon relative phrases. It contains some sixty of these divided into a dozen groups. It is from these groups, copied and recopied by the modern grammarians, that we have borrowed the expressions which figure in our appendices. Our intention, as every one will at once divine, was to interest the reader by showing him with what facility our process triumphs, in a few moments, over the difficulties which in other days so long hindered us, and which cost us so many efforts and so many written pages.

Our appendices furnish us with the occasion for a final and important remark upon the inner constitution of the relative phrase, and in particular the enclitic phrase. If examined, the phrase, "Continue, and try to pronounce well," is found to be composed of three distinct parts:—

1. "Continue,"—the motive which is the occasion of the relative phrase, and which serves as transition from the words of the pupil to those of the teacher.
2. "Try to,"—pure enclitic expression.
3. "Pronounce well,"—another motive acting as object or substratum to the enclitic.

MULTIPLIED FUNCTION OF RELATIVE PHRASE.

The same motive may thus serve two ends: it may be either the occasion of a relative phrase, or it may be the object, the substratum of one:—

1. Will you kindly → continue.
2. Continue, please—and try to → pronounce well.

In the phrase (1.) the motive "continue" is the object of the enclitic expression "will you kindly." In the phrase (2.) "continue" is the occasion of the relative phrase "try to pronounce well;" and "pronounce well" is the object of the enclitic "try to."

Owing to this double function—this double action of the motive of the relative phrase—there is not a single linguistic position that we are not able to turn round and deal with in our own way,—not an expression nor a proverbial or other form of words which we are not able to appropriate in the exact shape in which the wit or popular usage of the country may have moulded it—form, flavour, subtlety, grace, and force all resting intact.

2. *Correspondence of the system with the maternal process—The triumph of art—Correction of exercises—The teacher's power doubled—The question of accent—Free students.*

The objective language comes from the mouth of the pupil, and the subjective language from the mouth of the teacher. It is the dialogue of the mother and the child. The two languages are, therefore, perfectly distinct; they develop simultaneously side by side, marching abreast without confusion, exactly as in the lesson from Nature. The relative phrase arises quite naturally, without effort, with reference simply to the subject of the series or the manner in which it is presented. The two languages advance, one by the other, one in the other, one with the other. This is the faithful reproduction of the maternal process.

The relative phrase is not an empty form, a vain and foolish string of words; it is the expression of a real idea, of an actual impression or sentiment, of a real conception bearing upon some concrete fact, like the mother's observation or the child's reply.

Like the child, we can play with the same relative phrase

the whole length of the same exercise without offending reason, until it has penetrated our intellect, until it forms part of our thought, and, as we have said, becomes a veritable organ of thought. The study of the subjective expressions, that is to say, of the most abstract, and certainly the most arduous portion of the language, becomes, in our school, according to our prediction, actual play—a mere game. The grammar itself, that bugbear of childhood, becomes transformed into a quasi-attractive science, inasmuch as it reveals and explains to the scholar, day by day, the marvellous action of the human intellect, and of the genius of the people upon the forms of language. The relative phrase, by slipping into the enforced interval between two consecutive sentences of a given exercise, does not require a special period of time consecrated to its study. You develop the series, and obtain the subjective language into the bargain.

Far from standing in the way of the objective language, the relative phrase renders it firmer by adding to the movement of the facts that of the life of the spirit. Vocabularies and treatises upon pronunciation play no part in our instruction. Here is a still greater correspondence between our system and the maternal process. No intermediary comes between the words and the perception of the thought. These two identify themselves, and arrive simultaneously at the ear, and are thence transmitted to the understanding before being beheld by the eye or being translated by the hand,—in other words, before being subjected to the artificial processess of reading and of writing.

Upon all these points our process is in exact correspondence with that of Nature. But there is an additional feature which makes of our system an art, and consequently endows it with an incontestable superiority. Our series have a precision which is necessarily lacking to the natural series, and our exercises offer a richness of development which cannot be expected of those of the child's nurse. The order of succession and the co-ordination of the series are themselves reasoned out, while the child progresses more or less by chance, and often lingers long of necessity upon the same order of facts.

With regard to the subjective language, our school delivers it ready organised to the pupil. In Nature it is a slow-growing fruit, which regulates its maturity by that of the child. In six months our scholar can learn as much, and more, of the subjective language than could be learnt in six years outside the school.

The child has, however, an advantage which it is right to mention. Its ear is more tender, more sensitive, more impressionable. The sounds are engraved upon it with greater force and greater rapidity. But the more tempered will of the adult, a more continuous attention, and a more developed perseverance, these compensate, and more than compensate, for the privilege of early childhood. While conforming, therefore, to the prescriptions of Nature, we can do better, and teach more rapidly, than Nature herself. And is not the "conquest of Nature" the true field of art?

There is one duty which at present wastes the strength and the time of teachers of language; we mean the correction of exercises. Has it been fully realised that the ordinary proceeding condemns the conscientious professor to decipher a manuscript of more than 3000 pages a month, of more than 30,000 pages a year? Our method does away entirely with this long and painful labour, by rendering it absolutely useless. Upon what, I would ask, could a correction be made in our system? Where is the work which is not corrected ten times over before the end of the lesson? And where is the correction that a bright scholar could not make for himself? Is his oral lesson, think you, not perfect? And if he is not sure of the written reproduction, he has before him a faithful mirror, which will point out his mistakes to him more certainly than the most attentive professor,—his printed exercise.

A correction can be of no profit except to him who seeks to find out his faults. In our opinion, man should early begin to judge himself. Now this exercise, both moral and pedagogic, is within the reach of whosoever possesses, as in our system, a settled rule and a definite model. To deliver the teacher from the overwhelming drudgery of the correction of exercises is to increase his power tenfold; to increase tenfold the power of the teacher is tenfold to enlarge the field of study and the knowledge of the pupil.

When a native of any country takes upon himself to give a course of lessons in a foreign language, it is not long before he begins to hear behind his back discouraging remarks against his teaching. Were he the first philologist of his time, were be able to speak the language he teaches with greater elegance than any person, no matter who, in the country where this language is spoken, it would still be said his accent was not pure, and a foreign teacher will always be preferred.

Is it necessary thus always to recruit the ranks of our schoolmasters from foreign nations? Of this grave problem the system generally in use well knows it has no solution. Our system appears more happy in this respect. By its means the teaching of languages may become frankly, exclusively national, while yet challenging the severest criticism, and this privilege it owes to the organisation of the lessons upon the basis of the relative phrase.

In fact, arranged and conducted as we have set forth, the lesson is not only accessible to the willing student, but he finds himself in the position of being able to teach it just so soon as he has elaborated it himself. If desired, we can open our classes to adult foreigners, to which "*hospites,*" as we may term them, we should confide in our " ordered conversations " the exercise and the bandying about of the relative phrase.

In this manner a teacher of the pupil's own nationality can lead his class without fear and without reproach, having in his class and ready to his hand the foreign accent, and that a selected one. As to the "*hospites,*" we are quite sure hundreds of applications would be received from foreigners ready enough to learn our own language under such conditions.

3. *A declaration by a Minister of Education—The keystone of the edifice.*

One of the French Ministers[1] said some time back, speaking of the teaching of languages, that what was necessary was to seek some means, not of making the whole class of children sit still on the school-benches, but, on the other hand, of putting them to work, and of utilising the unconquerable need of movement of childhood upon the side of instruction; that the means should be found not of imposing silence upon a class, but rather of requiring them all to speak.[2] Possibly

---

[1] M. Jules Simon (Trans.).
[2] This principle has long been acknowledged and its practice attempted in the Kindergarten schools with much success in stimulating the intelligence and utilising the energies of the pupils. The present system advances a serious argument while indicating the means for the application of such a system to more advanced scholars (Trans.).

we have partly solved this problem. If we have had this good fortune, we owe it entirely to the discovery of the relative phrase.

The system of the relative phrases forms the keystone of our linguistic edifice. Without this, our method would remain barren of what may be termed "the moral element" of language. All language moves between two poles and upon two distinct currents. The two poles are external nature and the human soul—the non-Ego and the Ego. The two currents are the indefinite succession of tangible phenomena, and the permanent play of the faculties of the mind.

A language is the complex expression of these two kinds of facts. Our series correspond with one of these, and our relative phrases or interlocutory sentences to the other. The swallow builds its nest by mixing its saliva with clay; man builds up his language by allying the expression of the development of his mind to that of the movement of matter. One is the dough, the other the yeast.

FIGURATIVE LANGUAGE.

XIII.

OBJECT OF THIS STUDY—TWO PROBLEMS TO BE SOLVED.

Above the objective language, alongside and often at the heart of the subjective language, appears a third, the "figurative language." As its name indicates, it is not at all an original language; it is the language proper—the objective language—put to the service of the abstract ideas or conceptions of mankind, and lending thereto, if not a body, at least an appearance, a figure.

"I fall into the river,"—is objective language.
"I fall into error,"—is figurative language.
The second is visibly grafted upon the first.

Unfortunately, pedagogic science hardly separates at all these two languages, and teaches them mingled together pell-mell, just as the book happens to be printed, without rule, without method. Abstraction is a natural product of the human mind; therefore the metaphor, which is its form or its expression, deserves, as such, to be taken into consideration by linguistic science, and made the object of a somewhat serious study. Not only should this science instruct the scholar upon the character, properties, and usage of this important part of language, but it should also deliver humanity from many errors and disastrous myths, which have often no other root and no other nourishment than a vain symbolism.

The work we are here asking for has nothing in common with the treatises which used to be imposed upon us under the name of "figures of rhetoric." It is not, so to speak, the customary name by which a garment is known which we are in need of, but the secret of its shape and an harmonious adaptation to the conception it is called upon to clothe. The fanciful names of the rhetoricians no more represent the science of figurative language than the common nomenclature of the stars and constellations represent the science of astronomy.

The treatise which we have in mind should reveal to us the intimate relationships that the symbol bears to the abstract idea or conception which it is desired to translate. Without this previous study, the question of a rational system of teaching the figurative language cannot even be distinctly put. One is evidently the corollary of the other. Before storing the harvest in the granary, we must first gather the wheat into sheaves.

Linguistic science finds itself once more face to face with the two problems it has already had to solve with reference to the objective and the subjective language, namely—
 1. To set in order the material of the figurative language.
 2. To discover a rational process for teaching it.

These two chapters are neither so long nor so complicated as the previous chapters. In the first, indeed, we ought to set ourselves, not to distribute the entirety of the figurative language into its various categories, but simply to discover a principle which might preside over the arrangement in order of this last portion of the language; and the second problem will be solved as soon as we have discovered a logical means of attaching the metaphorical lessons to our series lessons.

FIGURATIVE LANGUAGE.

An Attempt at Organisation.

XIV.

METAPHORICAL THEMES.

*1. Origin of the metaphor—Its constituent elements—
Its definition.*

To set the material of the figurative language in order, we need, as we have said, a principle. This principle must be drawn from the very source of the metaphor itself—must be deduced from the function proper to the metaphor. It will most certainly be brought forth from a rigorous definition of this form of language. Let us try to trace back the metaphor to its origin.

The human mind, as we have seen in the episode of the mill, cannot dwell long upon a pure perception. In the mind, every perception tends to become metamorphosed into a conception. This is because, in order to assimilate an item of knowledge, it is necessary to transform it, exactly as the stomach transforms the food destined to nourish the body.

This work, this intellectual operation, is known under the name of generalisation. To generalise, is to pass from a perception to a conception; it is to raise the perception of the individual thing to the conception of the species or the kind; it is to pass from the actual and ephemeral fact to the conception of a constant and eternal fact; it is to cross the space which separates the contingent from the necessary, the variable from the absolute. The mind is the sense of the immutable, of the eternal, the crucible in which is elaborated and secreted these supreme forms of thought, the energy which transfigures every perception and makes thereof a "supernatural" product.

The perception of two or three imperfections of character enables us to sketch out, if not to constitute, the idea or the general conception of "vice," as the perception of several good qualities suffices for us to sketch out the idea or the general conception of "virtue."

There is the possibility, however, of establishing two categories of abstract ideas. The general conception of a "mill," for instance, is essentially distinguished from the general idea of "virtue." If we reflect, it is seen that their difference is derived from the difference of their origin. In fact, the first is born of the perception of an objective fact, while the second arises from the perception of a subjective fact. Although they are both, and from the same reason, direct products of abstraction, it is the last which bears exclusively the name "abstract idea."

The general idea of a mill being nothing more than the primitive perception in miniature, an extract, a kind of quintessence of this perception, is expressed naturally by the terms which translate the perception itself. From this it is seen that the figurative language is not made for this class of conception. The abstract idea, properly so called, is found under other conditions. A direct product of the perception of subjective fact, it has absolutely nothing of reality except as regarded in the mind; it is, indeed, for the mind that the word "immaterial" has been coined. The abstract idea is essentially immaterial—one might almost say, chimerical.

The terms which translate perception—that is, the real—are therefore found to be as improper as they are impotent to render these kinds of ideas.

Nevertheless the abstract idea is a product which deserves, as much as the perception, to figure in the commerce of minds. But a conception is only capable of transmission on the condition of being embodied in a tangible form. Where, then, are we to find a tangible form elsewhere than in the objective language? The mind will, therefore, be reduced to choose in the external world the phenomena which appear to it to have the greatest analogy with its abstract conceptions. Then, transporting the expressions proper to these phenomena into the superior region of abstraction, it will adapt them to its general conceptions.

If an abyss, for instance, appears to us to have certain resemblances to our general conception of error, we shall adapt to this conception the terms used for the abyss, and if "to fall into an abyss" is said, we shall also say, metaphorically, "to fall into error." Another time we may perceive a resemblance between error and a weed. We shall transfer in the same way to error the terms proper to the weed; and because we say "to uproot a weed," we shall consider ourselves authorised to say "to uproot an error." To thus transfer to some conception a term expressly made for a perception is to talk by metaphor. Note, in passing, that the word metaphor ($\mu\epsilon\tau\acute{a}$-$\phi\acute{\iota}\rho\omega$) is found to be the precise definition of the intellectual operation which it expresses.

But, it will be said, how can the immaterial be represented by the material, the subjective by the objective? And again: wherever there is metaphor there is necessarily comparison. How is it possible to compare facts which are not of the same kind? These two objections appear well founded, and as such deserve a reply.

We would remark, in the first place, that the metaphor is a linguistic form which can never be adequate to its object. It reveals it, manifests it, but cannot express it. It is a variable which approaches more or less its limit, but never attains it.

"To fall into an abyss" is the direct, immediate, and adequate expression of an objective fact.

"To fall into error" is the indirect, mediate, and intentionally symbolic expression of a subjective fact.

We would, in the second place, observe that the abstract idea of "error" is a generalised conception of the mind, and that the word "abyss" equally represents a generalised conception. Therefore, upon this ground, our two facts are of the same nature. From this it results that they are comparable together, so that, in a given case, the one may logically serve as symbol for the other.

By the light of this theory upon abstract ideas it is easy to determine the essential elements of every metaphorical expression. Let us analyse, for instance, the locution, "to uproot an error."

We find therein—

1. An abstract idea represented by the word "error."
2. A symbol unexpressed (that of a "weed"), but clearly indicated by the verb "to uproot."
3. A secret comparison between the abstract idea and the symbol.
4. The tacit identification of the idea with the symbol.

Such a simple conclusion at the end of an almost laborious investigation may perhaps recall to the reader the *mons parturiens* of the fable. But this disproportion between the end and the means is inherent in the solution of every psychological problem. In the intellectual field the slightest fact cannot be thoroughly established without relatively considerable developments.

2. *Ordinary symbolism—Construction of the metaphorical themes.*

The principle which we need to set in order the material of the figurative language should, and in fact does, spring from the preceding study or analysis. This principle may be formulated thus:—"The abstract ideas of mankind are not embodied in forms proper to themselves; they are manifested by the means of symbols taken from the external world, and therefore borrow their expression from the objective language."

From this principle it is easy to deduce the process to be followed for distributing in natural groups the general material of the figurative language. First, the list of the abstract ideas of mankind will be drawn up. The most elementary of dictionaries will contain their names; they will be collected from these. This done, they will be grouped into classes and families. Under the heading of "Virtue," for example, all the good qualities will be united; under the heading "Vice," the names of all the bad qualities will be placed, and so for the rest. We must warn the reader that the number of general abstract ideas is relatively quite small. It will certainly be impossible to discover more than fifty species.

When the groups have been constituted, the research will be commenced upon the symbols which relate thereto—those which the custom or the genius of the nation has consecrated. The same species may have several symbols. It is thus that the symbol of the abyss and of the harmful plant equally fit the abstract conception of error, as we can say both "to fall into" error, and "to uproot" error.

But what will yield us the symbolism of a people? How and where are we to find the various symbols destined for one and the same class of abstract ideas. The solution of this problem is perfectly simple.

Suppose we have given the general abstract idea of "vice." I open at this word the best dictionary at command, the last published, that, consequently, which includes all the others. If this dictionary is a good one, it will present a special paragraph, in which are gathered together, firstly, all the ordinary metaphors consecrated by usage to the abstract idea of vice, and secondly, those metaphors special to the great writers—new and original metaphors, as a rule, not very numerous. We shall find, for example, amongst them the following, which are set down at hazard:—

To leave vice.
To fall into vice.
To turn away from vice.
To become abandoned to vice.
To yield one's self to vice.
To withdraw from vice.
To plunge into vice.
To wallow in vice.
To uproot vice.
To renounce vice.
To shake off vice.

To repress vice.
To hate vice.
To fly from vice.
To cast one's self into vice.
To be ruled by vice.
To remain in vice.
To stagnate in vice.
To come out of vice.
To extirpate vice.
To propagate vice.
&c., &c.

Amongst these expressions we have chosen two which seem to be more particularly suitable for casting light upon the process in question; these are the expressions already mentioned :—

To fall into vice.
To uproot vice.

The two verbs, "to fall into" and "to uproot," clearly indicate that the popular imagination sees wickedness sometimes under the form of a miry abyss, sometimes under the form of a poisonous weed.

From the first symbol evidently come the expressions—

To fall into vice. To remain in vice.
To plunge into vice. To stagnate in vice.
To wallow in vice. &c., &c.

and those also that translate a movement away from "vice" :—

To tear one's self from vice. To escape from vice.
To turn away from vice. To fly from vice.
To withdraw from vice. &c., &c.

Considered in their totality, these locutions may provide the material for an exercise, or a fragment of an exercise, which we term "metaphorical theme." Moreover, the various parts of this double picture, resting upon a perfectly determinate objective fact, are capable of being set in order, and organised upon the model of the exercises in our series.

From the second symbol (weed) are derived the expressions—

To uproot vice. Vice germinates.
To extirpate vice. Vice takes root.
To propagate vice. &c., &c.

By setting these latter expressions in order around the symbol from which they arise, we shall obtain a second metaphorical theme analogous to the first.

In this way may be determined, one after the other, the various symbols under which the popular imagination represents the abstract idea of vice or wickedness. In the same way, the symbols of all the other abstract ideas of which the human mind is capable will be determined. The same symbol will serve for all the ideas of one group, and each symbol will furnish the occasion and the material of a metaphorical theme.

We have attempted to do this with the greatest works in those languages with which we are acquainted; and here again let us render unto Cæsar the things that are Cæsar's. On two occasions the dictionary has rendered us the greatest service: the first time for gathering together and forming into a system the subjective language—the relative phrases; and a second time, for an attempt upon the metaphorical language.

There exists a second means, an indirect means, of reconstituting the symbolism proper to the genius of each language, or rather of each nation. This process—certainly more instructive and more attractive than the cold-blooded study of national dictionaries, but less expeditious—would consist in gleaning, one by one, the metaphors contained in the literary masterpieces of each tongue.

By the aid of this metaphorical exegesis, the symbolism and the figurative language of each work or of each writer might be gathered together and set in order. In a future chapter (Method of Reading, Translating, and Assimilating Classical Works) we shall indicate the practical means of carrying out this important part of our labour.

FIGURATIVE LANGUAGE.

THE ART OF TEACHING METAPHORS.

XV.

TWO KINDS OF PROCESSES.

1. *Intrinsic rank of the figurative language—How assimilated in ordinary life—The part remaining to be done by Art.*

The figurative language represents the last linguistic conquest of man. Abandoned to his own resources, the child achieves it but slowly. Many persons only practise it accidentally, we might almost say that some never possess it.

FIGURATIVE LANGUAGE.

This fact is the condemnation of a legion of books written for the use of children, and which contain more metaphors than the most misty treatise upon metaphysics.

The figurative language cannot be taught—and therefore no attempt must be made to teach it—until after the language, proper or objective, has been learned. To follow a different course, as at present practised in most schools where the metaphysics of the sacred books comes before all the rest, is to begin the edifice by the ridge of the roof, to try to force the fruit before the bud. Worse than this, it is to accustom the child to take the effect for the cause, the shadow for the reality, the false for the true. In short, it is to teach him the art of deceiving himself—we might even say, the art of stupefying himself. The question of the order to be followed in the teaching of the three parts of language is therefore not one of pedagogic science alone—it is one of morality.

The figurative language should be engrafted, as we have said, upon the objective language. Now, before thinking of inserting a graft, we must possess a subject capable of supporting it. For instance, the child who has never seen a plant either uprooted or propagated will certainly not be able to understand the metaphorical expressions—

To uproot vice.
To propagate an error.

This is perfectly evident. Therefore, before teaching a metaphorical theme, we shall wait until the pupil thoroughly knows that series in which the symbolic fact serving as basis to this theme has been developed. Nothing is so vague as a metaphor; nothing is so light, vaporous, subtle, unstable, mobile, as this flower of language. We know only one means of fixing it in the memory: this is to link, knowingly and resolutely, the abstract idea to its symbol.

Between the objective and the figurative language is a perfectly natural transition stage—the subjective language. It will be observed, indeed, that a very large number of relative phrases include a metaphor, and that many metaphors are at the same time relative phrases.

To take courage,   To work with redoubled zeal,
To lose patience,   To hit the mark,
To take pains,   &c. &c.

these are expressions which assuredly represent metaphors; but under this other form—

Take courage!	Work with redoubled zeal.
Do not lose your patience!	You will attain your aim.
Take pains!	&c., &c.

they may play, if desired, the part of relative phrases.

In reality it is in great measure by the channel of the relative phrase that Nature transmits to each of us what figurative language we have at our disposal for the translation of our abstract ideas. We will even say Nature cannot do otherwise. Coming from such a teacher, the process cannot but be irreproachable, and it would be foolhardy either to disdain it, or to apply it otherwise than does Nature. It is therefore to the relative phrase that we shall, first of all, have recourse to transmit to our pupils the part of the figurative language that can be given to them in this way.

Nevertheless, it must be permitted to Art, here as elsewhere, to do better and more rapidly than Nature. In the first place, in yielding to us, by the process we have just described, the metaphorical expressions, Nature neglected to reveal to us the hidden symbols from whence these expressions arise. In the next place, these expressions strike our ears more or less irregularly and somewhat at hazard; and here assuredly is one of the reasons which cause the figurative language to remain all our life less familiar and more rebellious to the thought than the objective language. Lastly, and above all, whoever receives a metaphor wrapped up within a relative phrase assimilates this metaphor unwittingly. Now a treasure whose existence is not known is no longer a treasure.[1] Therefore there still remains something for Art to do.

If it can make mankind assimilate consciously the figurative language after having assimilated it unconsciously; if it can make this assimilation take place regularly and methodically; if, in fine, it can cause this last part of the language to be attached logically and harmoniously to the two others and to form with them a homogeneous whole, then Art will have

---

[1] The absence of conscious knowledge of the root of the metaphor, and the employment of figurative expressions as simple "relative phrases," is, of course, the cause of the use of mixed metaphors by unskilled rhetoricians (Trans.).

done what Nature does not accomplish, and cannot accomplish other than roughly; that is, Art will have conquered Nature. And Art can do this.

Our metaphorical themes will first make plain the unnamed symbols from which they borrow their development; then the diverse pieces of these themes will be set in order and organised in the direction indicated by the nature of the symbolic fact itself. It therefore only remains to discover between the figurative language and the objective language a natural relation which permits the exercises of the one to be harmoniously allied to the exercises of the other.

To study the figurative language indeed, in itself and for itself, separately and in the abstract, would be a perfectly barren labour, if not an impossible one. It would be simply to repeat our early experience with the dictionary. In the everyday practice of life the metaphorical expressions are mingled and interlaced continually with those of the language proper, coming one after the other, and linked together according to the secret dialectic of the natural facts upon which these expressions depend. But how are we to discover the relation which we need to carry out the synthesis of the two languages? How are we to determine the exact point of their junction?

The abstract language has no origin within itself. Its occasional cause is in the external world; therefore its roots reach down into the objective language. The two languages touch, therefore, at certain points. If these points exist, reflection can discover them. Let us see if we can find them.

2. *Search for a connecting link between the metaphorical theme and that of the series—Idea of dominants—Crossing and harmonious progress of the two languages.*

Every objective fact perceived by man provokes a judgment on the part of his mind. This judgment is the origin of generalised conceptions, and represents the raw material out of which abstract ideas are made. We have already stated and described this elementary operation, by which the understanding transfigures all that happens to fall within its field of action.

But if it transfigures isolated facts, it will also transfigure the groups of facts presenting, as in each exercise of our series, the synthesis of an end developed by its means. The groups of facts indeed, because they are more clearly determined, more clearly characterised than the isolated facts, draw the attention more forcibly, and give more strength to its judgments. In other words, as the mind treats the simple fact, so it treats the composite fact—that is, it submits the second as it does the first to abstraction and to generalisation. And what does it abstract? What product is yielded by this double operation? Beginning directly with the facts themselves, let us interrogate them; they will answer for us.

Read, or ask some one to read to you, any theme of our series. Without your being aware of it, there will spring up in your mind, or rather your mind will disengage therefrom, certain feelings, mental generalisations, which we call, and rightly, moral conceptions or abstract ideas. For instance, in our Series of the Shepherd, the scene that represents the fight between two rams will certainly awaken within you the abstract ideas or conceptions of ill-temper, of anger, of fury, of jealousy, and of brutality. In the Series of the Bird, the exercise which represents the father and mother feeding their young ones with their beaks will awaken in the same way the abstract ideas of love, tenderness, affection, devotion, &c.

These are associations of ideas which it is beyond the power of any one to prevent, and although not formulated aloud, the conceptions which are derived from this source are none the less realities. "Abstract" is a qualification which may be properly used in speaking about these products of the thought, for they are abstracted from facts belonging to the objective world. It is not only the above-mentioned themes and those which resemble them that give rise to abstract ideas within the mind; every development of an objective fact evidently enjoys the same property. The abstract ideas flash therefrom as the spark flashes from the flint, as the lightning from the cloud.

Let us now try to make use of this observation, and of the important fact that it reveals to us. Amongst the diverse abstract ideas that the development of a theme may give rise to in the mind, there is usually one which springs forth more naturally than the others from the general sense of this exercise. We will call this the "Dominant," because it dominates the subject as a whole. It is that which flows from it, which is deduced from it, which is disengaged the most quickly, that into which the whole theme seems most directly to resolve itself.

In the exercise where the shepherd's dog, at a mere sign from his master, does his utmost to gather the scattered flock together, what is the abstract idea which comes before all others? To our mind, it is not agility, nor courage, nor promptitude, nor even zeal, but rather obedience.

The Dominant: here is the intermediary of which we were in search; here is the true connecting link between the objective language and the figurative language. It is upon this dominant that the passage from one to the other will be effected, and this without embarrassment and without difficulty. Suppose, for instance, an exercise having as "dominant" the abstract idea which is represented by the term "courage." We shall construct the metaphorical theme of taking or losing courage, and we shall make it an appendix to the primordial theme. The one will be the complement and, as it were, the satellite of the other. It will be given as a lesson, and studied after the first.

It has been established that our series reproduced, or might reproduce, all the situations in which are presented either animate or inanimate objects. It has been established, besides, that every abstract idea proceeding at the same time from the mind which abstracts it and from the objective world whence it is abstracted, must perforce emerge from one or other of the facts developed in our series. Therefore, every abstract conception which the human mind can conceive will find occasion of expression within the limits of our system.

And if each theme of our series receives, as we have just indicated, a metaphorical theme as appendix, the figurative language will progress in our school as in practical life, side by side with the objective language. The two languages will not overlap sentence by sentence, but they will overlap exercise by exercise. They will none the less from this constitute a homogeneous whole, a firm and harmonious synthesis, analogous and pedagogically superior to that which is elaborated in the school of Nature.

To sum up and conclude: our method offers two means of transmitting the figurative language to the pupil, to wit, the relative phrase and the metaphorical theme, and it employs them both. The metaphorical theme, the logical complement of the series and its crown, leaves intact both the character and the unity of the latter, therefore modifies in nothing whatever the conditions and the mode of teaching it. It does not complicate the study of the objective language lesson, it illumines it; it does not increase it, it does not extend the material of work, it raises it, or, as we have said, transfigures it. Consequently this appendix does not constitute an overload of work either for the master or for the pupil. It is to the mass of the linguistic work as the salt is to the food of the body, as the yeast to the dough, a solvent—a solvent which, instead of overloading the conception or the memory, aids the intellectual digestion. Hence this deduction, a well-known and obligatory refrain of our chapters.

"The single master who suffices for three classes for the study of the objective language will be sufficient also for the teaching of the complete or integral language in its three portions—objective, subjective, figurative. And each lesson which had the virtue, after the work of assimilation, of transforming the disciple into teacher, will continue to enjoy this extremely important property."

XVI.

STILL ANOTHER QUESTION.

Our programme is fulfilled, the triple material of language is organised, our linguistic instrument is complete. Is there anything lacking to our exposition of the system? All the secrets of the construction of the said instrument have been revealed, as also the complex play of its mechanism. The raw material itself, which enters into the composition of this instrument, alone has not been studied. In other words, the system has been established directly upon the double base of the verb and of the sentence; but neither the properties of the verb nor the organism of the sentence have been dealt with thoroughly.

"Grammar" is the ordinary name for this study. When and how, in our system, will the grammar be dealt with and then practised ? This is the important question we have next to answer.

PART THIRD.

GRAMMAR.

I.

TWO OPINIONS UPON THE PRACTICAL VALUE OF GRAMMAR.

CONSIDERED as a means of studying languages, grammar, at the present time, is the object of two absolutely contradictory judgments. The one says :—The child proves to us every day that a language can be learnt perfectly without knowing grammar; therefore the grammar is useless, if not harmful, for the practical study of languages. The other says :—To learn a language is to learn words and to construct sentences; now this construction is subject to certain rules: therefore before all else it is necessary to study these rules. Which of these two judgments is wrong? which is right?

To our mind, both are well founded, and it is by reason of this that they are reconcilable. The reconciliation must take place upon the basis of a grammatical reform—a reform in theory, but above all a reform in practice.

Long before going to school the child uses grammar, and I assure you good grammar. He declines and conjugates; he uses the genders and numbers; he makes the verbs agree with their subjects; he determines, bends to his use, and adjusts certain direct or indirect complements long before he is assisted by a grammar. There is therefore a natural grammatical teaching, as there is a natural linguistic teaching. The science of pedagogy must seek to be inspired by the one as it should be inspired by the other, and the artificial process ceasing to be in itself in contradiction to that of Nature, our two contradictory judgments will evidently become reconciled.

But how are we to formulate the natural grammar, and how are we to apply it? If our linguistic system is really constructed upon the model of that of Nature, it ought to lend itself with the greatest ease to this new enterprise. We may attempt the task, and by basing it upon our system.

II.

DEFINITION AND DIVISION.

The various terms or elements which constitute "speech" or translate thought are subject amongst themselves to certain relationships, these relationships being determined by the work of the intellectual conception. The study of these relationships is termed "Grammar." They may be studied in two different ways. They may be studied in themselves and without connecting them with their determining cause, the mind; or they may be studied by starting from the mind to arrive at the form of speech. The first process gives a grammar which we might term "experimental;" the second leads to a grammar which is "rational." The first is multiple, that is to say, which varies with every tongue; the second is universal, that is to say, fits equally well all languages; it aspires to be one, as the human mind is one.

We have to choose between these two systems. We make choice, evidently and necessarily, of the second. The first process is suited to those who as yet know not, but seek. It is not suitable to a master who teaches, the first condition for teaching being to know. The second process, the only one truly pedagogic, proposes nothing less than the "unification of grammar." The psychologist-grammarian should determine the whole of the grammatical conceptions of the human mind, and from them draw up a well-thought-out series of questions, to which each language must be made to reply. This would be the ordinary teaching reversed. The latter, indeed, leaves the languages to set us their enigmas entirely at the chance of the teachers' fancy or that of their grammarians. In the system which we seek to establish, it will be ourselves who set the questions to the language. Instead of going uphill, we should thus go downhill, an infinitely less painful labour, and one which would lead us surely and in a short time to the knowledge of no matter what grammar. The prize is indeed worthy the pains. We will attempt to open up the path.

The practical study of grammar may be included under three heads :—

1. The study of the verb.
2. The study of the sentence.
3. The study of the moods and their expression.

The order to be followed is indicated. The study of the expression of the moods presupposes the knowledge of the simple sentence, and the study of the sentence presupposes the knowledge of the verb. We shall, therefore, begin by the study of the verb; we shall continue by the study of the sentence or syntax, and shall finish by the modal expressions.

STUDY OF THE VERB.

Exercises in the Conjugations (First Week).

III.

INDICATIVE (PRESENT ACTS).

We will again take our theme, "I open the door," and we will suppose the course of language-lessons to commence by this exercise. When it has been elaborated for the time required before the class and afterwards by the class themselves, we have stated that it is absolutely necessary to afford the class a rest, a relaxation, or rather a diversion, which shall be of profit to the intellectual effort by completing it and rendering it fertile, and this diversion we consider we have found in the act of writing out the exercise studied.

But this transcription may be done in several ways; it should, indeed, be varied with the varying aptitudes of the pupils. We give it first of all the form of a grammatical exercise.

1. *First Exercise.*

The pupil will write down the verb only, and this upon his slate, conjugating it in what is termed "the present indicative," in the present tense only, and according to a table prepared by the master in which the root part of the verb or radical is carefully separated from the variable part or the termination. We will present our examples in three living languages and one dead language :—

1. I   walk   we   walk
   thou walk est   you walk
   he   walk s   they walk

STUDY OF THE VERB.

2. je march e   nous march ons
   tu march es   vous march ez
   il march e   ils march ent

3. ich schreit e   wir schreit en
   du schreit est   ihr schreit et
   er schreit et   sie schreit en

4. perg o   perg imus
   perg is   perg itis
   perg it   perg unt

The pupil will conjugate in this way, in the language studied, the whole of the verbs of the first oral exercise, the whole of this work constituting the first grammatical lesson. A second oral exercise will be followed by a second "verbal" exercise, the third by a third, and so on. It is, of course, unnecessary to say that these exercises are only written by the pupil *after* they have been treated orally by the teacher. The verbal forms must, like all the others, be spoken first of all, and strike the ear before being presented to the eye or the hand. We have too often and too strongly insisted upon this principle and upon its consequences, for any further insistance to be necessary.

2. *Second Exercise.*

The verb will not be conjugated alone and in an abstract fashion, but rather with its subjects and its complements; and above all, the mistake must never be made of enumerating the terminations alone, but the termination must be connected to its radical:—

1. I walk towards the door.
   thou walkest towards the door.
   he walks towards the door.
   we walk towards the door.
   you walk towards the door.
   they walk towards the door.

2. Je marche vers la porte.
   tu marches vers la porte.
   il marche vers la porte.
   nous marchons vers la porte.
   vous marchez vers la porte.
   ils marchent vers la porte

3. Ich schreite auf die Thür zu.
du schreitest auf die Thür zu.
er schreitet auf die Thür zu.
wir schreiten auf die Thür zu.
ihr schreitet auf die Thür zu.
sie schreiten auf die Thür zu.

4. Ad portam pergo.
ad portam pergis.
ad portam pergit.
ad portam pergimus.
ad portam pergitis.
ad portam pergunt.

This second exercise still presents something abstract and factitious. We have already pointed out how pernicious in the study of languages is abstraction. It is, therefore, most important to hasten as quickly as possible to the concrete, the real.

3. *Third Exercise.*

The sentences will no longer be conjugated separately and isolated from each other, but the whole exercise will be put, for example, into the second person.

1. Thou walkest towards the door.
thou drawest near to the door.
thou arrivest at the door.
thou, &c.

2. Tu marches vers la porte.
tu t'approches de la porte.
tu arrives à la porte.
tu, &c.

3. Du schreitest auf die Thür zu.
du näherest dich der Thür
du kommst bei der Thür an.
du, &c.

4. Ad portam pergis.
ad portam accedis.
ad portam advenis.
ad portam, &c.

PRESENT ACTS.

Here all abstraction will have disappeared if the pupil imagines the action described to be performed by one of his school-fellows, in whom he can see, at will, either a second or a third person. Needless to say, this exercise can be equally well spoken in the plural as in the singular.

1. We walk towards the door.
   we draw near to the door.
   we come to the door.
   we, &c.

2. Nous marchons vers la porte.
   nous nous approchons de la porte.
   nous arrivons à la porte.
   nous, &c.

3. Wir schreiten auf die Thür zu.
   wir nähern uns der Thür.
   wir kommen bei der Thür an.
   wir, &c.

4. Ad portam pergimus.
   ad portam accedimus.
   ad portam advenimus.
   ad portam, &c.

As we have dealt with the exercise of the door, so we should deal with each exercise of the series developed in the course of the week. This will comprise the grammatical work for the first few days. Simple and elementary as this first operation is or seems to be, it deserves an attentive examination. We will discuss it before proceeding to the second week's exercise.

IV.

CRITICAL EXAMINATION OF THE PROCESS.

1. *Properties of our exercise in verbs.*

We begin at once the study of the conjugations from the first series and with the very first lesson; and it is the method itself which calls for and requires this evolution, while the linguistic theme serves us admirably as grammatical theme also. Furthermore, owing to the nature and the organisation of our exercises, we conjugate one after the other some fifteen or twenty verbs, without allowing any one of them to appear under the form of an abstraction. Few books, assuredly, can offer this advantage: "to force the pupil to think of an actual thing, to represent real facts while conjugating verbs."

Does this grammatical diversion, it may be asked, trouble or fatigue the pupils? All that we can say is, that it always has the advantage of amusing ours. But the irregular verbs! some one will exclaim. The irregular verbs, by our process, far from frightening the child, interest him even more than the other verbs. And this ought to be so; for in itself the regular verb is monotonous; now the genius of childhood is the enemy of monotony.

The result would evidently be quite other if, instead of giving him at any one time two or three irregular verbs to digest, we were to force him, as in most schools, to gorge himself with a parcel of fifty to eighty irregular verbs, and thus in the abstract, completely in the abstract, that is to say, stupidly. In our exercises the irregular verb stands out from the mass of regular verbs as black stands out from white, and for this reason impresses itself on the memory in characters almost ineffaceable. For us there are no longer irregular verbs in the language, or rather the irregular verbs, reappearing over and over again, continually seem to be the true regular verbs.

The grammar, at the beginning at any rate, becomes therefore like the study of the relative phrase, a mere "game." I hasten to add "a fertile game." It creates or awakens in the mind of the pupil, in a few days, a new sense, "the grammatical sense." Yes, a grammatical sense; this sense which you and I possess, which everybody possesses, and by reason of which, in the mother-tongue, we recognise intuitively and without recourse to any grammar whether a thing is properly spoken or not; by which we distinguish one mood from another, the form of one tense from the form of another tense, either when employed by ourselves or coming from the lips of others.

To be what it should be, the grammar ought thus to pass from the state of being in a book to that of becoming an organ of the mind. The method which can carry out this metamorphosis will have deserved much from the human mind.

But is not the grammatical work mentioned premature?

Does it respond to a real and actual need of the scholar? In other terms, does he learn the rules of a thing of which he knows nothing, or, to repeat the words of Condillac, does it load the memory of a pupil with an entirely unknown tongue? Does the abstract precede the concrete? Does the general come before the particular and the individual?

The reply to this question has already in part been made. Was not our first consideration to avoid everything that had the appearance of abstraction? Have we not applied ourselves precisely to transform the abstract into the concrete, to deal with the general by the particular? Moreover, the thing which we attempt to submit to rules is already known to the pupil; it is this column of verbs which we have just used to express a series of real, actual, personal perceptions.

Lastly, the exercise put into the second or third person is not more premature than it is at the time of the first giving of the lesson in the first person. Language is not formed to be employed in a solitary monologue, but, on the contrary, to bring us into relation with the minds of others. The need of speaking in the second, and above all in the third person, is perhaps more imperious than in the first person. The child (like Julius Cæsar) speaks at first only in the third person, even when speaking of himself:—

> Bertie fell down.
> Bertie hurt himself.

2. *Upon the unity of the conjugation.*

We have detached from the general conjugation one of its elements: we have isolated it and studied it separately. Are we right in so doing? Will not the unity of the conjugation suffer therefrom? Is it not important to respect this unity? And does the "present indicative" form a whole in itself—a definite, real, concrete whole? The following is our answer:—

Consider the little child. In what mood does he, when following Nature's process, speak his thoughts? Most assuredly it is not in the venerable supine, nor in the gerundive, nor even in the redoubtable but insecure subjunctive. He speaks in the indicative. And would you know why? It is because all that he speaks about is real. Now the indicative, as its name implies (that which "points with the index-finger"), the indicative is the mood of the real. And in what tense does this same child talk? Listen to him yourself, and you will soon notice that he hardly uses any other than the present. We have followed the course mapped out by Nature; therefore, if this road leads the child to success, we need not fear to miss it ourselves.

As to the unity of the conjugation, such as is commonly taught, such as is found in all the grammars without exception, it is not a "unity" at all; it is at most a table of contents, and still further, a very incomplete and badly arranged table, in spite of the plethora of bars and cross-bars amongst which, right or wrong, the grammarians strove to quarter the various movements of thought. It is a scaffolding which is based upon analogies too often quite untrue. Occasionally it is an enigma absolutely undecipherable. What, indeed, is more difficult to understand than that which has no reason for its existence?

The unity of the conjugation, such as we have all studied at school, only exists upon paper. That which is a unity is the container, but not the contained; it is the page on which the conjugation is written, but not this conjugation itself. The unity of the latter is purely a question of size of page or of typographic artifice. This is so true that he who studies in one grammar often cannot understand another.

If the classical conjugation formed a veritable unity, it ought everywhere and always to affect the same form, present the same organism and the same organisation. The artist cannot change according to his fancy the number or the order of the limbs upon the creature he wishes to reproduce. But can you quote two grammarians who completely agree upon this question, in our opinion the most elementary?

Such or such a form or "tense," as it is called, which one admits as necessary, is neglected by another as useless. What one calls "absolute" the other treats as "relative." One adjudges subjunctive what the other attributes to the conditional, and what still another places under the heading "optative." And, in point of fact, why is it that new grammars are published continually, if there is nothing to be changed in the old ones? Meantime, amongst this logomachy, what becomes, I would ask, of your unity of the conjugation?

But suppose that a book were to appear in which the conjugation presented an irreproachable unity. Would this table be profitable for the study of any given language? Our experience authorises us to say that it would be prejudicial to this study, and this paradox we explain in the following way. Every intermediary between the idea and its expression hinders the quick development of the latter. Just so long, for instance, as in order to employ a subjunctive form, it is necessary to remember the rule which commands it, and then to represent to oneself the small square in the table where dwells the form of which you are in need, you may be quite certain that you are not in a state either to speak or to understand any other person speaking in the language studied. Is not this exactly what happens to us with Latin or Greek after ten or even twenty years' study? Has Latin ever been better spoken than at that epoch in which the grammar was reduced to a few pages, or rather to a purely oral teaching? May we not say that the "practical" knowledge of this tongue has varied in inverse proportion to the thickness of the grammars?

It is the same with speaking as it is with reading. We only know how to read upon the day when we no longer have need to name the letters or to preoccupy ourselves about them. In the same way, we only know how to speak a language when we have no further need to consult the rule, that is to say, when, as we have said, the grammar has become an added sense, an organ of our intelligence.

What would be the effect produced by this ideal table of conjugations? Evidently this table will play the part of intermediary between the idea and its expression: it will hinder the grammatical sense from being born, and will hold the mind captive under its empire. Do not forget, moreover, that this ideal conjugation is an acknowledged abstraction. The mind having to struggle against two enemies at once, will inevitably succumb.

"But," it will be objected, "you are pleading against the conjugation; but the verb being the principal object of grammar, it is therefore grammar itself that you are attempting to batter down." Not at all, begging your pardon, but merely the manner in which it is taught. It is the process that we are attacking—that process that pretends to lead to the concrete by way of the abstract.

In the present systems, we are shown the conjugation on

paper: the eye is taught by means of lines and bars; we have to strive to form therefrom a "perception," a stereotyped view. No one seems to think of writing, not upon paper, but upon the thought, of forming of the conjugation a "conception." "But how can this be done?" you will ask. We will endeavour to show.

The unity of the conjugation may be assimilated to the unity of each of our series. The moods thereof represent the natural chapters or divisions. The diverse forms of these moods, so improperly called "tenses," are the themes thereof. Each mood forms a veritable and indivisible whole—a perfect unity; for it corresponds to a mode of existence of the mind. But, like the theme of the series, the "tense" forms in its turn an indivisible whole—a "unity" as perfect, but more true and more concrete, than that of the mood itself.

The conjugation may therefore be taught as a series: theme by theme, that is, tense by tense; that is, form by form; and if the distribution of a linguistic series in various themes, far from distraining the unity of the series, strengthens it by recalling it continually to the mind, neither will the partial and successive study of the "tenses," or time forms, prove prejudicial to the unity of the moods; and, for the same reasons, the unity of the conjugation will remain intact, provided only that the teaching proceeds rationally. The sun does not shine the less brightly because it shines over a wider extent.

Furthermore, this unity will gain considerably both in force and in precision: in force, as does everything which is developed in its constituent elements; in precision, as does everything which passes from the general and the abstract to the concrete.

Therefore, by studying the conjugation piece by piece and as a series, the unity of this conjugation will not be affected. Our proceeding is therefore justified; we are right in teaching each mood separately and each form separately. From this follow three practical consequences of the very greatest importance:—

1. The memory of the pupil will be relieved of the overwhelming burden of the conjugation learnt in its totality. To express each of his ideas, he will not need to unfold before his imagination the extremely complex pigeon-hole arrangement of this conjugation, with its forms, regular and irregular.

He will have only one wheel to set in motion; he will have only one form to regard at any one time.

2. This form, separated from the essentially abstract system of the conjugation, may be assimilated to the idea which it expresses, may be made to form one body with it, and so become stripped of all feeling of abstraction.

Thenceforward there is no intermediary between the idea and the form—a result absolutely impossible of achievement if a special form were forced, as in the classical process, to remain adherent to the whole of the conjugation, and if, in order to apply this single form, it were necessary to embrace and set in motion the whole body of the conjugation—that is to say, to imagine it in its totality. Riveted to an abstract whole, this form would inevitably remain abstract itself.

3. Lastly, and most important, this operation will prepare the awakening of the new sense of which we have spoken—"the grammatical sense." The form being identified everywhere and always with the idea, it will not be long before the pupil will apply the foreign grammar "by instinct."

3. *Our process and that of nature — Awakening of the grammatical sense—The indicative mood, the form of the present tense, and the third person—The series of the verb.*

Let us now compare our process with that of Nature, and see if they agree the one with the other. In the first place, the two results thereof are identical: the child also applies the conjugations "by instinct." Long before he has heard of conjugations, long even before he has learned to read, the child distinguishes perfectly well the moods and the time forms of the verbs. Whence comes this marvellous intuition?

We have already fully stated that, in learning the mother-tongue, the language forms one with the perception: what the child sees, that he speaks about directly and without intermediary, and his perception in early childhood being always that of an actual fact, he gives it the form which we know under the name of "the present." As with our method, therefore, the child commences with the present. Subsequently this form, owing to its frequency, becomes identified naturally with all that appears as present, and the child "instinctively" borrows this form whenever it wishes to express anything that it perceives as present—that is to say, this operation becomes after a time the effect of a true "feeling" or "sense." Does not our process equally lead to the same point?

The child plays about a very long time upon the present; he expresses therewith, so to speak, the whole of his individuality before passing to another tense. Hence the exceptional importance of this first form. It is to the entire conjugation what the verb is to the sentence—the soul or the substance. In all languages, the third person of the present tense contains in itself the complete germ of the whole verb. And this should be so, the third person being the first form that the child distinguishes and in which he babbles his infantile language. As we have said already, the child at first employs this third person even when speaking of himself—

Teddy is hungry.

The third person includes within itself the entire conjugation, which develops therefrom piece by piece according to the needs of the age or of the thought. It is in the third person that, at the commencement, the unity of the conjugations resides. It is not yet the unity of the oak, but it is the unity of the acorn; and as fast as a new form issues from it, the mind will easily recognise this form by its appearance as belonging to the same whole. In this manner the conjugation becomes a kind of "progressive" unity, which at no time hinders or burdens the development of the various parts.

Guided by this observation, we have adopted for the ordinary and constant form of our series the third person singular of the indicative mood, present tense. Like Nature, we make this third person the basis of our operations. We have had the idea of sometimes taking as point of departure, instead of the form of the present tense, that of the future or of the past tenses, hoping by this means to advance the knowledge of the verbs while saving time; but we soon perceived that the exercise lost in clearness and simplicity by so doing; that the assimilation took place with far greater trouble; and lastly, that with these forms it was not easy to ascend or re-descend to any other. We were forced to re-establish the verb upon its natural basis, "the present."

The present, or rather the form of the present tense, is a known quantity, and a constant one; the other forms are unknown quantities which are deduced from the one given.

THE REFORM OF GRAMMAR TEACHING.

Consequently, before conjugating, it is necessary to know and possess the form of the present. Our first step is therefore both in accordance with the prescriptions of reason and with the lessons of Nature, properly interpreted.

4. *Summary and conclusion—Grammatical teaching must be reformed, not abolished.*

To sum up the preceding considerations: the true grammar should begin, not by the study of the substantive and of the declensions, but by the study of the verb. The form of the present tense will be the object of our first attempts. This form will be conjugated not for itself—that is to say, abstractly—but with all the complements of the verb in the sentence given. This grammatical diversion is a relaxation for the scholar, a fruitful game which endows him with a new sense—the "grammatical sense." This exercise is not premature; it responds to a real and actual need. The study of the verb should be progressive; each form should be separated from the whole and treated in its turn. The child begins by the indicative mood, and by the present tense of this mood; we do likewise. This process changes in nothing the true unity of the conjugation, but, on the contrary, strengthens it.

No grammarian has been able as yet to draw up the table of the conjugation under a perfect and definite form. But even if this ideal table could be made, it would only prove pernicious to the study of languages, at any rate in cases where it was applied as are the conjugations of the present grammars. It would stand inevitably as an intermediary between the idea and its expression, paralysing the latter, exiling the mind into the void of abstraction, burdening the memory with the whole weight of its general organism, stifling the grammatical sense as a tyrant stifles liberty.

In itself everything included in the term conjugation belongs to the abstract. Now all good teaching should strive to bring the abstract to the concrete, the general to the particular. Words are but signs, that is to say, in reality a pure abstraction, which abstraction is intended to lead to the perception or the representation of a real and concrete fact. It is therefore wrong, radically wrong, in dealing with language, to act upon the principle so often advocated with reference to all and everything—"To proceed from the concrete to the abstract," which renders simple things difficult, and transforms what is easily represented in the mind into that which is nebulous and indefinite. It is this principle turned the other way round which we should follow in *teaching* languages. We should take the abstract and render it as concrete as possible. Our formula will thus be to proceed at once from the abstract to the concrete, that is, to transform whatever is abstract and render it concrete.

To attain this aim in the study of the verb we propose to assimilate the conjugation to a series, of which the various links, that is, the separate themes, would be what are termed "the tenses." Each form or tense would be elaborated separately, not in the vague form of the abstract, but upon the actual material of our series, and until the pupil applied it instinctively, spontaneously, intuitively. This process appears to us to offer great advantages:—

1. The mind deals with but one form at a time, and runs no danger of succumbing under the burden of the complete conjugation.

2. Each form being separated from its abstract whole, becomes rapidly identified with the idea, the perception—becomes embodied in it, and passes to the concrete.

3. Lastly, grammatical speech under these conditions may, and does, promptly become an instinct; in other words, is developed by intuition.

Compared with the process of Nature, our system will be found to have attained the same aims by the same means. Like the child, we begin by the indicative and the form of the present. Like him also, we make this form the basis of all our operations by dwelling, like him, upon the third person. Soon, like him again, from this third person we shall make all the other parts of the verb which it contains in germ spring successively forth.

Finally, the grammar of childhood is indeed a grammar of intuition; but this intuition—let no one be deceived upon this point—is the result of a prodigious labour. It is no more a gift than the ability of Henri Mondeux was a gift; and our method does not in reality propose any less aim than to discover, or rather to reveal, the mysterious process which creates this intuition, and endows the human mind with its power. Therefore, if we wish to speak a language with the surety and the quickness of the child, we must pass through the apprenticeship that he passes through. There is therefore a process to be followed; there is something to learn, something to be studied. We are, therefore, in accord, at least so far as regards the basis, with those who maintain that a language cannot be learnt without learning rules.

On the other hand, we have clearly demonstrated that there is only one road that leads to intuition, that which goes from the abstract to the concrete, from the general to the particular, from the imaginary to the real. Now, whether we realise it or not, all grammars and methods at present known lead, on the contrary, from the concrete to the abstract, from the real to the imaginary; and, consistent with themselves, profess a profound disdain for intuition, denying its efficacy, denouncing it, and chasing it away like an evil spirit. But is not this like seeking to make a river flow by damming up its source? Is not this trying to produce light by eliminating the sun? We find ourselves, therefore, equally in accord with those who reprove the ordinary teaching of grammar as useless, if not actually harmful, to the "practical" study of languages.

In itself the grammatical teaching is necessary; but such as is given in the schools of to-day has proved useless, nay, even harmful, for the acquisition and the practice of languages. Conclusion: we must not abolish the teaching of grammar; we must reform it.

STUDY OF THE VERB.

Exercises in Conjugation (Second Week).

V.

INDICATIVE MOOD—ACTS PAST, PRESENT, AND FUTURE.

1. *Six times or six periods—Definite times and indefinite times—Moments of precision.*

We have conjugated the verbs of our exercise, or rather the exercise itself, in the present tense. We could have conjugated it, and we can conjugate it, in the same manner, and with the same facility, in the past, in the future, and in other tenses, if they exist. This will be the task of the second week. Before doing so it will be necessary to give to the pupil a precise notion of the grammatical tenses.

Our explanation will be short and simple. We shall say to him :—

The human mind is capable of distinguishing or perceiving, within time in general, various "periods" or durations of time, sharply determined as regards their length, and taken as units, to wit, the period of a day, the period of a week, the period of a month, the period of a year, the period of the life of a man; lastly, a period which comprises all the others, TIME properly so called, or Eternity. These constitute the six periods of time, which we shall take as the basis of our grammar.

We will repeat them :—

The period or duration of a day, this is the first period.
The period or duration of a week is a second period.
The period or duration of a month is a third period.
The period or duration of a year is a fourth period.
TIME in general, or eternity, is a fifth period.

There is also the period or duration of time, not so definitely fixed, measured by the life of a man—Charlemagne, Napoleon, Shakespeare, yourself, myself, or any other person: this is the sixth period.

We must be careful not to omit this last; it is the key to some of the greatest difficulties of the conjugations. Without it a rational explanation of the forms of the verbs is impossible. It is the omission of due consideration of this period or duration which is the cause of the embarrassments and mistranslations of the grammarians. Why, indeed, should the duration of the life of the person who is speaking not take its place amongst the epochs in which he mentally places the facts about which he is thinking? We must not forget that every living individual involuntarily and inevitably considers himself as the centre of the world, as the substance of the universe, and connects everything with himself.

There will be, therefore, at least six periods or durations of time. With reference to the three forms hitherto regarded as the substance itself or the incarnation of time—the past, the present, and the future—we shall presently state their proper signification in grammar.

For the moment the three legendary tenses are dethroned. What will pedantry say to this? And how shall we be able ourselves to justify the number six? To the child all justification is needless. He will understand us perfectly and at once; for the six periods which we have just enumerated are to him real periods of time and not "abstractions" of time. He knows them as well as we do ourselves; he uses them constantly. They form a set of pigeon-holes, always present, always open before him, into which he is continually distributing his remembrances, his perceptions, his thoughts. The pedagogue will possibly be less docile; but we will pass on; we will try conclusions with him later.

A "day" may be past and gone; it is then called yesterday, the day before yesterday, last Monday, last Tuesday, the other day.

A day may be present; it is then called to-day.

A day may be future, that is, still to come; it is called to-morrow, the day after to-morrow, next Monday, next Tuesday, &c.

Past, present, future—these words do not represent "periods of time;" they represent "states" of the periods of time.

What we have said of the period of a day we can also say of the period of a week. A week may be past; it is then called last week, the other week, two weeks ago, &c. A week may be present, that is, still going on; it is then called this week. A week may be future or to come; it is then called next week, the coming week.

We have in the same way, last month (the month that is past), this month or the current month, next month or the coming month.

We have also, last year or the past year, this year or the current year, next year or the coming year.

TIME, properly so called, has only one state; it is always present.

Here we have a nomenclature which assuredly is within the reach of everybody's comprehension. All that is required to understand it, is to be able to distinguish a week or a month from a day, and to-day from to-morrow.

A day "past"—yesterday, for example—is a period of time begun and finished, that is to say, in relation to the present moment, limited behind and before. It is therefore "definite" (or finished), and grammar has rightly consecrated this term thereto.

A day "present" (to-day) is a period of time begun but not finished. It is not, in relation to the present moment, limited at its latter point; consequently it is "indefinite" (unfinished). Grammar has also consecrated this term.

What we have just said about the day applies to the week, the month, the year. But eternity being by its nature always present, can only be an "indefinite" (or unfinished) period of time. In the same way, the life of any person still living (you, me, this or that man) equally represents an "indefinite" (or unfinished) period of time.

What difference is there between a past time and a definite time? In ordinary language, very often none at all. Indeed, all time that is past may be considered as finished, and consequently as "definite." The two terms "past" and "definite" seem therefore perfectly identical. Are they so in reality, and ought they to be so? No.

"Definite" is a qualificative of the period of time. "Past" is a qualificative of the action that has taken place in TIME in general. It is the confusion of these two terms which has given rise to so many grammatical enormities, and so many mistranslations.

Each of the before-mentioned periods of time becomes imposed upon us as an indivisible whole. Nevertheless, each of them has various moments which might be called "moments of precision." The year has its months, the month its weeks, the week its days, the day its hours.

> Last year I killed a snake.

And if I wish to be precise:

> Last year, in the month of January,
> I killed a snake.

Observe that this addition does not here bring with it any change in the form of the verb. The definite (or finished) periods of time, such as yesterday, last month, do not admit of other divisions.

The indefinite (or unfinished) periods, such as to-day, this week, this year, also contain the natural moments, and these it may be important to indicate precisely, because with these the form of the verb does vary. Thus, the period "to-day" comprises five "moments," which we generally designate by the following terms:—

Up to now (this morning, or rather that part of to-day already gone)	ce matin	heute Morgen.
Just now	il y a un instant (tout-à-l'heure)	so eben.
Now	à présent	jetzt.
Presently	dans un instant (tout-à-l'heure)	sogleich.
This evening, to-night	ce soir	heute Abend.

"This week" divides naturally into two parts: that which is already fled, and that which has not yet passed. The same division applies to this month, this year, to the individual life, and to TIME properly so called.

2. *Natural association of the forms of the verbs with the times—The tense intuition.*

Our pupil now possesses a clear and precise notion—and let us hope an exact and complete one—of the grammatical times, and of their kinds, their different states, and their various appellations. What use will he make of this notion? Or rather, what use shall we make of it ourselves in order to teach him the conjugations, and especially those of the indicative mood? Nature has solved the question ever since man existed, or at least ever since the time he began to talk; the most ordinary common-sense should therefore lead us before all else to study her processes.

And first of all, let us lay it down as a principle that if there is a natural grammar, it must be simple—extremely simple—from the fact that all the world over it is understood and applied without ever having been studied. If, therefore, we encounter in it what may be termed "simplicities," we must not be either astonished or regretful thereat. One fact is certain, that the most unlettered of men—let us say the most ignorant—never makes a mistake in the time signification of his verb,—saying "went" for "has gone,"—however quickly he may speak. This proves that we have here one of the most simple of operations, one which has not the slightest practical connection with the abstract and metaphysical views and rules of our grammarians. If it were necessary, in order to employ what is commonly termed the "past indefinite," to have present in the mind the rule laid down by such or such grammarian who happens still to be enthroned in our schools, we should most certainly be in danger, not only of putting a past definite where a past indefinite should be given and *vice-versâ*, but often of not being able to speak at all: the rule being far from applying to all cases.

The employment of tenses, I repeat, should be, and as a matter of fact is, an extremely simple operation. It is this:—Every time we wish to state, not an abstract idea, but an actual fact which takes or took place within a certain time, *we always begin by mentioning or by indicating this time*:—

  Yesterday . . Arthur visited a friend.
  Last week . . Arthur visited a friend.
  Last month . . Arthur visited a friend.
  Last year . . Arthur visited a friend.
  Socrates . . died in prison.

When pronouncing the word "yesterday" I infallibly represent to myself the definite (or finished) period of time which this word recalls, and I choose naturally the verbal form destined and consecrated to all definite periods of time:—

  I visit ed
  thou visit edst
  he visit ed.

I repeat, and the attention of the reader is particularly directed to this point, never do we express a fact without previously designating by one of the preceding terms or by some analogous term, in which of the six "periods" of time the fact took place. Every one can convince himself of this by observing what himself he says. Suppress all indication of time in the phrase above given, and it will run :—

  Arthur visited a friend.

Something essential is lacking to this sentence: it is not complete under this form; involuntarily you wonder, "When ?"

NECESSITY OF SPECIFYING THE TIME.

Add to it any one of the six periods, and it leaves nothing to be desired:—

Last week Arthur visited a friend.

These six periods form, as we have said, a kind of set of pigeon-holes (everybody has the same set) into which we distribute, not letters, but the various acts which we wish to express, which thus find themselves categorically labelled, that is, determined as to time.

Now transport the fact into an "indefinite" (or unfinished) period of time; for example, into the period "to-day." To-day presents, as we have just said, several "moments":—

Up to now—this morning (or rather that part of to-day which is passed), } Ce matin.
Just now, Il y a un instant.
Now, A présent.
Presently, Dans un instant.
This evening, Ce soir.

If you will notice, you will find that you never express a fact as taking place in the time to-day without mentioning, or at any rate tacitly indicating, which of the moments the fact took place in.

To-DAY (some time up to now, not specified),[1] } I have spoken to my friend.
Just now, I have just spoken to my friend.
Now, I am speaking.
Presently, { I am going to speak. / I shall speak.
This evening (to-day), { I am going to speak; or, / I shall speak.

These words—this morning, just now, now, presently, this evening—express parts inseparable from the period termed "to-day." When pronouncing each of these terms, I represent to myself, therefore, by a well-known association of ideas, both the indefinite (or unfinished) period of time, "to-day," in its entirety, and a particular "moment" of this general time. It is, therefore, exactly the same operation as for the definite (or finished) periods of time.

---

[1] When the exact moment is specified, the form in English is different. (See next page)—(Trans.).

Let us replace to-day by to-morrow. When pronouncing "to-morrow" I represent to myself the future period of time evoked by this word (and of which "yesterday" is the image), and I employ naturally and spontaneously the verbal form habitually employed for this species of period:—

>I shall speak.
>Thou wilt speak.
>He will speak.

We ask, is there any operation of the mind more elementary, more easy to follow, than this?

In what exactly does the intellectual operation carried out by the man who speaks in these different tenses really consist? There is nothing, I fancy, more simple. He speaks not according to an abstract rule, but according to his own conception. He imagines to himself the time; he sees the time, that is, the day, or the week, or the year, &c., in which the act he wishes to express has taken place, takes place, or will take place; and according as this time is a definite (or finished) time, an indefinite (or unfinished) time, or a future time, he makes his choice of the first, of the second, or of the third form above given.

The person speaking is, therefore, his own arbitrator; his forms relate only to his fancy. He is guided and ruled by himself alone in defining by a word such as "yesterday" or "to-morrow" the time in which the act happened or will happen. Is not this the intuitive process *par excellence?* If one wished to explain what intuitive perception was, could a much better example be chosen?

This little word "yesterday," which the grammar disdains or hardly perceives—this worthless word is found to be the luminous beacon which guides in his speech the most ignorant as well as the most learned, and the most learned as much as the most ignorant, without ever allowing them to be led astray.

We may here open a parenthesis. The difference between the definite periods of time and the indefinite periods of time being thus clearly laid down, we can explain in passing various grammatical facts upon which light has never been clearly thrown until now. For instance, in English, when speaking of a past act within the period of time "to-day," we may say, and say with equal correctness—

>To-day   I have opened the door.
>To-day, at eleven o'clock,   I opened the door.

DEFINITE AND INDEFINITE PERIODS.

Why is this? In these two phrases has not the act taken place in an indefinite period of time, the period of time to-day? and is not "I opened the door" a form exclusively consecrated to the definite periods of time? Ought the verbal form to be thus in disaccord with the time? Is there here what is termed an exception to the rule? No, a true rule is susceptible of explanations; it cannot permit exceptions.

In the second case of the example here chosen, the moment is more exactly defined by the words "at eleven o'clock." There is no reason why, if we wish so to do, we should not conceive our period of time to be shorter than a day—to be a forenoon, an hour, even a minute. Whenever the exact moment is defined, it will be found that the act is represented as taking place in a short period of time separated from the present, which is, therefore, a definite (or finished) period of time, and the definite form, "I opened," is used whenever it is important to indicate the exact moment. Whereas if the act occurs simply in the period of to-day—some time up to now—its exact point being of no great importance, the form "I have opened" clearly expresses the larger unit of time "to-day." This phenomenon (which does not occur in French) might be said to result from the value accorded to time in England—whether the period of an hour or of a minute—the English proverb, "Time is money," thus appearing even in the conjugation.[1]

We will quote another example, which will serve to confirm our explanation. Some one asks you:—

"Have you read Molière?" (Avez-vous lu Molière?)

In this phrase the indication of time seems to be lacking. It is there nevertheless. Amongst our periods of time is that of the life of the individual who is, or may be, the author of the act expressed. In the foresaid example the author of the act therein referred to is "you." The word "you" gives the indication of the period of time. Does not "you" imply the idea of your life or your duration of existence? But your life is an indefinite or unfinished period of time. The act takes place, therefore, in an indefinite period of time, and hence the form, "Have you read?" (Avez-vous lu?), and not, "Did you read?" (Lûtes-vous?).

The expression, "Did you read the Pensées of Pascal?"

---

[1] This paragraph, and the other English examples, pp. 225, 233-4, are inserted by the Translators.

(Lûtes-vous les Pensées de Pascal?), would be incorrect standing alone, or would inadequately render your idea.

For the same reason we can say with equal correctness, "Horace wrote an ode on this subject," and "Horace has written an ode on this subject." The first phrase places the fact in the life of Horace, which represents a definite period of time. The second phrase places the fact in TIME properly so called, which represents an indefinite or unfinished period of time.

In French a similar phenomenon, but in the opposite direction to the English, takes place. In French is said, and can be said, with the same accuracy:—

> Hier, je fermai la porte.
> Hier, j'ai fermé la porte.

"Hier" (yesterday) is a definite period of time, and yet "j'ai fermé" is a form consecrated to the *in*definite periods of time. Here, again, who is the author of the act expressed? It is the "I" or Ego. This "I" represents an *indefinite* or unfinished period of time (for "I" am still living), of which yesterday is merely a moment of precision.

The act takes place, therefore, at the same time both within a definite period, yesterday, and in an indefinite period represented by the "I," that is to say, the duration of my life. This, then, simply is the reason why these two expressions are sometimes equally correct. It should be added that the second, the most irregular in appearance, is in France and Germany more employed than the first, which perhaps results from the predominance in man of the perception of the Ego. Evidently these facts and these rules may be considered as so many witnesses in favour of our system of the "periods of time."

3. *The ordinary period of time (yesterday, to-day, to-morrow, &c.)—The false period of time of the grammars (the past, the present, the future).*

Compare the words yesterday, to-day, to-morrow, this morning, &c., with the three terms by which the grammarians have thought fit to replace them—the past, the present, the future.

Yesterday, to-day, to-morrow, certainly represent something to us. By them and in them time takes unto itself a body; of the abstract it makes itself concrete,—as concrete as is possible for "Time" to be: it becomes almost perceptible; it becomes quasi-tangible. "To-day" is not a pure idea; it is a reality. "Yesterday" is not a chimera; it was a reality. "To-morrow" is not a vain conception comparable to a thought, a longing; it is a reality—a reality which is not yet, but which is to be.

By resting upon these realities of time, Nature remains faithful to her constant process of "going from the abstract to the concrete" (that is, transforming what is abstract and rendering it concrete). Now let us weigh these three other words—the past, the present, the future.

Every one of us, at school or at college, has read, written, copied, and recopied, during seven or eight years, the words "past" and "perfect." We have continually, so to speak, articulated these words with our lips and received them with our ears. Going to a grammar-school, is it much else, even in our own day, than declining and conjugating? Well, let the cleverest of those who have conjugated so long with us declare with sincerity whether they have seen in these words "past" or "perfect" much else than a vain termination:— *i, isti, it, imus, istis, erunt* or *ere, amav-i, isti, it, imus,* &c.

Who is he who has ever thought of seeing in these forms the "time reality" which they carry: yesterday, last week, last month, last year, the lifetime of Socrates or of Cæsar?

How is this? Nature conducts a thing essentially abstract —"Time"—to concrete realities; and the school can find nothing better to do than to push aside these realities and to cast the child into the void of abstraction—The Past! The Present! The Future!

But do you recognise that these three words represent abstractions to the second power? "Virtuous" is assuredly less abstract than "virtue." The substantive always surpasses, as regards abstractions, the corresponding adjective. To raise the adjectives "past, present, future," to the rank of substantives, and make of them "the past, the present, the future," is certainly to raise the abstraction to its second degree. Can you be astonished, after this, that the most profound philologist cannot, as we have so often said, accomplish in ten years what the humblest nurse-maid does in six months? Can you be astonished that the child feels and retains for the study of grammar that taste and tender affection which we all know.

By proceeding on the systems at present taught, by taking that which is concrete and transforming it into abstraction in order to teach the child, answer me, have you been walking with Nature or against her? Are you going towards progress, or are you not rather rushing into nothingness?

4. *Erroneous notions of the tenses in the grammars—Various causes of these errors: disdain of observation, traditional logomachy, confusion of the tense and the act, vain symmetry.*

Nature carries on her work continually beneath our eyes and in full daylight, and with a success that no one can contest. How is it, then, we may ask, that her work and her processes have struck no one's attention, and have remained so little understood by linguists? There are, we think, several causes of this.

We must denounce, as the first cause, a certain contrariety of the human mind. Man regards with disdain all that is simple and all that is within his reach: in everything at the beginning he prefers the longest way round. To discover the laws of language, it does not occur to him to study the child or the ordinary man who speaks under his very eyes, as it did not occur to the University to study Henri Mondeux in order to learn the art of mental calculation. The being who speaks before us produces the effect upon us of a common and well-known machine. To observe him, to study the secrets of such an ordinary operation, would appear derogatory to our dignity as a teacher. Lord preserve the scientist from seeking the laws of language in so lowly a place! Will not absolute truth be found rather in the metaphysical regions of the brain? It is here we must place ourselves, they think, to see truly and see far. It is here we must post ourselves to have the right of dictating rules for the languages, and of regulating them with authority. So much the worse for those languages that will not fit into these rules. It is for them to lend themselves to reason, and not for reason to bow before them.

It is, indeed, unfortunately from these heights that the greater part of our grammars have descended to us. We know not a single one that is based upon the direct observation of the human mind, and of the child day by day creating his language.

A second cause is a deplorable confusion of words consecrated by usage and sanctified by time—a confusion which grammarian bequeaths to grammarian as a tradition. This is the confusion of the time with the act that takes place in this time.

In itself, the time has nothing in common, and can have nothing in common with the expression of a fact, in the same way that the expression of a fact has nothing in common with the time. One is the container, and the other the contents—nothing more. The act is no more the time than the milk is the jug which it fills. The time can determine the form of the expression as the jug fixes the form of the liquid; but beware of identifying these two; if you do, you expose yourself to the error of attributing to the act that which belongs only to the time, and to the time that which belongs only to the act.

All the present grammars consider the tenses of indicative mood as times; they name them as such, and they deal with them as such. In ordinary grammar the past definite is a time, the past indefinite is another time; the imperfect is also a time, and the pluperfect is yet another time. The past future (a future which is passed!), the subjunctives—present, past, imperfect, pluperfect; the conditionals, and so to the gerund, the supine, all the forms indistinctly bearing the names of tenses, *i.e.* times. From this confusion grievous errors have arisen.

No! "I love," or "we love," or "thou lovest," or "you love," or "he loves," or "they love," is not a tense, *i.e.* a time; it is the expression of an "act," an act taking place in a present time as now or "ordinarily."

No! "I have loved," or "we have loved," or "thou hast loved," or "you have loved," or "he has loved," or "they have loved," is not a tense, *i.e.* a time; it is the EXPRESSION OF AN ACT, a past act which has taken place in an indefinite period, as to-day, this week, my life, &c.

For goodness' sake, let us not couple together the two adjectives past and indefinite. What is past is finished and cannot be indefinite or unfinished. Above all, let us not make this monstrous abstraction—"the past indefinite!"

Of what use can it be to set your pupils, and from the very commencement, this enigmatical contraction? Why discourage their patience by giving them this Gordian knot to unravel, whose ends you yourselves seem not able to find? Seriously, what is the real meaning of this expression—"past indefinite" (past which is not finished)? Is it worthy of science, is it worthy of a grammarian? Are you really in earnest when you pronounce these two words, which mutually contradict each other—"past indefinite"? And have you the right to be astonished that children cannot comprehend you, and especially cannot apply what causes you so much trouble to explain to them?

No! "I loved," or "we loved," or "thou lovedst," or "you loved," or "he loved," or "they loved," is not a tense, *i.e.* a time at all; it is the expression of an act, a past act, which took place in a definite period of time, such as yesterday, last week, last month, last year, &c. For the sake of science, for the sake of the children, let us not wed together these two adjectives "past and definite." It is clear that what is past is finished. Above all, do not make of these two synonymous adjectives a substantive—"the past definite!"— as if it were wished to maintain that two adjectives are worth one abstract substantive. Seriously, once more, do you think this play upon words (past which is finished) is worthy of a teacher? Cannot our language avoid this tautology? Is it really necessary that each classical book should reproduce and propagate indefinitely this strange term, simply because it has always appeared in our grammars?

And the imperfect tense, and the pluperfect tense, and the future anterior tense! What nonsense is not hidden by these words or these combinations of words? Can you be astonished that the child has great trouble to understand you, and that he confuses together, day after day and for ten years together, your imperfect with your past definite, your pluperfect with your past future, your subjunctive with your indicative or your conditional? Is there any wonder that he can do no better than yourselves with these enigmatical contractions?

If he is right occasionally, think not the honour is due to your definitions; he does it by intuition or by chance. Confusion of the time in which the act takes place with the act itself, confusion of the act with its form and its verbal expression, here we have a second source of the grammatical errors presented by our schoolbooks. And it is not the last.

DIFFERENT USES OF THE SAME FORM.

For reasons which we cannot go fully into here, the same form of the verb often serves in some languages to translate an act in different periods of time; in other words, the same form serves for several periods of time. For instance, in English—

> When he was at the seaside, he *would* rise at six.
> Yesterday he *would* not come with us.
> I *would* go now, if I were you.
> I am sure he *would* never cheat.
> If you were to work hard you *would* succeed.

In French—

> Autrefois j'aim*ais* à dessiner.
> Aujourd'hui je déjeun*ais* quand il est arrivé.
> Demain, s'il fais*ait* beau, j'irais à la campagne.
> A présent, s'il fais*ait* beau, je sortirais.
> Si tu t'appliqu*ais*, tu réussirais.

These five phrases are expressed in five different periods of time:—

Autrefois	—	hitherto	(definite period).
Aujourd'hui	—	to-day	(indefinite ,,).
Demain	—	to-morrow	(future ,,).
Maintenant	—	now	(present ,,).
Toi	—	thee	(life of an individual).

And for these five periods of time we have one ending, the form "AIS, AIT," that of the ordinary imperfect.

Here is a fact to which our grammarians do not seem to have given sufficient attention. Wherever there is a single form, they seem to say, there could not be several essentially different things. Hence superhuman efforts to reduce "two into one;" hence recourse to all kinds of subtleties to justify this new kind of contraction, and to silence at last this importunate sphinx, that so long has set the grammatical genius at defiance.

They have not seen, furthermore, that each mood answering to a general faculty of the mind admits, or may admit, as with the faculty itself, of divisions and subdivisions. Who amongst them, for example, has ever dreamt that the indicative may be a complex mood? Who has supposed that the subjunctive can be decomposed into three or four distinct moods, and that the conditional itself might be something entirely

P

different from a simple mood? Hence, again, these forced assemblages of forms and ideas in themselves radically heterogeneous.

The ordinary grammar, as we have said, being preoccupied solely with the forms of words, remains perfectly content with counting the various case-endings or verbal changes, grouping them as best it may, sorting them according to accidental analogies, without regard for the intellectual faculties from whence moods and forms are derived, thus becoming the impossible guide or handbook that we know it to be.

One may turn its pages over and over, may worry it for twenty years without finally being able to thoroughly comprehend what the subjunctive really is, without acquiring a really clear idea of the conditional, without being able to distinguish rigorously the past definite from the past indefinite or from the imperfect tense. As we have already said, nothing is more difficult to conceive than relationships that do not exist. It is much like the effect of looking into an unlighted peepshow. The spectator may imagine he sees something, but it is perfectly certain he does not see very clearly.

Another fruitful cause of grammatical errors is the love and search for symmetry. Symmetry! It is here indeed that grammatical pedantry is triumphant. What is called an "imperfect" tense has been placed in the indicative mood; symmetry requires that we also stick in an "imperfect" in the subjunctive. A pluperfect figures in this same indicative; in the name of symmetry a pluperfect is planted in the subjunctive. The particles will be dressed up, always for symmetry, in surnames such as past, present, future, and this *à priori*, and without questioning if a participle—that is, an adjective—can ever be past, present, or future, and without perceiving, for instance, that the pretended "present participle" is employed just as well for past and future tenses as for present tenses. Can one imagine how a mechanism so perfect, arrangements so well thought out, combinations so ingenious, and, above all, so natural, have so little sovereignty over the mind of the pupil, and seem to repel him rather than attract?

Let us leave sarcasm. We have attempted to lay bare the proceedings of Nature, we have equally attempted to lay bare the proceedings of the ordinary grammarians; knowing henceforth the route that we ought to take, and the breakers that we have to avoid, we can boldly set sail with confidence.

VI.

OUR PRACTICE IN THE FORMS OF THE INDICATIVE.

1. *First Exercise—Simple and momentary acts.*

The class is invited to quit the "present," and to transport themselves in thought into the day of "yesterday." Our lesson will therefore take a new form.

YESTERDAY—

1. I went to the door.
   I drew near to the door.
   I came to the door.
   I stopped at the door.
   I stretched out my arm.
   I took hold of the handle, &c.

2. J'allai à la porte.[1]
   je m'approchai de la porte.
   j'arrivai à la porte.
   je m'arrêtai à la porte.
   j'allongeai le bras.
   je pris la poignée, &c.

3. Ich ging zu der Thür.
   ich näherte mich der Thür.
   ich kam bei der Thür an.
   ich blieb bei der Thür stehen.
   ich streckte den Arm aus.
   ich fasste den Griff an, &c.

4. Ad portam perrexi.
   ad portam accessi.
   ad portam perveni.
   ad portam substiti.
   brachium porrexi.
   portæ ansam apprehendi, &c.

---

[1] *Allai*, with the short closed sound (6) as *allé* (Trans.).

Instead of practising the theme in the first person, we may practise it in the second or the third, as already explained.

YESTERDAY—

1. Thou wentest towards the door.
thou drewest near the door.
thou, &c.

2. Tu allas à la porte.
tu t'approchas à la porte.
tu, &c.

3. Du gingest zu der Thür.
du näherest dich der Thür.
du, &c.

4. Ad portam perrexisti.
ad portam accessisti.
ad portam, &c.

The following remarks are suggested by this new exercise:—

1. The act is entirely distinct from the time, and the exercise may be entitled, "A past act in a definite period of time."

2. The time (yesterday) is perceived as a concrete reality.

*3. There is, not identification, but simply alliance, aggregation, association between the act and the period of time, in that the act is placed by the mind—that is, thought or perceived—in the period of time of yesterday, and not worked or welded artificially to abstract terms, such as past, perfect, definite, &c. In a word, the translation of the act in the time takes place directly, without any intermediary—that is to say, by "intuition."

When we consider the pupil to be sufficiently familiarised with this form, we shall substitute the period of time "to-day" instead of "yesterday," and what we have then to express will be, "A past act in an indefinite period of time."

TO-DAY (some time UP TO NOW not specified) [1]—

1. I have gone towards the door.
I have drawn near to the door.
I have come to the door.
I have stopped at the door.
I have stretched out my arm, &c.

---

[1] The unit of the "day" is taken here; it may, of course, equally well be the unit of the week or year—that is, this week, this year, my life (Trans.).

THE PAST PARTICIPLE.

Aujourd'hui (ce matin).

2. J'ai marché vers la porte.
   je me suis approché de la porte.
   je suis arrivé à la porte.
   je me suis arrêté à la porte.
   j'ai allongé le bras, &c.

Heute.

3. Ich bin zu der Thür gegangen.
   ich habe mich der Thür genährt.
   ich bin bei der Thür an-gekommen.
   ich bin bei der Thür stehen geblieben.
   ich habe den Arm aus-gestreckt, &c.

Hodie.

4. Ad portam perrexi.
   ad portam accessi.
   ad portam perveni, &c.

The lesson, as presented in French, will give rise to the explanation of the rule of the participle. In a very few moments the pupil will have seized the idea, and will apply it to the lesson of the verb without the possibility of being deceived. The German and English lessons will give rise to the rule of the formation of the participles, and of the displacement of the prefixes and auxiliaries. This lesson will, moreover, give rise to an observation which applies to most of the modern languages, and justifies our manner of presenting the conjugation, as follows:—

When the act took place in an indefinite period of time, a period not yet finished, it is expressed by two terms, an auxiliary and a participle—"I have opened." The auxiliary in this combination has the form of the present:—

I have, thou hast, he has. } Ich habe, du hast, er hat.
J'ai, tu as, il a.

I am, thou art, he is. } Ich bin, du bist, er ist.
Je suis, tu es, il est.

The participle is that which expresses a fact already accomplished (the past participle of the ordinary grammars).

This composite form presents a perfect harmony with the conception. Indeed, in the phrase, "to-day" (or this week, this year), "I have opened the door," the mind distinguishes at once two facts, to wit—

    1. The act of opening the door.
    2. The time in which this act took place.

The act is past, but the time, *to*-day, *this* week, *this* year, belongs to the present time, and the words "to-day" (or this week, or this year), indicate that this period of time is still before the mind's eye.

The auxiliary corresponds to the time, the participle corresponds to the act. The time is present, the auxiliary, therefore, has the form of the present. The act is past; the participle therefore bears the form of the past.

The verbal exercise of the ancient language will be the occasion of a remark in the contrary direction. The Latin tongue has only one form for the two periods of time:—

(Yesterday), ... Portam aperui.
(To-day, some time up to now), Portam aperui.

The ancients represented to themselves the grammatical time in a manner rather different from ours. It is for the teacher to explain the why and the wherefore.

The grammatical work of our two first weeks, as above set forth, represents a well-determined whole. It will be useful to write out the synthesis of what has now been done, and to present it to the pupil as a memento.

We have put forward the idea that the indicative is not, as hitherto imagined, a simple mood. What, then, should be the character of the part or the chapter that we have been dealing with? The verb varies its forms according to the nature of the periods of time in which the act takes place. It may well be that these forms vary also according to the conditions or the ways of taking place of this said act. An act may, in point of fact, occur separately, or in combination with some other act; it may be momentary, or it may be continuous; it may be casual, or it may be habitual.

If the indicative really does comprise divisions and subdivisions, no doubt they owe their origin to differences of this nature. It is upon these differences that grammar must attempt to base the subdivisions. The acts to which expression is given in our linguistic lesson are successive acts. They

MOMENTARY ACTS. 231

occur separately, one by one, and momentarily—that is to say, they do not continue. It is easy to draw from this a characteristic distinction for our first grammatical chapter. Here is the synthesis which we shall present to our pupils:—

INDICATIVE.
SIMPLE AND MOMENTARY ACTS.

YESTERDAY	I opened the door.
TO-DAY—	
Sometime up to now not specified . . .	} I have opened the door.
Just now . . .	I have just opened the door.
Now . . .	I open the door.
Presently . . .	I am going to open the door.
This evening . .	{ I am going to open the door. { I shall open the door.
TO-MORROW . . .	I shall open the door.
HIER	J'ouvris la porte.
AUJOURD'HUI—	
Ce matin . .	J'ai ouvert la porte.
Tout-à-l'heure . .	Je viens d'ouvrir la porte.
A présent . .	J'ouvre la porte.
Tout-à-l'heure . -	Je vais ouvrir la porte.
Ce soir . .	Je vais ouvrir la porte.
DEMAIN . . .	J'ouvrirai la porte.
GESTERN . . .	Ich öffnete die Thür.
HEUTE—	
Heute morgen . .	Ich habe die Thür geöffnet.
So eben . . .	Ich habe die Thür geöffnet.
Yetzt . . .	Ich öffne die Thür.
Sogleich . . .	{ Ich will die Thür öffnen. { Ich werde die Thür öffnen.
Heute Abend . .	{ Ich will die Thür öffnen. { Ich werde die Thür öffnen.
MORGEN . . .	Ich werde die Thür öffnen.

N.B.—We regard here the list of times as a simple grammatical indication; for this reason we construe "ich öffnete, ich habe," &c., instead of "öffnete ich, habe ich," &c.

HERI	Ostium aperui...
HODIE—	
Hodie manie . .	Ostium aperui.
Modo . . .	Ostium aperui.
Nunc . . .	Ostium aperio.
Jamjam . . .	Ostium aperturus sum.
Hodie vesperi . .	Ostium aperiam.
CRAS	Ostium aperiam.

This synthesis will not possess the disadvantage for which we have reproached the tables of the ordinary grammars. As a matter of fact, we do not begin by this synthesis—we end with it. We do not bring forth from this table the knowledge of the verb and of the conjugation; it is the table, on the contrary, which is the fruit of this knowledge. Abstract in itself, this synthesis is concrete by reason of its object, and can only carry us back to this object, which is the harmony between the forms of the verbs and our conception of the periods of time. If the echo is not the voice, neither is it an abstraction of the voice. In the portrait of a well-known friend, we do not behold an abstraction of this friend, but the image of this friend himself.

2. *Second Exercise—Continuous and habitual acts.*

Instead of happening in a fugitive manner and casually, the simple act may have a certain duration, and may be perceived by the mind, sometimes as continuous, sometimes as habitual, sometimes as "frequentative." In these various cases the act presents a constant character, namely, it persists, "it keeps on."

Every language has a special form to translate this character. One expresses it by lengthening the final syllable, another by doubling the initial syllable; one by an "augment," the other by an added syllable, another by a special form or auxiliary.

In English this character is expressed by the syllable ING, or by the locutions "I used to" and "I would," or by the tense which in most grammars is termed the "present indefinite;"

CONTINUOUS ACTS. 233

or in many cases (for the past especially), where the act is itself necessarily a durative one, by the form of the simple past, thus :—" I dwelt, I studied " :—

> Now-a-days I am studying Latin.
> Formerly I used to bathe before breakfast.
> When at the seaside we would often bathe at six.
> Now-a-days I bathe before breakfast.

In French, for past actions, the verb takes the final long AIS, AIT, &c. (that of the ordinary "imperfect") :—

> Il y av*ait* une fois un homme et une femme.
> Ils habit*aient* près d'un forêt. . . .
> Dans ma jeunesse j'all*ais* à la chasse.
> Au collège de Séez on se lev*ait* à cinq heures.

In Latin, the syllable "bam" is added to the root form of the present: "amo" becomes "amabam." The Greek prefixes an augment. In German, for past actions, the syllable TE is annexed (to the regular verbs), "strecke" becomes "streckte."

1. The act whose character is to continue may be taking place at the present time, or it may be perceived in the three periods of time—in a finished or definite period of time, in an unfinished or indefinite period of time, and in a future period of time. The following are the forms which correspond, when the act is simple and alone, to these times :—

> Last year   I studied Greek.
> this year   I have studied German.
> now-a-days   I am studying Latin.
> next year   I shall study Russian.

For French we have the following forms :—

> l'année dernière   j'étudiais le Grec.
> cette année   j'ai étudié l'Allemand.
> maintenant   j'étudie le Latin.
> l'année prochaine j'étudierai le Russe.

These examples in the two languages show that whereas in English there is a particular form to express the actually continuing act with the termination ING : " I am studying Latin ;"

in French (as in most of the Continental languages) the form for the present continuous act is the same as that for the present momentary act: "J'étudie le Latin."

2. The act may be frequentative—that is, a single short act, but happening often—in which case in English a different form is employed for the past act or acts, i.e., in the finished or definite period:—

Formerly	I used to bathe (or I would bathe) before breakfast.
Hitherto (up to now)	I have bathed before breakfast.
Now-a-days	I bathe before breakfast.
Henceforth	I shall bathe before breakfast.

In French the forms for habitual acts are the same as for the continuous acts.

Autrefois	je dînais à six heures.
Jusqu'ici	j'ai dîné à six heures.
Maintenant	je dîne à huit heures.
Désormais	je dînerai à sept heures.

This section of the indicative presents in French, in German, and in Latin only one original form. The question arises, How are we to apply this form to our lessons? How can we exercise ourselves in its use? To what artifice must we have recourse to give rational opportunity for its practice? We shall call it forth by putting a simple question, the following, for instance:—"Every day you have opened the door; now what did you habitually do to open it? Habitually what would you always do to open the door, or what were you in the habit of doing to open the door?" To which, in English, the pupil will reply (according to the form of the question)—

Habitually:
I walked (or I used to, I would walk) towards the door.
I drew near (or I used to, I would draw near) to the door.
I came (or I used to, I would come) to the door.
I stopped (or I used to, I would stop) at the door.
Then I stretched out (or I used to, I would stretch out) my hand, &c.

HABITUAL ACTS.

In French he would answer to either of these—

2. J'allais[1] vers la porte.
   je m'approchais de la porte.
   j'arrivais à la porte.
   je m'arrêtais à la porte.
   j'allongeais le bras, &c.

In German—

3. Ich schritt auf die Thür zu,
   ich näherte mich der Thür.
   ich kam bei der Thür an.
   ich blieb bei der Thür stehen.
   ich streckte den Arm aus, &c.

In Latin it will be—

4. Ad portam pergebam.
   ad portam accedebam.
   ad portam subsistebam.
   brachium porrigebam, &c.

We will now crown this short exercise as in the previous one, with a synthetical table.

INDICATIVE.

CONTINUOUS AND HABITUAL ACTS.

Formerly	I dined / I used to dine / I would dine	at six o'clock.
Hitherto	I have dined	at six o'clock.
Nowadays	I dine	at eight o'clock.
Henceforth	I shall dine	at seven o'clock.
Autrefois	Je dînais	à six heures.
Jusqu'ici	j'ai dîné	à six heures.
Maintenant	je dîne	à huit heures.
Désormais	je dînerai	à sept heures.

3. *Third Exercise.—Two acts occurring within the same period of time—Simultaneous acts—Imperfect, anterior, and posterior acts—Pluperfect acts.*

The phrase, "Yesterday my friend came in while I was eating my breakfast," is the expression of two acts, viz., to come in and to eat. These two acts are combined or connected by the

---

[1] With the long open *é* sound (Trans.).

conjunction "while." The word "yesterday" indicates the grammatical time in which these two actions took place, and "while" establishes their order of succession in this time. What name are we to give to the system represented by these two acts? We might name them conjoint acts, conjunctive acts, acts co-ordinated within the same period of time. We propose to use, as being most exact, the latter expression— "Two acts co-ordinated within the same period of time."[1]

When two actions occur within the same period of time, they may occupy therein, in relation to each other, four different positions. Two actions may, first of all, occur together, that is, they may be "SIMULTANEOUS," and under this condition three distinct cases may present themselves.

1. The two acts may be both continuous, and therefore develop parallel to each other—

  Yesterday, while I was dining, he was working.
  Hier, tandis que je dînais, il travaillait.

This relation may be graphically represented by two parallel lines, thus—

  ——————— while I was dining,
  ——————— he was working.

These two acts may be termed "Parallel Acts."

2. The two acts may be both momentary, and therefore occur at the same moment—

  Yesterday, as I closed the door, he arrived.
  Hier, en même temps que je fermais la porte, il arriva.

This relation may be represented by two points placed opposite each other, thus—

  • as I closed the door,
  • he arrived.

and the two acts may then be termed "Coinciding Acts."

---

[1] The passage following, as far as page 240, is developed somewhat differently in the original. Upon careful comparison of the two languages, however, the development given above seems to be the true one, the greater difference in form between verbs expressing long and short acts in English having served to show more clearly the psychological distinctions latent in the tense forms. The terms "Parallel, Simultaneous, Consecutive, Posterior, Imperfect, Anterior, and Coinciding Acts" have been proposed as indicating with exactitude the time relations expressed. The translation of the author's exact text is given for comparison in the Appendix.—(The Translators.)

CO-ORDINATED ACTS. 237

3. The two acts may be one continuous and the other momentary, still being contemporaneous—

  Yesterday, while I was dining, he arrived.
  Hier pendant que je dînais, il arriva.

In this case the continuous action had commenced before the other, and was still going on; the first action was not ended, was not completed, when the second began. Grammar seems to have discovered the true name of this first act, "Imperfect Act;" it receives the form of the continuous acts,—in English ING, in French the final AIS. We may represent this relation of the two acts by two lines, one of which begins before and ends after the other, thus—

  ——————————— while I was dining,
    ——   he arrived.

4. Lastly, if two actions do not occur together, one of them may, in relation to the other, occupy two different positions in time; it may follow it, or it may precede it. We may represent in each case these relations by two straight lines following each other, thus—

  Yesterday,
   after I had been dining, he arrived.[1]

  To-morrow,
    he will arrive   before I have been dining.

The terms Anterior and Posterior (expressing acts anterior or posterior the one to the other) therefore will apply to these acts. The term anterior is one already employed by the grammars.

If we now transport all these relations into definite (finished), indefinite (unfinished), and future periods of time, the following are the forms that we shall obtain, first in English and afterwards in French.

---

[1] In ordinary usage the distance of the time, either in the past or in the future, of the acts imagined and expressed, usually causes what may be termed a fore-shortening of the act; so that unless the length or duration of the act were important, we should use the forms: "Yesterday, he arrived after I had dined," and "He will arrive before I have dined." In cases where the duration of the act is important the above construction is used; as, "The doctor will test your lungs after you have been running" (Trans.).

ACTS CO-ORDINATED IN THE SAME PERIOD OF TIME.

A.—Parallel Acts (*both continuous*).
(To work and to dine.)

YESTERDAY	while I was dining	he was working.
TO-DAY	while I have been dining	he has been working.[1]
TO-MORROW	while I am dining	he will be working.

B.—Consecutive and Simultaneous Acts.

A Momentary act: to arrive, in relation to another act:
1. To a Continuous act: to dine. | 2. To a Momentary: to close the door.

YESTERDAY (Definite, or finished, period of time).
He arrived

	Posterior act.		*Posterior act.*
before	I had been dining.	before	I had closed the door.
	Imperfect act.		*Coinciding act.*
while	I was dining.	as	I closed the door.[2]
	Anterior act.		*Anterior act.*
after	I had been dining.	after	I had closed the door.

TO-DAY (Indefinite, or unfinished, period of time).
He arrived[3]

	Posterior act.		*Posterior act.*
before	I had been dining.	before	I had closed the door.
	Imperfect act.		*Coinciding act.*
while	I was dining.	as	I closed the door.
	Anterior act.		*Anterior act.*
after	I had been dining.	after	I had closed the door.

TO-MORROW (Future period of time).
He will arrive

	Posterior act.		*Posterior act.*
before	I have been dining.	before	I have closed the door.
	Imperfect act.		*Coinciding act.*
while	I am dining.	as	I close the door.
	Anterior act.		*Anterior act.*
after	I have been dining.	after	I have closed the door.

---

[1] For the time NOW, the two acts being both in this time, it is natural that they both take the form of the "present;" they have no special form resulting from the co-ordination—NOW, while I am dining, he is working. Further, the time NOW only enduring for a moment, two consecutive acts cannot take place within it. The time NOW, therefore, does not appear in the table.

[2] On certain occasions the same act, as already pointed out, may be considered either as continuous or as momentary, according to the circumstances. We shall thus have forms such as: "He arrived before I had dined," and *vice-versa*: "He arrived while I was closing the door." But it is not necessary to repeat these forms in the two columns.

[3] In English, these forms are the same as for Yesterday—the statement: before, while, or after, at once carries the two acts into a definite past period of time, in specifying the exact moment of to-day.

TABLE OF THE COMPOUND INDICATIVE.

ACTES CO-ORDONNÉS DANS UNE MÊME PÉRIODE DE TEMPS.

A.—Actes Parallèles (*tous deux continus*).

(Travailler et dîner.)

Hier . .	. tandis que je dînais . . .	il travaillait.
Aujourd'hui .	. tandis que je dînais . . .	il travaillait.
Demain . .	. tandis que je dînerai . . .	il travaillera.

B.—Actes Consécutifs et Simultanés.

Un acte momentané : **arriver**, en relation avec un autre acte :

1. Avec un acte continu : dîner.	2. Avec un acte momentané : fermer la porte.[1]

Hier (Temps défini).
Il arriva

	Acte postérieur.		*Acte postérieur.*
avant que	je dînasse.[2]	avant que	je fermasse la porte.
	Acte imparfait.		*Acte coïncidant.*
pendant que	je dînais.	en même temps que	je fermais la porte.
	Acte antérieur.		*Acte antérieur.*
après que	j'eus dîné.	après que	j'eus fermé la porte.

Aujourd'hui (ce matin) (Temps indéfini).
Il est arrivé

	Acte postérieur.		*Acte postérieur.*
avant que	je dînasse.[2]	avant que	je fermasse la porte.
	Acte imparfait.		*Acte coïncidant.*
pendant que	je dînais.	en même temps que	je fermais la porte.
	Acte antérieur.		*Acte antérieur.*
après que	j'ai eu dîné.	après que	j'ai eu fermé la porte.

Demain (Temps à venir).
Il arrivera

	Acte postérieur.		*Acte postérieur.*
avant que	je dîne.[2]	avant que	je ferme la porte.
	Acte imparfait.		*Acte coïncidant.*
pendant que	je dînerai.	en même temps que	je fermerai la porte.
	Acte antérieur.		*Acte antérieur.*
après que	j'aurai dîné.	après que	j'aurai fermé la porte.

[1] It should be noticed that in this table the forms of the French verbs are everywhere the same for the momentary as for the continuous acts.

[2] As is seen, this table includes certain forms of the conjugation which the grammars usually place in the subjunctive mood.

The employment of the tense termed the pluperfect (French *Plus-que-Parfait*) appears to us to be governed by the following conception:—

In the same way that the day now present, which we term "To-day," has been preceded by another day termed "Yesterday," and will be followed by another day termed "Tomorrow," so also any day which has fled, designated either specially, as "December 3rd," or in a general manner by the expression "a certain day," has been preceded by a day termed "the day before," and followed by a day termed "the next day, the day after." Hence we have the following table:—

>On a certain day (3rd December 1891, for instance) a sportsman killed two hares.
>PREVIOUSLY (THE DAY BEFORE, two days before that . . .) he HAD KILLED six hares.
>The next day, or the day after that (two days after that . . .) he killed two more hares.

>Tel jour (le 3 décembre 1891, par exemple) un chasseur tua deux lièvres.
>AUPARAVANT, (LA VEILLE, l'avant-veille . . .) il AVAIT TUÉ six lièvres.
>le lendemain (le surlendemain . . .) il tua deux autres lièvres.

So, in considering the act of dining upon any particular day as having already been accomplished, we say:—"On a certain day, at eight o'clock."

>already, I had dined.
>déjà, j'avais dîné.

These tables afford us the following new forms:—
In English—
>I was dining.
>I had been dining.
>I had dined.
>I have been dining.

In French we have six new forms:—
>J'eus dîné.
>j'ai eu dîné.
>j'aurai dîné.
>(que) je dînasse.
>(que) je dîne.
>j'avais dîné.

PRACTICE OF THE TENSE-FORMS.

The question now arises, How are we to adapt these forms to our language-lessons? We do it in a very simple manner.

1. The teacher will provoke the first by a question similar to the following: "Yesterday you opened this door; how did you do it?"

The pupil will reply, "First of all, I walked towards the door."

T. Well, and when you had walked towards the door, what did you do next?

P. After I had walked towards the door, I arrived at the door.
    after I had arrived at the door, I stretched out my arm.
    and when I had stretched out my arm, &c.

T. Hier vous ouvrîtes cette porte : comment vous y prîtes vous ?

P. D'abord je marchai vers la porte.
    après que j'eus marché vers la porte, j'arrivai à la porte.
    après que je fus arrivé à la porte, j'allongeai le bras.
    après que j'eus allongé le bras . . .

Or, in French the form might be used—

HIER je marchai vers la porte, avant que j'allongeasse le bras ;
    j'allongeai le bras, avant que je prisse le bouton ;
    je pris le bouton, avant que je tournasse le bouton ;
    je tournai le bouton, avant que je tirasse la porte. . . .

2. In English for the time TO-DAY the forms are the same as for yesterday (see table previously given) ; but in the French, to the question, "Aujourd'hui (ce matin) comment avez-vous ouvert la porte ?" the pupil will reply—

AUJOURD'HUI j'ai marché vers la porte ;
    quand j'ai eu marché vers la porte, je suis arrivé à la porte ;
    quand j'ai été arrivé à la porte, je me suis arrêté à la porte ;
    quand j'ai été arrêté à la porte, j'ai allongé le bras, &c.

3. To the question, "To-morrow how will you open this door?" the pupil will reply—

To-morrow I shall walk towards the door;
>after I have walked (*i.e.*, shall have walked) towards the door, I shall stop at the door;
>after I have stopped at the door, I shall stretch out my arm, &c.

In French, to the question, "Demain comment ouvrirez-vous cette porte?" he will reply—

Demain je marcherai vers la porte;
>après que j'aurai marché vers la porte, je m'arrêterai à la porte;
>après que je me serai arrêté à la porte, j'allongerai le bras;
>après que j'aurai allongé le bras, je prendrai, &c.

4. To the question, "Yesterday you opened the door, but *previously* what had you done to open it?" the pupil will reply, employing the form of the verb called the pluperfect:—

>Previously I had walked towards the door.
>I had stopped at the door.
>I had stretched out my arm.
>I had taken hold of the handle, &c.

"Hier vous ouvrîtes cette porte : mais auparavant qu'aviez-vous fait pour l'ouvrir?"

>Auparavant j'avais marché vers la porte.
>j'étais arrivé à la porte.
>j'avais allongé le bras.
>j'avais pris la poignée, &c.

When the pupil has thoroughly assimilated these new forms by practising them, he will be presented with the foregoing synthetical table. It is not necessary to repeat these examples in the other languages. It must be perfectly evident that the exercises can be practised in any and every language spoken.

The foregoing sections do not even yet exhaust all the forms of the indicative, but all may be equally presented according to the manner in which the facts or the elements of the facts are conceived by the mind. And it will be seen that this mood has not a single form which might not be exercised or conjugated naturally, and without abstraction, upon the lessons of the series.

Nevertheless, however effective these exercises may appear, our method does not remain content with this first elaboration of the forms of the verbs. It possesses, indeed, the secret or the means of rendering the conjugations permanent. This method consists in the continuous employment of the relative phrases or interlocutory sentences. By the use of these sentences both master and pupil will conjugate constantly without appearing to do so. Transposing, as occasion may require, their own thoughts in all the various grammatical times or tenses, they will be able to vary indefinitely, both regularly and irregularly, all the verbal forms of the expressions they employ. Thirty thousand relative phrases represent thirty thousand opportunities of practising the forms of the verbs. It is not too much to believe that whoever has accomplished this work will know how to conjugate.

STUDY OF THE VERB.

EXERCISES IN CONJUGATION (THIRD WEEK).

VII.

THE CONDITIONAL AND THE SUBJUNCTIVES.

1. *First Exercise—The conditional.*

To any first fact, real or supposed, the human mind has the faculty of associating a second. If the expression of the first represent a "condition," the expression of a second represents a "conditional fact." The two together form the object or material of what is termed in grammar "the conditional mood." For the reason that every man has the faculty of conjecturing and of associating one fact to any other fact, every language possesses a "conditional mood." The error would consequently be very great if any grammarian were to venture to deny the existence of this mood to any language whatever.

This mood may lend its form to another mood, or it may borrow them of this latter; but in itself this mood exists for the reason that it responds to an energy inherent in the human mind. Moreover, this mood is necessarily complex; it has to translate—

1. The supposed fact or condition.
2. The fact which rests upon this or is made conditional.

Without pretending here to exhaust the question, the above statement is seen to be true from the following forms of the conditional in English:—

YESTERDAY (Finished period).

If it had been fine . . { I should have played (or been playing).

TO-DAY (Unfinished period).

If it had been fine . . { I should have played (or been playing).

Now (Present time).

If it were fine . . . I should play (or be playing).

TO-MORROW (Future period).

If it were to be fine . . I should play (or be playing).

THE CONDITIONAL MOOD.

In French we have forms such as the following :—

                HIER (Temps défini).
S'il avait fait beau   .   .   J'aurais pêché.
            AUJOURD'HUI (CE MATIN) (Temps indéfini).
S'il avait fait beau   .   .   J'aurais pêché.
              MAINTENANT (Temps présent).
S'il faisait beau   .   .   .   Je pêcherais.
              DEMAIN (Temps à venir).
S'il faisait beau   .   .   .   Je pêcherais.

This table, therefore, presents us with the following new forms in English :—

        I should have played, &c.
        I should have been playing.
        I should play.
        I should be playing.

In French we have two only—
        J'aurais pêché, &c.
        Je pêcherais.

These forms will adapt themselves to our lessons of the series as easily and as naturally as those of the indicative have been found to do. You have simply to ask the pupil the following question: "If you wished to open this door, what would you do?"

And he will be obliged to answer you in what is termed the conditional mood, present tense—

        I should go towards the door.
        I should draw near to the door.
        I should get to the door, &c.

"Si vous vouliez ouvrir cette porte, que feriez-vous?"
        J'irais vers la porte.
        Je m'approcherais de la porte.
        J'arriverais à la porte, &c.

Put the same question to him again, simply replacing the idea of "now" by that of "yesterday" or "this morning," and you will be answered in what is termed the "conditional past." "To-day—some time up to now—if you had wished to open this door, what would you have done?"

Answer :—

I should have walked towards the door.
I should have drawn near to the door.
I should have got to the door, &c.

"Ce matin, si vous aviez voulu ouvrir la porte, qu'auriez-vous fait ?"

J'aurais marché vers la porte.
Je me serais approché de la porte.
Je serais arrivé à la porte, &c.

2. Second Exercise—The subjunctives.

What is usually termed "subjunctive" is a mood essentially complex. All the grammarians, on the contrary, seem to have determined up to the present to consider and treat the subjunctive as if it were a simple mood. Hence the inability of the grammar to formulate the law of the forms attributed to this mood, and to determine their usage. This expression: "I wish it may be fine" (je désire → qu'il fasse beau temps), is composed of two entirely distinct portions :—

1. To be fine weather.
2. To wish.

"To be fine weather" represents an objective fact; "to wish," represents a subjective fact. It is the alliance of these two facts which, properly speaking, constitutes a "subjunctive." This word "subjunctive" (joined beneath), therefore, expresses only half of what it really means. Hence the error of the grammarians, who see the "subjunctive" exclusively in the second part—"(that) it may be fine" (qu'il fasse beau temps)—of the whole expression.

The reader will not have forgotten our attempt to clear up the question of the subjective language, and, in particular, of the sentence termed by us the "enclitic." Well, what the grammarians designate by the word "subjunctive" is nothing more nor less than the object or material of our enclitic phrase. Now, of these two—objective and subjective—elements, which, think you, is it that commands and governs the other in the complete phrase ? Evidently the subjective element.

But this element is as diverse as the faculties of the mind are diverse. Therefore that subjunctive which requires one enclitic may easily be quite different from that subjunctive which commands some other enclitic. We come, therefore, to

THE SUBJUNCTIVES. 247

this conclusion, that grammar contains not one subjunctive, but several subjunctives.

The first thing to be done is to distinguish and to count them. We have previously said that the enclitic expressions could be and ought to be classified and distributed in categories. As many categories as may be found for the enclitics, so many different kinds of subjunctives will there be. We shall have, for instance, the Subjunctive of the Possible, the Subjunctive of Doubt, the Subjunctive of Desire, and so forth.

This work of classification does not enter into the scope of the present work. The reader will probably dispense with any deeper research into the theory of the conjugation. Let it suffice, firstly, to count the various forms which the grammars generally connect with the subjunctive mood; and, secondly, to show how they can be adapted to the lessons of our series.

The grammars accord the four following forms to the subjunctive in English :—

    That I open (or may open).
    That I should open (or might open).
    That I shall have opened (or may have opened).
    That I should have opened (or might have opened).

In French—

    Que j'ouvre.
    Que j'ouvrisse.
    Que j'aie ouvert.
    Que j'eusse ouvert.

1. If you put to the pupil the following question: "To open this door, what will it be necessary that you do?" he will answer by the subjunctive present:—

It will be necessary—
    that I walk towards the door.
    that I draw near.
    that I arrive.
    that I stop.

"Pour ouvrir cette porte, que vous faudrait-il faire?"
Il faudrait—
    que je marche vers la porte.
    que je m'approche de la porte.
    que j'arrive à la porte.
    que je m'arrête à la porte, &c.

2. If you put the following question: "Yesterday, to open this door, what would it have been necessary for you to do?" he will answer in what is termed the imperfect of the subjunctive:—

It would have been necessary—
> that I should walk towards the door.
> that I should draw near.
> that I should stop.

"Hier, pour ouvrir cette porte, que vous aurait-il fallu faire?"

Il aurait fallu—
> que je marchasse vers la porte.
> que je m'approchasse.
> que j'arrivasse, &c.

3. Put this third question: "Before opening the door, what will it be necessary to have done?" and he will reply in the perfect of the subjunctive:—

It will be necessary—
> that I shall have walked.
> that I shall have drawn near.
> that I shall have arrived, &c.

"Avant d'ouvrir la porte, que vous faudrait-il avoir fait?"

Il faudrait—
> que j'aie marché vers la porte.
> que je me sois approché de la porte.
> que je sois arrivé à la porte, &c.

4. To the question, "What would it be necessary to have done?" he would reply by the pluperfect of the subjunctive:—

It would be necessary—
> that I should have walked.
> that I should have drawn near.

Il faudrait—
> que j'eusse marché vers la porte.
> que je me fusse approché, &c.

Still less, perhaps, than with the indicative does our method remain content with these elementary exercises for the subjunctive. It has at its disposal some three or four thousand enclitic expressions. Care will be taken that these are not brought into play until both the enclitics themselves and the verbal forms they command are completely assimilated.

There need be no fear. By the use of the enclitic relative phrases the forms of the subjunctive will become as familiar to the pupil as those even of the "indicative mood, present tense," itself. There is no necessity to speak here of the imperative, nor of the infinitive, nor of the participle, the exercise of these three moods being permanent in the practice of the relative phrase.

We here end this too long chapter by the enunciation of two truths which manifest themselves from one end of it to the other:—

1. The grammar, so far as concerns the conjugation, may really become ONE, as the human mind is ONE.

2. No method, classical or non-classical, exercises or works the conjugation of the verb to anything like the same extent as does our own.

STUDY OF THE SENTENCE.

ELEMENTS OF THE SENTENCE, THEIR FUNCTIONS.

VIII.

SPOKEN ANALYSIS OF THE SENTENCE.

1. *Various functions of the terms of a sentence—The pupil's initiation into this knowledge.*

Syntax, as now understood, has for its object the study of the laws or rules of the sentence. In any sentence there are two things to be considered and determined :—

1. The functions of the constituent elements of this sentence.
2. The arrangement of these elements—ordinarily termed the construction of the sentence.

"Syntax" is, therefore, hardly a correct term, as it only expresses the half of what it really means. How ought we to study the first part, and how do we study it ?

Let us return once more to our theme of "Opening the Door,"—for what good purpose will it serve to change the example if the method of teaching remains, from the first exercise to the last, always identical ?

Je marche vers la porte.

When the teacher gives the lesson, this sentence is detached, as we have seen, from the rest of the theme; then it is concentrated for one moment in the verb "marche;" then it blossoms out finally, by unfolding or evolving from itself, first the subject and then the complement of the verb. But is this manner of presenting the phrase really anything else than an analysis—an analysis at the same time both grammatical and logical ? Will it be necessary, think you, to unmake and remake many such sentences before the student learns to distinguish the subject from the verb, the verb from its complements ? Where is the child who, at the first hour, at the first lesson, at the first phrase, will not comprehend this "spoken" analysis ?

The second sentence will then be decomposed, and afterwards recomposed like the first, and so with others. I repeat, the development of our theme, by reason of this mode of giving the lesson, is nothing else than a practical model of logical and grammatical analysis. The functions of each element of the sentences will themselves be studied as to their real signification, as soon as the time for it arrives, which will be whenever the pupil manifests the need of knowing them and of investigating the obstacles which he will not fail to encounter. To explain this more fully :—

In the first phrase, for instance, he will hear—

Je marche *vers* la porte.

In the second he will hear—

Je m'approche *de* la porte.

In one case he will hear "vers la porte," and in another "de la porte." In German he will hear "die Thür," and another time "der Thür;" in Latin he will hear in the same way sometimes "ad portam," and sometimes simply "portæ" or "porta." You may be quite sure that the child will be mistaken at first in the use of these terms, which will immediately lead him to ask the teacher the reason of their diversity. And if, by reason of an indolence happily uncommon, the pupil neglects to put this question, it will be the province of the teacher to provoke it.

An important problem is, therefore, put forward by the pupil, and the teacher will be led to explain to him that amongst the verbs some are complete in themselves and others are incomplete. "I sleep," for example, is a complete verb, because this expression is explained by itself and without recourse to another word; it translates in itself alone a complete situation, a complete state of being. "I go," "I draw near," on the other hand, are incomplete verbs, owing to the fact that their expression has not a finished sense, and requires to be completed by another word indicating "where" I go to and "to what" I draw near.

The class are thus prepared to receive the notion of complements, direct and indirect. The three fundamental complements are then brought forward, corresponding to the questions "what," "to what," "by what," put after the verb, and to each of these a numerical order is assigned.

   What?   First complement.
   To what?   Second complement.
   By what?   Third complement.

Then adding to this list the complements of place, the complements of time, the complements of aim, the complements of means or of manner, and the others, if there are any, we obtain a general framework which enables us to reduce to one page only, and to embrace in one glance, the fifteen or twenty chapters of the ordinary syntax. More than this, these categories being psychologically established, our framework will be capable of being adapted to any and every language, so that here again we shall have constructed a chapter of general or rather of universal grammar. The cause or the origin of "cases" and of inflections in those languages which have varied terminations is thus found to be quite naturally explained. There remains the question of teaching them.

2. *A starting-point and a direction.*

We shall ask the reader's permission to open this new chapter by a series of exceedingly elementary questions:—

Did the nurse of Horace learn off and repeat over to her little charge all the declensions of the Latin grammarians? Apparently not. Did Horace nevertheless manage to learn Latin? It certainly appears so. Did he speak it better and more fluently at four to seven years of age, and before having read the grammars and books of his time, than the cleverest of our classicists of thirty to forty years of age, who may have read the whole collection of Latin authors? Many will dare to maintain the affirmative.

Another example:—

Do the mothers of modern Greece begin teaching their babies with the Greek declensions? They would be extremely embarrassed if they had to do this. Do they always make a correct use of the cases? Probably not always. In spite of this, do the little Greeks learn to speak Greek as well and as quickly as the little English children learn to speak English? We have proof that they do. Do these Greek children speak better and more fluently at four to seven years of age, and before knowing how to read, than the most erudite of our philologists, who may know by heart the masterpieces of Greek literature? It is indisputable and not disputed.

Might it be possible to do better than Nature in this question of the study of languages? Perhaps. With the aid of the grammarians have we ever done as well as Nature? Never. Why not? And what process would it be necessary to adopt to do at least as well as Nature? That is the problem or the riddle which we have to solve.

The following is the order of procedure that the dialectic which has guided us in the solution of the anterior problems has shown to be best:—

1. To determine well the process of Nature.
2. To place the classical process and our own side by side.
3. To decide which of these processes most nearly approaches that of Nature.

IX.

THE COMPLEMENTS—CASES OR INFLECTIONS—DECLENSIONS.

1. *The art of declining out of school.*

How is it that the child before he has been to school manages to learn the cases, the inflections, the terminations—in a word, the declensions? Up to what point in this respect does what we have called the natural grammar carry us? Or is it quite by chance that this knowledge is acquired, and, consequently, is this labour susceptible of no explanation? Let us remark, first of all, that reason admits of no effect without a cause; therefore, in our judgment, the acquisition of the declensions and their practice in the every-day intercourse of life is certainly not the work of chance.

The "cases" serve to express a certain small number of relations of things one to another, which recur always and everywhere the same. The human mind grasps these relations very much in the same manner as it grasps the numbers; and in the same way that a person may be able to calculate without knowing figures, so he can apply, and does apply, the declensions without being acquainted with the written and abstract representation of the cases.

Man grasps these interrelations directly upon the facts

themselves, without any intermediary, that is, intuitively, and he expresses them as he conceives them, intuitively. That is how the child assimilates the cases, and how he familiarises himself with the various inflections of nouns and adjectives. Here occurs a phenomenon exactly similar to that which we have described with reference to the periods of time and the forms of the verbs in the conjugations, only instead of half-a-dozen periods of time, the mind can grasp a score or so of these interrelations. The child does this in playing without being aware of it and without apparent effort. We have in this, therefore, as for the application of the forms of the verbs, an operation essentially simple, and having in it nothing which puts us in mind, for instance, of those painful efforts necessary to overcome the difficulties of the first lessons in Latin at the grammar-school.

The *written* declension is the product of a subtle operation. To constitute this declension, it is necessary first to abstract the sign of each relation—that is, to detach it from the term to which it is welded; secondly, to consider and study this sign in itself; then to compare it with the signs of all the other relations; and lastly, to set in order and organise this general review.

Nature knows absolutely nothing of this operation—that is, of the art of declining. With the child and the uncultured man, the mind goes directly from the perception of the relation to the sign of this relation, and from the sign directly to the relation. He soon becomes very quick at this work, and very shortly sign and relation appear to him inseparable—as inseparable, in fact, as two halves of one and the same whole. In the one he sees the other.

By reason of this direct interchange between these relations and these signs, the mind actually acquires a new sense—the sense of interrelationships. We might even say, the intellectual substance comes forth from its native limits, spreads itself towards the external objects, reaches them, penetrates them, takes up a position between them, and connects them logically together. Hence the child's prodigious rapidity in finding, without apparent effort, the exact expression of each relation; hence this surety and this volubility of speech which we know not how to admire too much, and which it is absolutely necessary should be explained; hence, lastly, this spontaneity, at which the linguist who declines—that is, who never goes directly from the relation to the sign, that is, never attains the sign except in passing by the intermediary of the abstract table of a written declension—never does and never can arrive.

We have now revealed the process of Nature in its essentials; it remains to determine the degree of perfection with which Nature carries out her work. Let us, first and rapidly, sketch out the history of the interrelations and their signs.

In itself a relation between objects is a pure abstraction, and has no existence outside the terms which it unites. At first, therefore, the sign of the relationship was not separated from the terms of this relationship, but was fastened, welded to one of these terms, usually the first. It thus becomes placed between the two, a natural enough position for an expression acting as a connecting link. "Port-æ cardo;" *æ* is here the sign of relationship connecting *porta* to *cardo*, and this sign is seen attached to the first term—*port-æ*.

It might be said that the mind, conceiving with difficulty a relation apart from objective realities, could not resolve to grant it the right of being represented by a separate and independent sign, and consequently retained it captive and enchained to one of the two terms which it has a mission to unite. At this period the language would be under the dominion of the case or the inflection pure and simple—

> Italiam venit.
> Lavinia venit littora.

As it develops, the human mind experiences the need of a more severe exactitude and precision. The case-endings as signs gradually become too vague, too imperfect, too inconvenient; in a word, the "cases" are found to be insufficient. The relation between objects commences to play an important part in the sentence; it claims the right of being represented by a special sign, and Nature at last abandons to it those fragments of words and syllables that we are acquainted with:—*de, a, ab, e, ex, ad, sub*, &c.

The relationship then found itself enfranchised, and the preposition in some measure dethroned the case-ending. The ancient inflection was, however, maintained alongside this new sign, as if for witness of the first condition of the relationship and to recall its true character, "abstraction."

    ad port-am pergo.
    ad port-am subsisto.
    in pute-um se immisit hircus.

The relationship between objects then became possessed of two signs instead of one. It is to this era of language that the Latin language, amongst others, belongs.

Still later, one of the two signs was deemed superfluous, and, as such, condemned to be suppressed. The languages cast their useless baggage to the winds; the case-ending disappeared, and the preposition received the exclusive privilege of representing the relationship.

I go	towards	the door.
I draw near	to	the door.
I arrive	at	the door.
Je vais	vers	la porte.
Je m'approche	de	la porte.
J'arrive	à	la porte.
Ich gehe	nach	der Thür.
Ich komme	bei	der Thür an.

The languages of the first age have ceased to exist, at least upon the continent of Europe, and those of the third age refuse to recognise declensions. It is, therefore, to the languages representing the second age that what we have already said and what remains for us to say upon the subject of declensions applies.

If our historic idea is well founded, the case is a thing essentially decayed and variable—one, therefore, paying little respect to rules. This logical presumption finds itself amply confirmed by experience.

When speaking of the conjugation, we have put forward as an incontrovertible fact, as a matter of common observation, that neither the child nor the ignorant man makes mistakes in their mother-tongue as regards periods of time—that is to say, never confounds them one with another. We have equally demonstrated that the confusion of the forms of the verbs which are attached to these periods of time is also impossible. Is it the same when we come to the cases?

THE DECLENSIONS IN NATURE'S METHOD.

Go through those countries where almost every one knows how to read and to write—Germany, for instance; listen to the talk of the ordinary villagers from the school, and see if they are always quite sure of the use of the cases. Try to get hold of some of the letters written by the peasants in this language, of which the spelling is perhaps easier than that of any save Latin, and examine if the article, to say nothing of the other declinable words, is always treated according to the strict rules of grammar.

If you are at all observant, you will soon come to the conclusion that Nature is often at fault from the point of view of declensions; that she takes but little notice of the school teaching in this respect, and violates without scruple the most solemn dictates of the official grammar. In the rare regions, such as districts of Roumania, where Latin is yet spoken by the people, the most diverse terminations are either rendered through the nose with an obscure sound, or else crammed down the throat, and, as we say, "swallowed." In either case, their differences of sound are strangled or become confounded together in the vain sound of the fall of the voice.

This, then, is the avowal of Nature. She confesses herself fallible in the region of declensions; she avows herself clumsy in practising the "cases." But everything in Nature justifies its existence, and this appearance of clumsiness and of negligence possibly hides within itself for the pedagogue a most precious lesson. Let us consider for a few moments the proceeding which we have just pointed out. Let us attempt to extract therefrom the principles or the various teachings it may contain.

1. In Nature the mind passes from the relationship to the sign, and from the sign to the relationship, directly and without recourse to any intermediary. In itself, all relation between things is an abstraction; nevertheless, at the moment the mind grasps it, this relation becomes a reality. It borrows, so to speak, its existence from the two things it unites. It lives in them and by them. Consequently its expression represents something other than a mere void and empty abstraction.

What *is* truly abstract is this detached termination separated from its whole, and destined to stand for relationships which may be, but which are not yet. What *is* abstract is this *à priori* concept, this assemblage, this factitious scaffolding of terminations, termed the "declension." Here, again, Nature remains faithful to her eternal process; she works only on the concrete and real, and bears witness once again that she has as great a horror of abstraction as she was supposed to have of a vacuum.

2. Nature "practises" the cases; she does not decline; she takes no notice of any grouping made from the point of view of a declension. I repeat, she "practises" the cases, and this practice is constant and permanent. This exercise is not abandoned at the end of a month or at the end of two months to make place for another. It is continuous; it endures as long as the use of the language itself endures. And this exercise gives birth to a sense, the sense which we might call "the sense of interrelationships."

3. Nature never commences by the raw expression of a relation between objects; she attaches it first to the concrete part of the word, to its positive element. She never amuses herself, as does the school, by determining the expression of a relationship before being put into possession of the two terms of this relationship. In *portæ*, for example, *æ* is the sign of a relationship. *Porta* is one of the terms of this relationship, but where is the other term? This juggling with case-endings pure and simple is utterly foreign to Nature.

4. In itself the form of the inflection is transitory. Nature feels this, and treats this inflection as a thing merely accessory. Hence her negligence, and consequently her clumsiness in the use of the cases. Hence her indifference with reference to the solecism, and, I would say, her disdain for the grammatical thunderbolts it evokes. Hence this mobility, this instability of the case-ending, which becomes modified from one dialect to another dialect, from one river-bank to another river-bank, from one hamlet to another hamlet—which becomes changed from one generation to another generation.

It may be said that Nature roughs out the cases, and leaves to the school the trouble of perfecting the system and of regulating their usage. And if, indeed, the case has become anything at all, it is to the school rather than to Nature that this is due. The latter, on the one hand, points out to us the defect in her breastplate, and thereby, possibly, the means of vanquishing her; on the other hand, she teaches us to distinguish the essential from the accessory, to see in the play of the case-endings not an end but a means, and thus puts us on the alert against the attractions and the perfidious advances of abstraction.

Let us now develop, side by side, in parallel, and, so to speak, contradictorily, the two rival artificial processes—that of the classical school and our own.

2. *The art of declining at school.*

I do not think there can possibly be anything in itself more abstract than an inflection, a case-ending : *a, æ, am, æ, arum, as, is, i, um, o, u, ibus,* &c. :—

Ros a.   Ros æ.
Ros æ.   Ros arum.
Ros am.   Ros as.
Ros æ.   Ros is.
Ros a.   Ros is.

For myself, I cannot forget that I spent more than three months in trying to guess what it was that was wanted of me when I was told to study these figures under the form of letters. My teacher long despaired of his pupil. I confess my stupidity to a great extent gave him this right, in spite of the ardour of my zeal, and a desire to do well which nothing could discourage. Without having any comparison whatever in view, we might recall that the celebrated Alexander von Humboldt used to amuse himself by recounting how, up to his fifteenth year, his grammatical "fooleries" earned him the qualification of "dunce."

In reality, I fancy this is the history of all children condemned to pass through the wearisome phase of the classical declensions and conjugations. At college no pupil is despaired of, but he is usually riveted, in the name of experience to be acquired, fifteen or twenty months together (in the earlier forms) upon the interesting table of regular and irregular declensions of nouns and adjectives. Coming from this, the pupil finds himself sometimes capable of making a substantive and an adjective agree in gender, number, and case, and this brilliant result usually calls forth alike the joy of the teacher and his praise.

Let us speak the truth. However captivating for a man the right study of languages may become, let us frankly confess that the study of the declensions never had, and never can have, the slightest attraction for any one. Let us say further than this, that however the length and complexity of their table may be reduced, this work never becomes anything but a "torture." It is therefore by a torture—for this labour extends over two years at least—by an absolute torture that the classical school commences the study of languages—*Mala dulcis avi domum!*

Of a surety, it needs all the suppleness of the fibre of childhood to withstand such strains. Try yourself—you, a grown man or woman—to take your seat on the child's form and to study there, by his side, whichever language you please, by subjecting yourself once more to the method which is imposed upon him in order to learn Latin or German. Try, I say, and let us see how far your perseverance will take you.

To obtain this astonishing resignation from the child, there is but one way: to render him unconsciously an accomplice in the outrage thus directed against himself. This is the part that the school has learnt to play.

The declension, in point of fact, forms, as it were, a portal to the classical grammatical edifice. Now pupil, professor, and grammarian all alike work too long at this portal for the idea ever to come into their minds to put for one single moment a question as to its high value or its absolute necessity. If sometimes the shadow of a doubt comes to disquiet their faith in this respect, it is dismissed immediately as a suggestion of the spirit of error, or rather it is responded to by this proud and disdainful saying—*We* have learnt thus! Our fathers have always so learnt! Our children shall learn in the same way! Which is as much as to say, "No one can learn otherwise."

You are right, if your children are only required to know languages as you know them yourselves; then your resolution is wise, and the way is excellent; you may be assured that they will not outstrip you. And if it be determined, moreover, that it is absolutely necessary for them to learn the declensions by the process gone through by yourselves, we should be the first to counsel you in no wise to change the established order. For if you do not devote the whole of their childhood and the whole of their early zeal to this study, you may be assured that in later life they will seldom have the courage to undertake it.

According to our personal conviction, it requires more than

courage to devour this sweet morsel so cruelly spiced with abstractions; it requires the faith and the innocent inexperience of childhood. If at ten years of age you do not know the classic declensions, you stand a very great chance of never knowing them. Whether this may be said to the glory or to the shame of the art which prepares or the art which teaches the declensions, is a question which we need not, at this present moment, discuss; we content ourselves with stating a fact which the partisans of the ancient system themselves oppose to us as a principle.

We find, then, in the classical school all the efforts, both of teacher and of pupil, are concentrated upon the declensions. Any one would suppose that the whole language was contained therein. Ten years and more of his life are given to this work, and the pupil takes the shadow for the reality, and no one even thinks of forewarning him, or dares to undeceive him. If the declension is all, a solecism will be considered even worse than the use of a barbarism; and, in fact, the second is usually far from having the virtue of the first in exciting the thunders of the master.

The abstract—this is both the starting-point and the goal of the classical school. Nature, on the contrary, knows but the concrete, rests only upon the concrete, sees but the concrete. The school and Nature work, therefore, in exactly opposite ways. The first is always striving to make the river flow towards its source.

Let us now compare our process with the preceding one.

3. *Practice of the declensions in our system.*

From the very first lesson on our system the question of declensions is raised by the pupil himself, and the teacher profits by the occasion to determine the theory of the complements and to explain the origin of cases and of declensions. But he will put aside for a future lesson the task of organising the general table of the declensions, and designedly leaves to grow yet greater this desire of the child to know their usage in a more precise and definite manner.

Ordinarily, after the twelfth lesson all the possible case-endings have appeared. The hour has then arrived when the promised table may be drawn up. But who will construct this table, and where will it be taken from? Will it be copied out of the grammars? Will the teacher dictate it?

The pupil knows all the case-endings by having heard and practised them. Therefore the Case for him is not an unknown thing, nor an abstraction. Instead of borrowing the declension from such or such a book, it will be created piece by piece; and as all that the teacher does is simply to aid or direct, it will be the class themselves who carry out this work. Each pupil will henceforward comprehend and know to its very roots a table which is of his own construction. This table will be in no way an abstraction; it will respond, in fact, to a reality, it will represent knowledge previously acquired.

The table, once arranged, must next be used. The teacher will be the first to make use of it: he will refer to it when elaborating before his class each of the sentences, each of the exercises in the series which he is giving. Afterwards the pupil will himself take up these themes, and reproduce them by making use of the same table, rectifying his phrases by means of it in the same way as did the teacher.

An entire series is thus elaborated, two series, twenty series, the whole ordinary objective language. This is not all. Beyond the ordinary series, there are the Scientific Series and the Literary Series. We have stated, and shall shortly demonstrate, that the conceptions of the classical authors may be arranged in series and transcribed sentence by sentence on the model of our linguistic lessons. Now, over this creation at second-hand which we undertake with each work, this same table should preside. Not a sentence, not a phrase, which is not rectified according to this table, not an expression which is not subject to its control.

Is not this enough? Shall we have worked upon the declensions as long and as thoroughly as the ordinary school teaching? Do you think that our pupils will know them and be able to handle them as well as theirs?

Let us now say a few words upon the manner in which a table of declensions may be conceived and constructed, and we will apply our ideas to Latin. It must be borne well in mind that this question of the cases has been raised by the class themselves, and that the teacher is bound to join with his pupils in the search for the best possible solution. This process presents two advantages: in the first place, the pupil will take more interest in the subject; and in the second place, the solution arrived at will be graven upon his mind with all the characteristics of a personal discovery.

CONSTRUCTION OF TABLE OF DECLENSIONS. 263

The pupil has been led to distinguish two sorts of inflections —those of the terms which complete the verbs, and those of the terms which complete the nouns. He certainly will have the idea of separating these two kinds of complements. This distinction might be made by means of a bar, and we shall then obtain the first table in the following form:—

<pre>
          port—a
              æ
            ———
             am
              æ
              a
</pre>

Below the bar are placed the three endings that *porta* may take when it acts as complement to a verb or to a preposition; above the bar, the form which *porta* may take when it acts as complement to a noun, *portæ—cardo;* and on the first line the form which *porta* presents when acting the part of subject in a sentence.

We shall next indicate the function of each case-ending, and our table will become—

<pre>
    port-a   subject.
         æ   complement of noun.
         ———
        am   1st complement of verb.
         æ   2nd complement of verb.
         a   3rd complement of verb.
</pre>

The complement of a noun answers to the question "Of what (or whose)?" asked after the noun.

The complement (1) of a verb answers to the question "What?" asked after the verb.

The complement (2) answers to the question "To what?"

The complement (3) answers to the question "By what?"

We can again make these four questions figure in our table, which then takes the definite form—

<pre>
    What?   port-a   subject.
    Of what, whose?   æ   complement of noun.

    What?   am   1st complement of verb.
    To what?   æ   2nd complement of verb.
    By what?   a   3rd complement of verb.
</pre>

The plural will be constructed in the same way, and the whole of the first declension will be contained in the following synthetical table:—

TABLE OF THE FIRST DECLENSION.

a	æ
æ	arum

am	as
æ	is
a	is

This form is the one that would be adopted after two or three days of practice. The four other declensions will be collected into analogous tables, so that the five together might be held, as the saying is, "in the hollow of one's hand."

What advantages has this table over those of the ordinary grammar? In the first place, that of simplicity and of brevity. The pupil can and does embrace it in one glance.

A second advantage is its precision and its clearness. The bar that divides it in two reminds the pupil constantly that there are two kinds of complements, and therefore two kinds of case-endings. The grammarians seem never to have invented any method to enable the child to distinguish the flexion belonging to a complement of the noun from the flexions belonging to the complements of the verb. Whole weeks of explanation are therefore necessary to enable him to grasp the rule of the genitive case, "liber Petri" (Peter's book).

A third advantage is the natural order of the cases. I have often wondered, and I still wonder, why it is that in the ordinary grammars the ending destined for the first complement comes after that used for the second complement.

ros a
ros æ

ros æ, 2nd complement of verb.
ros am, 1st complement of verb.
ros a, 3rd complement of verb.

I confess I see no reason whatever for this inversion. Possibly, indeed, there is none. An insignificant detail, it will be said, a slight imperfection such as will happen anywhere.

Slight for you, perchance, but not for the child, who has thus to work amongst disorder, believing himself to be working amongst order. To put in the second rank that which should be in the first, to put in the first that which should be put in the second, what more likely than this to lead the learner astray? Could you do much more even if you wished to set a trap for his inexperience?

We have thus re-established the natural order, which is at the same time the logical order. In our table, the first complement comes first and before the second, and the second comes second and before the third. Here, certainly, is an innovation which has not needed any very great intellectual effort to make, and yet there is no one, so far as we are aware, who has said a word against the illogical arrangement here pointed out.

Our table commends itself, we think, also by the clearness of its terminology. We have replaced those surnames ending in *ative* and *itive* which usually no pupil really understands, nor can be made to understand, by expressions which we believe to be as exact as they are simple.

A final property of our table, and the most important, is that of reducing, as we have said, the whole syntax into a few lines. Syntax, in fact, has for its object the determination of the functions which devolve upon the terms of any sentence. Now these functions naturally find themselves determined by the very denominations which we have proposed.

"I give the poor man a coat." I give what? A coat (compl. 1), vestem. I give to whom? To the poor man (compl. 2), pauperi. And without any difficulty, and without hesitation, the pupil gives the phrase, "Vestem pauperi do."

"The shepherd strokes the dog's back with his hand."

He strokes what?—the back (compl. 1), dorsum.
He strokes to whom?—the dog (compl. 2), cani.
He strokes by what?—by his hand (compl. 3), manu.

And the pupil with the same surety (after a remark upon the Latin use of the third complement) produces the following phrase, "Dorsum cani manu remulcet pastor."

In what does the work of the teacher here consist? He aids the pupil in fixing the order of the complements, that is, in determining the true function of each term. Given the system of our series, together with our mode of teaching, and it can be seen that this work of syntax is perpetual in our language-lessons. It commences with the first sentence of the first lesson, and it ends only with the last sentence of the last series. Who, then, can accuse us of not teaching grammar? Can the school be named which at any time worked and practised the syntax to the extent that does our own?

4. *Parallel of the two processes.*

There are, therefore, two manners of teaching the declensions. Which is the best? To judge, we must compare them. The classical school puts the child to the study of the declensions before he knows what may be the object of this study and for what it may afterwards be of service to him. It is imposed upon him six months before he has need of it, two years before he puts it seriously into practice. With us, it is the pupil who solicits the explanation of the cases. The study of the declensions is, therefore, always premature in the classic school. It is not so with us, because with us the practice begins from the very first day.

Ad portam pergo.	ich gehe nach der Thür.
portæ appropinquo.	ich nähere mich der Thür.
ad portam pervenio, &c.	ich komme bei der Thür an, &c.

The pupil should know why it is that we find in one place *portam*, in another *portæ*, farther along *porta*.

At the classical school the pupil declines for the sake of declining. He learns, or thinks he learns, the declension for itself; he studies it, therefore, in a state of abstraction. With us it is in order to apply it immediately that he asks for it; it is in order to join it to something concrete, to realise it in the expression of an actual fact. There the declension is an end; here it is a means. There it is the form that exclusively preoccupies both teacher and pupil; here the essential goes before the accessory; the foundation goes before the form, as it does in Nature.

There, for term after term, the students dwell upon empty declensions. The child will decline and conjugate without truce or pity substantives, adjectives, pronouns; verbs—active, passive, neuter—and the rest, occupied solely with the termination, that is to say, with the accessory. With us, the explanation of the declension barely requires one hour. There, abstract tables, confused, badly arranged, are taken from the official grammars and imposed upon the pupil like so many dogmas. With us, it is the pupil himself who organises them, and the table represents in his eyes a synthesis—never an abstraction.

At the classical school, the declension is an intermediary which continually interposes between the perception and the expression of a relation between objects. The pupil never goes directly to this expression; he never reaches it save through the table of declensions. With us, he goes directly to the expression of the relation, applies it intuitively to the relationship which gives rise to it, then verifies it or rectifies it, if need be, by means of the table. The latter method finishes exactly where the former commences. With one, the student first speaks his thought and then corrects the form of its expression; with the other, he first of all manufactures a termination, then adapts it to his thought. The first operates intuitively, the second mechanically.

Which of the two processes approaches most closely to that of Nature, who, absolutely ignorant of the art of declining, goes directly, as we have said, from the relationship to the sign, and from the sign to the relationship—always practising, always working, upon the real and the concrete?

There is one objection which a good many persons formulate against our system; this is the proper moment to answer it. "You do away," they say to us, "with all the difficulties, and you leave nothing to the child's individual efforts. Afterwards let but the smallest obstacle occur, and he will dash against it and bruise himself. The mind must be hardened as well as the body."

We think so too; but we lay one condition thereto, that the mind in the end should overcome the difficulties and not succumb to them, for otherwise the best teacher would be he who was most incapable. Can we believe that defeat is the best school for victory?

We make the study of Latin too easy! What an objection! Our method makes the study of languages too easy! This is the old complaint of the stage-coach against the railway. Steam also has done away with many obstacles, has smoothed many rough roads, has even eliminated mountains. Is there lack of obstacles to-day? Has human energy become weakened from that day forth?

We make study too easy! Too fruitful, you mean. Is this a defect to cast in the teeth of a method? Do you qualify as bad a machine that will thresh a hundred sheaves of wheat an hour more than the ordinary threshing-machines? By the aid of the railway you can now accomplish in an hour what hitherto you could not do in a day. If with our methods you find you can learn in an hour what at present you cannot learn in a day, you would begin to think your faculties injured! You would think your means diminished, your forces decreased! You would regret the obstacles against which you used to exhaust yourselves in vain!

If, during the time you are wearily mumbling over one book of Virgil, we can assimilate this author entire, would you declare your work greater than our own, and more fruitful? For ten obstacles which your pupils have encountered on the way, and which have been for them the occasion of nine defeats, ours have encountered a hundred, which have been for them the occasion of ninety victories. Can you not decide which have taken the better way? We make the study of languages too easy! Does the lever destroy the power of man because it doubles the effect of each of his efforts?

Hitherto youth has exhausted itself in the study of one language; henceforth it may exhaust itself in the study of ten languages. Progress does not destroy the obstacle; it transforms it or shifts its position. However swift a scientific method may be, life will always be too short to discover all that is true, to see all that is beautiful, to learn all that is good.

Our duty is to gain knowledge by the shortest and easiest routes, and not to wander about after the fashion of the pilgrim, who imagines he is increasing his merits by wearing thorns in his shoes.

X.

THE PREPOSITION.

We have hitherto considered and dealt with the cases in themselves, apart from the prepositions, which are continually found joined thereto, and which, in appearance at least, govern

THE PREPOSITION.

them. Let us devote a few lines to the study of this element of the sentence, and explain how we practise them in our system.

The preposition is intimately connected with the verb, often even forming a part of it. It might be termed a detached morsel of the substance of the verb. It fulfils, with regard to the verb, the office of first body-servant. Its function consists principally in indicating the direction in which the action takes place, in defining exactly the point upon which it bears, in marking the end to which it tends.

Considered from this point of view, the preposition plays a very important part in the sentence, and in connection therewith we may put three principal questions to every linguistic method, and more particularly to our own:—

1. Does the preposition occupy a place in the method relative to its importance?
2. How does its assimilation take place?
3. How is its play upon the other terms of the sentence revealed and studied?

The exercises of our series reproduce, or may reproduce, all the acts and all the situations possible; it is therefore certain that the complete play of the preposition will be reproduced therein. So much in the first place. Moreover, the number of the prepositions is very restricted—as restricted, in fact, as the number of relationships they serve to express. These terms are therefore extremely general terms, an essentially current coinage, which, consequently, should be found everywhere.

Therefore, in the twenty-five phrases which ordinarily compose each theme of our series, there is plenty of room for their appearance; I will add, there is the chance for the greatest number to be effectively called up, and to be called up several times over:—

I go	towards	the door.
I draw near	to	the door.
I arrive	at	the door.
I stop	at	the door.
The door turns	on	its hinges
Je vais	vers	la porte.
Je m'approche	de	la porte.
J'arrive	à	la porte.
La porte tourne	sur	ses gonds
	&c. &c.	

If the verb occupies the first rank in our series, we may say that the preposition occupies the second rank. It has a right to this rank by the very considerable function it fills in the language as a determinative. Our method therefore accords it a place fully adequate to its importance.

How does the assimilation of the preposition take place? This problem is the immediate corollary of that which we have just solved in relation to the cases or the inflections of nouns. We shall not draw up, as do the ordinary grammars, an abstract list of these prepositions and of the cases they govern. No; this is an abstract work, a barren task.

We shall take them, we shall grasp these prepositions living; as living as the idea of which they are the embodiment; as living as the action of which they translate a phase; as living as the object upon which they rest; as living, in fine, as the organism of the phrases of which they form part. The preposition will be learnt in the phrase and by the phrase.

Will this assimilation be swift and will it be easy? Will it be swift? At the end of the tenth lesson the pupil will know them all. At the end of the twentieth he will make use of them with the same ease and the same surety as a professional philologist. He will know them, not in their definition—this is impossible—but in their sense or inner value, almost as one knows one's own personality without being able to define it.

Will this assimilation be easy? It will be as easy—I will say as instantaneous—as the conception itself of the relationships they express; and if these relationships are stamped on the mind, this assimilation will be equally stamped upon the mind, and will operate automatically.

This will be found difficult, you think? Possibly, for those who treat the preposition as a pure sign, an abstract sign, a sign deprived of its idea. In this condition I believe it to be not only difficult, but impossible. Count, indeed, the movements of the lips and tongue required from your pupil to learn these fifteen or twenty unfortunate syllables; and by the caricatures which usually grin at you from this wretched page of the school-grammar you may judge both of the weariness of the pupil and of the uselessness of the labours—always to be recommenced because always fruitless—with which he must periodically toil in this ungrateful field.

Will it be easy? you ask. We answer:—After the first week the preposition will be part of the very thought of our pupil, and it will be at the tip of his tongue as certainly as it is in his mind. It needs the heavy bandages of prejudice to prevent the reading of this conclusion in the mere state-ment of the premisses.

In those languages which have no declension, the preposition exercises no influence on the form of its complement. On the other hand, in the languages which have preserved the inflection, it compels its complement to take a particular and determinate case-ending. We have previously given the explanation of this double representation of the relationships. Whether this fact be due to the cause indicated, or whether it be the consequence of a real relationship of subordination, the result in practice is the same; we may say that the preposition "governs" the case in a similar manner to the verb.

We have spoken of the relationships that the verb sustains with its complements; we have mentioned how the mind goes from the one to the other, conceives the one in and by the other. The same theory entirely applies to the case before us. It applies to it even more directly than to the first case. In point of fact, the relationship contained within the ordinary verb is found therein in a latent state; it is enveloped therein, and is divined rather than seen—*Portæ appropinquo.*

On the other hand, this relationship becomes, so to speak, visible and tangible in the body of the preposition which is its special sign, its own particular expression—*Ad portam pervenio.* The play or the action of the preposition on its complement is learnt, therefore, like the rest, by force of practice; a practice direct and constant, from which in good time springs forth "Intuition."

The rule is the eggshell, destined to disappear as soon as the life shall have emerged.

XI.

THE PREFIX.

There yet remains for us to speak of one term which, by its form and its nature, must be considered as closely related to the preposition; perhaps it is even nothing else than this

preposition momentarily disguised. We refer to the "prefix."
In the greater number of the European languages the prefix
plays but a very minor part. German alone puts it particularly forward, and accords it a special and independent position
in the sentence. It is, therefore, in this language that it is
best studied.

The prefix is the sign of a sign; it is the instigator, or, if
you will, the prelude to another sign. It calls for, it provokes
either a *forte* of the voice or a gesture of the hand, commonly both, which begin the signification of the verb or which
finish it—
   Ich will die Thür auf-machen.
   Ich mache die Thür auf.

In these two sentences the hand and the voice aid, one may
say, the word *auf*, the one by the spontaneous movement, the
other by a special accent, the two dictated by instinct, or
rather commanded by the idea. This prefix is, therefore,
really the sign of a sign. As such, it is, in the true sense of
the word, "indefinable." It is a something that a book will
always be powerless to explain. The more the subject is
expounded, the less you are likely to comprehend. *An, auf,
ver, zer*, are signs so essentially abstract, so general, that they
no longer have any appreciable limits. There exist no other
terms more general that are capable of circumscribing them,
that is, of defining them. They are verily "indefinable."

There is nothing but a gesture or a modulation of the voice
that can render them. They do not represent a word, but
the fragment of a word, and of that the most intimate, the
most subjective, the most personal part of the word, namely,
the "accent," and in the accent the "intonation." There are,
therefore, only two means of manifesting the inner signification of the prefix—the tone of the voice and the gesture of
the hand.

Which is the method that has recourse to these two means
and which recommends them? Is it that which is based upon
the principle that a language can be learnt without a master,
or which condemns you to pick out this language piecemeal
from a dictionary, where it is not, cannot be, and never will
be? Try it and see.

The German language possesses about a dozen of these
terms. Well, these twelve syllables alone constitute an

obstacle which I take to be insurmountable by the usual methods—I repeat, "insurmountable."

Do you know in what—for the nations of the Latin race in particular—lies the difficulty in learning German? I can tell you; for I have waged over this ground a battle of more than three hundred days. I might possibly have been able to triumph over all other obstacles, but I succumbed, and I was bound to succumb, before that of the prefix. Combine these twelve or fifteen determinatives with the five hundred root words of the German language, and see what a formidable array the product of the composed terms will become. I struggled, therefore, practically against infinity; and he will equally have to struggle against infinity who does not attack the prefix upon the side which we shall now indicate.

The prefix is the most redoubtable rampart of the German language; but if you can once manage to conquer this, you will practically dominate all. The same may be said of Greek with its prepositions, which we regard as veritable prefixes. These two languages are two impregnable fortresses with the ordinary means. German is equal to Greek, and Greek equal to German, as languages which cannot be assimilated by means of the dictionary and the grammar. And yet these two languages, Greek and German, so rebellious to all the efforts of the classic school, should be, and in reality are, two of the easiest languages for European nations to learn.

If, indeed, their words may be composed and decomposed at will, this simply proves that the elements of these words are still distinct, while in other languages the most diverse elements are mixed and confounded together, and often absolutely unrecognisable. In such languages, each separate term has to be conquered as an original term, *sui generis*, and there are some thirty thousand or more of them. Whereas, in the former, it is sufficient to know a small number of elementary words, with the secret of their combinations, to know them almost all.

Let us base these generalities on facts and figures. We have said elsewhere that the expression of the objective language experienced by a human individuality—yours or mine—might be written out in a book of some four thousand pages. Now if a person had studied in French the first three thousand pages, we would not, therefore, guarantee that he could correctly express and understand the last thousand. But, on the other hand, experience has abundantly shown us that he who has gone through the first two thousand of our themes in Greek or German is then perfectly able to express and understand the other two thousand.

It is a remarkable fact that the pupils who have studied with us in Greek even the first eighty themes of our Series of the Shepherd find themselves all at once able to understand the Greek authors at first sight, while a person who has gone through the same themes in French is yet unable to decipher thoroughly even the easiest of the French writers. To what is this due? Evidently to the difference in the constitution of the two languages.

The constitution of a language depends in great measure upon the part to be played therein by the prefix. Our eighty themes represent a total of two thousand phrases. Now these two thousand phrases, inasmuch as they express the most elementary situations, movements, and acts of life, must contain, or very nearly so, all the roots of the language. They contain, besides, and necessarily, all the prefixes—the prefixes wedded to the roots, and forming with them the greater part of the alliances and combinations of which they are capable. Let the art of teaching make of this raw material the same use that Nature knows how to make, and the phenomenon which we have just stated will explain itself.

In fact, in the course of these eighty themes the pupil certainly has the opportunity of familiarising himself with the two essential and constituent elements of the language; he very soon finds himself able to work upon this material by himself, and from it form new combinations capable of expressing the rest of his own individuality. So much said, how are we best to teach the use of the prefix?

The prefix, let us remember, is a sign which provokes either a raising of the tone of voice or a gesture of the hand, both of them for the purpose of either commencing the signification of the verb or of completing it.

    Ich drehe den Griff *um*,
    Ich will die Thür *auf*-machen,
as in English—
    I turn the handle *round*,
    I will pull the door *to*.

Considered thus, the prefix, like the preposition, is part and parcel of the verb. As such, it will partake with the verb in the ruling position accorded by us to the verb in the sentence. But it is not only in our written system that the verb occupies a privileged place; it is above all in the oral expression of the lesson and of its sentences. The prefix marching always side by side with the verb, will share the same advantages; it will be given forth, proclaimed separately, along with the verb or as part of the verb, and we shall take pains to define it separately with a gesture of the hand or an emphasis of the voice. That is our manner of teaching or of translating the prefix.

Our elementary Series of the Shepherd, as we have said, contains two thousand sentences; this alone, therefore, offers us two thousand opportunities of producing this translation of the prefix by accent or gesture. Worked upon in this manner, does the prefix require many weeks to be assimilated by the mind? Will its virtue and its inner sense long escape the intuitive perception of the scholar?

Have you never wondered how it is that the German child manages to solve the twelve formidable enigmas set to him, continually and in rivalry with each other, by the twelve sphinxes which reign as autocrats over his mother-tongue? Observe him attentively, and you will see that accent and gesture are the only interpreters to which he has recourse—gesture, which "points" or figures the action; and accent, which imprints upon it a definite character.

The constitution of our series, the form of our lessons, our mode of teaching, all permit us not only to practise the prefix as Nature practises it, but to practise it even better than Nature can do.

STUDY OF THE SENTENCE.

CONSTRUCTION.

XII.

TWO SORTS OF CONSTRUCTION—NATURAL ORDER AND LOGICAL ORDER.

The materials are now all before us, properly trimmed into shape; we have nothing further to do but construct. Two styles offer themselves to us, the antique style and the modern style. Will our method adapt itself better to one than to the other of them, or will it accommodate itself equally well to both? Let us see, first, in what each of these two constructions consists.

In the very ancient languages every term employed to complete another term was placed before this other. Instead of saying, for instance, "upon the table," they said "the table upon." The modern languages still present certain vestiges of this archaic construction. In English we have "thereon, thereby, therein," &c., and in French the words "là-dessus, là-bas, là-dedans," &c., are composed according to this rule. It is this ideal which, to a considerable extent, governs the Latin sentence. The Roman said—

   Ad portam pergo, To the door I go,

and not

   Pergo ad portam, I go to the door.

Here, then, we have the antique order: I call it the "natural order." It is, in fact, more natural than the other. It begins by the determinate to finish by the indeterminate. Consequently, the expression remains concrete from the beginning to the end. Greek, according to this rule, is not as ancient in its method of construction as Latin. Its construction is almost that of modern languages.

If the verb is loaded with several complements, the order to be followed in the distribution of these complements is that presented by our general table of declensions. Write down first of all the first complement, continue by the second, and finish with the third :—

"Dorsum cani manu remulcet opilio."

To the rule we have just enounced it is necessary to add a second commanded by cadence and harmony, and with which the first is often obliged to enter into combination. The adjective will be separated from its substantive by one or several terms :—

"Tityre, tu patulæ recubans sub tegmine fagi,
 Silvestrem tenui musam meditaris avenâ."

By this arrangement the phrase presents itself in harmoniously balanced periods, and it avoids the continuity of monotonous consonances.

Such are the rules which preside over the construction of the antique phrase. Their application is as easy as their exposition is simple.

Modern construction obeys a principle diametrically opposed to that of the ancients. Every term which completes another is placed after this other. This rule, it must be noted, is no more absolute than the first, but it is the ideal towards which the modern sentence visibly tends :—

I go towards the door,

and not

Towards the door I go.

This inversion is only permissible in poetry, precisely for the reason that poetry especially seeks for archaic forms of expression. Cadence and harmony are here again admitted to their full rights, and the dominant rule is not always rigidly applied.

The term "logical" seems to us to characterise the order which presides over the construction of the modern phrase. Here the word which is most indeterminate is the starting-point, and the phrase as it develops proceeds by determining it more and more precisely. In the phrase, "I go towards the door," "I" is completed or determined by "go," and "go" is completed or determined by "towards the door"—"I go towards the door." So in French—"Je vais vers la porte." When the verb has several complements, it is usually the cadence or the harmony which decides their place.

The languages in which the prefix plays an important part,

as German (and, to a minor extent, English), should possess, and in fact do possess, a construction of their own. German presents four species of expression:—

1. Those in which the verb has either no prefix at all, or in which it is welded thereto as an inseparable prefix:—

   Ich öffne die Thür.
   Er zerbricht Holz.

In this case the sentence is constructed according to the "logical" order.

2. The phrases in which the verb carries a separable prefix:—

   Ich mache die Thür auf.

In this case the two parts are separated, and enclose between them, as in a frame, all the complements of the verb. Regarded closely, it is the logical order which presides over this construction. In reality, "auf" is nothing else than a determinative of "mache;" as in English, "I pull the drawer *out*," "I lift the jug *up*."

3. The phrases which are commanded by an enclitic verb:—

   Ich will → die Thür auf-machen.
   Versuchen Sie → die Thür auf-zu-machen.

There are in this case two verbs in the phrase, and all the complements are enclosed or enframed between them. This form is a compromise between the antique construction and the modern construction. The enclitic is in the place which it should occupy in a modern sentence, but the second verb, "auf-machen," is preceded by its complement, "die Thür."

4. The phrases which occur introduced by a conjunction:—

   Wenn ich die Thür auf-mache.
   Wenn ich die Thür auf-machen will.

These constructions partake more of the antique than of the modern form. In the above phrase "will" is preceded by its complement "auf-machen," and "auf-machen" is preceded by its complement "die Thür." The entire phrase is enframed between the conjunction "wenn" and that of the two verbs which has a personal form, "Ich will."

These are the four types of construction which a German sentence can present. If we add to these four that in which some complement usurps the place of the subject, or in which

CONSTRUCTION BY THE CLASSICAL PROCESS. 279

this subject leaps by way of the verb to re-establish the balance, as—

Die Thür will ich auf-machen,

we shall have exhausted all that we have here to say upon the construction of German.

XIII.

PRACTICAL STUDY OF THE CONSTRUCTION IN AN ANCIENT OR MODERN FOREIGN LANGUAGE.

We have just seen that the Latin phrase is constructed in a different form to the French or English phrase, and the German phrase differently to either of these two types. The man, therefore, who has never spoken any other language than, say, English or French, is incapable of constructing properly a single phrase in either Latin or German, even if he is in possession of all the elements of those languages. Consequently, if he wishes to learn one of those languages, what is required of him is that he should study the construction of the phrase in this language itself. So far as regards our mother-tongue, each of us has learnt the construction directly while learning to think, and we apply it intuitively. Our own language is not, therefore, the place to study it, at least with the view of its practical application. Hence the problem in question may be formulated as follows :—A pupil is accustomed to think and to speak according to the "logical" order; to what exercise must he submit himself in order to learn to think and to speak with the same facility in a foreign language in which the phrase is constructed according to the "natural" order? The classical school possesses, or believes it possesses, a solution to this problem; our method proposes a new solution. Let us compare them.

1. *Construction by the ordinary process.*

We will suppose that the lesson to be given in class is one of the Eclogues of Virgil :—

"Tityre, tu patulæ recubans sub tegmine fagi,
Silvestrem tenui musam meditaris avenâ.
Nos patriæ fines et dulcia linquimus arva,
Nos patriam fugimus : tu Tityre, lentus in umbrâ,
Formosam resonare doces Amaryllida silvas. . . ."

The classical school brutally uproots the sentence from its surroundings to submit it to a species of anatomical dissection. It breaks it up without pity, or at least pulls it to pieces like a child its toy; then, replacing its elements in the logical order, makes therefrom a modern phrase. This is what is called construction:—

"Tityre, tu recubans sub tegmine fagi patulæ,
Meditaris musam silvestrem avena tenui,
Nos linquimus fines patriæ et arva dulcia;
Nos fugimus patriam; tu, Tityre, lentus in umbra,
Doces silves resonare Amaryllida formosam. . . ."

To teach the antique construction the school destroys it, makes it disappear, and substitutes in its place the modern construction. I ask if this is really the means to familiarise the mind with the Latin construction? I ask, how many years are needed to be able, by this strange proceeding, to follow intuitively the natural order—to apply intuitively the antique form of construction? Instead of bringing the logical order back into the natural order, you force the natural order into the form of the logical order. Were ever means and end more contradictory? As well might one, as some one somewhere has said, practise balancing a chair on the tip of one's nose in order to strengthen the arms.

In thus reading Latin the wrong way round, in speaking it, in writing it the wrong way round, I do nothing but weave the web of Penelope. It is quite evident that by so doing I shall never be able to thoroughly learn this language, which is, nevertheless, one of the easiest of all languages ever spoken on the face of the earth. Nay, further, the more I read it, the more I speak it, the more I write it in this way, the less shall I know of it.

For observe, between my thought and the antique form of this thought you again place an intermediary. I am obliged to reach the antique construction by way of the modern construction. You condemn me to construct the natural order out of the logical order, which is as much as to say to manufacture light out of darkness. Instead of clearing away all obstacles which might hinder my thought from going straight to its expression, you vastly increase them.

No! never—however much I work, I should never know Latin; this language would never become for me a natural organ of my thought; never would one of its books bring up before me the true soul of the author; never will the beating of his heart quicken mine. Virgil, Cicero, thus dessicated, can never be other than dry bones—corpses!

This is whither the methods of the classical school lead us. Let us see where our own will lead.

2. *Construction by our method.*

From the very first lesson, from the very first sentence, we put before the pupil the antique construction; we force him to think according to the natural order, and to accommodate his phrases to this new manner of imagining things. Let us try this first of all upon one of our series, and let us take yet once more our old exercise, "Ostium aperio."

The teacher gives the first word, *pergo*. Then attacking the phrase by the complement, and making it start into life by the gesture of his hand and the accent of his voice, he says—

  Pergo.   Ad ostium pergo.

Have we not here both analysis and synthesis? Analysis when the master, dividing the sentence into two parts, sets the verb by itself; synthesis when he builds up around this verb the complete phrase and allows it to blossom forth as upon its natural stem.

appropinquo	Ad ostium appropinquo.
pervenio	ad ostium pervenio.
subsisto	ad ostium subsisto.
apprehendo	ostii ansam apprehendo.
torqueo	ostii ansam torqueo.
recludo	ostium recludo.
vertitur	cardinibus vertitur ostium.
stridet	cardinibus stridet ostium, &c.

Here, then, is no intermediary between the idea and the antique form destined to translate and to manifest it; no construction after the fashion of modern speech. Here it is directly, and without recourse to any mediator, that the idea goes to the form, and that the form comes to the idea and adapts itself to the idea. Of anatomical dissection there is none. As soon as the phrase issues from the mouth, it is living. It lives already in the verb, which is the abbreviation of it; and it is thence, as from a focus, that the Promethean spark springs forth to animate its various members and complements. With us the phrase never appears in the state of a corpse, and a corpse, moreover, cut up into pieces as in the word-for-word or interlinear translations of the classical school.

And nevertheless all is distinct in our sentence. It is a team in which the various guiding reins never get mixed. We owe this advantage to the elevated and firm seat in which we have been able to place our charioteer, "the verb."

The first part, we think all will confess, is gained: the master has made his class think in Latin; he has initiated them into the secret of the antique construction; he has familiarised them with what we have termed the natural order of the words. More than this, the scholar has, without knowing it, deserted the logical order—the form to which his thoughts are habituated—to follow the natural order, a form contrary to his habits of thought. A few more exercises and the pupil will no more be able to construct his sentences otherwise than could the ancients themselves. He will not seek for the antique construction; he will apply it by instinct.

From the first series you will lead him to the second, from the second you will conduct him to the third, and when all the complements possible have found opportunity to manifest themselves and to play their part around the verb, when the pupil possesses that basis of the language of which we have so often spoken—then open Virgil, and, going from sentence to sentence, sow the verbs (or their substitutes) first. From this seed will ripen the brilliant harvest so highly prized. Your scholars shall gather it sheaf by sheaf, and this book shall be for them no more a barren field. Virgil will no longer be for them what he was for us, "a dead body."

recubans	Tityre, tu patulæ recubans sub tegmine fagi,
meditaris	silvestrem tenui musam meditaris avenâ.
linquimus	Nos patriæ fines et dulcia linquimus arva,
fugimus	nos fugimus patriam.
(lentus)	Tu, Tityre, lentus in umbrâ,
resonare	formosam resonare doces Amaryllida silvas.

The classic issues absolutely intact from this operation. It is neither mutilated nor violated by the book in a horrible word-for-word translation, nor is it disorganised nor massacred by a wordiness without shame and a knowledge without taste.

The smallest blemish, the slightest scratch of the sacred text is spared. The length of the typographical line is the sole thing we do not consider ourselves bound to respect. It cannot be here a question of verse. When the pupil has heard the text, he will be able to open the ordinary edition and therein scan the syllables at will. We would, however, point out that even the versification is only deranged typographically.

It must, of course, be thoroughly understood that the reading of the classics only comes *after* the study of the series proper. One is the necessary condition of the other; it prepares for it as the expression of the facts of ordinary life prepares the child for the immediate and fluent reading of the books of his mother-tongue. He who passes from the grammar direct to the literary masterpiece is forced to have recourse to the anatomical dissection commonly known as "construing" or "word for word" translation.

The solution of the problem which we have presented is the natural product of the general mechanism of our system—a product, indeed, so natural that one would hardly even suspect that there is here a formidable difficulty vanquished. This solution is, as it were, the resultant of all the principles which lie at the root of the system. It follows from the central idea of the series, from their inner construction, from their written and spoken form. It is the immediate corollary of the axiom which has raised the verb to the first rank in the phrase.

This verb, which allows the sentence to fold itself up, to gather itself together, to contract itself, to force itself into one single term, afterwards to expand itself to make all the various complements that it encloses spring forth—the verb plays in the sentence a part that is not without analogy with that of the heart in the human body.

It is this double movement of contraction and expansion which our method of teaching can enable the sentence to make that explains the easy triumphs of our method, as it explains elsewhere the miracles of life. No matter what language we take, or under what form a phrase occurs, if there is a verb in this phrase and if there are complements, these complements must come either before or after the verb. We have shown that our process accommodates itself as well to the one as to the other. It is therefore applicable to all languages.

THE MODAL PHRASES.

XIV.

CLASSIFICATION AND PRACTICE.

1. *Definition of the modal phrase—Its constituent elements—Their relations.*

When, in our school-days, we dealt with phrases such as the following:—

I think you are crying,	Credo te flere,
I think that he is reading,	Credo illum legere,
I think that he has read,	Credo illum legisse,

   Je crois que vous pleurez,
   je crois qu'il lit,
   je crois qu'il a lu,

we dealt with "modal phrases." When we recited the rules of

   Suadeo tibi ut → legas,
   Timeo ne → præceptor veniat,
   Cave ne → cadas,
   Dignus est → qui imperet,
   &c., &c.

we were still elaborating "modal phrases."

Various writers have special names for these syntactical forms. The modern grammars usually content themselves by attempting a rule or a definition of what is understood by the word "subjunctive," and refer for particular cases to the dictionaries. A treatise therefore remains to be written which should comprise the complete series of the locutions analogous to those just given, and which would classify them according to a rational principle.

The modal phrase is always composed of two distinct parts, each part with its own verb, but one of them subordinate to the other. The part which governs the other usually expresses a mental fact, an attitude of the mind either active or passive.

I think that →	you are crying.
I advise you →	to read.
I am afraid that →	the teacher will come.
Take care →	not to fall.
He is worthy →	to command.
That will make you →	reflect.

The first part is nothing else than an enclitic relative phrase. The second part expresses some fact appertaining either to the exterior objective world or to the interior subjective world. To which of these two parts should the name of "modal" be applied?

The first is "modal" in so far as it decides the "mood," that is, the form of the second, and the second is "modal" in the sense that it clothes this form. But that one of the two which is the determining cause of the mood, that is, the first or enclitic phrase, is the true modal phrase, and to it this denomination is here applied. The two elements of the complete modal phrase are welded the one to the other either by a preposition or by a conjunction. The conjunction, therefore, forms part of the modal phrases, and cannot, consequently, be the object of any special theory.

2. *Establishment of the moods—Vicious circle of the classical school—Our process.*

In the chapter upon relative phrases we first of all determined the intrinsic value of the enclitic and the part which it plays in the language; then we sought a practical means of teaching it. But that which constitutes precisely its character of "modal," that is, its particular relations with the subordinated sentence, yet remains for us to study. In other words, the enclitic has been dealt with as "enclitic," and not yet as "modal." What will be the best manner of procedure in this new study? Let us examine first of all how the ordinary grammars proceed; and we must here ask the reader to permit us the necessary recapitulation.

The distinct terminations special to the moods known as "subordinate" have first been counted; then the attempt has been made to put them in order. As the basis of the order desired, the grammarians have adopted, not a real principle, but a vain symmetry. We have already stated what confusion may be engendered by a conception so narrow, a starting-point so badly chosen as this.

The ordinary grammar draws up at once and *à priori* the system of conjugations of "subordinate" moods; then a hundred pages or so later it will treat of "modal" or subjunctive phrases. These phrases are divided into some ten groups, and each group is based upon one of the forms of the pre-established conjugation. The modal phrase is thus subordinated to a form of conjugation; the cause is subordinated to the effect, resulting in a wandering round and round with the fullest confidence in the most perfect of vicious circles. Hence these perpetual contraventions of rules and these interminable lists of exceptions.

Our process will be the exact reverse of that adopted by the classic school. Where, indeed, does the first cause of the subordinate moods reside? Is it not in the idea expressed by the modal phrase? Is it not the modal phrase which "governs" in one place the subjunctive, in another place the conditional, elsewhere the imperative or the supine?

We shall commence, then, not by arranging the inflections in paragraphs, but by classifying the modal phrases. We shall then determine the mood to which each of our established classes corresponds. It may very well be that a single form serves two different moods. If so, we shall state the fact, we shall explain it if we can, but we shall guard ourselves from distorting it by any attempt to reduce "two into one." It may equally happen that our moods thus deduced do not agree, either as to their number or as to their form, with those of the usual grammars. We shall not attempt to reconcile the two systems; the starting-point being changed, the destination will also be changed.

3. *Ordinary practice of the modal phrases and the moods—Our process.*

The moods once established and organised, it remains for us to exercise them, to practise them. How does the classical school acquit itself of this task? It places before the pupil eight or nine types of modal expressions; then, dictating to him a set of detached phrases, says to him, "You are to make each of these phrases into one of the types consecrated in

ERRORS OF THE ORDINARY PRACTICE. 287

your grammar, and you will do this in such a way that your phrase shall agree exactly with its model."

Always the same process, and always the same faults.

1. This work is *written* instead of being oral.
2. An intermediary is placed between the idea and its expression.
3. The intellectual operation is mechanical instead of being intuitive.

The multifold criticisms of which this process has been the object in previous chapters will absolve us from insisting here upon the fundamental vice which condemns it to utter barrenness. As to our own process, we have set it forth at length in the chapter upon enclitic phrases. To this chapter we refer the reader.

ANNEXES AND COROLLARIES OF THE SYSTEM.

I.

THE ORTHOGRAPHY—SPELLING.

Orthography has for its object the written representation of the terms of a language. The greater portion of these terms are formed of two distinct parts, namely, an invariable element named the "radicle," and a variable element termed the "inflection" or termination. The radicle can only be learnt by the eye. To read and read, to write and write, over and over again, that is, to look at or retrace by the eye the representation of speech, these are the sole means of learning the spelling of this first part of the words. The termination is a more or less conventional thing. As such, it is susceptible of rules, and comes under the scope of the grammar.

Can the knowledge of orthography in its two elements be acquired directly by the practice of our method? This property of the system is too evident to all for there to be any need for us to stop to again demonstrate it.

The method embracing each language in the totality of its terms and its expressions, both the eye and the hand will have the opportunity of becoming familiarised with the radicle of all the terms which form part of it; and this taking possession of the roots will be as swift as it is easy. For example, when the theme "open the door" has been fully elaborated in the manner we have explained, it is absolutely impossible that the spelling of the word "door" should not thereafter be engraved for ever on the pupil's memory, or that the fancy should take him to write this radicle otherwise than as so often encountered in the course of the lesson. All the advantages which the method can offer for the study of languages it also offers for the learning of the spelling either of a foreign language or of the mother-tongue.

II.

READING.

From the spelling to the reading is but one step. Every method for the teaching of languages should contain within itself a method for the teaching of reading. Indeed, if a book is a good one for teaching how to speak and write a language, it must be equally so for teaching to read.

Recall the properties of our series; examine once more from this point of view the arrangement of our lessons and the order of the sentences; remember the mode of giving the lesson by the teacher and the process followed by the scholar, and you will be able, perhaps, to judge whether or not our method may become the most practical of all the methods of teaching children to read yet brought forward.

What book is the best to give into the hands of the child immediately after teaching him the alphabet? In the first place, it must be a book devoid of all metaphor, and of all metaphysical conceptions—a book expurgated of all those abstruse religious sentiments with which too often the books for earliest childhood are crammed. Let us reserve these matters for a riper age. The little child, however much you may try, cannot at first be made to understand metaphor. Now, no one can read well what he understands ill.

Reading is the first serious effort demanded of the intelligence of the child. Here we have one of the most arduous steps to be undertaken, and we should direct our energies to clearing the road instead of encumbering it with obstacles. The first reading-book must, therefore, be simple—as simple as childhood itself—as simple as the life the child leads around its mother's knee.

And what should this book be about? It should deal with the knowledge that the child itself already possesses. The child should find out, with an ever-increasing interest in the reading-book, the expression, the translation of its every-day life, and not endless reflections upon wickedness it knows nothing of, and upon virtues which as yet it does not possess.

The child gets up in the morning, dresses himself, eats, drinks, and plays; let him read the story of his getting up, of his dressing, of his breakfast, the description of his little games.

T

All these things written down will have for him the attraction of a revelation. Is it not, indeed, the progressive revelation of his individuality? He sees his mother or his nurse light the fire, draw water from the spring, sweep up, wash, dust the room: let him read the story of the pump or the well, and that of the washing-tub. He sees, or should see, his father or some of the men on the farm chopping wood, haymaking, reaping, gardening, driving; let him read the story of the woodman, the haymaker, the reaper, the gardener, the drayman, &c. He sees, or should see, living around him a cat, a flock of sheep, some horses, fowls in the farmyard, birds, bees, flying beetles, butterflies, flowers, trees, all sorts of things; open before him the history of the rodents, the quadrupeds, the birds, the insects, the plants, and there will be no lack of interest. So much for the material of the book. But what form shall we adopt?

First of all, each reading lesson must have a determined length, a length calculated upon the effort that can be sustained by a frail intelligence without fatigue. Experience has demonstrated to us that a lesson of twenty to thirty sentences is the ordinary measure of the effort of the little child.

Next, what typographic form are we to give to this lesson? We could write the sentences one after the other, just as they come, without troubling ourselves either about their beginning or their end, so that if the size of page were large enough the whole might be given on a single line. Or we may write down these sentences one beneath the other upon separate lines, so that the eye not only distinguishes them without effort, but can embrace them in one look, and grasp them at a glance.

We have to choose between these two types. To which of the two will pédagogy give the preference? I imagine to that which promises to smooth, and thereby to shorten, the path of the scholar. For this reason it is the second of these we shall take. The book sought is therefore found to be identical with that of our elementary series, identical both as regards material and form. Our method, therefore, really carries hidden within it a method of teaching reading—a method as simple and easy as is its method of teaching foreign languages, and practised in exactly the same way.

And if instead of the usual A B C books—books as abstract as they are arbitrary—and the mechanical alphabets of to-day were substituted a truly rational alphabet, an alphabet in which each letter speaks and itself tells its origin, name, and virtue (and this alphabet is possible, because we ourselves use it[1]), then the great task of teaching reading will be the work of a few weeks, or rather (with a phonetic spelling) a game of a few days. Better even than this, the child will not *learn* to read; he will read as he speaks, by instinct, spontaneously, intuitively. And this is as it should be.

Doubtless the eye will not be able to dispense with a certain apprenticeship. When the child first walks alone, he gropes prudently to feel the ground under his feet. When he reads for the first time, the eye will attack each word slowly, with circumspection; but he will not spell the words—he will read; he will not syllabify—he will read direct; he will not gather part of an idea by gathering part of a word—he will gather the entire idea by grasping the entire word.

Do we ever see our scholars when learning Greek amusing themselves by spelling or "a-b-abbing" the words? When shall we rid school-work entirely of this absurd, this idiotic habit of putting the child everywhere and gratuitously to puzzle his little brain over abstractions? For regarded carefully, spelling and dividing words into syllables are operations really as abstract as the calculation of the binomial theorem or the discussion of an analytic formula.

Yes, with our Series reading becomes, like the rest, a mere game; so much so indeed, that the children know how to read without ever having learnt. The child's first lesson of reading is then always a language-lesson. He reads that which he has just heard, that which he perceives directly, that which he has just spoken himself; he reads the speech he has just assimilated, the words which are still vibrating in his ear. He does not guess, he does not decipher upon each line one or several logographs, puzzles in words; he *recognises* quite naturally the expression of his thought.

This was the method of the Greeks, who all knew how to read, even the slaves. It is, in certain parts of Germany (and of England), the present method. The scholar in Germany does not spell, does not syllabify—he reads. To-morrow, if we would, all our school-children could do the same. Simply let the school do away with its alphabetical abstractions.

---

[1] The question of the alphabet will be more fully explained in other works (Trans.).

III.

DRAWING—ITS RELATION TO LANGUAGE.—THE ILLUSTRATED SERIES.

Let us shake for the last time the tree of our linguistic system; perhaps there may fall from it yet another forgotten fruit. Each of our themes forms a thoroughly determinate whole; its totality presents what is termed a picture, and may, if desired, be reproduced otherwise than by writing. If we think of it, it is a subject ready prepared for drawing. No object is forgotten in our series, and the general situations of animals or of things are found therein faithfully retraced. Why could we not attempt, in a series of sketches, to reveal to the child the fundamental, generating, substantial lines of all beings or objects mentioned therein, as they arise upon the scene in the lessons of the series?

The art of teaching drawing appears to us to be at exactly the same point as the art of teaching language. There exists as yet no method of teaching drawing which does not reproduce the same errors as those of the present grammars. Every one of them begins by abstraction. To commence by lines, squares, geometrical figures, is to commence by abstraction; it is to "spell" the form; it is to exclude intuition, to prevent inspiration.

To commence by the nose, the eyes, the ears, is again to begin by abstraction. If it is not "spelling" the form of the object, it is "syllabifying" it. Beginning by the head is a superior process to the two preceding. The pupil no longer works altogether upon the abstract; and the teacher, if he is clever, can provoke intuition, can awaken inspiration. But, whatever he may do, this head is part only of a whole—it is not a true whole.

To read isolated words is not really "to read," and to draw parts of objects or isolated objects is not really "to draw." That a thing may be rightly drawn, it must bear the shade of the objects that surround it; it must be limited, defined, by these objects. We only really read when we enounce a complete phrase; we can only really draw when we reproduce that which corresponds to the phrase, namely, "a group."

We will venture the statement that the true point of departure of drawing is the group, and not the line; it is synthesis, and not analysis; it is the phrase, and not the word, exactly as for language. This principle, dictated to us by logic, is confirmed by experience. Observe the early attempts of any child having the promise of an artist in him, and you will be struck with one fact that allows of no exception. It is not geometric lines, not noses, nor mouths, nor even heads, that first solicit the pencil of the future artist, but always groups, and nothing but groups. *It is the relations between the things* which first captivate him; and it is the intuition of these relations which attaches him to the things themselves. That he shall feel emotion, it is distinctly necessary that Nature should say something to him, express something to him. It is this expression that the little artist essays to translate; it is that which we term "the ideal."

Each of our themes is the expression of a group of facts, and of facts simple, elementary, well known to the child, and already "lived" by him. These facts are set in order, harmonised, as they are in Nature. The child perceives or conceives the true relations that these facts have with each other. Our Series appear to us, therefore, to be able to serve as the basis of a decidedly rational system of teaching drawing. Our system will lose nothing by being interpreted by another art, while this other art would gain in clearness by being guided by language, and following the language in all its evolutions.

Language and drawing are two revelations of Nature which cannot do otherwise than complete each other without ever contradicting each other.

To those who would reproach us with wishing to perform too much with a linguistic method, we will answer that in Nature everything is strictly knitted together, that the whole being of man rests upon language, that language is the marvellous placenta to which is attached, and by which is fed, every product of the intelligence and of the activity of mankind.

IV.

THE TIME NECESSARY TO LEARN A LANGUAGE.

The arena is prepared, its limits defined; the obstacles are all numbered, the difficulties estimated. What time will be required by a runner of average force to reach or pass the goal? In other words, how many months are necessary to learn a language by means of our method?

To learn a language is, as we have said, to translate one's own individuality into this language. Our complete series represents the expression of a strong human individuality of about fifteen years of age. Every calculation taken, we have found that our own may be written within a book of 4000 pages, divided into fifty or sixty chapters, each presenting the development of a general series consisting of from fifty to eighty separate themes or exercises. Each of these themes contains, on an average, twenty-five sentences. The complete expression of our individuality will therefore be represented by 25 times 4000; or 100,000 sentences. On an average, our pupils assimilate five themes in an hour; 4000 divided by 5 gives the quotient 800. It is therefore 800 hours that is required for the complete study of a language. Let us say 900 to have something in hand and to allow for the unforeseen.

Nine hundred hours spread over the entire year or 360 days, reduces itself to two hours and a half a day, or an hour and a quarter in the morning and an hour and a quarter in the afternoon. The complete study of a language within the year is therefore an easy task. Nine hundred hours spread over six months, that is, over 180 days, is equal to five hours a day, say $2\frac{1}{2}$ hours in the morning and the same in the afternoon. Whoever, therefore, can and will give up five hours a day to the study of a language will with certainty have assimilated the language at the end of six months.

An objection will here be made to us: let us at once deal with it. Five times 5 are 25. Is it possible to assimilate twenty-five pages of a foreign language per day? Is it even possible for them to be given as lessons?

In the chapter upon "The Construction of the System" we endeavoured to bring into light a property of our series which is a direct and emphatic reply to the objection quoted. We will recapitulate it. A single series—that of the quadruped, for example—gives us possession of the first basis of a language, that which may be termed its "substance." The second series rests upon the first, and borrows therefrom two-thirds of its expressions. The third is fed in the same proportion at the expense of the two first; and so on for the others. The same terms are repeated again and again indefinitely from one sentence to another sentence, from one aim to another aim, from one theme to another theme, from one series to another series.

At the end of the first series the pupil, therefore, finds himself in possession of a crowd of expressions which he has only to apply in the second; the study of the second will facilitate yet more that of the third and of the following ones. At the end of the first month our pupils are generally able to receive and assimilate up to twelve exercises in the hour. From the second month forward the pupil, therefore, can finish his daily task in two hours.

As regards the teacher, it is quite evident that he requires no more time to give than the pupil needs to learn the lessons. We must not forget, moreover, that the successive acquisition of the lessons day by day facilitates the teacher's task and abridges it. But the writing? Where will the pupil find time to write out the twenty-five pages a day?

The speech of man, we have said, is continuous. Our entire life has therefore been spoken by us. But who of us has written it out in all its details? To know our native language, the foreigner is no more bound than we are ourselves to write out the hundred thousand sentences which express our individuality. He will write as many of them as he can—the more the better. The essential part, however, is that he should speak them all.

Here we may parenthetically remark that of our 4000 themes 2000 or more will appertain to science properly so called. Have we not defined our system as "the sciences by the languages and the languages by the sciences"? Consequently, with our system, and by reason of it, and it alone, the time given to languages is not stolen from the sciences. It is as much given to them, indeed, as to the languages themselves. By our system pupils learn the sciences and obtain the languages into the bargain.

Nine hundred hours! This is the time necessary to assimilate the entire series, that is to say, the objective language. But this language does not constitute the whole of language. Alongside or above the series there is the subjective language; there also is the figurative language, and there is the grammar. Will it be necessary to devote special and supplementary hours to the study of these three parts.

We will refer the reader to the chapters in which they have been treated in full. We have shown how far the figurative language is attached to and hangs, so to speak, upon the themes of the series; how the relative phrase, enclitic or other, is taught with and by the same themes; lastly, how the grammar is exercised upon them, and is applied to them without opposing or hindering their development.

The figurative language slips into the interval between the series; the relative phrase fills up the interval between the sentences; the grammar commands and guides the whole. The objective language, under the form of the series, represents a penetrable body, having the property of aggregating others to itself without increasing its volume.

Nine hundred hours! I repeat, the study of a language requires 900 hours. Whether a person have or not what is called the "gift for languages" (and each of us receives it on being born), there is the total amount of time which it is necessary to devote to it. There we have the price, the exact price of a language. He will appear and will be reputed to be the most clever and the most gifted who is able the soonest to invest the capital required.

From the defensive we will pass to the offensive. In the first place, what must we think of those teachers of languages who engage to include an entire language in ninety pages, to teach it to you by opening their mouths ninety times, to make you assimilate it by honouring you with forty-five visits, or to deliver it to you complete on receipt of the fiftieth ticket?

Our judgment will be brief. Justice condemns for cheating persons less qualified for it than these. He who sells a piece of goods that he knows he cannot deliver is not an honest man. A language is a whole world to conquer. Now, no one can conquer a world by executing haphazard a dozen marches and a couple of dozen countermarches.

Next, let us judge the official scholastic programmes from

the point of view of the study of languages. Two hours of French or of German a week make a total of eight hours a month, say eighty hours for the whole scholastic year. Eighty divided by 10 gives a quotient 8. It is, therefore, eight full days that the school accords to the children for learning a modern language.

Eight days a year—a little over a week! This figure eight is in itself at once a criticism and a judgment—a judgment so severe that we can hardly allow ourselves to translate it into the vulgar tongue. Eight full days to conquer a language!!!

The course, it is true, is spread over ten months, but these ten months are quite evidently nothing but a delusion; and whatever any one may say, a course of ten months at two hours a week will never represent more than eight full days. Further, eight days spread over fifty weeks have not even this value.

A rower who, in order to progress up a river, should struggle against the stream two hours a week, and all the rest of the time should allow himself to drift down with the ordinary current, would be more likely to get to the sea than to the river's source. The scholar who is learning a foreign language floats alternately upon two currents opposed to each other, and of unequal force. If he will not be carried away by the stronger, that of his mother-tongue, it is absolutely necessary for him to have recourse to extraordinary means.

Then you count for nothing, we shall be told, the tasks, home-lessons, writing exercises—the personal work, in point of fact—from one class to another, as a means of keeping the pupil to his work. Alas! experience has proved to us, and thoroughly proved, that this work is not only unfruitful, but disastrous. Remember our own attempt on the German authors and dictionaries. Our work was assuredly at least worth that of the collegian, as much for the quantity as for the quality of it. And to what result did our efforts, so severely classic, lead us?

Either the pupil does over again an exercise already done, which is much the same as beating a sheaf already well threshed, or he makes up a new one himself, which is as much as if one delivered into the hands of a workman who knows not his trade an ingot of gold from which to manufacture a watch. The raw material may be squandered, but converted into a watch—never!

There can only happen to your scholar what happened to ourselves. He will falsify his pronunciation, pervert his accent, fabricate vicious expressions, and confiding to the eye what should be confided to the ear, he will perceive syllables, but will always forget the thought in the language he is studying; and therefore, try as long as he may, he will never properly assimilate it. We know, besides, that the virtue of first impressions is that they are never eradicated. This is the point to which, as regards languages, personal work, such as is inculcated by the ordinary school, at present leads.

We shall be told, again: But we give up nine or ten years to continue, complete, and perfect our linguistic teaching. Ten times 80 are exactly 800 hours. Is not this your amount? No; it is not our amount. In point of fact, whoever does not, within the space of the four seasons of one year, manage to learn practically all there is to be learnt of the basis of a language, will never learn it.

We have many of us studied Latin and Greek for ten years. Who among us is there who can be said to thoroughly know Latin and Greek? No; it is *not* the amount we require. In ten years the public school should give us ten languages. In this same time a child's nurse, who should change her situation each year, would teach the bulk of her language ten separate times.

The evolution of the language may be made to, and ought to, follow that of the seasons. While the year performs one revolution, the child expresses all the phenomena which it unfolds successively before him. And if from one day to the next he applies, that is, repeats while modifying and extending it ceaselessly, the language which expresses his individuality of one day, so also, from one year to the next, he will recapitulate the language that expresses his individuality of a year.

That which the young child performs so easily cannot be impossible to the adult; and if, as we ourselves did at Berlin at first, he finds himself after a year's effort less advanced than the little child, there can be little doubt it is because he is on the wrong road; and what is not less certain is, that if he does not see fit to change his route, he will not attain his aim any more the second year than he did the first. In the second year the learner can recapitulate after the manner of the child, and can enter into possession of his acquisitions. It is impossible for him to recommence his campaign.

Last and supreme objection: Man has not to learn languages only, and the time given up to the study of languages is lost for that of the sciences.

In the ordinary system this is true, but not with ours. On the contrary, by the languages we teach the sciences, and by the sciences we teach the languages. Who does not see in this system an immense simplification of methods of teaching? In itself the thing is logical. We shall try to show shortly that it is realisable.

V.

THE TEACHING OF LANGUAGES BROUGHT WITHIN THE REACH OF ALL—LINGUISTIC APTITUDES OF WOMEN.

In the hands of a clever workman even a bad tool sometimes accomplishes wonders. It has been remarked that the authors of methods otherwise defective employ them always themselves with success. It is right, therefore, to inquire whether our system, which may be fruitful when practised by its author, acts equally well when some other person attempts to apply it.

We have exposed in its entirety the secret of our process of teaching. It is for the reader to judge whether our directions are or are not easy to carry out.

And if we are further pressed to give our own opinion in this respect, and to base it upon certain facts, this is what our reply would be: In the first place, it is, of course, fully understood that the composition, the writing, the arrangement of the book itself remains entirely as given by the author. If, in order to apply our system, each teacher had to construct it for him or herself, its application might as well be renounced at once. We have spoken of the inherent difficulties of this kind of work; no one knows them better than he who has spent a large part of his life in overcoming them.

To impose a similar task upon every teacher would be to declare the scheme impracticable at the very outset. We start, therefore, with the assumption that this system is definitely constructed, and that the instructor has only to apply it.

We believe that we have demonstrated that the pupil who has thoroughly assimilated one of our themes is in a state to be able to teach it in his turn almost as well as ourselves. Remember once more that they were little children who aided us to translate our individuality in German, as afterwards in English and in other tongues, and that we owe the development of our series to the simple workmen who figure as actors therein. It was a ploughman who told us the Series of Tilling the Ground; it was a shepherd who gave us the Series of the Shepherd, and a woodman who gave us that of the Woodman.

Our reply, therefore, to the question put is: "Whosoever knows how to speak a language is capable of teaching in this language our Elementary Series, those which reproduce the basis of the language."

If this be so, our method is likely to open up a new career for the activity of women. It gives, in fact, into the hands of women the whole elementary teaching of foreign languages. Women have, indeed, a far greater aptitude than men for this kind of teaching. A woman's tongue is more subtle and more supple than that of man; her ear more delicate, her accent more pleasing and more penetrating; and for children her devotion is only equalled by her patience.

In our own public and private classes we have always found that the girls assimilate a language (ancient or modern) much more quickly and much more correctly than the boys. In the countries where languages are most cultivated it is always the woman who speaks them best and who knows them most thoroughly. If she has not already outstripped man in the teaching of languages, this is because of the imperfection of the methods which are imposed upon her. The abstract is the bugbear of childhood. Our method, by combating and suppressing it everywhere, places (or so, at least, it seems to us) the teaching of foreign languages well within the reach of woman.

If our system when practised by man is worth anything, we are convinced that it will double its value on the day that the application of it is undertaken by women teachers, and the language of our new generation cannot but gain in purity, in nobleness, in elegance, and, I might add, in decency. If it were permitted to us to chose for our method an interpreter and an apostle, we should certainly chose a woman. The practice of our system is therefore well within the reach of every one.

VI.

CAN A LANGUAGE BE LEARNT WITHOUT A TEACHER?

Can a student learn a foreign language without a teacher? The greater part of the authors of modern methods maintain that he can, and this declaration may be considered as the most efficacious cause of their success. Ollendorf owes to this in great part the 200 editions of his works. A volume, in fact, costs less than a teacher. What answer does the classical school make to this question? It commences by a negative and ends by an affirmative.

From the lowest form to the highest the classical method gives to the scholar a whole legion of masters in order to teach him Latin. What means this long array of pedagogic forces, unless it be that the individual must be considered as incapable of arriving by his own unaided efforts at knowing a given language. Looking at it from another point of view, however, and taking into consideration the means to which recourse is had, we might conclude that the study of language is a purely personal work.

The classical master, when placing in the hands of his pupils a grammar and a dictionary, says to them, in effect: "The whole language is contained within these two books, and the smaller one will teach the use of the larger. When you are hungry, you do not ask other people to eat for you; in the same way, it would be of not the slightest use to you if your teacher learned the grammar for you, searched in the dictionary for you, construed the phrases for you, wrote out exercises for you. What you must set yourself to do is to carry out all this work for yourself." I ask if it is possible to affirm more categorically that the study of a language is an individual, a personal labour?

How does the classical school reconcile its teaching with its practice? In a manner as ingenious as it is original. "It does not propose," its professors say, "to teach languages, but only how to learn to learn them!" Begging the question in this manner, the classicists hesitate to draw the conclusion. We are therefore obliged to do so for them.

"Here is a hammer, a square, and a chisel, and there lies a block of marble," the classical school says to its disciples,

"You have here everything that is needed for carving any statue you please. You will now set to work and carve from this block the statue of the Emperor of China, whom you do not know, and it must be a good likeness."

There you have exactly the task imposed upon the Latinist who begins in the studio of the classical school; the grammar is the hammer, chisel, and square; the dictionary is the block of marble, and the statue of the unknown Emperor of the Celestial Empire represents the language to be constructed. One need not feel astonished if the apprentice toils ten years, fifteen years, twenty years, all his life, without ever being able to bring about the desired resemblance. The pupil is condemned to "recognise" a thing which he has never seen, to discover a language he has never heard. What is required of him is to draw the language forth from his brain, where it is not and never has been; or from a book, the dictionary, where it may be found in much the same state as the Madonna of Raphael in the artist's colour-box. Will your disciple, after such a training, however long it may be, have even learnt how to learn?

To conclude. Work which is solitary and purely personal will never produce an efficient knowledge of a language. We base this thesis upon axioms or principles already thoroughly established. The receptive organ of language is not the eye—it is the ear. But in order that the ear may receive, speech must be produced; therefore to study a language it is necessary to have a master—that is, a person who speaks before the pupil.

Each language has a pronunciation proper to itself; each sentence has its note, each word its accent; these three things have their effect, not upon the eye, but upon the ear; therefore to study a language a master is needed, a person who pronounces and accentuates before the pupil.

The forms of things are presented to the intelligence by the eye, but it is the ear to which is confided the duty of transmitting to the intelligence the sounds, the words, together with the ideas of which they form the body; therefore to study a language we require a master—that is, a person whose mouth articulates the syllables and utters the sounds.

The written language, that which is transmitted to the memory by the organ of sight, is graven thereon with difficulty, and the impression of it is ephemeral; the spoken language, that communicated to the mind by the ear, is graven thereon instantaneously, and the impression of it is almost ineffaceable. Therefore, once more, to study a language we require a master—that is to say, living speech, whose vibration shall set in motion the organ of thought itself.

He who boasts of having assimilated a language without recourse to the speech of others, either does not know this language or deceives himself. Language is the connection of mind to mind. In order that it shall be something more than a mere abstraction lacking consistence, it must be the direct and real product of the intercourse of two or more minds.

PART FOURTH.

THE AUXILIARY SERIES.

THE creations of literature, the sciences, the trades, the arts may become the material for fresh series. We designate these by the general name of "Auxiliary Series."

They are useful but not indispensable for the knowledge of a language. They do not give the first basis of a language—they presuppose it. They nourish it, maintain it, amplify it, complete it—they do not create it. They are to the ordinary series what the heat of the sun is to the field of corn; they do not supply it, but they ripen it.

STUDY OF THE CLASSICS
(LITERARY SERIES).

OUTLINE OF A NEW PROCESS FOR TRANSLATING, READING, AND ASSIMILATING THE CLASSICAL AUTHORS.

I.

PUTTING A LITERARY WORK INTO SERIES.

1. *Principle and point of departure.*

The study of a language is incomplete and mentally sterile if it does not include the literary masterpieces of this language. Every such masterpiece therefore requires not only that the student should read and comprehend it, but should assimilate it. We know too well what the ordinary processes of teaching the classics can do in this respect; we know how much we ourselves retained of them on leaving the sixth form at school.

A practical and rational method for reading, translating, and assimilating the great classical works yet remains to be found and organised. This method should be, it seems to us, the direct product and the natural corollary of a linguistic method worthy of the name; it should bear witness in favour of this result, and should end, so to speak, by consecrating it. If our system is what we believe it to be, it bears within it this second method, or rather it is itself this method. Let us attempt to demonstrate this.

Every literary work represents a series of conceptions linked together by the logic personal to the author. Each conception therein is developed in its turn by a series of distinct sentences; and it has been already demonstrated that this development has its natural limits, and that its measure is a constant one in all the works which deserve the name of masterpieces.

U

Therefore every literary work is capable of being decomposed into themes of a determined length, each one representing the development of a particular conception. From this it follows that every literary work can be transcribed under the form of one of our Linguistic Series. Therefore, finally, it may be treated exactly as one of our series themselves is treated. The scholar will assimilate a book of Virgil, a book of Homer, a chapter of Herodotus, a chapter of Tacitus, exactly as he assimilates the Series of the Ploughman, the Series of the Plant, the Series of the Insect.

But may it not be said that to assimilate a literary work thus, conception by conception, sentence by sentence, is to do over again the work of the author himself? If our method renders this work possible, it is really what we have claimed for it—a veritable method for reading, translating, and thoroughly assimilating the classical masterpieces. And if, along with this, it delivers into the hands of the master the secret of rendering this assimilation as rapid as the exposition of the lesson itself, as instantaneous as speech, I maintain that this method comes very near to realising the ideal to which the teaching world aspires.

Its success will depend upon two things :—

1. The mode of transcription of the classical work;
2. The elaboration of the exercises furnished by this transcription.

We will describe or repeat how this double work should be carried out.

2. *Transcription of a classical work into literature lessons.*

Given a classical work to be studied :—

1. We draw up, first of all, a list of the diverse and successive conceptions of the author; then, dissecting, detaching these conceptions one from another, we form therefrom a series of scenes or pictures, that is, of distinct lessons.

2. Each of these themes is divided in its turn into its separate sentences, and each sentence is placed on a line by itself.

3. Each sentence has a centre around which gravitate its various elements, which is, as it were, its soul. The soul is the "verb," or the term which takes the place of the verb. We detach this verb from the sentence, and place it in full

view in a column arranged to the right-hand side of the page.

4. Each conception is capable of being still further subdivided; it presents, usually, two or three distinct groups of sentences, which form the various "moments" of this conception. We term these divisions "steps" (paragraphs), and we mark these stopping-places by the sign (—). Between two consecutive steps of our text we also leave a rather larger space than between two lines of the same group.

As is seen, the arrangement of our literary themes or lessons is in every way similar to that of the ordinary series. We have transcribed and lithographed under this form the greater part of the classical authors. A book of Virgil, for instance, gives us an average of a series of seventy themes, each having twenty-two to thirty sentences. A book of Homer furnishes thirty-five to forty lessons. The "Ars Poetica" of Horace yields thirty-six.[1] We may point out that the Greek and Latin prose writers are already divided in the current editions into small chapters, which usually correspond to our own divisions.

5. In the same way that there is, for the development of the various conceptions of the mind, an average length, so also there is an average length for the separate sentences, and it is this that decides the size of page of our transcription. If this size be well chosen, the greater number of the sentences will go upon one line. It is well to avoid double lines, for two reasons. In the first place, irregularity is always painful to the eye; in the next, the unity of the thought seems to call for the unity of the line. The intelligence takes it in more easily in this state.

6. Whenever a phrase is composed of two portions, an enclitic and a subordinate sentence, we usually write these parts upon two separate lines, connecting them together by the conventional sign (→). Placed at the end of an enclitic expression, this sign serves both to bring this expression into relief, and to draw the pupil's attention more forcibly to it.

The organisation of our literature lessons is dominated by a fact which we have already pointed out, and of which it is

---

[1] Printed privately by the author for the use of his French students. They will form part of the practical course (Trans.).

important here once more to remind our readers. This is, that our transcriptions reproduce the exact text of the author, without ever either altering the terms or the construction. The length of the typographic line alone is not respected. Need we hesitate to sacrifice the arbitrary to the logical? When questions of methods of teaching are before us, there is one interest which should guide the orders of the publisher or the printing foreman, and this is the pedagogic interest.

3. *Specimens of transcriptions.*

To make still more clear the process which we have just described, it appears to us that it would be well to offer sundry short examples of the transcriptions of authors. We will take one of the fables of La Fontaine, a fable of Phædrus, one of Grimm's fairy-tales, and a scene from "Romeo and Juliet." A longer work, such as a book of Virgil, would doubtless be a more striking example, but the length, already considerable, of the present work will not allow us to occupy so much additional space. Moreover, the lessons which follow will amply suffice for a first trial. He who thinks well of the system will be able to avail himself of the collection of our transcriptions of the classical authors.

THE LION AND THE GNAT (La Fontaine).

I.

The Outrage and the Duel.

— "Be off, thou paltry insect, thou excrement of the earth."	be off
It was in these words that the lion spoke one day to the gnat.	spoke
The gnat declared war against him;	declared
"Thinkest thou," said he, —	thinkest thou
"that thy title of king affrights me,	affrights
or even disquiets me?	disquiets
An ox is more powerful than art thou,	is powerful
and I can lead it whither my fancy pleases."	can lead
— Hardly had he finished these words	had finished
than he himself sounded the charge,	sounded
and became both herald and challenger.	became
At first he keeps a safe distance,	keeps
then, taking his time,	taking
dashes at the lion's neck,	dashes
and drives him nearly mad.	drives
The quadruped foams at the mouth,	foams
and his eye glitters;	glitters
he roars.	roars
All hide,	hide
all quake in the neighbourhood,	quake
and this universal alarm is the work of a gnat.	is the work
— The miserable wretch of a fly harasses him in a hundred places,	harasses
stings him sometimes on the spine, sometimes on the nose,	stings
sometimes creeps up his nostrils.	creeps
His rage then rises to the utmost.	rises

* * * * *

THE LION AND THE GNAT.

II.

Triumph and Ruin.

—The invisible foe triumphs,   triumphs
and laughs to see —   laughs
that there is not a tooth nor a claw of the   is tooth
    irritated beast
but does duty in bringing blood.   does duty
The unhappy beast tears his own flesh,   tears
lashes his tail against his flanks,   lashes
vainly beats the air,   beats
and his extreme fury wearies him,   wearies
overthrows him.   overthrows
He is utterly defeated.   is defeated

—The insect retires from the combat with   retires
as he sounded the charge,   [glory;   sounded
so he sounds the victory,   sounds
goes here and there to announce it,   announce
and meets on his way the ambush of a   meets
he there likewise meets his death. [spider;   meets

—What things may we be taught from   may be taught
I can see two,   [this?   can see
of which the first is, that —   is
Amongst our enemies the smallest are   are to be feared
    often the most to be feared;
the other, that —   is
Through perils great one may have passed,   may have passed
To perish from the slightest thing at last.   perish

*   *   *   *   *

CANIS ET LUPUS (Phædrus).

I.

Pereo fame.

— Quam dulcis sit libertas breviter proloquar.	dulcis sit proloquar
— Cani perpasto macie confectus lupus forte occurrit,	occurrit
Salutantes dein invicem	salutantes
ut restiterunt:	restiterunt
L. Unde sic, quæso, nites ?	nites
Aut quo cibo fecisti tantum corporis ?	fecisti
Ego, qui sum longe fortior,	sum fortior
(ego) pereo fame.	pereo
— Canis simpliciter:	dixit
C. Eadem est conditio tibi,	est eadem
præstare domino si par officium potes.	præstare
L. Quod (officium) ? inquit illa.	quod est
C. Custos ut sis liminis,	custos ut sis
furibus tuearis et noctu domum.	ut tuearis
L. — Ego vero sum paratus;	sum paratus
nunc patior nives imbresque	patior
in silvas asperam vitam trahens;	trahens
quanto est facilius mihi —	est facilius
sub tecto vivere	vivere
et otiosum largo satiari cibo !	satiari
C. Veni ergo mecum.	veni

* * * * *

CANIS ET LUPUS.

II.

Regnare nolo liber ut non sim mihi.

— Dum procedunt ·	procedunt
adspicit lupus a catena collum detritum cani :	adspicit
L. Unde hoc, amice?	unde est
C. Nihil est.	nihil est
L. Dic, quæso, tamen.	dic
C. — Quia videor acer,	videor
alligant me interdui,	alligant
luce et quiescam,	ut quiescam
et vigilem	vigilem
nox quum venerit.	venerit
Crepusculo solutus,	solutus
qua visum est vagor.	vagor
Affertur ultro panis;	affertur
de mensa sua dat ossa dominus,	dat
frusta jactat familia,	jactat
et quod fastidit quisque pulmentarium.	fastidit
Sic sine labore venter impletur meus.	impletur
L. — Age!	age
si quo abire est animus,	abire
est licentia?	est licentia
C. Non plane est, inquit.	non est
L. Fruere quæ laudes, canis;	fruere
regnare nolo,	regnare
liber ut non sim mihi.	non sim liber

* * * * *

Die drei Spinnerinnen (Grimm).

I.

Das faule Mädchen.

— Es war ein Mädchen faul,   es war
und wollte nicht spinnen;   spinnen
die Mutter mochte sagen was sie wollte,   sagen
Sie konnte es nicht dazu bringen,   bringen
Endlich übernahm die Mutter einmal Zorn und Ungedulb,   übernahm
daß sie ihm Schläge gab,   gab
worüber es laut zu weinen anfieng.   weinen

— Nun fuhr gerade die Königin vorbei,   fuhr vorbei
und als sie das Weinen hörte,   hörte
ließ sie anhalten,   anhalten
trat in das Haus,   trat
und fragte die Mutter, —   fragte
warum sie ihre Tochter schlüge,   schlüge
daß man draußen auf der Straße das Schreien hörte.   hörte

— Da schämte sich die Frau —   schämte sich
daß sie die Faulheit ihrer Tochter offenbaren sollte,   offenbaren
und sprach: sprach
„Ich kann sie nicht vom Spinnen abbringen,   abbringen
sie will immer und ewig spinnen,   spinnen
und ich bin arm   bin arm
und kann den Flachs nicht herbeischaffen."   herbei schaffen

— Da antwortete die Königin: antwortete
„Ich höre nichts lieber als spinnen,   höre
und bin nicht vergnügter   bin vergnügter
als wenn die Räder schnurren: schnurren
gebt mir eure Tochter mit in's Schloß,   gebt
ich habe Flachs genug,   habe
da soll sie spinnen so viel sie Lust hat."   spinnen

* * * * *

Die drei Spinnerinnen.

II.

Drei Flachskammern bei der Königin.

———

—Die Mutter war's von Herzen gerne zufrieden.　　　war zufrieden
Die Königin nahm das Mädchen mit,　　　　　　　　　nahm mit
und fuhr nach dem Schloß zurück;　　　　　　　　　　fuhr zurück
als sie in's Schloß gekommen waren,　　　　　　　　 gekommen
führte sie es hinauf zu drei Kammern,　　　　　　　 führte
die lagen von unten bis oben voll vom feinsten Flachs.　lagen voll

—„Spinn' mir diesen Flachs,"　　　　　　　　　　　　spinn'
sprach die Königin,　　　　　　　　　　　　　　　　　sprach
„und wenn du es fertig bringst,　　　　　　　　　　 fertig bringst
so sollst du —　　　　　　　　　　　　　　　　　　　sollst
　　meinen ältesten Sohn zum Gemahl haben;　　　　 haben
bist du gleich arm,　　　　　　　　　　　　　　　　 bist arm
so acht' ich nicht darauf,　　　　　　　　　　　　　achte darauf
dein unverdroßener Fleiß ist Ausstattung genug."　　ist Ausstattung

—Das Mädchen erschrak innerlich:　　　　　　　　　 erschrak
denn es konnte —　　　　　　　　　　　　　　　　　　konnte
　　den Flachs nicht spinnen,　　　　　　　　　　　 spinnen
wär's dreihundert Jahr alt geworden,　　　　　　　　wäre geworden
und hätte jeden Tag von Morgen bis Abend dabei gesessen. hätte gesessen

* * * * *

Die drei Spinnerinnen.

III.

Die Verzweiflung.

— Als nun das Mädchen allein war,   allein war
zu weinen, fieng es an —   fieng an weinen
und saß so drei Tage   saß
ohne die Hand zu rühren.   rühren

— Am dritten Tage kam die Königin;   kam
und als sie sah, daß —   sah
noch nichts gesponnen war,   gesponnen war
verwunderte sie sich.   verwunderte sich
Aber das Mädchen entschuldigte sich damit, daß —   entschuldigte sich
es, vor großer Betrübniß   vor
über die Entfernung aus seiner Mutter Hause,   über
noch nicht hätte anfangen können.   anfangen

— Das ließ sich die Königin gefallen,   gefallen
sagte aber beim Weggehen,   sagte
„morgen mußt du mir anfangen —   anfangen
    zu arbeiten.   arbeiten
Als das Mädchen wieder allein war,   allein war
wußte es —   wußte
    sich nicht mehr zu rathen   rathen
    und zu helfen.   helfen

* * * * *

Die drei Spinnerinnen.

IV.

Drei seltsame Weiber.

—In seiner Betrübniß   in
trat das Mädchen vor das Fenster.   trat
Da sah es drei Weiber herkommen: herkommen
davon hatte die erste einen breiten Platschfuß;   hatte
die zweite hatte eine so große Unterlippe,   hatte
daß sie über das Kinn herunter hing,   herunter hing
und die dritte hatte einen breiten Daumen.   hatte

—Die blieben vor dem Fenster stehen,   blieben stehen
schauten hinauf,   schauten hinauf
und fragten das Mädchen was ihm fehlte.   fragten
Es klagte ihnen seine Noth;   klagte
da trugen sie ihm ihre Hülfe an,   trugen an
und sprachen: sprachen
„Willst du uns zur Hochzeit einladen,   einladen
dich unser nicht schämen,   schämen
und uns deine Basen heißen,   heißen
auch an deinen Tisch setzen,   setzen
so wollen wir dir den Flachs wegspinnen,   wegspinnen
und das in kurzer Zeit."   (thun)

—„Von Herzen gern," antwortete es: antwortete
„kommt nur herein,   kommt ein
und fangt gleich die Arbeit an."   fangt an

* * * * *

Die drei Spinnerinnen.

V.

Das rasche Flachsspinnen.

— Da ließ es die drei seltsamen Weiber herein,   ließ herein
und machte in der ersten Kammer eine Lücke   machte
wo sie sich hinsetzten   hinsetzten
und ihr Spinnen anhuben.   anhuben

— Die eine zog den Faden   zog
und trat das Rad;   trat
die andere netzte den Faden,   netzte
die dritte drehte ihn   drehte
und schlug mit dem Finger auf den Tisch;   schlug
und so oft sie schlug,   schlug
fiel eine Zahl Garn zur Erde   fiel
und das war aufs feinste gesponnen.   gesponnen

— Vor der Königin verbarg sie die drei Spinnerinnen,   verbarg
und zeigte ihr,   zeigte
so oft sie kam,   kam
(zeigte ihr) die Menge des gesponnenen Garns,   zeigte
daß diese des Lobes kein Ende fand.   fand
Als die erste Kammer leer war,   leer war
gings an die zweite,   ging
endlich an die dritte   ging
und die war auch bald aufgeräumt.   war aufgeräumt

* * * * *

Die drei Spinnerinnen.

VI.

Treue und Dankbarkeit.

———

— Nun nahmen die drei Weiber Abschied,   nahmen
und sagten zum Mädchen: sagten
„Vergiß nicht, was du uns versprochen hast: vergiß
es wird dein Glück sein."   wird sein

— Als das Mädchen der Königin die leeren Kammern und   zeigte
     den großen Haufen Garn zeigte,
richtete sie die Hochzeit aus.   richtete aus
Der Bräutigam freute sich, daß ⟶   freute sich
er eine so geschickte und fleißige Frau bekäme,   bekäme
und lobte sie gewaltig.   lobte

—„Ich habe drei Basen,"   habe
sprach das Mädchen,   sprach
„und da sie mir viel Gutes erwiesen haben,   erwiesen haben
so wollte ich sie nicht gern ⟶   wollte
     in meinem Glück vergessen.   vergessen
Erlaubt doch, daß ⟶   erlaubt
ich sie zu der Hochzeit einlade,   einlade
und daß sie mit an dem Tisch sitzen."   sitzen
Die Königin und der Bräutigam gaben ihre Einwilligung.   gaben

* * * * * *

Die drei Spinnerinnen.

VII.

Die Hochzeitfeier.

— Als nun das Fest anhub,   anhub
traten die drei Jungfrauen in wunderlicher Tracht herein,   traten herein
und die Braut sprach: sprach
„Seid willkommen, liebe Basen."   seid willk.
„Ach!" sagte der Bräutigam,   sagte
„wie kommst du zu der garstigen Freundschaft?"   kommst

— Darauf gieng er zu der einen,   gieng
der mit dem breiten Platschfuß,   mit
und fragte: fragte
„Wovon habt Ihr einen solchen breiten Fuß?"   habt
„Vom Treten," antwortete sie,   habe
„vom Treten."   habe
Da gieng der Bräutigam zur zweiten,   gieng
und sprach: sprach
„Wovon habt Ihr nur die herunterhängende Lippe?"   habt
„Vom Lecken," antwortete sie,   habe
„vom Lecken."   habe
Da fragte er die dritte: fragte
„Wovon habt Ihr den breiten Daumen?"   habt
„Vom Faden drehen," antwortete sie,   habe
„vom Faden drehen."   habe

— Da erschrak der Königssohn,   erschrak
und sprach: sprach
„So soll mir nun und nimmermehr meine schöne Braut —   soll
ein Spinnrad anrühren.   anrühren
Damit war sie das böse Flachsspinnen los."   war los

*   *   *   *   *

SHAKESPEARE.
Romeo and Juliet.

Act III., Scene 5.

I.

— *Jul.* Wilt thou → be gone ?　　　　　　　be gone
It is not yet near day:　　　　　　　　　　　is not day
it was the nightingale, and not the lark,　　was nightingale
that pierc'd the fearful hollow of thine ear;　pierc'd
nightly she sings on yon pomegranate tree.　sings
Believe me, love,　　　　　　　　　　　　believe
it was the nightingale.　　　　　　　　　　was nightingale

— *Rom.* It was the lark, the herald of the　was the lark
　　morn, no nightingale.
Look, love, →　　　　　　　　　　　　　look
what envious streaks do lace the severing　do lace
　　clouds in yonder east.
Night's candles are burnt out,　　　　　　burnt out
and jocund day stands tiptoe on the misty　stands tiptoe
　　mountain tops.
I must →　　　　　　　　　　　　　　　must
be gone and live,　　　　　　　　　　　be gone
or stay and die.　　　　　　　　　　　　stay

— *Jul.* Yon light is not daylight:　　　　is not daylight
I know it, I;　　　　　　　　　　　　　know
it is some meteor　　　　　　　　　　　is meteor
that the sun exhales,　　　　　　　　　exhales
to be to thee this night a torch-bearer,　　be torch-bearer
and light thee on the way to Mantua:　　light
therefore, stay yet;　　　　　　　　　　stay
thou need'st not →　　　　　　　　　　need'st
to be gone.　　　　　　　　　　　　　be gone

* * * * *

SHAKESPEARE.
Romeo and Juliet.

Act III., Scene 5.

II.

— *Rom.* Let me—be ta'en,   be taken
let me—be put to death.   be put to death
I am content,—   am content
so thou wilt have it so,   have so
I'll say,   will say
yon grey is not the morning's eye,   is morning's eye
'tis but the pale reflex of Cynthia's brow;   is reflex
nor that is not the lark,   is the lark
whose notes do beat the vaulty heaven so   do beat
    high above our heads;

— I have more care — to stay,   stay
than will — to go;   go
come, death,   come
and welcome!   be welcome
Juliet wills it so.—   wills
How is't, my soul?   how is
Let's talk;   talk
it is not day.   is not day

*   *   *   *   *

SHAKESPEARE.
Romeo and Juliet.

Act III., Scene 5.
III.

Jul. It is, it is;	is day
hie hence,	hie thee
be gone,	be gone
away!	away!
It is the lark,	is the lark
that sings so out of tune,	sings
straining harsh discords and unpleasing sharps.	straining
— Some say —	say
the lark makes sweet division;	makes division
this doth not so,	doth not
for she divideth us.	divideth
— Some say —	say
the lark and loathed toad change eyes;	change
O, now I would —	would (that)
they had chang'd voices too!	had changed
since arm from arm that voice doth us affray,	doth affray
hunting thee hence with hunt's-up to the day.	hunting
— O, now be gone;	be gone
more light and light it grows.	grows light
Rom. More light and light;	grows light
more dark and dark our woes. . . .	grows dark

* * * * *

SHAKESPEARE.
Romeo and Juliet.

Act III., Scene 5.

IV.

— *Nurse.* Madam!   madam!
Jul. Nurse?   nurse!
Nurse. Your lady mother's coming to your   is coming
the day is broke;   [chamber: is broke
be wary, look about.   be wary
Jul. Then, window, let day in,   let day in
and let life out.   let life out
Rom. Farewell, farewell!   farewell
one kiss,   (give) one kiss
and I'll → descend.   will descend

— *Jul.* Art thou gone so?   art gone
Love, lord! ay, husband, friend!   my love!
I must hear from thee every day in the hour,   must hear
for in a minute there are many days: are many days
O, by this count I shall be much in years   shall be in years
ere I again behold my Romeo.   behold
Rom. Farewell!   farewell
I will omit no opportunity →   will omit
that may convey my greetings, love, to thee.   may convey

*   *   *   *   *

SHAKESPEARE.
Romeo and Juliet.

ACT III., SCENE 5.

V.

— *Jul.* O, think'st thou —	think'st
we shall ever meet again?	shall meet
Rom. I doubt it not;	doubt not
and all these woes shall serve for sweet discourses in our time to come.	shall serve
— *Jul.* O God!	God!
I have an ill-divining soul;	have ill-divining
methinks —	methinks
I see thee,	see (thee as dead)
now thou art below, as one dead in the bottom of a tomb:	art below
either my eyesight fails,	fails
or thou look'st pale.	look'st pale
Rom. And trust me, love,	trust
in my eye so do you:	so do you (look)
dry sorrow drinks our blood.	drinks
Adieu! adieu!	adieu!
— *Jul.* O fortune, fortune!	fortune!
all men call thee fickle:	call fickle
if thou art fickle,	art fickle
what dost thou with him	what dost thou
that is renown'd for faith?	is renown'd
Be fickle, fortune;	be fickle
for then, I hope —	I hope
thou wilt not keep him long,	wilt not keep
but send him back.	send back.

* * * * *

II.

ELABORATION OF A LITERARY SERIES—OUR METHOD OF TEACHING.

1. *One of La Fontaine's Fables.*

In our transcription, the fable of "The Lion and the Gnat" is divided into two portions, the first numbering twenty-two, and the second twenty-five sentences. Each theme is divided quite naturally into three paragraphs, and therefore comprises three distinct steps. The teacher will recount first of all the subject of the fable, not with the details and in the terms used by the author, but freely, bringing up the whole situation in his own words.

He will then begin the first step of the first lesson by the phrase which has as its verb "Be off." He throws, as it were, this verb (be off) down in front, then upon it builds up the phrase. "Be off, thou paltry insect," &c., giving to each term its proper value, and justifying its use in this place or objecting to it. During this time each pupil writes down in a column to the right of his exercise-book the verb: "Be off."[1]

The second sentence develops from the verb "spoke." The master will first enounce this verb; the class will inscribe it beneath "be off," and then will listen to the teacher as he finds out and reconstructs piece by piece the phrase used by La Fontaine. The third sentence will be "created" in the same manner, then the next and the next, to the end of the first step.

The most backward boy in the class will then be asked to go through the entire "step," and to reconstruct each phrase with the aid of the verb, the whole class carrying out the same work silently to themselves.

A second scholar is now asked to discover the logical sequence of the verbs, and with them to reconstruct from the beginning the entire step, by conceiving it as the author must have conceived it.

---

[1] For greater clearness the exercise is here expressed in English; the French text and the corresponding relative phrases are given in the Appendix (Trans.).

At this moment the disciple has become equal to the master; he is ready to pass to the second conception. The second step is then taught and assimilated as was the first, and the third as the two others.

After the conquest, the entering into possession. Silence will be called for, and while the teacher goes away to teach a similar lesson in an adjacent class, each pupil will write out, either from memory alone or by the aid of the verbs previously set down the first part of La Fontaine's little masterpiece.

On the teacher's return, the least advanced pupil will be asked to read out his second-hand creation. He will give it sentence by sentence, the others calling attention, by correcting them, to the slight imperfections that may have escaped him. After this, the second part of the fable will be elaborated in the same way, and the aim proposed will be attained, viz., "The pupil will have done over again the work of the author he is studying."

As regards the manner in which the teacher constructs each phrase before his class, this will vary with the teacher, and will depend on his capacity and his aptitude. It seems to us impossible to represent one of our lessons by writing, or to give our own personal process for an example. We may, however, formulate a precept which will stand as a definition of this process :—

"The teacher should strive, not merely to read the phrase of the author, but to create it, to cause it to be born, laboriously and with pains, as the author himself must have done; substituting successively one term for another, in the manner of an algebraist who transforms indefinitely the formula before him into another and simpler one." This pedagogic precept evidently implies the thorough and exhaustive discussion of each term of the classic studied.

In every literary lesson of this kind there are two sorts of expressions particularly important and particularly difficult to appropriate: these are the "metaphors" on the one hand, and on the other what we have termed the "relative phrases." The pupil will be required to glean these two species of expressions, and to write them out in a list apart at the end of the text. By means of the collection of the first species of expressions he will appropriate to himself the imaginative ideas of each writer, and this work will very quickly form his literary taste and judgment. The collection of the relative phrases will deliver into his hands the secret of expressing the most delicate and finest relationships of ideas and of things; and this exercise, by sharpening his mind day after day, will endow it finally, and in a short time, with that precious quality which is termed "tact or refinement."

Here, for example, are the metaphors that may be gathered from the fable "The Lion and the Gnat":—

to finish a word.	declare war.
to take time.	sound the charge.
rage rises.	sound the victory.
fury wearies.	announce the victory.
fury overthrows.	meet his end.
fury defeats.	pass through peril.

After an author, or at least a work, has been entirely gone through, all the metaphors will be brought together and grouped into order according to some system that shall enable them to be embraced at one glance, and consequently to be looked through often. We have already explained in the chapter upon the figurative language how a metaphorical theme is constructed. Evidently it is to this process that we should have recourse to set in order the metaphors of the authors we are studying.

The pupil will therefore glean, as we have expressed it, all the metaphors of the authors read by him; he will attempt to deduce therefrom the various "symbols" which they reveal, and upon these symbols he will construct his metaphorical themes. Thus will gradually be elaborated for him, and by him, a sort of systematic dictionary of the figurative language of each writer,—a precious spring, always pure and always wholesome, from which he may draw boldly and extensively. If, indeed, there is one species of riches which is common, and should remain common to all the members of the same race of mankind, it is the symbolism of their language, that which characterises, expresses, and defines their race.

After the metaphors we should attack the relative phrases. The following are those which will be noted by the pupil in the above fable, or which the teacher will aid him to discover :—

to think that →	to triumph.
to be affrighted.	to rise to the utmost.
to be disquieted.	to laugh to see that →
to be powerful.	to do one's duty in →
to lead anything whither one's fancy pleases.	to be defeated.
	to retire with glory.
to keep one's distance.	to sound the victory.
to take one's time.	&c. &c.
it is the work of →	

The following proverbs are also found :—

1. Amongst our enemies the smallest are often the most to be feared.
2. Through perils great one may have passed, to perish from the smallest thing at last.

The expressions followed by the sign (→) are enclitics.

It is not sufficient, however, merely to copy out these abstract formulæ; it is not enough merely to draw up a list of these fragments of thoughts. To become fruitful of result they will have to be grafted upon something solid. Transferred, amalgamated, wedded to what we have termed "the motives" of the relative phrases, these formulæ will give place to concrete expressions, to interlocutory sentences such as the following :—

Cont.[1]	I think that → you know what follows.
P. att.	Do not think that → thou canst learn without taking pains.
Take p.	Thinkest thou that → a language can be learnt without pains ?
Cont.	And let nothing affright you.
Cont.	The construction of such a simple phrase need not affright you.
V. gd.	I can see you are not affrighted.
Cont.	If you make a mistake, let not that disquiet you.
V. gd.	Your memory is becoming more powerful day by day.

---

[1] *Cont.* Continue, go on.   *Sp. b.* Speak boldly.
P. att. Pay attention.   *W. dn.* Well done.
V. gd. Very good.   *Att.* Attention.
B. g. ch. Be of good cheer.   *Take p.* Take pains.

V. gd.	In constructing a phrase no one is more powerful than art thou.
V. gd.	You lead the language whither your fancy pleases.
Slowly.	Take your ease: keep, as they say, a safe distance at first.
Slowly.	Take your time.
Cont.	And first, picture the fact clearly in your mind.
Cont.	And first, give the verb.
W. dn.	That is the work of a clever scholar.
B. g. ch.	You will triumph.
B. g. ch.	We shall triumph.
V. gd.	I am triumphant — to see you doing so well.
V. gd.	I laugh to see — that there is no further difficulty for you.
Att.	Do your duty by — clearly imagining the fact you have to express.
Att.	Do your duty by — speaking distinctly.
Sp. b.	Your duty is — to know it well.
V. gd.	You are not yet overcome.
Cont.	Show me that — you are not yet defeated.
V. gd.	From the combat you will retire with glory.
V. gd.	You can now, I think, sound the victory.
Att.	Mind the little words: amongst our enemies the smallest are often the most to be feared.
Att.	Through perils great one may have passed, To perish from the slightest thing at last.

We have already explained in the chapter on the relative phrases how the exercise of these phrases is combined with the study of the series. The literary themes can be, and are, treated in the same manner. As one pupil reconstructs the phrase of the author, the master or a fellow-pupil answers him with one of the preceding formulæ. He gives it once, twice, until it is graven upon the memory of all, and becomes for the whole class, as it were, a species of current coin.

What we have thus done for a fable of La Fontaine we have done, or we will or might do, for all the classical masterpieces—in Latin, Greek, German, French, Italian, Russian, Arabic, Sanscrit, &c. Prose or poetry, sciences or literature, all kinds (save only that of the empty vocabulary, essentially antipathetic to a system basing itself on life and desiring life everywhere), all kinds may be dealt with by this process.

This we affirm from experience we have already obtained. Now let us enumerate the advantages presented by this mode of teaching.

The pupil produces not a composition open to criticism, but a masterpiece. This creation is not the privilege of those only who are clever, it is the work of the less gifted of the class as well as the more gifted. The progress of those that are weak imposes no hindrance upon those that are strong. Art thus re-establishes the equality of intellects by re-establishing the equality of wills—that is, of attentive forces.

The art of reading well has for its first condition the need of a good accentuation. But to accentuate a phrase well the reader requires to know upon what word or upon what syllable the stress of the voice is to fall, and in order to know this word or syllable it is necessary to have first definitely determined the various parts that the terms which compose the phrase have to play, and to know exactly what each of these terms is intended to reveal. The work of exegesis which we have just described thus represents as useful a lesson of speaking or reading as it does of literature. The pupil who has composed over again with us the fable of La Fontaine will assuredly be able to speak it and to read it.

The whole class knows the fable to its very roots. I defy time itself to efface it from the memory of any one of our pupils. Yet he has not learnt it "by heart"—he has created it with his judgment. He has not confided its terms merely to his lips, as we so often force little children to do—he has kneaded it into his own substance; he has moulded it with his thought; in other words, he has made it his own by "conceiving" it in his mind. The work before him is really his own work; he would almost have the right to sign it with his name. And because it is his own work he has not the power to forget it.

How much time have we spent upon the creation of this masterpiece? On an average we need a quarter of an hour to elaborate a theme of about twenty-five sentences. When a problem was read out to Henri Mondeux, the last word had hardly been pronounced when the shepherd-boy gave back the answer. After a certain number of exercises carried out under conditions such as we have described, the memory of the child absorbs it almost as quickly as it can be spoken. Make a trial of the process yourselves, and you will soon see what is the capability of the memory, or rather the genius of the child, when he is placed under the dominion of logic and of mental representation.

The scholar gathers from success in the earliest days a knowledge of his personal power, and this confidence in himself has immediately the effect of redoubling his energies. Instead of requiring a spur, he will need a brake. A school conducted upon methods having this effect may well produce men of genius. Every man yet created loves his work—above all, when this work is constantly successful; and the love of the work done applies also to the labour which produces it. Our process is therefore a preventive to idleness, which is far better than its punishment. It creates the taste for work; it even gives rise to a passion for labour and study. From the very first day it lights the sacred fire.

Each scholar feeling himself a creator, every one is attentive—every one is entirely occupied with his own effort, his own creation. Therefore the words "imposition and discipline" will sound like barbarisms in the ears of our children. But for the words to remain always barbarisms, we must not forget that the human strength has certain very precise limits, and that if a sermon or a lecture three-quarters of an hour long exhausts a grown man, it will certainly *à fortiori* exhaust the child. Many of our pedagogues have not yet understood this axiom. It is for this reason that, in the eyes of children, the master is not a master, but an enemy. He is this indeed, because in the person of the child he does violence to, and cruelly wounds, human nature itself. He is more than an enemy—he is a tyrant.

The correction of exercise-books is no longer needed; all the exercise-books are perfect. In and by our process composition and correction are synonymous, and represent one and the same operation. The recitation of lessons also is no longer called for. Every one knows his lesson thoroughly. At the College of Caen, as I dare say elsewhere, this recitation of the lessons used to take an hour. It was always our despair, and it ought to become so for every conscientious professor. The children were enervated, or rather exhausted, before the real work of the class had even commenced.

No more dictation lessons. This deplorable exercise is

severely interdicted in many of the German schools. The German pedagogues stigmatise it by the name of "the abuse of confidence," and they are right. It would be better simply to copy; the pupil at least would not make mistakes, and to copy he does not need a master. During the time that he scribbles and blots one page under dictation, he might assimilate it and read it over twenty times. Therefore we have no more corrections, no more recitation of lessons, no more dictation.

How much time have we thus gained! What weariness have we spared our pupils! How many impositions have we avoided! How much good feeling drawn to the master! The child will no longer see in the man set to form his mind and morals an enemy and a tyrant. He will love him, he will be drawn to him as the most worthy and the most estimable of his friends. We shall see the child running to school with the same ardour as to the village fair.

By substituting everywhere lectures for silent study, our process suppresses in those schools which adopt it the ungrateful duty of monitor. It raises this personage to the position of assistant-master or of preceptor to beginners, with all the title and authority of an educator. It is upon him that falls the duty of teaching the elementary part of the languages. We have demonstrated that our method puts this teaching within the reach of every one. The teaching of the sciences will be for the learned professor.

An honest and devoted nurse sometimes occupies a larger place in the child's heart than even its own mother. The despised elementary language teacher will have, under the method that we propose, the first fruits of the scholar's affection. More than this, the prestige which the knowledge of languages gives will perhaps make of him a personage more regarded than the learned science master himself.

To all these advantages let us not forget to add that translated by the formula often evoked in this book:—"For three classes one master." While the scholar is writing out his lesson, that is, is giving a tangible form to his conception, the master could be training a second class, then a third, delivering to each of these the germ or the raw material of a creation similar to that already given—"One harvest is ripening while two others are being sown!"

A LATIN LESSON.

2. *A Page of Virgil.*

ÆNEID, Book II. v. 544.

Instead of the lesson which we have just elaborated, we may substitute a theme in a classic tongue. Let us take, for example, from our transcription of the Æneid, the 45th theme of the Second Book.

THE DEATH OF PRIAM.

Nunc morere!

—Sic fatus senior,   fatus est
telumque imbelle sine ictu conjecit;   conjecit
rauco quod protinus ære repulsum,   repulsum
et summo clypei nequicquam umbone pependit. pependit
Cui Pyrrhus: dixit
"referes ergo hæc   referes
et nuntius ibis Pelidæ genitori: ibis
illi mea tristia facta   narrare
degeneremque Neoptolemum narrare me- narrare
Nunc morere!"   [mento. morere

—Hoc dicens,   dicens
altaria ad ipsa trementem traxit   traxit
et in multo lapsantem sanguine nati,   lapsantem
implicuitque comam lævâ,   implicuit
dextrâque coruscum extulit (ensem)   extulit
ac lateri capulo tenus abdidit ensem.   abdidit

—Hæc finis Priami fatorum: finis fuit
hic exitus illum sorte tulit,   [gama, tulit
Trojam incensam et prolapsa videntem Per- videntem tul.
tot quondam populis terrisque superbum reg- regnatorem
    natorem Asiæ:
Jacet ingens littore truncus   jacet
avulsumque humeris caput   avulsum
et sine nomine corpus.   sine nomine.

* * * *

One remark with reference to the transcription of this exercise. How is it that amongst the number of professors who have undertaken the literal line-for-line translations, no one has had the idea, in the first place, of numbering the various distinct conceptions of the classic authors, and of constituting with each of them a separate exercise analogous to our own; and in the next place, of separating the sentences instead of dealing with single words; and, lastly, of arranging these sentences for the student in the order in which they are presented by our transcriptions?

The explanation of this fact is very simple. The Literary Series is the immediate corollary of our Linguistic Series. To conceive the one it is necessary to have first conceived the other. The high value of the verb in the language, its preponderance in the sentence, the amplitude of the intellectual effort of mankind, the measure of each one of our conceptions, the average length of the sentence, the part to be assigned to the ear, with the principles or precepts which devolve therefrom, and which constitute, in very truth, the art of teaching languages—these are the data which it was necessary to have possessed to be able even to formulate the problem. It will be remembered by what mere chance it was that we ourselves were enabled to unite them.

If, besides this, we keep in mind the blindness in which the spirit of routine, under the form of a word-for-word translation, has kept our humanists until the present time, one need not be astonished that they have stood so long close alongside our idea without ever even having caught a glimpse of it. So much having been said, let us show how the lesson of Virgil is given.

The end to be attained is: "To enable the work of the author to be reproduced by the pupil." The master first gives a free translation in his own words of the conception or the scene of Virgil; then beginning the first sentence of the first step he gives it in English—

"Thus spake the old man."

He strikes once more the term "spake" alone, and from this throws forth the Latin verb "fatus est," which he says again and again (fatus est—fatus est); and on this verb he builds up the phrase—

"Sic fatus est senior."

The pupil writes down on the margin of his exercise-book the verb "fatus est;" and then the master enounces the next sentence—

"And, without force, he cast an impotent javelin."

He repeats "cast," and then substitutes "conjecit;" establishes this verb solidly, and upon it as foundation raises the sentence—

"Telumque imbelle sine ictu conjecit,"

evoking the subject, evoking the complements, evoking the grammar and the genius proper to Latin, constructing always according to this genius, *i.e.*, placing that which completes before that which is completed. Meanwhile, each pupil inscribes "conjecit" beneath the "fatus est." After the second phrase the third is expounded; after the third the fourth, and so on until the whole of the first step is finished, at which point a halt is made.

Now the teacher and pupil exchange parts. The teacher has just given what we term the theme of the first step; the pupil, by listening and interpreting mentally each Latin phrase, has made the translation of it. Next in his turn the pupil gives the Latin of this mental translation. The master gives him the verb, "fatus est," and, if need be, the English phrase corresponding thereto, and the pupil should be able to find the sentence—

"Sic fatus est senior."

The master then challenges him afresh with the verb "conjecit." The pupil takes up the gauntlet and responds by the phrase—

"Telumque imbelle sine ictu conjecit."

The master gives him the third verb, and the pupil returns the third sentence, and so on to the end of the paragraph. The second step is attacked and carried like the first, and the third like the two others. A second pupil will wish to go through the whole of the theme with the sole aid of the verbs written on the margin of his exercise-book; another may solicit the favour of being allowed to reproduce the whole from memory.

The class have thought with Virgil, have spoken his words, have penetrated to the height of his genius, have assimilated a fragment of his art. Without reading Virgil directly, without translating him, without copying him, the pupils have actually conceived and rewritten the scene from the great master, and this work has required for pupils at this stage at most ten or fifteen minutes of time. The conception of Virgil has passed entire into the conception of the scholar. This is much—but it is not yet enough.

Every student now opens his book of transcriptions, and each separately looks rapidly through the work hitherto done in common. Then the books are closed, and in the exercise-book, which bears the verbs on its margin, the pupil recomposes, opposite these verbs, the corresponding sentences. Lastly, the correction is carried out in the manner we have mentioned, by the reading aloud of a single copy. At this moment, the conception of Virgil will have passed by all the senses of the scholar—first the ear, then the tongue, then the eye, and lastly the hand. Henceforth it will form part of his individuality; "he can never forget it."

We may point out further, that the exercise of the grammar has been constant though no grammar has figured in the class, and that the pupil has learnt the whole crowd of expressions without having once turned to his dictionary.

The metaphors and the relative phrases will next be noted or gathered together, and at a second reading—that of the whole book—they will be made the object of a special exercise. The relative phrases will furnish the elements of what we have called "An ordered conversation."

Under what conditions will this second reading take place? By the ordinary processes it is little less laborious than the first. The same difficulties are encountered; the same faults are committed; the same time is spent or wasted; and the utter weariness engendered ends by making odious to the student both the classical work and the name of its author.[1] But an entire book of the Æneid, for example, read through by means of our transcriptions, requires about two hours. Done from memory and aloud in class, together with the conversation by means of the relative phrases, it takes some three or four hours.

Seventy to ninety Latin lessons worked through in a morning! At this rate we have been able boldly to undertake to thoroughly learn, not only a few scraps of certain clas-

---

[1] "Horace, whom I hated so."—BYRON.

sical masterpieces, but these masterpieces themselves in their entirety.

The study of authors by means of our transcriptions is therefore as rapid as it is easy, and it is not the less fruitful.

Might not the language, we shall be asked, be learnt by the reading of the authors alone? Might we not do without the ordinary series? The present work is a continual demonstration of the negative. No; the reading of the classics, however long, persevering, and obstinate it may be, will never lead you to the true and thorough knowledge of the language.

If I were to desire to maintain the contrary hypothesis, should I not be opposed with the contradiction of the sorrowful experience achieved after so many years by all the schools and colleges of the world? All of these make their students read the Latin authors. Which of them, I ask, has discovered the true secret of teaching Latin? To learn a language, let us recollect for the hundredth time, is *not* to translate a book; it is to translate our own individuality into this language. We have pointed out how this human individuality is constituted. Now there is no classical work which contains this individuality; or rather it can only be found therein as Homer in the dictionary.

You have gathered together, we will suppose, all the materials for a house. The totality of these materials cannot be called a house, and will not really be a house, until the day on which these materials are grouped together and set into a certain definite order. In the same way, let us admit that all the elements that form part of your individuality can be found in the literature of a language. For these elements to represent your individuality, they must be first united, then grouped, then set into order in a certain manner—that is to say, brought together into what we have called the Ordinary Series.

Moreover, these are the only means to assure Latin being spoken and used in ordinary life. And if Greek is usually less well known than Latin, it is simply because it is less spoken. I used to read, re-read, and have read to me, during more than twenty years, the Greek and Latin classical works, and this exercise did not give me possession of either Greek or Latin. A desperate and continued reading of the German classics did not prove of greater benefit to me. I finally applied to these languages the system of the series—that is to say, I translated my individuality into these languages. Since then, but only since then, have I felt that these languages have become my own. Language is an edifice which has its summit, its crowning point, in its literature. This summit is always something quite other than the foundation. It presupposes this foundation, but it never can take its place.

The process of which we have just given a description may be brought to bear upon a literature lesson in German, in French, or in Arabic, as well as Latin. We have chosen the latter in order to put to rout once more the absurd prejudice which proclaims the necessity for two methods of teaching languages—the one for ancient languages and the other for modern.

Whoever the man who thinks and who writes may be, he does it by linking conception to conception, sentence to sentence. The work will be read well by that man who knows how to discover these links, and to accommodate his march and his length of step to the march and the step of the author.

Two more observations, and the exposition of our "method of translating, reading, and assimilating the classics" will be complete. The class have reproduced each of the foregoing themes in two manners: first orally, and then by writing. It is, perhaps, hardly necessary to state that this second exercise is not continual. One may undertake to read the principal masterpieces of the literature of a language, but not of writing out the whole of them by hand. The written theme has specially in view the art of composition. This art may be quite well taught to the student in making him reproduce, not all the models, but a certain number of them only.

The student must not be made to read for the mere sake of reading, but in order to understand and to learn. The book must therefore be one adapted to the age and the knowledge of the reader—that is to say, the reading must be graduated. Our system itself supplies us with a rule or a principle for establishing this graduation. The works will be classified according to their relation to the objective language such, as we have defined it. The tale, for instance, being the reproduction of the facts of every-day life, is the kind that approaches most nearly to our elementary series. The first exercise of reading in a foreign language will be given, therefore, by means of a collection of tales written in this language. Is not this also the first book understood, sought for, and assimilated by the child in his own language? After the tale will succeed the epic poem; to the epic will succeed the history; to the history the other kinds of literature,—all called forward in an order corresponding to the degree of their affinity with the Elementary Series or the objective language.

THE LANGUAGES BY THE SCIENCES AND THE SCIENCES BY THE LANGUAGES.

I.

THE SOLIDARITY OF THE SCIENCES AND THE LANGUAGES.

"Reduce the number of subjects taught!" This is the cry we hear continually; and from year to year this cry will grow louder—"Reduce the subjects!" The burden imposed on childhood surpasses the measure of its forces; the day's length of study exceeds the day's length of life. Instead of building up, edifying, this task overwhelms and crushes; instead of developing, this labour simply exhausts; therefore, "Reduce the subjects!" A cry so universal cannot but be the symptom of a real disease :—" Vox populi, vox Dei !"

Count, indeed, the sciences that the human mind has created or organised during the last fifty years; reckon up and measure the chapters which are added to each of them from one day to another, and you may well be astounded at the task laid upon the modern teacher and the modern scholar. Therefore, "Reduce your subjects," repeat the crowd.

But to do this we should have to omit some of the sciences. Now the suppression of science now-a-days is almost equivalent to the amputation of a limb. Let the ablest man be so good as to point out which are the superfluous sciences, and which parts are to be cut out. The schoolmaster who should announce his intention of striking out of his curriculum physics, for example, or chemistry, or some branch of natural science, would be to-morrow the object of universal reprobation, and would very soon lose all his pupils. And he would deserve it. Is not school the place to teach the sciences? Where else can our children learn them?

Thus the same voice that cries "Reduce the subjects," cries at the same time, "Do not alter the list of subjects." How are we to reconcile injunctions so contradictory? Is it not the predicament of the sick man who calls for the doctor, but pushes away the remedy prescribed?

This is because, as a matter of fact, the duty of the school is to add to, and never to take away from, human knowledge. The school is at one and the same time the first representative and the first instrument of progress. Its mission is to give light and still more light, and never to hide the candle under the bushel. "Reduce your subjects" does not mean "Suppress science;" it means, "Reform your methods."

It is not science, it is routine that must be suppressed; it is not knowledge which must be decreased, but the time which must be lengthened; it is not the load which must be diminished, but the power that must be doubled; it is not the comparatively feeble horse, but the steam-engine which must be called upon to draw the train which carries the modern fortune.

Every human science borrows its expression from language. To teach a science is to speak this science; to learn a science is again to speak this science. The knowledge of it is usually nothing else than speech — speech "set in order." Why is it that this speech *par excellence*, could not be utilised for the study of language properly so called? Why cannot the material of this science be used as a linguistic theme?

There is in school one ogre who devours not the flesh, but the time of children, who consumes their force and their life. This ogre is the study of language. For one hour given to the study of sciences the scholar spends four upon that of language under the form of grammar, spelling, dictation, of Greek, of Latin, of French or German. Whence is this disproportion? Why would not the lesson on zoology or botany serve as the theme for the lesson of spelling? Why should not the lesson on physics or on history be employed as the theme of a lesson in German or French?

Yes! between science properly so called and that of language there exists a profound solidarity, of which linguistic science should have been able long ago to make wonderful use. While studying languages we might study the sciences, and in studying the sciences we can study the languages. This is the point, the true point, upon which the attempts of reformers of the curriculum should be brought to bear.

Let the pedagogic science find the secret of making a science-lesson out of a language-lesson, and a language-lesson out of a science-lesson, and it will have trebled or quadrupled the time and the force of both master and pupil. Then the studies will be harmonious and the work properly balanced. Then the list of subjects will be found light. More; they may even be trebled and yet be found light.

How is it that this reform yet remains to be carried out? It is because it can only be accomplished upon the basis of a method which equally suits either the revelation of scientific truths and the translation of the forms of language. Where is this method? Until the present moment has the problem even been formulated?

Perhaps we may be permitted to apply in passing, and briefly, the principles of our linguistic method to the study, for instance, of the natural sciences, to that of the exact sciences and to that of history, in order to see if our humble essay might not prove to be the preface of that system for which pedagogic science has been waiting so long. We will commence by the end—that is to say, by history.

II.

THE LANGUAGES BY HISTORY AND HISTORY BY THE LANGUAGES.

1. *Necessity of a reform in the teaching of history.*

The teaching profession should renounce resolutely all those manuals or abridgments which present history to the minds of childhood in an altered, chopped up, mutilated form. It should seek to replace all these bad books by complete treatises, in which the life of the people and the instructive play of causes and effects develop with all the richness of truth. History is the grand school in which the future should gain its instruction—a school of politics and morals. Until now what have figured almost exclusively on the walls of this school are certain names and dates, in which are enshrined a few more or less important facts. Pedagogic science ought to pass the sponge over these insipid abstractions and replace them by living pictures.

It should resuscitate the past with its splendours and its miseries, with its heroisms and its deficiencies, with its passions, noble or criminal; it should reproduce, with all its incidents, the great drama of liberty struggling against despotism.

This is the kind of history I should wish to teach to my children; but where is the book that realises this ideal, and that I can put into their hands?

All the histories are composed and written for minds which meditate, analyse, and synthetise—for men of forty years old and upwards. But where is the history that is composed and written to be assimilated by children and youths? It is in vain that we ask them of pedagogic science.

Do not be deceived. All the so-called historical works "prepared for the use of children" are perfectly inaccessible to the child, and even to many grown-up persons. Between these books and all the others I see absolutely no difference other than the title—"For the use of children," and this title is a misnomer. Examine them yourselves. Are the chapters in these books thought out, shaped, or distributed differently to those in other books? Are the occurrences more detailed and placed in better sequence? Is the synthesis more logically connected? Has the style less of metaphor, less of rounded periods, less of pomposity? All these histories, I repeat, have nothing special in them; the most celebrated, so far as I have yet seen, have nothing truly pedagogic either in their basic idea or in their form.

And in this there is nothing very astonishing. The problem of a reform in the teaching of history has hardly as yet been put. If languages are badly taught in the great schools, what must we say to their teaching of history? History, real history, is too often not taught at all. Open the books and see if history is to be found therein, you who know what history is. See if the child can draw therefrom lessons and principles which may serve him and direct him when he becomes a citizen and has to exercise his rights.

Why are there throughout the country so many divisions and so many political parties? It is in great part because we do not know our country's history, or because each man has a history of his own, and not the impersonal history of a healthy pedagogic science; because the little that we do know of it has not been learnt at school where it is practically prohibited—but from newspapers; because we have oft-times the passion of it, but not the reason—the error of it, but not the truth.

History, real history, practically taught, practically written, here is the sacred book, the bible of the future. But this book is not yet written. The profession of teachers must set themselves courageously to this task, and create for their own use a method for teaching history such as that which we have attempted to create for the teaching of languages. And the creation of this book is of the first necessity. History and the reading of history, and meditation therein, must be for the future citizen a sacred daily duty. History must become an essential part of our moral personality. It is important, therefore, that this history should be true; and it is equally important, seeing the richness and the extent of the material, that it should be in the highest degree easy of assimilation.

In fact, it will not be in a volume of 300 pages that you will recount—I will not say the history of the world, nor even the history of the nation, but one single epoch of this history. It is therefore necessary to find a system so simple, so practical, that the pupil has but to read in order to know, has but to look in order to retain, has but to turn over the pages to refresh his memory. Is such a system possible? And would it be possible to-day to establish the basis and trace the chief outlines of it? We will attempt it. We may be able to prove that our project deserves to be considered as something more than a mere chimera.

2. *History put into Series.*

History is the story of the passions, the aspirations, the tendencies, that is, the various and successive ends which have been pursued by a people, and the means by which they have attempted to attain them. History represents, therefore, a tissue of ends and of means. But wherever there are "ends and means" there is opportunity and place for SERIES. Therefore the series, the basis of our linguistic system, may become the basis of a historic method. We should proceed to establish, to weave, this new kind of series in the following manner:—

Given a certain historical fact—the Seven Years' War, for instance, or the reigns of Louis Quatorze of France or of King Charles I. of England, or a special moment in any one of the reigns, such as the Wars of the Roses—we shall study with care the men who have played a part in this political act, and the passions which have moved them; we shall count minutely the various ends into which their movements may be resolved; we shall draw up a catalogue of these ends or aims, not according to an alphabetical list, but according to their chronological succession. Then seeking the means by which these various ends have been attained as time passed on, and expressing them in the same order in which they succeeded, or should have succeeded, each other, we shall arrange them upon the model of our Linguistic Series. Putting the Life of the People into series—this is at one and the same time both the foundation and the plan of an historical method; we will indicate here, briefly, the work of detail, and the form of the edifice.

The general history of events will be found divided into a considerable number of particular stories, which form so many pictures or scenes. Each scene will contain one simple and unique fact, strongly brought into relief by the style and the movement of the phrase. This scene will occupy a special page, and will bear a title as simple as itself, of which the text of the page is the development. On this page the order of succession in time will be rigorously followed—an order of which far too little account is taken even in the most elementary text-books of history, and which, nevertheless, is certainly the secret of precision and of clearness, as it is the condition of prompt and easy assimilation. For, indeed, *what is memory if it is not the logical classification of facts in the mind?* If, therefore, the facts are already classified, the mind will grasp them and will retain them so much the more rapidly, and the less able pupils will be able to remember them as well as the most gifted.

We shall have none of these reflections and prognostications such as fill up our present text-books and dishearten the child, for the reason that he is not able to understand them, and is still less able to distinguish them from the real history of facts. The facts, nothing but the facts—the facts with the dramatic movement of causes and of effects—the facts which speak for themselves and cause the reader to think—the facts interpreted solely by the accent of the professor—these are what we require. And in the expression of them we must have none of those gross and empty metaphors that the child understands not, which mislead rather than guide him, and which cause him to take vain shadows for living realities.

Conceived on these lines, history may be written in quite a

different fashion to that we now know. We shall write it in simple and short phrases, which course after one another, having all the rapidity of the movement with which the life of the people is unfolded.

1. Each phrase will only express one idea or one simple fact.

2. Each phrase will be distinct from that which precedes and from that which follows it, both on the paper as well as in the mind, *i.e.*, each sentence will be placed line by line as in our Linguistic Method.

We have shown the justification for the use of this form of the printed page when speaking of the themes of our series: the same reasons justify the use of it for our historical themes.

The method is sketched out: let us suppose that it is constructed; how are we to apply it? This question is one that is not less grave than that of the method of teaching our Linguistic Series. In order to fix ideas and to facilitate our explanation, we reproduce on the following page an historical theme taken almost at hazard from one of our lithographed transcriptions. This scene has no other pretension than that of showing the typographic form of our Historical Series.[1] An isolated theme can with difficulty be made to give any exact idea of our historical treatises: it would be necessary at least to devote an entire chapter to the subject.

---

[1] This specimen history-lesson has been also given in the French, as it then equally illustrates the property of the system of forming advanced language-lessons from the history of the country whose language is being studied (Trans.).

BATTLE OF ROSSBACH.
November 5, 1757.

— On the morning of the 5th, Soubise com-   commanded
manded the attack.
The army deployed in a long line,   deployed
with the idea of turning the Prussians,   turning
and enclosing them in a circle of fire. [tent,   enclosing
Frederick remained perfectly still within his   remained
tranquilly following the movements of the   following
    enemy.
At noon he sat down to table as usual.   sat down
The French continued to advance;   advance
drums were beating,   were beating
bands were sounding triumphal marches;   were sounding
nothing stirred in the Prussian camp.   stirred
The French attributed this calm to fear,   attributed
and could not comprehend such apathy.   comprehend

— It was two o'clock in the afternoon;   was
Frederick came quickly out of his tent,   came out
and gave the order, "To arms! March!"   gave order
In the twinkling of an eye the tents are   struck
    struck, folded,
orders cross in the air,   cross
and the battalions hasten to the place assigned.   hasten
"Forward," cried Frederick a second time,   cried
and the army threw themselves on the foe.   threw themselves

— A rain of fire and bullets fell upon the   fell
    French.
Prince Henry took their infantry in flank.   took
Seidlitz attacked them in the rear with his   attacked
    cavalry.
This violent and unforeseen movement of the   acted
    Prussians acted as a surprise;
the amazed Imperialists took to flight.   took
The French maintained their position until   maintained
disputing the ground foot by foot. [dusk,   disputing

*   *   *   *   *

BATAILLE DE ROSSBACH.

5 Novembre 1757.

—Le 5 au matin, Soubise fit sonner la charge ;   fit sonner
l'armée se déploya sur une longue ligne :   se déploya
il s'agissait de tourner les Prussiens,   tourner
et de les prendre dans un cercle de feu.   prendre
Frédéric resta immobile dans sa tente,   resta
suivant tranquillement les mouvements de   suivant
    l'ennemi.
A midi il se mit à table comme à l'ordinaire.   se mit
Les Français continuaient d'avancer,   avancer
les tambours battaient,   battaient
la musique jouait des marches triomphales ;   jouait
rien ne bougeait dans le camp prussien.   bougeait
Les Français attribuaient ce calme à la peur   attribuaient
et ne pouvaient s'expliquer tant d'apathie.   s'expliquer

—Il était deux heures de relevée :   était
Frédéric sort précipitamment de sa tente,   sort
et crie : " Aux armes ! à l'ennemi ! "   crie
En un clin d'œil les tentes sont arrachées, pliées ;   arrachées
les commandements se croisent dans l'air,   se croisent
et les bataillons courent à la place assignée.   courent
" En avant ! " cria une seconde fois Frédéric,   cria
et l'armée se rua sur l'ennemi.   se rua

—Une pluie de feu et de balles s'abattit sur les   s'abattit
    Français.
Le prince Henri prit en flanc leur infanterie,   prit
Seidlitz la prit en queue avec sa cavalerie.   prit
Ce mouvement violent et imprévu des Prussiens   agit
    agit comme une surprise ;
les Impériaux épouvantés prirent la fuite.   prirent
Les Français tinrent bon jusqu'au soir,   tinrent bon
et disputèrent le terrain pied à pied.   disputèrent

*   *   *   *   *

3. *The teaching of the history lessons.*

A history lesson is a play in two acts; we have the work of exposition by the master, and then the work of assimilation by the pupil. Let us deal first with that of the master. In beginning the lesson, the master does not read; he improvises. Nothing cools the ardour of a class of children more than reading; the book acts as a screen, and both paralyses the feelings of the teacher himself and hinders his thoughts from radiating to the minds of his hearers. A picture, a chart, such as would be illustrative of the facts he wishes to enforce, should be the only auxiliaries of a good teacher of history. To the eyes of the pupil, the professor should be a living history. He needs not only to know history, but to appear permeated therewith.

He must not, therefore, have his historical lessons written out exactly as he is to give them; their titles at most may act the part of programme, as memoranda or notes. He will abandon himself to the inspiration of the moment, to his own conception, and will expose the facts as if he saw them or knew them, with order, with clearness, with precision, and with warmth, giving emphasis to those that deserve emphasis, and this in language half-conversational, half-academic, and with an occasional humorous turn which will serve to place the fact in relief in the memory.

The block of marble is drawn from the quarry, trimmed, roughed out; the inspiration is communicated. We next endeavour to perfect the statue. After having made the facts speak for themselves, the teacher will make the book speak. Now he reads; but this exercise is not an ordinary reading; it is a translation, the translation of a scene already well known to all, and in which, shortly before, the whole class were vividly interested. This exercise presents itself as the solution of a fresh problem of which the following is the statement:—
"To find the best expression possible of the historical drama to which the class have just been giving their attention."

From this point of view the reading has a great interest. Rest assured that here we have discovered a method for keeping each pupil attentive. The teacher reads, comments upon, criticises each phrase,—carries out, in fact, a work analogous to that which we have described when speaking of the reading of the classical authors. So much for the teacher's part: now let us investigate that of the pupil.

In the first place, he knows to its roots the history he has before him. What he lacks is the expression of it. How can he conquer this? Nothing is more simple. We may point out at once that our historical lessons are all as exactly and definitely organised as our linguistic lessons. The theory that we have developed when dealing with these equally applies in its entirety to the history lessons.

This stipulated, the pupil will proceed as follows:—Covering up the text, he will read aloud the verbs one after the other, and on each verb he will build up the corresponding phrase. He will elaborate in this way, piece by piece, the first paragraph or step, and going through it a second time, he will thoroughly assimilate it. He will do the same with the second and with the third step. It will require, we have found, five to seven minutes for a pupil to learn, in this manner, a history lesson such as that given. This result is rich in consequences: we will refer to them farther on.

The teacher now asks the dullest in the class to repeat the lesson. He ascertains that this child knows the page, and will conclude from this that all know it. To what exercise will he now pass? This will depend upon the age and the ability of the children before him. If he is dealing with beginners who do not yet know how to write correctly, he will simply give them the lesson to copy out, or perhaps he will dictate it carefully, pronouncing each word separately, or possibly will have it dictated by one of the scholars.

This exercise will advantageously replace that of the usual dictation exercise and the writing lesson, and will, moreover, be a diversion and an opportunity for the pupils to digest the lesson. If the class are already well drilled in spelling, if serious mistakes need be no longer feared, the history lesson will become the material for a literature lesson in composition. In such a case, these are the conditions under which the work would be carried out:—

Each pupil will copy into his exercise-book the series of verbs from the history lesson, then closing the printed book, he will reproduce in writing the phrases corresponding to the verbs. The correction of these exercises will be as short as they are easy. It will be sufficient for the teacher to have one copy read out aloud. Each pupil will correct his phrase according to that which is judged perfect. If the class is still further advanced, the history lesson will be reproduced as a true narrative after a single reading or a single hearing, and without other help than the logic of the facts.

There remains yet one other category of pupil—those who, trained by these various exercises, have learnt to think for themselves, that is, to seize the true relations of things, and who along with solid principles have acquired the forms wherewith to express all their conceptions. These will treat the history lesson from a higher point of view; they will trace the portraits and sound the praises of the great men whose actions are before them; they will paint the battles; they will judge the revolutions; will give their appreciations of the legislation, will give over again the speeches of the great politicians, attempting to revive in these compositions the ideas and the passions which have agitated bygone times, seeking by these means to epitomise each epoch, to characterise each historic moment.

Studied in this way, history will inevitably enter at each lesson deep into the mind and the heart of the child, and will early make a man of him. Our aim can now be seen; history is considered by us first of all as a science, and is treated as such; afterwards it is used as a literature lesson, marvellously suitable for forming the language and the style of the pupil.

Prepared as we have just indicated, history is a collection of narratives, in which we set down successively the forms and turns of expression most habitual and most important in literary composition. By means of these narratives the literary education of a class will be carried on day by day. The principal advantages of this method of proceeding are these:—

1. Each history lesson forms one complete narrative, of a length suitable to beginners.
2. The facts are analysed and developed in this lesson methodically.
3. Order and movement are given to them.
4. The pupil will quickly learn to control his thought by means of these short and rapid phrases, which are used to translate the facts of the narrative.
5. Each phrase being a whole in itself, the pupil is forced to give equal care to every phrase.

HISTORY AND LITERATURE COMBINED.

In ordinary compositions one phrase compensates for another—the best for those less well turned. But in our scenes each part is well in view. Each sentence requires to be considered separately, to be balanced, put into cadence. Teachers well know that this is the last thing to be obtained (when it *is* obtained), even with the most promising of their scholars.

The firm material of history is far better for beginners, is infinitely easier to deal with than are the subjects usually proposed, by which the idle imagination alone is excited, while the pupil generally knows not from which side to commence the attack. The brevity and facility of the history compositions will enable either one or several to be given every day. These exercises being all polished to the point of perfection, or nearly so—every effort being fruitful, every hour producing its result—little time will be needed to form a taste and a genius for narrative in the pupil's mind.

The history lesson is, therefore, really a literature lesson as well, and in our opinion one of the most practicable that a teacher can propose to give in class. For this reason the historical series is the first auxiliary we propose to the purely linguistic series.

When the basis of the language has been conquered, reading lessons and recitations are needed, in which all the terms, both real and figurative, recur, so to speak, in their free state, and as called forth by the incidents. What more convenient could be imagined, either for the teacher who recounts or for the pupil who listens, than these historical series ?

What reading-lessons easier, and at the same time more profitable, than these could the student undertake ? What subject more advantageous to his mental progress could he study ? His eye has never to take in more than one line at a time, his mind has only one sentence to grasp. He descends from thought to thought with surety, without possibility of mistaking the sense. By reason of the natural order which links incident to incident, he can divine, so to speak, each phrase even before reading it. The "Steps" mark the precise points at which he should stop, or at which the recital should be broken off, so that he may read over what he has already understood, in order to take thorough possession of it. We need not again refer to the verb, which announces the idea as the dawn announces the day.

Up to the present time, no really practical book, it seems to us, has ever been written for the use of those who wish to perfect themselves in the study of a language, or to keep up their knowledge of it, while at the same time giving useful and interesting information. History treated in the manner we have here indicated appears to us to be able fully to satisfy this need.

Amongst the advantages of this method, there is one which we certainly ought to indicate in concluding, as it answers at the same time an objection which cannot fail to be levelled at us. Would it be believed? this process, which enables us—nay, which forces us to descend into the very smallest details, in order to really make the actions and the men live over again, actually has the advantage of brevity over all the others.

We have put into series on this system the French historian certainly farthest beyond rival in this respect—Voltaire; we have narrated and written out the reign of Louis XIV. in 250 themes or lessons, without omitting a single one of the facts contained in the work of this great writer. And the book by Voltaire, in the edition of a similar size of page, has 600 pages! over 300 of which must therefore be explanations, remarks, or other matter not absolutely necessary to the progress of the story.

There remains the difficulty of execution. We who are engaged upon the work know better than any one else can possibly do how much labour may be spent in arranging a treatise of history in this way; but when one feels oneself to be at last on the right track the work becomes easy. Two things suffice to succeed: faith and courage.

We are now in a position to calculate the length of time that a history course carried out under these conditions will require. Each whole lesson given by the teacher will usually embrace one well-determined episode, decomposed into at least five or six different movements, which give rise to as many separate page exercises. These exercises are to the whole lesson what the paragraphs of a book are to the chapters.

At the end of our treatise "Project for County High Schools" (Projet d'Ecoles Cantonales), an episode of the

Frondist war is given, forming the material of one ordinary lesson. To this treatise the reader who desires to know more of our history lessons is referred. Basing our calculations upon this lesson, we are able to estimate the amount of history work accomplished every day. An episode properly prepared is given easily within half-an-hour, and five themes can be learnt in thirty-five minutes. On an average, one hour, therefore, will be sufficient for the elaboration of five historical themes, comprised in one episode.

It is always better that a complete episode should be given at each lesson. Experience has demonstrated to us that the longest of these episodes seldom exceeds ten pages—that is, ten exercises. When such a case presents itself, the whole hour is devoted to the study of this episode, and the next day the whole hour is given to the literary work of the lesson. The result is exactly the same—ten exercises in two hours. At the end of the 300 days of the scholastic year the pupil will thus have been able to assimilate a volume of 1500 pages. Compared to what is now obtained even in the best schools, this result must appear prodigious, and represents at least the work of three years. Added to this, these 1500 exercises have been conscientiously elaborated and conquered by all the pupils. I repeat, by all.

With regard to the written work, this must be put to the credit of the literary tasks. What we have already said upon this point should be remembered; each theme should be elaborated orally, but not all of them need be written out on paper.

One such series may be given in English, another in French, this one will be given in German, and that in Italian; by history the languages will be studied, and by the languages the history will be studied.

4. *Geographical Series.*

The teaching of history is involuntarily associated in the mind with that of geography.

If the teaching of geography is capable of reform, this reform must be based upon a reform in the maps. It is in this direction that we have attempted to solve the problem. In our " Projet d'Ecoles Cantonales "—Réforme des Méthodes, p. 37— we have set forth our process at length. We there state how we have been able to reproduce by drawing the true configuration of a given region; how the apparent relief of the surface increases, becomes more precise, as our maps are withdrawn further from the eye; how the map by this means, by rendering possible the collective teaching of geography, becomes a thoroughly pedagogic instrument; how each continent is subdivided into regions, natural or climatic; how each region is itself put into series—that is, decomposed into its various countries and subdivisions; how each theme of this new series is taught and elaborated; and, lastly, how the geographical theme may be converted into a linguistic theme.

III.

THE LANGUAGES BY THE NATURAL SCIENCES AND VICE VERSA.

To determine first the diverse ends of each being or of each force, then to reveal the means, still more diverse, by which these ends become realities, is not this, in point of fact, the true object of the teaching of all science, physical or natural? If this definition is correct, the principles of our method should adapt themselves admirably to the material of physical or natural science, both for defining the conquests of scientists, as well as for popularising them. We repeat, wherever there are means and ends, there is the possibility of series. Now, the series, the properly organised series, is incontestably the most practical, the most clear, one may say the only logical, form under which truth may be manifested.

In reality, scientific men, whether they know it or not, pass their lives in reading, deciphering, then in constructing such series, or in preparing the material for these series. The oral teaching of every good professor is nothing more than the development of a series. Given from his lips, the series is almost always perfect, the end being presented as an end and the means as means. But the book which reproduces his teaching is seldom irreproachable. Too often it flings ends and means together into a confused heap. Here we have the true reason why a course of lectures is always found more helpful than a printed book.

We have here once more, therefore, a reform to be attempted, namely, a reform in scientific text-books, one which cannot but be of considerable service to the scientific man himself, to the science which he cultivates as well as to the teaching of it. An example will more fully explain our idea.

There exists no good treatise on botany which contains less than 400 ordinary pages. To assimilate the contents, the student is obliged to meditate upon them for days and weeks together, and finally himself re-edit—that is to say, "set in order"—the material which they comprise. Now, the series of a tree—that of the oak, for example, following this member of the vegetable kingdom from the moment the acorn drops to the ground and takes root, right through to the moment when it becomes in its turn a fruitful tree—will encounter on its path all the phenomena of vegetation imaginable, from the birth of the cells, the development of the roots, the circulation of the sap, to the formation of the wood, to the blossoming of the flower, to the mysteries of reproduction. The linguist who should construct this series would, therefore, on the one hand, have to recognise, to count, to determine one by one the various and successive ends proposed by Nature in the plant; and on the other, to observe and express the ways and means by which each one of these ends is variously attained.

Now, each problem solved or posed by science corresponds, or ought to correspond, to an end or aim of Nature. How many different problems could the greatest botanist in the world enounce upon the complete development of an oak? We may boldly advance the statement that he would be greatly embarrassed, in spite of the richness of the material before him, if he were asked to formulate two hundred. Therefore the contents of all the botanical treatises in the world (speaking of the principles and the theory of botany) might well be comprised within a series of 200 themes.

The science of botany would therefore gain considerably in precision, if its expression were elaborated according to the principles of our method. It would gain still more in clearness if the problems set by it were to succeed each other in the rigorous order of a series, where each theme presented the logical development of a particular problem, that is to say, the means by which Nature successively accomplishes each of her aims.

The written science would thus become the rival and the perfect image of the reality. Problems as yet unsolved, being brought fully into view, would more directly attract the attention of scientific men to them, and the conquests of science would become, at the same time, both more certain and more rapid.

What we have said with respect to the science of botany applies equally to all other sciences. As a method of exposition, our system seems to us, therefore, capable of rendering the greatest services to true science. What use can the study of language make of this property of the system? It can make an immense use—one so great, indeed, that our method would be impossible if the sciences could not be taught by the series.

In fact, the material of which our series is constructed, as we have stated in the chapter on the construction of the system, is natural history itself—it is the translation of the life of the plant, the translation of the life of the insect, the life of the bird, the life of the quadruped, the play of the elements; it is the expression of the general life of mankind, and its development by and in the trades, the arts, the industrial occupations; all this is organised—as living as that reality itself which the method attempts to interpret.

Everything is fixed, defined, immutable in Nature; ends and means, all are contained therein, all are linked together. Where could linguistic science possibly find material more fruitful, or one easier to put to its use? Is not the principle of causality, which rules over the order and the harmony of the world, the sole basis that should be adopted by a method aspiring to be truly rational?

The work carried out for science and by science will serve also, therefore, for the study of language. In return for this, linguistic science should set in order, define, popularise the revelations of physical science, and consequently should offer a system of which the true definition will still be—

"The languages by the sciences,
The sciences by the languages."

It has needed some courage on our part to resist here the temptation to put into series either a chapter of physics, or the history of a plant, or an entomological study by Réaumur. But we have explained at the commencement of the book how the series of a quadruped, the series of a plant, or the series of an insect should be constructed. We must content ourselves with this general indication, and must reserve the elaboration of the scientific series for definite scientific works.

IV.

THE LANGUAGES AND THE EXACT SCIENCES.

It should be stated, in the first place, that the exact sciences are just those which are taught with the greatest success in the ordinary schools. What is the reason of this? Open a book of mathematics, and you will find a series of lessons, termed theorems, developed separately and methodically. Their enunciation exactly corresponds to the expression of the "ends" or aims of our linguistic lessons, and the demonstration by deduction answers to the development of the successive "means" by which our ends are attained. The books, therefore, which treat the exact sciences do really present these sciences under the form of series.

It is, in fact, to this disposition of their lessons that the teaching of the exact sciences in our present schools owes its successes, or rather its triumphs. The mathematical books therefore bear telling witness in favour of our system.

The fact now stands revealed—our system is not new; it is as old as the sciences, which have applied it instinctively for centuries.

But that which is even better than the mathematical books, and which still more resembles our series, is the verbal lesson or exposition of the teacher. The book often presents two deductions, or two fragments of deductions, upon the same line. The teacher gives forth only one sentence at a time. He stays and rests, as we do, upon this sentence; his accent isolates it, so to speak, and sets it alone upon its own line. The book often omits a connection or a deduction; the teacher, who speaks in order to be understood, never commits this fault, or, if such an omission occurs, he at once corrects it. It is for this reason that the student usually prefers his own notes and exercises to the most learned of printed books.

What, then, we may ask, is lacking to the geometric or algebraic theorem for it to be a perfect linguistic theme?

Nothing, or next to nothing, so far as regards its basis. The nature of the exact sciences specially lends itself to the principles of our system. In fact, there is nothing more rigid than mathematical deduction. It is no longer, it is true, the relationship of succession in time which links idea to idea, phrase to phrase, but the logical relationship of principle to consequence, which is not less inflexible than the former[1] (*vide* "Ecoles Cantonales," p. 36). Let but a teacher be ruled to some extent by pedagogic science, and his book will be as perfect as his lecture. The arbitrary disposition of the typographical line spoils the book; it paralyses or lames the straightforward march of reason; it embarrasses deduction, it lessens or obscures the evidence.

If a mathematical theorem were written as it should be written, any scholar would be able to assimilate a book upon mathematics just as easily as a book upon history. The exact sciences are, indeed, nothing but the development of pure reasoning—reasoning never contradicted, altered, or corrupted by sentiment.

It is, therefore, the form, and more particularly the written form, or the printed book, which yet leaves something to be desired in the teaching of the exact sciences. Let but treatises be written in which the theorems are grouped and classified in families, in which deduction is rigidly conducted and thoroughly developed, in which the sentences, simplified and disentangled from each other, occupy their natural place, and stand each on its own separate line as they do in our series; in which the paragraphs, after the manner of our steps, are multiplied as necessitated by the ideas and according to the varied play of the data, and the mathematical theorem will present all the properties of a linguistic theme. It could be given and afterwards assimilated in the same way, and in any language desired; and the study of mathematics, instead of opposing and hindering the study of languages, would serve it as an auxiliary.

However restricted the language of the exact sciences may be, this language certainly has its value. In default of colour, it can give to the science of language the precision, the swing,

---

[1] Why should not the exact sciences themselves be reformed, so that they also might be the study of facts according to their order of succession in time? This is perfectly possible (Trans.).

the force, the feeling of pride and of independence which spring from truth. Witness the style of Pascal.

Grant a reform in the method of teaching languages and sciences, both in written text-books and in the manner of giving the lessons, and languages and sciences will lend each other mutual aid and compete in rivalry for the advancement of each other. Then the more the languages are studied the better will the sciences be understood; the greater the work done on the sciences the more the languages will be exercised. The sciences will be benefited by the time given to the languages: the languages will be benefited by the time devoted to the sciences.

In this way we shall have reduced the number of subjects, while at the same time making the lessons more fruitful, while making them produce double and treble harvest; in other words, we shall reduce the labour while multiplying the work done.

One good result always draws others in its train. This reform delivers into our hands the secret of forming complete minds. The teacher will cease to be a mere huckster of vain declensions and pure abstractions, and the student will cease to be the fraction of a man. His knowledge will become the harmonious compound of science and of literature, of science and of morality, of science and of art.

PART FIFTH.

GREEK AND LATIN.

I.

THE VALUE OF GREEK AND LATIN.

1. *The interest of the race.*

My name is a compound of five letters. Taken separately, these letters are to me nothing more than they are to all the world besides. Grouped in a certain fashion, they form a word which has the virtue of exerting a very peculiar effect upon my mind : it is the name of my father, the name of my mother ; it is my own name ; it is a part of myself—it stands for myself.

This word includes for me a whole world of ideas, of sentiments, of remembrances. It contains and sums up the existence of beings who are or have been the most closely connected with my own existence. For me this name cannot perish; it is for me dearer and more sacred than even the portraits of those whom it recalls. The portrait can show but one moment of an existence, the name translates its totality.

To renounce this name, to barter it for another, seems to me to be almost impossible. I should feel myself committing the blackest of impieties, the meanest of apostasies. I should feel as if I were denying the name of my father and mother, blushing for their life of self-sacrifice, despising their love. Such is the virtue of a family name.

I am bound by ineffaceable ties to the cottage in which I was born, to the orchard which was the scene of my childish games, to the village where dwelt my mother, to the village church and the village chimes. When I hear the words "my country," it is to these scenes that my soul takes wings.

I cling to the persons, old and young, whom then I knew,

or rather all these things belong intimately to my being; they are as if welded to me; they form part of my very self. Hence this sorrowful emotion when one of them passes away from earth; hence this rending of my very substance which translates itself to the external world by a sigh or by tears. It is a part of this substance which is torn violently from me; it is a part of my being which dies, a living image which goes out upon the hearthstone of my life.

Such is the virtue of our earliest remembrances; and it is within the depths of this double sentiment that the domestic and religious traditions have their roots.

As with individuals, so the races have also their name—a name which expresses them and defines them—a name which includes the facts of their life, the archives of their existence; and this name is—their language! It is bequeathed from generation to generation as an entailed patrimony. The language has all the virtues of the family name; the race by whom it is spoken clings to it as to a part of itself, and deems it imperishable.

Is it possible to imagine a nation decreeing the abolition of the language of its forefathers?

As with individuals, the races have their reminiscences, their childhood's earliest remembrances; they are termed "traditions." And these traditions constitute the basis of the racial characteristics; they are their substance. If these were to perish, the races would perish. It is the living source from whence the three great arteries of the Good, the True, and the Beautiful draw their sustenance.

For the Latin races, Latin is the language of their forefathers; it is the true name of the race, and its literature contains a part of the substantial traditions of this race, more especially that of the Law.

Greek is not the language of their forefathers, but it is that which brings in a golden sunbeam the traditions of the True and the Beautiful, which, joined to the traditions of the Roman law, rendered the Renascence possible. The Greek language is so encrusted within the languages of our own day, that, to get rid of the one, we should have to destroy the other. For the Latin races the Roman tongue furnished the raw material, but Greek fashioned it: the material is Latin, but the construction is Greek. If Latin is the original name, we might say that Greek is the surname. One represents the essence, the other the manner of existence.

The surname often says more to us than the original name, and even becomes a title. And if Greek has become a distinctive title of a race, have they any right to renounce it?

The life of nations is as a balance; one of the scale-pans carries their past, the other carries their future. The State is the pivot upon which the whole is supported. It is formed for both of them, and, as its name (*status*) seems to imply, it is by means of the State that the equilibrium—that is, the conciliation of opposed and apparently antagonistic forces—takes place.

Although the attributes of the State are as yet but ill-defined, there are certain functions which belong to it by nature. The State is before all else the representative of the race; to it are confided the interests of the nation. It has the charge, like the Vestal virgins of Rome, of maintaining upon the altar of the country that which may be termed the sacred fire of the race, and to watch not only that this shall never go out, but that it shall never diminish or languish in the least degree. To it, therefore, is confided the sacred keeping of the ancient mother-tongues of the race. The interests of the race imperatively demand the maintenance of the Greek and Latin tongues: "Caveant consules!"

2. *The interest of the individual.*

The study of ancient languages has received a name so true, so just, so profound, that we might almost say it had fallen from heaven: this name is—"THE HUMANITIES!"

To study these languages is to make a man of one's self! Every harmonious being has two poles. To be complete, the man of to-day should be grafted upon the man of ancient times. There is something lacking to him who has not studied "the humanities." His personality is ill-balanced: he himself dimly feels this. He may be thrice as gifted as the humanist who stands before him, yet by instinct he will everywhere yield the highest places to the humanist. This may be noticed more particularly in the writer and the thinker. The exclusively modern man is timid. He has no confidence in himself—he lacks assurance. Whence comes this? It is because he can feel no solid base whatever beneath his feet. He rests, indeed, only upon himself, But a man's self is not a base: it is a gradual "growth."

That which gives the humanist his strength is the basis upon which he rests. He feels within himself two personalities—the ancient man, in whom no further change will occur, and in whom the race is personified, and the new man or individual, engrafted upon the first, nourished by it, and destined to change—that is, to live and to produce. It is like the tree with its unchangeable trunk, and the graft which borrows therefrom its juices, to transform these successively and periodically into leaves and flowers and fruit.

The harmonious alliance between these two beings, the racial man and the individual man, this it is that makes the great man, the man of genius, the useful man, the good citizen, the man *par excellence*, who unites within his own personality a House of Commons and a House of Lords, a Senate and a Chamber; the two moving in accord, the one sustaining the other—the one vivifying the other. The truly great man will disappear from off the earth on that day when the individual—that is, egotism or the rule of the "ego"—becomes exclusive.

I have just spoken of the great writer. It has been stated above that there are two manners of constructing a sentence—that is, two manners of conceiving the form of a thought: the one antique, the other modern—the one natural, the other logical.

These two constructions are the two wings of an author. He who has but one of them will never wing an harmonious flight in the world of ideas. In this respect the study of Latin, even if imperfect, has a considerable value.

As regards its form, it is the most antique of the languages spoken on the European continent—a quasi-primitive language. It is in the Latin school, therefore, that we can best study the antique manner of thinking and of speaking. The great writer, like the great man, is he who can amalgamate in their right proportions the antique step to the modern gait, the natural movement to the logical movement, in the same way that a truly classical work is an harmonious composition of these two spirits and the two processes.

It is owing to this hidden virtue that Latin has not succumbed under the criticisms (otherwise well founded) of its detractors; it is this incontestable merit that has made it deserve the privilege of being adopted as the first basis of literary education of all the nations who have schools at all, both of the Latin or the non-Latin races. Let us add, that if this language has its adversaries, it is not in reality the language itself that is attacked, but the absurd and irrational method by which it is applied, which cause it alone to absorb a good third of the student's life.

In our opinion, there is no tongue which presents so perfect and tempered a mingling of antique and modern as the French language. Hence, perhaps, that secret charm which captivates all nations; hence that singular prestige which has caused the French language to be considered the human language *par excellence*. For all these reasons, the "humanities" should remain dear to us and to our children. Let the State protect and foster them, for they are the source not only of beautiful forms of expression, but still more of precious traditions which aid in forming good citizens.

The interests of the race, however, are not always in accord with those of the individual. It may be that what is obligatory for the race should remain optional for the individual. The race has an unlimited time before it, while the days of the individual are numbered. For the individual the first duty is to live. If it be necessary, he will alienate even his family title-deeds, and no one has the right to make of this a crime. Therefore the State cannot absolutely impose upon a free man the obligation to partake of "the humanities," whatever other social interests may be invoked to do so.

The true source of riches is the good use of time—"time is money," as the proverb has it. Is it making good use of time to give twelve years of one's life to the study of a language which we are assured can never be thoroughly learnt? My time belongs to me. I beseech you, leave me to dispose of my own goods as I think fit, otherwise do not call me free.

I have said that the duty of the State is to protect, to foster —I did not say to *impose*—the humanities. Now, it will protect them, will foster them, will even propagate them, if it can reduce the length of time necessary to be given to them; if, instead of selling them to its subjects at the ruinous price of ten years of their lives, it were to grant them at the price of a few months, and more particularly, if, besides it could guarantee them to be delivered complete—that is, fruitful. Now this the State can do if it will.

II.

CONDEMNATION OF THE PROCESSES APPLIED TO THE STUDY OF ANCIENT LANGUAGES.

1. *Ten years and ten masters.*

Are ten years of one's life under ten teachers absolutely necessary to learn Latin? Why is the very same child who can learn English, or French, or German, without going to school at all, obliged, when he goes to school, to give ten years to the learning of Latin? The question seems to us to be very well put: we demand a frank and precise answer.

Let no one here attempt to make the triflingly subtle distinctions or antitheses between the spoken language and the written language, the every-day language and the literary language, the living language and the dead language, the practical language and the philological language. Whether it be acknowledged or not, there is for each language a definite foundation, a first footing, upon which is based all its ulterior developments, literary or otherwise. This foundation is no more dead in Latin than in German. To teach it, it is necessary to speak Latin as one would speak German.

Now, a person either possesses this foundation or he does not possess it. When he has learned it, he knows, or at least he understands, all the various "languages" which constitute this language; and when he does not possess it, he understands none. This foundation of the Latin tongue was taught by every Roman mother to her child within the circle of one year. Who can doubt this? Does the present school teaching deliver it to our children at the end of forty or of fifty seasons? Who will dare affirm that it does? Does it even know this foundation of the Latin tongue itself? We should not care to guarantee this.

Let us here lay down a principle:—The perfection of a linguistic method is, or should be, in inverse ratio to the number and the cleverness of the teachers required by its use.

I am aware that the classical school will acknowledge with

difficulty any such principle, for it goes against its very constitution; and, as we have said, the privileged classes were always enemies to reform. But, nevertheless, a principle is a principle, and the above statement is evidently one. In fact, the more defective a system, the greater are the efforts required on the part of those who apply it; the worse the method, the harder one has to work. What heavy labours are not spared to the workmen of to-day by new types of machinery that a child can direct with one hand! What services have not been rendered—first by the sail, and then by the propeller blade, instead of the galley oar—to our modern sailors!

Compare the post of ancient days with the telegraph of to-day! Where once it required coachmen, and horses, and carriages, and legions of servants, all that is now necessary is the attentive eye of a slim girl, calmly watching a dial-face which thinks and speaks for the whole universe. I repeat, the perfection of a method is in inverse ratio to the efforts which its use necessitates.

If this principle is true, was ever a system more imperfect than that of the classical school? The plethora of teachers which it declares absolutely necessary for its working is either a formidable abuse, or else the indication of a vice more formidable still.

What do we find? It requires the combined efforts of eight or ten graduates—that is to say, the knowledge which represents more than two hundred years of study—to produce in ten years—what? A result which the humblest of mothers can realise infinitely better than ourselves in two or three terms! We shall be reminded of the number of the pupils. But why do not our colleges have also twelve professors for German, twelve for Italian, twelve for arithmetic? Are these languages and these sciences less difficult than Latin?

Be it not forgotten, it is not against the teachers themselves that we are here instituting proceedings, but against the methods, against routine. The time has come when the truth may be spoken without need of tenderness of feeling for that egotism of cliques or of castes which everywhere hinders the march of progress. The upholders of national education should dare to cast to the winds those calamitous traditions which it has received from the enemies of progress.

No, it is not necessary to spend ten years of one's life in

learning Latin. It no longer needs the combined efforts of ten Masters of Arts.

> Ad portam pergo,
> ad portam appropinquo,
> ad portam pervenio,
> ad portam subsisto,
> brachium porrigo,
> ansam apprehendo,
> ansam torqueo, &c.

Is it necessary to hear this lesson twice to know it? Is there any need of making a word-for-word translation, or to construe it—that is, to pick it to pieces? Is it necessary to turn up the dictionary or to worry over the grammar? Of all the languages spoken in Europe, is there one in which this exercise is easier than it is in Latin?

When a child strikes itself against an obstacle, it often avenges itself with its foot or its fist. Do not let us act like children. If we find ourselves incapable of teaching Latin, do not let us lay this incapability to the nature of this language itself, but rather to our own want of skill in teaching it.

2. *The dictionary, or the discipline of the vicious circle.*

We shall not here undertake the enumeration of all the vicious errors adopted and followed by the classical school in teaching the ancient languages; as well might we repeat our entire book. We shall content ourselves with examining the lever or the general tool which is placed in the hands of the student to enable him to carry out his various linguistic labours: we refer to the dictionary. The dictionary being used in every lesson, every translation, and every reading of the classic authors, we shall, when treating of it, reach all three of these fundamental operations of the ordinary grammar school teaching.

Let us first of all give the definition of this grave and austere volume. It is the complete collection of all the terms of a language considered separately. It is this language dissected. The language is not to be found in a dictionary in a living, but in a dead state—the state of a corpse, and, moreover, of a corpse cut up into pieces, one in which the elements are subjected to a semblance of classification. This classification rests upon no principle, but merely upon a convention. The classification has therefore no linguistic virtue; it has no usefulness for the determination of the value of the terms. These terms are classified by the simple chance of their initial letters; they are arranged in what is termed alphabetical order.

The making of a dictionary has its difficulties, but this work does not affect either the teacher or the pupil. The tool is given into their hands ready made; they have only to use it.

The dictionary, we have said, is a collection of isolated words; therefore it contains nothing but generalities—that is, abstractions. The problem to be solved is therefore this: with the abstract to form the concrete; with the dead to make the living; "out of darkness to bring forth light."

Let us take an example. A pupil proposes to translate into Latin this every-day fact, "I raise my hand to my head." He turns up his dictionary, and at the word "raise" he finds the following expressions: *tollo, attollo, erigo, effero, augeo,* &c. He has several expressions before him, of which he has to choose one. Which shall he decide upon? If the dictionary formed a true system, it would be sufficient to have the key to make the choice. But the dictionary is a dead body, and as such is dumb. Once more, what will make the way clear to the student, and guide him rightly in his choice?

I have known scholars who thought to construct good Latin by taking from amongst the words served up to them by the dictionary those which appeared the most strange to them. An expression was considered to be so much the better Latin the less it resembled the corresponding expression in their own tongue.

A child is taken with its eyes blindfolded into an unknown land; he is placed at four crossways, then given his sight and told, "You must open your eyes; here are four roads, choose you that which leads the most directly to Rome, and take care you choose aright." We know that all roads lead to Rome, but we also know that from any one point to another there is only one straight line. There is, therefore, only one road that is truly direct.

The embarrassment of the child in such a predicament would be great, or rather it might be great; for what he is most likely to do is to laugh at you, and he would be right to laugh. What you propose to him cannot be seriously meant. To make a choice he must at least know in which direction Rome lies.

This is exactly the case of our young Latinist. To choose between four significations of the word "raise," he should know the connection of each, not only with the abstract word "raise," but the idea expressed by the sentence in his own language. In other words, he requires to know the precise meaning of the four Latin words. And if by chance—a chance which presents itself, as we know, just as often as not—neither of the four words served up by the dictionary is the correct word—what then?

It stands confessed, to be able to construct rightly a Latin theme by the aid of the dictionary, it is necessary already to know Latin! We defined, and we had the right to define, the study of languages by the dictionary as "The discipline of the vicious circle."

But we shall be told: "Raise" is not the whole of the phrase. If the student comes to grief over the verb, possibly he will be more lucky with the other words. I will suppose that this does happen, although there are good reasons to suppose the contrary. To what result would this lead? Remember that we are requiring not the translation of isolated and abstract words, but of organised phrases. Now, the word that rules the whole sentence, that imprints upon it its character, and that makes it what it is, is the verb. If you confess yourself incapable of translating the verb in the exact sense indicated by the sentence, you may throw down your pen, close the dictionary and trouble yourself no further with the construction of Latin sentences.

Yes, it certainly is the verb that causes almost the whole of the difficulty with foreign languages. It is for this reason that our method concentrates upon the verb all the energies of the mind of the pupil, and all the efforts, all the attention, all the art of the teacher.

The classical school will reply: There are dictionaries and dictionaries. A practical dictionary should give abundance of examples, and should reproduce, as occasion required, a part of the literature of the language. Then the pupil reads, compares, and, after this excellent exercise, chooses his word. Do you believe a child will do this? "Sic notus Ulysses?" A child who compares expressions in a language he does not know! And how clever he is at this operation!

Every comparison presupposes an ideal. Whence, think you,

is the scholar to obtain his ideal of Latin? If he already possesses this ideal, he has no need to search; in other words, he would not require to study Latin. Your "practical!" dictionary puts the difficulty a little further away, but it in no way solves it. The pupil strays abroad in rather a wider circle, but the circle is always a vicious one. To learn Latin, you use a dictionary; but to use a dictionary you must first know Latin.

We professors, when we are obliged to have recourse to a dictionary, even for a French expression in the dictionary of the Academy, nay, even in the monumental work of Littré itself, sometimes hesitate for a considerable time over the choice of a single expression; and yet we condemn a child of twelve years old to find out in their school dictionaries the exact expression of any of the hundred thousand sentences required to translate the human individuality into Latin. The classical pedagogy, in default of other virtue, seems at least to have that of being very childish and very simple!

Just consider: in order to translate into Latin the ordinary expression, "I stop at the door," I myself had to read, not the school dictionary [1]—which does not contain it and does not know it—but two or three classics. After I had learnt the German dictionary by heart, I translated with some confidence, "Je mets mon chapeau" (I put on my hat), by "Ich lege meinen Hut zu" (instead of "Ich setze meinen Hut auf").[2] I should certainly have composed a Latin phrase in the same excellent taste, if I had taken counsel of the Latin dictionary to say in Latin, "I stop at the door."

You are sure you have chosen correctly when you have the good fortune to come across the complete phrase in the dictionary. But consider what this means. . . .

Why should I be made to turn up words in the dictionary at all? Would it not be simpler to give me by word of mouth the correct expression at once? If the dictionary is fairly complete, you have the pupil condemned to go through two, three, five, ten columns! All this to find one unhappy word— a word which he cannot always find, which he even finds but seldom, unless the dictionary were an encyclopædia, containing

---

[1] Quicherat.
[2] As if in English "Je mets mon chapeau" were translated, "I put my hat" (Trans.).

all that has been said or that might be said, in which case the whole of one's youth would have to be given to the study of the dictionary. What an amount of time and effort lost! It is true that the classical school makes cheap of time. It asks ten years to bring even its incomplete operation to a termination!

I hear a new protest on behalf of the necessary book. The mind, it is said, only preserves long that which it has had trouble to assimilate. Now, the time that the pupil gives to determining an expression is the graver which engraves it upon his memory.

Very good! But suppose this expression is false, which happens at least as often as not; it is then an error that the mind of your student broods over, keeps warm, assimilates! And if the expression happens to be correct, let us see exactly to what the duration of this incubation is reduced. The egg is only being hatched while actually under the hen. The word is only subject to its incubation while actually under the eye of the student. Now, how long does it remain under his eye! Just the duration of one glance. For you can hardly put to the credit of the incubation the time lost by the student in turning over the leaves of his dictionary. If the incubation of anything whatever goes on during this time, it is the expression in the pupil's own language, and not the translation of it, which he does not yet know.

Then, again, no sooner has the student caught sight of it than it is written down: he does not willingly expose himself to the chance of losing a treasure that has cost so much trouble to discover. And this is to what the duration of the pretended incubation is reduced! Could an expression given directly and orally by the master, or that given by an interlinear translation, have a more ephemeral effect than this?

Another objection by the classicists: We do not begin, they say, as you seem to imply, with a complete dictionary; but, graduating the difficulties, we put into the hands of the pupil a vocabulary made expressly for translating a certain text. The lesson-books, after giving the course of exercises, contain also a dictionary in which are to be found all the words given in the lessons, and in the exact sense that they are employed.

Very good! Here, then, at last, we have a practical dictionary. The pupil, at any rate, has no longer any need to fear that he may be deceived. But now, perhaps you will kindly explain to me what pleasure and what profit you can find in making him turn over and over for two hours at a time even this lesser heap of paper, in order to enable him to put into Latin ten lines which you might very well teach him to express to perfection in a few minutes? It is, indeed, very much as if a mother, when her child asked the name of some object, instead of giving it to him directly herself, were to refer him to the people down in the village.

There prevails among the teaching bodies of all countries at the present time a curious disease which we may call by the name of "vocabulomania." While this disease lasts, the study of languages cannot make progress.

Dictionaries are made for teachers and not for scholars. The lesson manufactured by means of the dictionary represents a labour worse than barren. By this exercise, not only does the pupil not conquer the language, but the little that he does learn is mostly false. The acceptable expressions that come from his pen from time to time are reminiscences. He owes them, either to the actual voice of the teacher, or to the reading of authors undertaken aloud in class. In these two cases it is his ear, in which these expressions still vibrate, that dictates them to him; it is never the dictionary that inspires him to give them.

A disastrous councillor for translating into Latin, will this same dictionary prove a better aid for translating from Latin into the pupil's native tongue? The degree of perfection of an instrument can be established by means of two data:—

1. The degree of perfection of the product itself.
2. The time necessary for producing it.

Twenty candidates present themselves for the examinations. A Latin paragraph of fifteen or twenty sentences is given to them. They are allowed two hours or so to divine the signification of these few sentences. The faculty is triumphant if it so happens that only one half of them are plucked.[1]

And, nevertheless, it is not practice that these unlucky ones require. They have been manipulating their instrument for some nine years at least. They certainly ought, it would seem, to know it thoroughly to the depths of its resources.

---

[1] And in France a dictionary is often allowed to candidates as well! (Trans.).

And, be it noted, there is no question here of Greek or of Sanscrit, but of translating Latin, where, for a French student, every word shows its meaning, and even for an English student every other word is akin to words in his native tongue.

Nine years of practice! Two hours to interpret fifteen or twenty sentences! Two or three mistranslations in half a page! The dictionary is condemned. It is not less clumsy an instrument for translating from, than into, a language.

We now come to the third operation, the reading of classics. We have no need to add to what others have said upon this subject. The most bitter of criticisms, the most cutting of ironies have vied with each other in heaping insults upon the classical processes of teaching. Notwithstanding this, the classical school perseveres in its errors. This is because, if the ancient system is condemnable and condemned, nothing has yet been brought forward which might replace it.

The pupils on our system assimilate in five minutes that which they could not manage to interpret correctly on the old system in two hours by the aid of the dictionary. "Five minutes against two hours!" This ratio is sufficiently eloquent in itself for there to be any need of commenting further upon it, but it requires a little explanation.

In the classical process the phrase is read out once, twice, often a third time. Then a halt is called and the attempt is made to divine the meaning. Then the phrase is rearranged in the modern or "logical construction." The pupil makes a mistake; the teacher brings him back again. Finally, the scholar grasps, or fancies he grasps, the author's idea, and ventures upon an equivalent phrase in his own tongue. It is generally wrong; the master attempts to correct him, substitutes another phrase, and often still another.

Place your watch in front of you and see how long this operation takes. Multiply this time by two thousand, and calculate how long it will take you to translate a book of Virgil—how many years will be needed to read the entire Æneid. I should add that, if one pupil has construed aright, you are not by this assured that all the others have heard and understood thoroughly. If you are a good teacher, you should now recommence, and have the sentence repeated by those pupils suspected of inattention. It must not be forgotten also that in this estimate, already so heavy, the time devoted to what is termed preparation is not included.

Against this labour let us place that of our method. We have already explained how, by our process, each conception of the author becomes the conception of the whole class; how each of his thoughts becomes the thought of each of our pupils; how we proceed, not from word to word, but from sentence to sentence, doing the work of the author over again, not by translating it, but by composing it in the language itself, without the possibility of making mistakes or mistranslations, without the need of recourse to construction and reconstruction, nor to repetitions and readings always requiring to be begun over again. Expending one-fifth or one-sixth the time, we get through five times or ten times the work. This is our secret, the whole of our secret.

The instrument put into the hands of the child to work upon the languages is defective from all points of view. Consequent upon the false principle that the study of a language may be a personal and solitary work, the use of the dictionary is the occasion of an incalculable waste of time, and seems to have been designed expressly and solely to kill time and occupy students during the intervals between classes.

The slowness of the process discourages the child, paralyses his energy, and, little by little, kills his will, like all the exercises which have come down to us from the Jesuits. If incomplete or poor, the dictionary is of no use at all; if complete, it is impracticable. It should be banished from all elementary classes, and a logical and fruitful process of teaching should be made at last to replace this pitiful delusion—the barren and pernicious discipline of the vicious circle.

III.

THE FEAR OF IMPROVEMENT—SCEPTICAL DISDAIN OF THE OFFICIAL SCHOOLS AND THEIR SECRET AVERSION TO REFORM.

1. *A last contest.*

We have stated our opinion upon the importance of Greek and Latin. But if it were only possible to buy the knowledge of these languages at the price of the ten best years of our lives, we should be the first to advise against the study of them. To the modern individual they certainly are not worth the price. We have exposed the vices of the methods of teaching applied to these languages. If it be insisted that these methods should be maintained, it will be necessary to insist that the ten years of study shall also be maintained. If this is done, we may feel perfectly assured that modern requirements will not hesitate to cast overboard entirely the study of Greek and Latin.[1] And the decision would be wise.

German can be learned in six months. Why should the grammar-schools and colleges demand twenty times as much for Latin? Is it incapacity on their part, or is it speculation? In any case, we cannot consent now-a-days to be victims to trickery or to suffer by the incapacity of others. Therefore, if we wish to save "the Humanities," the methods must either be reformed or a process must be invented which will enable an ancient language to be learnt at school as rapidly and as thoroughly as a modern language can be learnt in the family.

But can anything be discovered that the official teaching has not yet discovered? This seems to be the great objection of the members of the teaching profession and those that govern it. Even supposing that a method might be discovered for teaching German in six months or a year, can we hope to discover one for teaching Latin within the same time.

This insidious and contradictory formula is the last entrenchment of routine. If we can cast down this inner fortress, reason will be forced to acknowledge our victory. Yes, there is a process for learning Greek or Latin as well as German in six months or a year, and this process is the Series Method. One final blow we must strike against this absurd prejudice, which refuses to admit that the same system may be applied to several languages.

Your system, we are told, appears to be excellent for the study of modern languages, but it would be absolutely impossible to apply it to the study of the ancient languages.

Why so, if you please? Upon what do you found such a presumption? One of two things must be true: either we apply, after having discovered it, the true process of Nature, or we do not apply it. If we do not apply it, our system will

---

[1] We find already in England strong indications that this prophecy is very rapidly being fulfilled (Trans.).

not be less impotent for modern languages than for ancient languages. If we do apply it, why should we not achieve the result achieved by Nature herself? Once more we ask, Did the mothers of ancient days possess and follow other pedagogic principles than those possessed and followed by the mothers of the children of to-day?

If we really have discovered this maternal process, by what right do you doubt its success with Greek and Latin? Do you find these two languages to be of such peculiar nature that it is necessary to invent special methods for them? From the official objections one would really think that, in order to have the gift or the secret of teaching Latin, it would be actually necessary to have been a Roman matron of the time of Numa or Vespasian!

But Latin is a dead language, they cry; a dead language cannot be treated like a living language. Why not? Whence do you take the premisses of this conclusion? What influence can the qualification of dead or living exert upon the teaching of a language? Is German less a dead language than Latin itself in the countries where no one speaks it—as with ourselves, except in the class-room? It is true that not much greater success is usually achieved with it than with the dead languages. Its quality of "living" is not of very great use to it.

Let us repeat a reflection previously uttered. A language which is spoken is not a dead language. Now, in order to teach a language, we have said it is necessary to speak it. Therefore, from the point of view of teaching, there are no dead languages.

At bottom the prejudice we are combating has no avowable motive whatever; and it is a strange thing, but we find this prejudice chiefly amongst the professors themselves. If we press them to justify their opinion, they have usually nothing to say but that "it is their feeling," and that is all. A professor ought to know that a feeling is not a reason. This sceptical disdain, this aversion of the school for any reform of the school, this fear of anything better, must have some reason for its existence. Let us set forth these reasons, and judge them in the full light of day.

The sentiment in question appears to us to have its origin in three distinct causes. The first is the imperfection itself of the modern linguistic methods. All of them, in fact, have aimed at solving the problem of the ancient languages. But the verdict of experience has not been given in their favour. And in this there is nothing astonishing. Systems radically incapable of teaching us a living language cannot pretend to be in possession of the secret of teaching an ancient language. This non-success has had the effect of discrediting everything terming itself a linguistic method. We know how mankind is too apt to reason, and how at one bound it raises this generalisation—

"A certain modern method is proved worthless,
Therefore all are worthless."

And this has been to the triumph of the dictionary process of learning languages.

The second cause is the feeling which is to be found more or less at the root of every contradiction, namely, personal egotism. We have stated that the objection of which we are speaking is generally made by members of the teaching profession. Unconsciously their judgment is dictated by personal interest and a feeling of *amour propre*. By their interest; for does not our system institute an indirect attack upon their position? What becomes of the present methods if the teaching of languages can be simplified to the extent we have indicated? By their *amour propre;* for why could not they as well as others have discovered a better system, if any better system could exist than that of the present colleges? These unworthy feelings, however, would never be allowed weight by those who saw in a new system a true means of helping forward the cause of education.

A third cause, and the principal one, is the knowledge of the difficulty of a really effective reform. This reason is a legitimate one, and deserves to be taken into consideration.

In the first place, a professor has always present to his mind the remembrance of his long struggle with the classical languages, and it is extremely difficult for him to believe that any one can triumph over them with less effort than he was obliged to expend upon them himself. He has, besides, his every-day experience, ceaselessly reminding him of the amount of pains it costs to obtain even the most moderate linguistic development in the schoolboy mind. Therefore by training, if not by nature, the teacher is very sceptical when mention is made of the virtue of certain methods. For him the imbecility of the mind does not come from the defectiveness of methods, but the powerlessness of the methods finds its explanation in the imbecility of the mind. In our opinion this is to take the effect for the cause; but it must be admitted that it is extremely difficult for any one who is committed to the practice of the ordinary methods not to fall into this error.

To all this is added the difficulty of working upon a dead language. One can conceive, it may be objected, that you might be able to construct your series in a living language, either by actually going to the country where this language is spoken, or by having recourse to the knowledge of a native of this country. But how could you manage to construct your series in a language which nobody now speaks?

This is a grave question, and one which it is proper to answer, not by general considerations, but by precise facts.

2. *Solution of the conflict.*

We will concede, in the first place, to our opponents that the task is an arduous one; we will grant that the enterprise is even more laborious than they themselves suspect. Having made this reservation, we justify in the following manner our position and our statements.

Suppose for a moment that our method had been constructed in the time of Cicero or of Demosthenes. Applied to the two classical languages then "living," they would have rendered the teaching of these languages as easy as that of German or of French or English to-day. In fact, grant that this method is an excellent one for the living languages, is it not confessed thereby that it would have been "of old" equally excellent for Greek and Latin? But can a method which was a good one for these languages in the lifetime of Cicero cease to be excellent when applied at the present day?

There remains, therefore, to be proved that if our system had been created at the time of Cicero, it would not have sensibly differed from that which we have constructed or, believe ourselves able to construct, at the end of the nineteenth century. Cicero and Demosthenes are dead, and with them every one who spoke their tongue. But there remains to us the written Latin and Greek literature. The following, then, is our plan of work.

We shall take—ourselves or the reader of these lines—the set of pigeon-holes of our Series—Domestic and Rural, Animal and Vegetable, the Harvest, the Shepherd, the Feast, the Battle, the Ship, &c., with the subjective and metaphorical categories—and setting this up before us, we shall open a first author—Phædrus, for example. Each of his sentences translates either a fact of our Series, or one of our relative phrases, or a detail of one of our metaphorical themes. We shall first of all mark these sentences by special signs, then we shall throw each sentence into the pigeon-hole that is waiting for its reception. Our transcriptions of the classical authors, in which each sentence is placed separately line by line, will be of immense service to us in the execution of this work. After Phædrus we shall take Quintus Curtius; after Quintus Curtius, Virgil or Livy; after Virgil, Tacitus, or such other as is thought best. We shall strip in this way one after the other the small number of Latin authors that is left to us.

They are not, be it observed, abstract, isolated words that we shall dispose in our pigeon-holes, but sentences—complete expressions. It is for this reason that the dictionary can be of no use to us whatever. And, moreover, is not the dictionary quite incapable of responding to the greater part of the demands of our pigeon-holes?

As we proceed, we shall indicate by figures the chapter, paragraph, or verse of the author. This will be our hall-mark. By thus declaring the origin of each expression, our work will confound incredulity and defy criticism.

Suppose this work to be accomplished and our pigeon-holes filled, will it be difficult, then, for us to construct our Series in a language that is no longer spoken? And, constructed under these conditions, will our system be sensibly different from what it would have been if put together by some person in the time of Cicero or of Demosthenes? This system will, therefore, have resuscitated two of the most illustrious of the dead, and henceforth Greek and Latin can be taught exactly as are the living languages.

And notice one fruit of this labour: by studying the Series the pupil will assimilate the whole of the expressions of the classical masterpieces. The Series finished, let him open any book whatever, and he will find himself in the presence of a language he already knows well; he will never, in fact, meet in these books any expression which does not figure in the Series. He will, therefore, read this language, and will understand it as each of us reads and understands a book written in his mother-tongue. For that pupil Greek and Latin will be surely something other than "dead" languages.

"But how will you deal with the terms of entirely modern creation," some one accustomed to judge of things only from their smallest side will be sure to object, "terms such as powder, gun, cannon, steam, electricity, telegraph, &c. ?" Our method preoccupies itself solely with the sentence and with the verb. It must not be forgotten that we know a language thoroughly when we thoroughly know these two elements. As to this dozen substantives of modern creation, we can, at need, graft them upon the ancient languages exactly in the same way as they have been grafted on the modern languages. One may know a language perfectly, and yet be ignorant of these few technical terms. If a river receive the water from sundry gutters or from a few fresh runnels, it is not thereby any less the same river.

I know of only one further objection to our system. Who will engage to do this work? Who will undertake this dissection of two great literatures? It cannot be expected that this should be imposed upon the ordinary teacher. To carry it out, it would be necessary to have complete possession of the vast system of disposition, and all the secrets of the "Series." Our answer is: This work is in part accomplished; it is already over twenty years since the labour was commenced.

What might be termed "the error in Greek and Latin teaching" is not an error special to the English school, or the French school, or to any school; it is German, Swiss, Russian; it is European, it is universal. Every school in the world cultivates it in rivalry with its neighbour. All, without exception, treat Greek and Latin practically under the same process.

At no time in the world's history has the question of reform been so much agitated as at present. At no time have the errors of the classical systems been criticised with so much vehemence, nor the entrenchments of pedantry assailed with so much resolution. If a new way can be opened, the time is certainly ripe for it; the reform is no longer a mere idea—it is an urgent need. And with so much in its history that points to liberty, the nations will not fail to honour France for being in the vanguard of progress in the scholastic world as it is in the social world.

IV.

THE DYING DIALECTS—AN ARK OF SAFETY.

A nation is not a homogeneous whole, as the politicians of the present day—in an interest quite other to that of its happiness—wish to make the world believe. The great races are not vast families issuing from a single stock, but assemblages of tribes, at one time distinct, and often enemies to each other.

Hence, alongside each general language we have special languages called dialects, which survive among the tribe by which they are spoken, as the man is survived by the name which he has made illustrious.

Europe still abounds with minor languages of this kind. We have said that the races bear a name which sums up their life and defines their character; this name is their language. The dialects are, therefore, as the residues of civilisations which have preceded our own. Each of them represents a chapter in the annals of the human race. For this reason the dialects deserve to be immortalised. History will have hard things to say in after years of the levelling despotism of our time, which has declared war not only against the liberty of nations, of tribes, and of families, but even against their languages themselves.

Unity in variety—this is Life; unity without variety—this is Death. Therefore the dialects should be allowed to live, and with them the races and the tribes that speak them. A state desiring to be something more than a mischievous abstraction, must rest upon strong and numerous individualities. True unity is something quite other than a dull uniformity.

The dialects have a great value, not only as the repository of the thoughts and of the life of another age, but still more as the substratum of the general modern languages.

The dialects are, therefore, worthy of attention from the triple point of view of history, of linguistic literature, and of their influence upon the national character. Everywhere care is taken to preserve the stone monuments of earlier ages; science cannot permit political vandalism to raze to the ground and bury out of sight the chief monument of those very ages. But where is the ark that shall shelter and save the sacred archives of the civilisations of which ours is the resultant? The dictionary perhaps, or possibly the libraries?

Let us try to estimate the chances of safety that a language could find in these two sanctuaries. The dictionary, as we have seen, only preserves a language in the state of a dead body, and of a dead body in pieces. To reconstitute a language by means of the dictionary is not less impossible than to reconstitute the world by the aid of the fourscore prime elements known to chemistry. Let a German, for instance, attempt to find out in Littré the expression of his whole individuality in French! Or let a Frenchman try to express his own in German by the aid of the dictionary of Grimm! It could not be done. The dictionary is, therefore, perfectly powerless in itself to save a language from oblivion.

Do the libraries offer better guarantees of safety? Yes, assuredly, but upon one condition: this is, that the dialect possesses a rich literature. But where is the dialect that enjoys this privilege? Indeed, a dialect is a dialect, only for the reason that it has not, or has no longer, any literature.

And, moreover, if a literature is an eminently fit sanctuary for the preservation of a given language, it should be thoroughly recognised that this language itself cannot be extracted therefrom but with infinite pains and precautions. We will go further, and maintain even, that, without a system such as that we have set forth, this operation is practically impossible. Therefore, literature abandoned to its own resources is found to be almost equally powerless with the dictionary for perpetuating either the knowledge or the usage of any dialect whatever.

That service which the two great means of which we have just spoken—the dictionary and the literature—are incapable of rendering to the dying dialects, or those which are condemned to die, our method of Series now comes forward to offer. Have we not demonstrated that this system is a mould

CONCLUSION.

from which may be cast, palpitating with life, the whole human individuality of no matter what period of time! And if this is so, nothing will be easier, once the system is written in a first language, than to transpose it into Breton, Basque, Alsatian, Bohemian, Coptic, Welsh, Gaelic, and all the other idioms at present existing.

Being the direct and spontaneous expression of an individuality thinking in each dialect, this translation will represent the complete system of this dialect in its living reality, one which will spare the philologists of the future that laborious exegesis now needed, ending only in incomplete resurrections, always open to dispute and always disputed.

The dialects, therefore, need be henceforth in no fear of either dying or of being forgotten. They will be transmitted as a tradition; they will be within the reach of all, and will be learnt like an ordinary language, not in ten long years, but in a few short months; not at the schools of the universities, but in those of the village, or rather round the paternal hearth.

We must bring to a close with this last application of it the exposition of our system. It has shown itself capable of resuscitating the dead languages; there but remained for it to discover the secret of rendering imperishable the tongues ready to die, thus yielding for its last fruit a fruit of life.

This volume is but the preface to the system. Even now the work is in hand of putting together the material already collected. If the work prove good, help will not be lacking; and it has long been demonstrated that when human power is added to human power, it can remove mountains and incline oceans.

The complete work will have, and should have, two chapters—the written book, and the school wherein it is practised. To write the book, Science will lend its treasures, and, if need be, its legions. The school might be offered by one of the many scholastic or commercial bodies that would benefit from it.

APPENDIX.

I.—THREE FRENCH SERIES LESSONS.

LA POMPE.

I.

La femme se rend à la pompe.

— La femme prend le seau par l'anse,	prend
la femme lève le seau,	lève
la femme traverse la cuisine,	traverse
la femme ouvre la porte,	ouvre
la femme franchit le seuil,	franchit
la femme sort de la cuisine,	sort
la femme se retourne,	se retourne
la femme ferme la porte.	ferme
— La femme quitte la cuisine,	quitte
la femme s'éloigne de la cuisine,	s'éloigne
la femme se dirige vers la pompe,	se dirige
la femme s'approche de la pompe,	s'approche
la femme parvient à la pompe,	parvient
la femme s'arrête près de la pompe,	s'arrête
la femme lève le seau,	lève
la femme allonge le bras,	allonge
la femme place le seau sous le tuyau de la pompe,	place
la femme lâche l'anse du seau.	lâche

* * * * *

1. Femme (fille, fillette, bonne, servante, garçon, domestique, serviteur . . .).
2. Seau (arrosoir, urne, cruche, broc, seille, jatte, baquet, vase, vaisseau, ustensile . . .).
3. Cuisine (maison, logis, demeure, domicile . . .).

LA POMPE.

II.

La femme pompe de l'eau.

— Elle étend le bras,	étend
elle saisit le balancier,	saisit
elle hausse le balancier,	hausse
elle abaisse le balancier,	abaisse
elle hausse le balancier,	hausse
elle abaisse le balancier,	abaisse
le balancier grince,	grince
la pompe tremble.	tremble
— L'eau monte dans la pompe,	monte
l'eau coule par le tuyau,	coule
l'eau tombe dans le seau,	tombe
l'eau frappe le fond du seau,	frappe
l'eau bruit au fond du seau,	bruit
l'eau tournoie dans le seau,	tournoie
l'eau écume dans le seau,	écume
l'eau monte dans le seau,	monte
l'eau monte, monte et monte encore,	monte
elle emplit le seau ;	emplit
la femme lâche le balancier.	lâche

* * * * *

1. Balancier (le bras, le levier, le manche, la machine, le machin, l'affaire . . .).
2. Pompe (le corps de pompe, le cylindre, l'intérieur, le dedans . . .).
3. Tuyau (le conduit, le canal . . .).

APPENDIX I.]

LA POMPE.

III.

La femme emporte l'eau à la cuisine.

— La femme se penche vers le seau,   se penche
prend le seau par l'anse,   prend
et le retire de dessous le tuyau ;   retire
elle ferme le poing gauche,   ferme
elle appuie le poing gauche contre sa hanche,   appuie
elle se penche du côté gauche,   se penche
et fait ainsi équilibre au poids de l'eau.   fait équilibre

— Elle tourne le dos à la pompe,   tourne
elle quitte la pompe,   quitte
elle s'éloigne de la pompe,   s'éloigne
elle se dirige vers la cuisine,   se dirige
elle s'approche de la cuisine,   s'approche
elle arrive à la porte,   arrive
elle ouvre la porte,   ouvre
elle franchit le seuil,   franchit
elle entre dans la cuisine.   entre

— Elle referme la porte,   referme
elle traverse la cuisine,   traverse
elle porte le seau d'eau à sa place ;   porte
elle se penche,   se penche
et pose doucement le seau d'eau à terre,   pose
elle lâche l'anse du seau,   lâche
se redresse,   se redresse
et reprend haleine.   reprend
Puis, elle emploie l'eau aux usages ordinaires du   emploie
    ménage.

*   *   *   *   *

—Place (le lieu, l'endroit, le coin . . .).

APPENDIX II.

CO-ORDINATED ACTS—THE AUTHOR'S TEXT.

(*See* p. 236.)

THE following portion of the text has been replaced by the translators by a slightly expanded development, after careful analysis and comparison with all the English forms (which were not given in the original) :—

When two actions occur within the same period of time, they may occupy therein, in relation to each other, four different positions.

1. They may take place parallel to each other, that is, simultaneously :

"*While* he was enjoying himself, I was working."
"*Tandis qu'*il s'amusait, je travaillais."

This relation can be expressed by two parallel lines.

2. One of the two actions may have commenced before the other, and be still going on—it was not ended, it was not complete when the other began. Grammar has discovered the true name of the first—"Imperfect Act," and it receives the form of the Continuous Acts,—[in English ING], in French the final AIS :

"Yesterday, he came *while* I was eating my lunch."
"Hier, il arriva *pendant* que je déjeûnais."

We may represent this relation by two lines, one of which begins before and ends after the other.

3. The two acts may be contiguous or follow immediately one after the other :

"Yesterday, *just as* I had dined (done dining), he came in."
"Hier, *sitôt que* j'eus déjeûné, il arriva."

Grammar once more affords us an exact denomination by which to designate the first of these acts—the word "Perfect" (that is to say, a perfected act). The first act, indeed, is accomplished or perfect when the other begins.

We may represent this third relation by two lines, the second of which will begin opposite the point at which the first finishes.

APPENDIX.

4. Lastly, the first action may have been finished for a certain time at the moment the second act commences:

"Yesterday, I had *already* dined (been dining) when he arrived."

"Hier, j'avais *déjà* diné quand il arriva."

Here, the first action is more than perfect when the second occurs. The term Pluperfect (that is, Act, plus or more than perfect—Plus-que-Parfait), furnished by the grammars, therefore in every way suits the first of these two acts. We may represent this relation by two straight lines which follow each other at a certain interval.

If now we transport these four relations into definite (finished), indefinite (unfinished), and future periods of time, the following are the forms we shall obtain:—

ACTS CO-ORDINATED IN THE SAME PERIOD OF TIME.

A.—SIMULTANEOUS ACTS.

YESTERDAY	while I was dining ...	he was working.
TO-DAY	while I have been dining ...	he has been working.
TO-MORROW	while I am dining ...	he will be working.

B.—CONSECUTIVE ACTS.

YESTERDAY (definite or finished period of time).

He arrived

while	I was dining.	*Imperfect act.*
just as	I had dined (been dining).	*Perfect act.*
already	I had dined.	*Pluperfect act.*

TO-DAY—this morning (indefinite or unfinished period of time)

He arrived

while	I was dining.	*Imperfect act.*
just as	I had dined (been dining).	*Perfect act.*
already	I had dined.	*Pluperfect act.*

TO-MORROW (future period of time).

He will arrive

while	I am dining.	*Imperfect act.*
just as	I have dined (been dining).	*Perfect act.*
already	I shall have dined.	*Pluperfect act.*

[Appendix II.]

ACTES CO-ORDONNÉS DANS UN MÊME TEMPS.

A.—Actes Simultanés.

Hier	tandis que je dînais	il travaillait,
Ce Matin	tandis que je dîne	il travaille.
Demain	tandis que je dînerai	il travaillera.

B.—Actes Consécutifs.

Hier (temps défini).
Il arriva

pendant que	je dînais.	*Acte imparfait.*
sitôt que	j'eus dîné.	*Acte parfait.*
déjà	j'avais dîné.	*Acte plus-que-parfait.*

Aujourd'hui, Ce Matin (temps indéfini).
Il est arrivé

pendant que	je dînais.	*Acte imparfait.*
sitôt que	j'ai eu dîné.	*Acte parfait.*
déjà	j'avais dîné.	*Acte plus-que-parfait.*

Demain (temps à venir).
Il arrivera

pendant que	je dînerai.	*Acte imparfait.*
sitôt que	j'aurai dîné.	*Acte parfait.*
déjà	j'aurai dîné.	*Acte plus-que-parfait.*

APPENDIX III.

LE LION ET LE MOUCHERON (La Fontaine).

I.

L'Outrage et le Duel.

— Va-t-en, chétif insecte, excrément de la terre !	va-t-en
C'est en ces mots que le lion parlait un jour au moucheron.	parlait
L'autre lui déclara la guerre :	déclara
Penses-tu, lui dit-il, —	penses-tu
que ton titre de roi me fasse peur,	fasse peur
ni me soucie ?	soucie
Un bœuf est plus puissant que toi ;	est puissant
je le mène à ma fantaisie.	mène
— A peine il achevait ces mots,	achevait
que lui-même il sonna la charge,	sonna
fut le trompette et le héros.	fut trompette
Dans l'abord il se met au large ;	se met
puis prend son temps,	prend
fond sur le cou du lion,	fond
qu'il rend presque fou.	rend fou
Le quadrupède écume,	écume
et son œil étincelle ;	étincelle
il rugit.	rugit
On se cache,	se cache
on tremble à l'environ,	tremble
et cette alarme universelle est l'ouvrage d'un moucheron.	est l'ouvrage
— Un avorton de mouche en cent lieux le harcelle,	harcelle
tantôt pique l'échine et tantôt le museau,	pique
tantôt entre au fond du naseau.	entre
La rage alors se trouve à son faîte montée.	montée.

* * * * *

LE LION ET LE MOUCHERON.
II.
Triomphe et Ruine.

— L'invisible ennemi triomphe,	triomphe
et rit de voir →	rit
qu'il n'est griffe ni dent en la bête irritée	n'est griffe
qui de la mettre en sang ne fasse son devoir.	mettre en sang
Le malheureux lion se déchire lui-même,	se déchire
fait résonner sa queue à l'entour de ses flancs,	résonner
bat l'air qui n'en peut mais ;	bat
et sa fureur extrême le fatigue,	fatigue
l'abat ;	abat
le voilà sur les dents.	voilà
— L'insecte du combat se retire avec gloire ;	se retire
comme il sonna la charge,	sonna
il sonne la victoire ;	sonna
va partout l'annoncer,	annoncer
et rencontre en chemin l'embuscade d'une	rencontre
il y rencontra aussi sa fin. [araignée ;	rencontre
— Quelle chose par là nous peut être enseignée ?	enseignée
J'en vois deux :	vois
dont l'une est que →	l'une est
entre nos ennemis les plus à craindre sont	à craindre
souvent les plus petits ;	
l'autre, que →	l'autre est
aux grands périls tel a pu se soustraire	se soustraire
qui périt pour la moindre affaire.	périt.

APPENDIX III.] **Le Lion et le Moucheron.**

(RELATIVE PHRASES OR INTERLOCUTORY SENTENCES.)

Cont.[1]	Je pense que → vous savez la suite.
F. att.	Ne pense pas que → tu puisses apprendre quelque chose sans cela !
D. t. p.	Penses-tu que → l'on puisse apprendre une langue sans cela ?
Cont.	Et que rien ne vous fasse peur.
Cont.	La construction d'une phrase ne doit pas vous faire peur.
Tr. b.	On voit que vous n'avez pas peur.
Cont.	Si vous faites une faute, que cela ne vous soucie.
Tr. b.	Votre mémoire devient de jour en jour plus puissante.
Tr. b.	Pour bâtir une phrase nul n'est plus puissant que toi.
Tr. b.	Vous menez la langue à votre fantaisie.
Lent.	Mettez-vous, comme on dit, au large.
Lent.	Prenez votre temps.
Cont.	Et dans l'abord représente-toi bien le fait.
Cont.	Et dans l'abord produisons le verbe.
B. dit.	C'est là l'ouvrage d'un bon écolier.
Cour.	Vous triompherez.
Cour.	On triomphera—nous triompherons.
Tr. b.	Je triomphe → de vous voir si bien marcher.
Tr. b.	Je ris de voir → qu'il n'est plus de difficulté pour vous.
Att.	Mettez-vous en devoir → de vous bien représenter le fait que vous exprimez.
Att.	Faites votre devoir → de bien prononcer.
Att.	Fais ton devoir → de parler correctement.
P. har.	Qui fait une faute souvent n'en peut mais.
Tr. b.	Vous n'êtes pas encore sur les dents.
Cont.	Montrez que → vous n'êtes pas encore sur les dents.
Tr. b.	On ne peut pas dire : le voilà sur les dents.
Tr. b.	Du combat vous vous retirerez avec gloire.
Tr. b.	Vous pouvez, je crois, sonner la victoire.
Att.	Prenez garde aux moindres mots : entre nos ennemis les plus à craindre sont souvent les plus petits.
Att.	Aux grands périls tel a pu se soustraire qui périt pour la moindre affaire.

---

[1] *Cont.* Continuez.   *D. t. p.* Donne toi de la peine.
F. att. Fais attention.   *P. har.* Parlez hardiment.
Tr. b. Très bien.   *Cour.* Courage.
Lent. Lentement.   *Att.* Attention.
B. dit. Bien dit.   *Ap. v.* Appliquez-vous.

APPENDIX IV.

CERTIFICATE OF THE FRENCH MINISTER OF PUBLIC INSTRUCTION TO M. TEMPIÉ, WHO PROVIDED FUNDS FOR EXPERIMENTAL COURSES IN GERMAN.

[Copy]

PARIS, *Le 9 juin* 1888.

A Monsieur TEMPIÉ.

MONSIEUR,—Monsieur le vice-recteur de l'Académie de Paris m'a transmis un rapport sur les résultats obtenus dans l'enseignement de l'allemand à l'école normale d'instituteurs de Paris par Monsieur Gouin, qui a été autorisé à faire l'application de sa méthode dans cet établissement.

Cet essai a permis de constater d'une manière certaine qu'en moins de 300 leçons les élèves suivaient une conversation ordinaire, comprenaient un exposé fait en allemand, savaient donner eux-mêmes une leçon, démontrer les règles de la grammaire et écrire correctement.

Je crois devoir vous adresser mes félicitations pour les résultats dûs à votre initiative.

Monsieur le vice-recteur m'informe que vous auriez l'intention d'établir à Paris, dans un local que vous demanderiez à la ville, des cours de langues vivantes où votre (la) méthode pourrait recevoir une utile application. Ce projet mérite d'être pris en considération, et je verrais avec plaisir que la consécration donnée par cette lettre aux résultats déjà obtenus pût décider les conseils généraux à vous envoyer des boursiers pour suivre ces cours. Recevez, Monsieur, l'assurance de ma considération très distinguée.

Le Ministre de l'Instruction Publique et des Beaux Arts,
LOCKROY.

APPENDIX.

[*Translation.*]

To M. TEMPIÉ.

PARIS, *June 9th*, 1888.

SIR,—Monsieur le Vice-Recteur de l'Académie de Paris has forwarded to me a report upon the results obtained in the teaching of German at the Normal School of Preceptors, Paris, by M. Gouin, who has been authorised to carry out the application of his method in that establishment.

This trial permits the definite statement to be made that in less than 300 lessons the pupils followed an ordinary conversation, understood a lecture given in German, knew themselves how to give a lesson, to demonstrate the rules of grammar, and to write correctly.

I think it my duty to congratulate you upon the results due to your initiative.

Monsieur le Vice-Recteur informs me that you have the intention of establishing in Paris, on premises which you will ask of the town, classes for the teaching of modern languages in which the method might receive a useful application. This project deserves to be taken into consideration, and I should see with pleasure that the official recognition given by this letter to the results already obtained might decide the General Councils to send you exhibition scholars to follow these courses. Receive, &c.

The Minister of Public Instruction and Fine Arts,

(Signed)   LOCKROY.

INDEX.

	PAGE
ABSTRACT IDEAS, absence of, in the child	55
and metaphors	184, 193
words, futility of studying	155
Abstraction	182, 209, 221, 257, 291
Accent	151, 272, 330
Acts, present	201
not tenses	223
simple and momentary	227
continuous and habitual	232, 235
co-ordinated	236, 238–9, 389
parallel and coinciding	236
anterior and posterior	237
pluperfect	240
Æneid	94, 333, 337, 375
Alphabet, a rational	291
Analysis and synthesis	7
and early lessons	107
of the sentence	250
Ancient and modern languages, to be studied in the same manner	141, 166, 367, 377
Annexes and corollaries of the system	288
Appendix	388
Arabic referred to	6, 166, 329, 339
Arbitrary, the, in language lessons	45
Article	123
Artificial method	85
Association, logical	42, 90
of word and thought	84
of time and act	228
Atrophy of linguistic powers	139
Attention of pupils	95
Auxiliary Series	304
"BATTLE OF ROSSBACH"	348–9
Berlin University	25
family in	56
philosophical bout at	57
Bird, Series of	51, 62
Book, A B C	290

INDEX.

	PAGE
Book, form of teaching	290
reading	289
of Nature	59
Botany, the teaching of	342, 357
Breathing, and the length of phrase	93
CAEN, studies at	8
Cadence	277
"Canis et Lupus"	311
Cases	253
knowledge of, by Germans	257
instability of	258
Certificate by M. Lockroy	395-6
Child, method of	4
a hackneyed riddle	5
learns no grammar	17
living language of	35
logical order of	34
linguistic work of	40, 47
subjective language of	52
curiosity of, cause	124
learning a language easy to	128
distinguishes by accent	152
instinctive grammar of	196, 203
and the present tense	207
and the German, prefix	275
enjoyment of school	332
Chinese referred to	6, 161
Cicero revived	380
Classes, at Berlin	25
Classics, author's antecedents in	9
study of	305
organisation of	381
Classical process, Greek	10, 30
declensions	260
construction	279
subordinate moods	285
time given in	297
and teachers	301
Complements of verbs	251, 263
Concentric Series	107
Conception, mental	39, 88
length of	93, 94, 96
of an author	305
Conditional mood	244
Conjugation, study of	198
unity	203
perfect	209
tables of	231, 235, 238-9
practice of	227, 241
permanent	243
Conjunction	285

INDEX.

Construction, ancient or natural	276
modern or logical	277
German	278
by the classical process	279
by the Series method	281
Construing abrogated	283
Continual talk, the	79, 82, 295
Conversation in German	14
Co-ordinated acts	236, 238, 389
Curiosity of child	124
"Death of Priam"	334
Dead languages	166, 378
Declensions, Latin	252
in the classical school	259
study of, a torture	259
on the Series method	261
construction of table	262
Definite periods of time	213, 219
Dialects, the dying	383
Dictation	331, 342
Dictionary, learning off by heart	27, 32
cure of the fear of	58
totality of, contained in the Series	65
use of, in the classical school	301
condemnation of, as an instrument for study	369
Discovery of the Series system	38
Discipline, strict and lax	143, 162, 331
Dislike for the study of languages explained	128
Difficulties, in construction of Series	88, 299
of ordinary process	164
of reform	379
Diversion necessary to pupils	95, 132, 198
Domestic Series	123, 124
Dominant, the	87, 193
Drawing, art of teaching	292
"Drei Spinnerinnen"	313
Ear, as the organ of language	33, 47, 48, 56, 128, 139, 303
as tuning-fork or standard	140
Early reminiscences	362
Elementary Series	96
given by workmen	300
teachers	332
verbs	134
Enclitics	146, 265
uniformity in all languages	146
classification	147
Virgil's	148
method of teaching	163
constitution of	176
in German	278

INDEX.

	PAGE
Enclitics in the classics	307
English, first lesson in	174
employment of definite tense	219
Equality of intellects	131, 330
Errors of the classical school	33, 35, 127, 222, 264, 280
Everyday language	75, 289
Exercise, construction of	67
properties of	70
value of	75
difficulties of construction	84
length of	94
Eye, futility of teaching by	33, 48, 134
FAILURE	30
Figurative language	55, 182
based on domestic life	75
organisation of	183
art of teaching	189
Fire, Series of	106, 112
First lesson	133, 165
in eight languages	168
Fowl, Series of	51
French, first lesson in	171
employment of indefinite tense	220
a difficult language	273
the human language	366
GAME	37, 148
Gifts of Nature	5, 210
Gift for languages	6, 31, 296
Generalisation	38, 89, 185
Geography, the teaching of	355
German, attempts of author to learn	9
roots	12
thinking in	56
first lesson in	173
conjugations	231
prefix	271
an easy language	273
Goethe, translating	15, 17, 49
Grammar	196
author's study of German	11
a quasi-attractive science	178
practical value of	196
psychologic basis	197
a game	202
unity of	203, 249
reform of	209
natural	215
Grammatical sense	202, 207, 209
Greek, author's knowlege of	10
pronunciation	137

	PAGE
Greek, teaching of	166
first lesson in	169
declensions	252
grammar	253
an easy language	273
and spelling lessons	291
must be spoken	338
value of, in education	364
compulsory	377
Grimm, "Die drei Spinnerinnen"	313
HAMBURG UNIVERSITY	9
History, teaching of	343
the sacred book	344
put into Series	345
specimen Series	348
method of teaching	350
advanced students of	352
and literature combined	353
in foreign languages	355
Homer, length of scenes in	94, 307
Horace	252, 307
Hospites	180
Humanities	364
Humboldt, Alex. von, a dunce at school	259
IMPERFECT ACTS	226, 237
Incubation of language	43, 95, 393
Indefinite periods of time	214, 219, 229
Indicative mood	203, 211
simple	231
continuous and habitual	235
co-ordinated	238-9
Individuality, weaving of, by nature	39
formation of, by language	48
translation of	49, 88
formed within one year	50
mystic ladder of	51
expressed in 100,000 sentences	294
Instinct	5, 207
Intellectual effect, measure of	93, 331
Intelligences equal	81
Interlocutory sentences	157, 328, 394
Inter-relationships	253
Intuition	210, 218, 224, 228, 271
Italian, first lesson in	170
JACOTOT, absence of theory	8
system of	22, 90, 92
formula of	47
Japanese	6

INDEX.

	PAGE
LA FONTAINE	309
Language, may be learned in six months	6
art of learning	38, 48
subjective	53, 60, 144, 159
objective	53, 60, 61, 127
figurative	55, 60, 182, 189
limit of	65
inarticulate	123
ease of learning	128
psychological difference	151
time necessary to learn	294
a whole world to conquer	296
the name of a race	363
Languages, two different	52, 149, 177, 181
by the sciences and *vice versâ*	341, 356
study of, an ogre at school	342
Latin, teaching of	166
construction of exercises	166, 276, 279
first lesson in	168
grammar	205, 253
conjugation	232
belongs to second age of language	256
spoken in Roumania	257
cases	263
study of, made too easy	267
no longer a dead language	282
modal phrases	284
ordinary knowledge of	298
now requires ten masters	301
method of teaching	335
must be spoken	338
value of	363
difficulty of translating into	370
Life of the people put in Series	346
Line by line arrangement	71, 94
Linguistic method, need of	1
an art	86
"Lion and the Gnat"	309, 392
method of teaching	325
Literature and history combined	353
Literary Series	305, 335
specimen	309
method of teaching	325
classification of	339
Logic of the child	35, 90
Logical order of construction	277
MATHEMATICS	359
Means and end	43, 52, 71, 79, 92
of demonstration	7
Memory	33, 82, 91, 134, 346
Mental railway	2, 4

INDEX.

	PAGE
Metaphors	183, 191
of a classical author	327
Metaphorical Series	194
Method, artificial	85
of teaching	129, 159, 189, 198, 261, 281, 325, 350
one only, of learning languages	146
Mill, visit to	36
child's series of	43
generalisation of	89
Mind, faculties of	148
Mind's eye, seeing in	39, 97
Mnemonic properties	80
Modal phrases	284
Moments of precision	214
Mondeux, Henri	6, 210, 330
Moods	285
Mother's Series	83, 123, 150
Motive of Relative phrases	155, 176
Mystic ladder of individuality	51
NAME, properties of	362
Native teachers	179
Natural forces tamed	3
Natural method	5, 24, 85, 91, 92
order of construction	277, 365
sciences	356
Nature, process of	6, 35, 38, 44, 128, 178, 253, 293
logic of	40, 43
school of	91, 257
order of	92
secrets of	35, 59
at fault with the cases	257
Necessity of specifying the time	216
Norwegian, first lesson in	175
Nursemaid, her series	83, 123, 150
can teach the bulk of a language in six months	128, 221
OAK, Series of	49
Object lessons	22
Objective language	53
organisation in Series	61
method of teaching	127
Ollendorf, absence of theory	8
German method	18
appreciation of	19
study of	20
failure of	21
use of the substantive	45, 67
hideous confusion of	90
without a master	301
Oral exercise, to come first	133
Ordered conversation	163, 337

INDEX.

	PAGE
Order of Nature	92
and disorder	91
natural and logical	276
Organ of language	33, 47, 127
Orthography	288
PARSING in practice	131
Participle	226, 229
Pascal, quoted	59, 84
style of	361
Past, present, and future	213, 221
Perception of the will	37
and conception	39, 41, 48
Periods of time	211
Perpetual speech	79, 83, 295
Personal work of the student	135, 267, 297, 301
Phædrus, "Canis et Lupus"	311
Phrase, measure of	93
Plant, Series of	63
Ploetz, systematic vocabulary	24
Pluperfect acts	240, 390
Prefix	271
Prendergast's system	92
Preposition	256, 268
Present tense, importance of	208
Project for county high schools	354, 355, 360
Pronunciation, falsification of	57, 302
good	82
reason of false	136, 298
figured	138
Psychology, language a chapter of	80
Psychological classification	147
Pump, Series of	96, 99, 386
Punishment, a diversion	95
QUIETISTS, objections of	3
READING	205, 289, 330
the classics	339
Reading-book, child's first	289
Reading-lessons in history	353
Reduce the subjects	341, 361
Reform of language teaching	127, 142
of grammar	209
of teaching reading	289
of teaching drawing	292
of teaching history	343
of teaching geography	355
of mathematics	360
of text-books	361
of teaching Greek and Latin	377
Relative phrases	54

INDEX. 405

	PAGE
Relative phrases, definition	145
classification	149
motives	155
double function	177
of a classic author	327
Relationships, logical	42, 50
between things	253, 293
Remembrances, virtue of	362
Robertson, absence of theory	8
system of	23, 90, 92
Romeo and Juliet	320
Roots, Greek and German	12
true, of tongues	19
Roumania, knowledge of Latin in	257
Routine	91, 139, 260
Rule for construction of a classic phrase	329
Russian, referred to	166, 329
SACRISTI!	153
Sanscrit, referred to	6, 329
Saying and doing	37
Sciences by the languages	295, 341, 356
Seasons and the language	298
Sentence, study of	250
Sentences not words	45
Series of verbs	49, 51
definition of	61
material of	61
construction of	62, 65, 86, 97
of the Mill	42
of the Bird	51, 62
of the Plant	50, 63
of the Bee	64
of the Wood-chopper	69
the nursemaid's or mother's	83, 123, 150
pedagogic measure of	87
of the Pump	97, 99
of the Well	104, 108
of the Spring	105, 111
concentric	102, 107
of the Baker	105
of the Fire	106, 112–119
of the Stove	107, 120
co-ordination of	122
domestic	123
indoor and outdoor	124
rural	125
of the Shepherd	125, 273
technical	126
of the Games	126
of Opening the Door	129, 160
method of teaching	129

INDEX.

	PAGE
Series, specimen, in eight languages	174
metaphorical	194
for reading-lessons	289
for drawing-lessons	292
literary	309
historical	345, 348-9
geographical	355
spoken	356, 359
scientific	356
mathematical	359
classical	381
specimen in French	386
Series method, applicable to all languages	6, 166, 283, 329, 385
Shakespeare	320
Simplification of teaching	142, 361
Spanish, first lesson in	172
Spelling	288, 291
Spring, series of the	111
State, duty of, in preserving languages	364
Steps or divisions in exercises	72, 307
Stove, Series of the	120
Students at Berlin	25
Style	277, 327, 361
Substantive	45
Substantives, general and specific	76
Substitutes	73, 77, 82, 103
Subjective language	52
its organisation	144, 157
method of teaching	159
Subjunctives	246
Succession in time	42, 71, 92
Symbols of metaphors	186, 327
Symmetry, vain search for	226
Syntax	250, 265
Synthesis	7
Systematic vocabulary	24
TEACHER, one for three classes	142, 162, 193
necessity of a	301
Teacher's task simplified	135
spoken series	359
Teaching must assume the character of a game	129
Tenses and acts	204
various use of same	225
Theory	8
Thinking in the foreign language	57, 130, 141
Thought and words	122, 139
Third person	203, 208
Time in general	212, 228
always mentioned	216
necessary to learn a language	294, 368
Traditions	363

INDEX.

	PAGE
Tragen, inner meaning of	16
Transcription of a classical work	306
Translation, Goethe and Schiller	15, 16, 31
judgment of	17, 141, 370
Typographic form	290, 307
VALUE of Greek and Latin	362
Variants	104
Verb, importance of	45, 283, 306
Series of	50
principal part played by	67
concentration of attention upon	82, 131
definition by position	102
study of	198
Verbs, of ends and of means	77, 79
irregular	202
complete and incomplete	251
Vicious circle of the dictionary	371
Virgil, translating	49
length of scenes in	94, 307
enclitics in	148
assimilation of	268, 306, 337
Eclogues, construction	279
no longer a dead language	282
specimen of transcription	335
method of studying	336
Vocabulary	24, 65, 73, 373
Vocabulomania	374
Voltaire's History	354
WEB of language	46
Well, Series of the	108
Women teachers	300
Wood-chopper, Series of	69
Words, inner sense of	15
number of, in a Series lesson	73
and thoughts	122, 139
Writing	179, 295, 339
Written Series	84
words	140
ZEITWORT	46
Zoology	342

THE END.

Lightning Source UK Ltd.
Milton Keynes UK
UKHW021832080321
380000UK00004B/69